John Welsh

VERTICAL GEAR CUTTING MACHINE

Courtesy of Gould and Eberhardt, Newark, New Jersey

Modern
Shop Practice

A General Reference Work on

Machine Shop Practice and Management, Production Manufacturing, Metallurgy, Welding, Tool Making, Tool Design,
Die Making and Metal Stamping, Foundry Work,
Forging, Pattern Making, Mechanical
and Machine Drawing, Etc.

Editor-in-Chief
HOWARD MONROE RAYMOND, B.S.
President, Armour Institute of Technology

Assisted by a Corps of

MECHANICAL ENGINEERS, DESIGNERS, AND SPECIALISTS IN SHOP
METHODS AND MANAGEMENT

Illustrated with over Two Thousand Engravings
SIX VOLUMES

AMERICAN TECHNICAL SOCIETY
CHICAGO   U.S.A.
1928

Editor-in-Chief

HOWARD MONROE RAYMOND, B. S.

President, Armour Institute of Technology

Authors and Collaborators

EDWARD R. MARKHAM
Instructor in Shop Work, Harvard University and Rindge Technical School
Consulting Expert in Heat Treatment of Steel
Formerly Superintendent, Waltham Watch Tool Company
American Society of Mechanical Engineers

CHARLES L. GRIFFIN, S. B.
Assistant Engineer, The Solvay-Process Company
American Society of Mechanical Engineers

HOWARD P. FAIRFIELD
Professor of Machine Construction, Worcester Polytechnic Institute
American Society of Mechanical Engineers

JOHN LORD BACON
Consulting Engineer
Formerly Instructor in Forge Work, Lewis Institute
American Society of Mechanical Engineers
Author of "Forge Practice"

BENJAMIN B. FREUD, B. S.
Associate Professor of Organic Chemistry, Armour Institute of Technology
Member, American Chemical Society
Member, American Electrochemical Society

ERVIN KENISON, S. B.
Associate Professor of Drawing and Descriptive Geometry, Massachusetts
Institute of Technology

GEORGE W. CRAVENS
Mechanical and Electrical Engineer
Chief Engineer, Elkhart Carriage and Motor Car Company

H. B. PULSIFER, S. B., Ch. E.
Professor of Metallurgy, Lehigh University
American Chemical Society
American Institute of Mining Engineers

❦

FRANK E. SHAILOR
Mechanical Engineer
General Manager, Detroit Welding and Manufacturing Company

❦

FREDERICK W. TURNER
Head, Department of Pattern Making, Mechanics Arts High School, Boston

❦

WALTER H. JAMES, S. B.
Instructor, Massachusetts Institute of Technology

❦

GLENN M. HOBBS, Ph. D.
Head, Technical Department, W. M. Welch Scientific Company, Chicago
Formerly Instructor in Physics, University of Chicago
American Physical Society

❦

WALTER W. MONROE
Instructor in Pattern Making, Worcester Polytechnic Institute

❦

LAWRENCE S. SMITH, S. B.
Instructor, Massachusetts Institute of Technology

❦

C. C. ADAMS, B. S.
Switchboard Engineer with General Electric Company

BURTON L. GRAY
Instructor in Foundry Practice, Worcester Polytechnic Institute
Member, Foundrymen's Association

OSCAR E. PERRIGO, M. E.
Consulting Mechanical Engineer
Expert Patent Attorney
American Society of Mechanical Engineers
Author of "Modern Machine-Shop Construction, Equipment, and Management," "Lathe Design, Construction, and Operation," etc.

ROBERT VALLETTE PERRY, B. S., M. E.
Professor of Machine Design, Armour Institute of Technology

HAROLD W. ROBBINS, M. E.
Formerly Instructor, Lewis Institute, and Armour Institute, Chicago
Special Writer and Technical Investigator

EDWARD B. WAITE
Formerly Dean, and Head, Consulting Department, American School
American Society of Mechanical Engineers

WILLIAM C. STIMPSON
Formerly Head Instructor in Foundry Work and Forging, Department of Science and Technology, Pratt Institute

JOHN JERNBERG
Instructor in Forge Practice and Heat Treatment of Steel, Worcester Polytechnic Institute
Member, Swedish Engineering Society

JESSIE M. SHEPHERD, A. B.
Editor, American Technical Society

Authorities Consulted

THE editors have freely consulted the standard technical literature of America and Europe in the preparation of these volumes. They desire to express their indebtedness, particularly, to the following eminent authorities, whose well-known treatises should be in the library of everyone interested in Modern Shop Practice.

Grateful acknowledgment is also expressed for the invaluable cooperation of the foremost manufacturers and engineering firms in making these volumes thoroughly representative of the best and latest practice in machine and pattern shops, foundries, and drafting rooms, and in the construction and operation of machine tools, and other classes of modern machinery; also for the valuable drawings and data, suggestions, criticisms, and other courtesies.

C. L. GOODRICH

Joint Author with F. A. Stanley of "Accurate Tool Work," "Automatic Screw Machines and Tools"

OSCAR E. PERRIGO, M. E.

Author of "Modern Machine-Shop Construction, Equipment, and Management"; "Lathe Design, Construction and Operation"; "Change Gear Devices"

JOHN LORD BACON

Author of "Forge Practice"

JOSEPH V. WOODWORTH, M. E.

Author of "American Tool Making," "Punches, Dies, and Tools for Manufacturing in Presses," "Dies, Their Construction and Use for the Modern Working of Sheet Metals," "Gages and Gaging Systems," "Grinding and Lapping," "Drop Forging, Die Sinking and Machine Forming of Steel," etc.

FREDERICK A. HALSEY

Author of "Methods of Machine Shop Work," "Handbook for Machine Designers and Draftsmen"

WILLIAM KENT, A. M., M. E.

Author of "The Mechanical Engineer's Pocket-Book," "Strength of Materials," "Steam Boiler Economy," etc.

FRED H. COLVIN

Author of "Machine-Shop Calculations"; Joint Author with F. A. Stanley of "American Machinist's Handbook," "Machine Shop Primer," "Hill Kink Books"; Joint Author with Lucius Haas of "Jigs and Fixtures," etc.

HARRY HUSE CAMPBELL

Author of "The Manufacture and Properties of Iron and Steel"

HUGO DIEMER, M. E.

Author of "Factory Organization and Administration"; Joint Author with G. H. Resides of "Wood Turning"

F. A. STANLEY

Joint Author with F. H. Colvin of "American Machinist's Handbook," "Machine Shop Primer," and "Hill Kink Books"; Joint Author with C. L. Goodrich of "Accurate Tool Work," "Automatic Screw Machines and Tools"

HENRY M. HOWE, B. S., A. M., LL. D.

Author of "Iron, Steel, and Other Alloys," "Metallurgical Laboratory Notes"

JOSHUA ROSE, M. E.

Author of "Mechanical Drawing Self-Taught," "Modern Steam Engineering," "Steam Boilers," "The Slide Valve," "Pattern Maker's Assistant," "Complete Machinist"

P. S. DINGEY

Author of "Machinery Pattern Making"

ROBERT GRIMSHAW, M. E.

Author of "Steam Engine Catechism," "Boiler Catechism," "Locomotive Catechism," "Engine Runner's Catechism," "Shop Kinks," "Saw Filing"

JOSEPH G. HORNER

Author of "Pattern Making," "Hoisting Machinery," "Tools for Machinists and Woodworkers," "Modern Milling Machines," "Engineers' Turning," "Practical Metal Turning," etc.

THOMAS E. FRENCH, M. E.

Author of "Engineering Drawing"

WILLIAM JOHN MACQUORN RANKINE, LL. D., F. R. S. S.

Author of "Applied Mechanics," "The Steam Engine," "Civil Engineering," "Useful Rules and Tables," "Machinery and Mill Work," "A Mechanical Textbook"

WALTER LEE CHENEY

Joint Author with Fred H. Colvin of "Machine-Shop Arithmetic," and "Engineer's Arithmetic"

GARDNER C. ANTHONY, A. M., Sc. D.

Author of "Elements of Mechanical Drawing," "Machine Drawing," "The Essentials of Gearing"

CHARLES W. REINHART

Author of "Technic of Mechanical Drafting"

SIMPSON BOLLAND

Author of "The Iron Founder," "The Iron Founder's Supplement," "Encyclopedia of Founding," "Dictionary of Foundry Terms," etc.

THOMAS D. WEST

Author of "American Foundry Practice"

WILLIAM RIPPER

Author of "Machine Drawing and Design," "Steam," etc.

OSCAR J. BEALE
Author of "Handbook for Apprenticed Machinists"

❦

JAMES LUKIN, B. A.
Author of "Possibilities of Small Lathes," "Simple Decorative Lathe Work," "Turning for Beginners," "The Lathe and Its Uses," "The Forge and Lathe," etc.

❦

O. M. BECKER
Author of "High Speed Steel—Its Manufacture, Use, and the Machines Required"

❦

F. W. BARROWS
Author of "Practical Pattern Making"

❦

L. ELLIOTT BROOKES
Author of the "Automobile Handbook," "Practical Gas and Oil Engine Handbook," "The Calculation of Horse-Power Made Easy," "20th Century Machine-Shop Practice"

❦

STANLEY H. MOORE
Author of "Mechanical Engineering and Machine-Shop Practice"

❦

CHARLES C. ALLEN
Author of "Engineering Workshop Practice"

❦

BRADLEY STOUGHTON
Author of "The Metallurgy of Iron and Steel"

❦

F. W. TAYLOR, M. E.
Author of "On the Art of Cutting Metals"

HORIZONTAL INCLINED-RAIL MILLING MACHINE MILLING RACKS.   STEEL
BARS SHOWN IN FOREGROUND PRIOR TO BEING
INSERTED IN MACHINE

Courtesy of Ingersoll Milling Machine Company, Rockford, Illinois

Foreword

A LITTLE more than a century ago the first prime movers were invented and developed, and mechanical development had its beginning. With the development of machines came the development of mechanics to run these machines, to fabricate the parts and to assemble them into the finished articles. The evolution of both machines and mechanics has been marvelous, the accuracy of workmanship today being easily two hundred times that of a century ago, and the speed of manufacture probably much more than this. Since that time one industry has helped to develop others until today the mines produce ore in large quantities to supply the iron, copper, and other metals; the great steel mills supply the raw or fabricated material; the foundries and forging shops fashion the many castings and forgings for the intricate machines to be built; the immense shops machine the parts and assemble them for the market. Everywhere we turn we find a manufactured article which has gone through these various changes from raw material to finished product.

¶ "Production" methods have enormously increased the output of our shops and the machines which have made this development possible are of a diversified character—speed lathes, planers, multiple drillers, grinders, milling machines, stamping machines, die presses and the jigs, tools and dies which go with them—all of these have contributed to the accuracy and speed of manufacture. The demands of the automobile industry have done wonders in hastening this development as the manufacture of the parts in duplicate was absolutely necessary in order to cheapen the price of the assembled machines. The fact that many of the present-day automobiles are shipped "knocked down" to assembly plants without ever having been put together is an eloquent testimonial to the accuracy with which the duplicate parts are built. Another contributing factor in modern production methods is the development of high speed steels which enable the operators to run the machines at speeds hitherto unattainable.

¶ And yet with all this wonderful development of the machines themselves and the design of what are termed "automatics," the workman has not lost his skill. In fact, one trip to a well-organized scientific machine shop will teach any skeptic that the intelligent workman who has contributed so largely to the mechanical developments of the past twenty years is more skilled, more intelligent, certainly better paid, and more interested in his work than ever.

¶ But this same skilled mechanic is today a specialist. He has no opportunity to build a complete machine or even a small part of one; his active work is carried on along rather narrow lines. Consequently, it is all the more necessary for him to have a standard reference work to help him in other shop lines with which he is unfamiliar. "Modern Shop Practice" is such a work—one which has been tested through six editions—and the practical treatises on the various shop subjects have been supplied by well-known teachers and practical men and are strictly up to date. The authors have at all times kept in mind the practical nature of their subjects and numerous shop kinks and other helpful suggestions have been introduced. It is the hope of the publishers that this new edition will supply the needs of both the skilled mechanic and the layman who is interested in mechanical affairs.

¶ In conclusion, grateful acknowledgment is given to the authors and collaborators—engineers and designers of wide practical experience and teachers of recognized ability—without whose cooperation this work would have been impossible.

Table of Contents

VOLUME VI

*For page numbers, see foot of pages.

†For professional standing of authors, see list of Authors and Collaborators at front of volume.

ERECTING UNIVERSAL MILLING MACHINES IN BROWN AND SHARPE FACTORY

Courtesy of Brown and Sharpe Manufacturing Company, Providence, Rhode Island

BLUEPRINT READING

INTRODUCTION

Definition of Blueprint. A blueprint as used by engineers and by workmen in the various industries is a reproduction of what is known as a *working drawing*. A working drawing, as made by the draftsman, shows by means of lines what the piece, machine, or construction is, gives the necessary working dimensions and whatever other data the workman needs to know in order to build the piece or the structure; in other words, it is the drawing by which the workman does his work and to which he looks for his information when building the structure or machining the part. However, it is essential that the working drawing itself be preserved for reference in the drafting room, and therefore a blueprint is made from the working drawing and this is what the workman uses at his machine or in the field. The lines, numerals, and letters on the original working drawing are black on a white background but these appear on the blueprint as white lines on a blue background; hence the name *blueprint*.

Process of Making Blueprints. Blueprints are contact prints; that is, the blueprint paper and the working drawing are in contact with each other while exposed to the light. Blueprint paper is a strong rather tough white paper coated with a solution which is sensitive to sunlight and turns blue when exposed to sunlight and then washed in clean water. Those firms which use large numbers of blueprints often coat their own paper. Most firms, however, buy it already coated with the prepared sensitive solution. In making a blueprint, the working drawing is laid face down on a sheet of clear glass and the blueprint paper, cut to a size slightly larger than that of the drawing, is laid on the drawing with the colored, or sensitive, side next to the drawing and by means of a clamping frame is brought and held firmly in close contact with the drawing. The holding frame is then tipped and held in a position to allow the sun or other strong light to shine squarely through the glass. The light thus passes through those parts of the drawing on which there is no ink and effects a chemical change in the light-sensitive blue coating. The light does not shine, or pass, through the inked lines of the drawing, the lettering, or the numerals. After a short exposure to a strong light the clamps are removed and the blueprint paper is taken out of the frame and thoroughly washed in clean water. The parts upon which the strong light shone turn a rich blue color; those parts which came under the inked lines were not affected by the light rays and wash up a clean sharp white.

Importance of Blueprints. The blueprint from a properly made working drawing should contain *all* the information needed by the workman in his work and he should never ask for information until he is positive that it is not on his blueprint. It is well also for him to understand that his blueprint is an exact reproduction of a drawing on file in the drafting room and that, if he implicitly follows instructions and dimensions as given in his blueprint, he is protected in any argument which occurs over his work; in other words, if his work checks up with the blueprint he has worked from, any errors found in results are squarely up to the draftsman.

What Blueprints Should Show. A blueprint is in a sense a picture of the piece, machine, or structure which is to be made or built. This picture is made up of views; for example, front view, top view, end view, etc. These views are made up of lines which would show clearly to the eye if the part, machine, or structure were viewed from the several positions noted; for example, a front view consists of those lines which would be clearly seen if the observer were viewing the part or machine from the front. The blueprint should also contain all the essential dimensions and indicate clearly from what surfaces they are to be taken. In most cases, this is done by using a distinct arrowhead with the point resting against the line which represents the surface or the outline from which the measurement starts or from such a working line *extended;* that is, the line which represents a surface edge is lengthened to make it convenient for placing the arrowhead. Another arrowhead is placed against the line representing the surface where the measurement stops, and the two arrowheads are connected by a line called a dimension line and the given dimension is placed either in this line or directly over it. Fig. 1 shows this. The blueprint will probably also contain lettered directions; some surfaces are to be ground, and the word "grind" may be lettered on those surfaces, others are to be polished, and on those the word "polish" may be placed.

Reading Blueprints. To be able to read a blueprint is as essential to a workman's success as to be able to read printed matter. To read blueprints readily, he must know some of

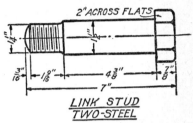

Fig. 1. Detail Drawing of Link Stud

the principles of making drawings. This is somewhat equivalent to learning the alphabet in learning to read printed text. The workman should first understand that a blueprint is a record of instructions given him to read. Second, he should realize that the language used by the draftsman in making his drawing is largely a language of lines and that, unless he knows how to read lines, the instructions recorded on the blueprint are essentially in a foreign language.

To read a blueprint, the first thing is to study the several views until one has a good mental picture of what he is to construct. As the blueprint is a flat surface, it is necessary for the workman to use his imagination to make the lines and views lift up from the paper. When a clear-cut mental picture has been formed, the dimensions should be studied until understood. Next all the lettered text should be read and considered. Carelessness in any one of these three respects is not to be excused.

GENERAL DIRECTIONS FOR READING BLUEPRINTS

Method of Obtaining Views. The drawing or blueprint is nothing more than a condensed book of instructions for making an object. Its lines and symbols are a universal language which the workmen of all nationalities can read. The blueprints shown in this section consist of separate drawings or diagrams. These diagrams are known as views and are obtained by projecting the outlines of the piece point by point onto an assumed plane. In the case in hand, the paper on which the drawing is made is the plane, and as the blueprint is an exact reproduction, line for line and point for point of the original, it also can be said to be the projecting plane. As an aid in understanding what the draftsman did when he made these *views* and why they are placed on the paper as they are, let the reader imagine that with a sheet of paper he has made a *box* having all the corners and all the sides square with each other. Assume that the paper box is transparent as glass is transparent and that a piece of work might be hung inside the box centered with the sides and corners. Let us now in imagination hang various objects one at a time in this paper box centered squarely with its transparent sides through which they may readily be viewed. If the first object selected is a perfect cube, for example, an ordinary playing dice, then, viewing this from every side of the box, it is at once evident that all the views are the same in outline. If the outline dice is drawn, with a pencil, on each side of the box, as seen through that side, we will have six outlines all of the same size and shape. If an ordinary playing domino is substituted for the dice, the views when looking into the top and the bottom of the box will be alike in outline. Those seen when looking into the right and the left ends will also be alike, as will the views seen when looking through the back and the front sides of the box. If the pencil is used as before, six outlines are shown, but instead of their being each like the other, there are three pairs of views, each pair distinctly different from the others. If these penciled views are labeled top, bottom, front, back, right end, and left end, and the paper box is cut along its corners and the paper then tacked flat on a board, we have a drawing of the piece, giving six views labeled top, bottom, etc.

Instead of doing all this box work, the draftsman first trains his hands to use in a neat and skillful manner the various tools. He also trains his hands to produce and his mind to remember the various outlines. In addition, he must learn to imagine what he is going to make a drawing of, or, as it is termed, see the thing in space, which means form a reasonably complete *mind* picture of the piece he is to draw. By using his tools in a certain conventional manner, he gets all the views he wishes on a sheet of paper tacked flat on a board.

Number of Views Needed. It will be recalled that in viewing the domino centered in the box, while we had six separate views, certain views duplicated and three views were sufficient to show clearly the outline of the piece. When drawn, some parts need several different views; others need only a single view.

Interrelation of Views. In reading blueprints, it will be observed that the top view and the front view center, line for line and point for point, on the same *vertical* center line, also that the front view and the end view center, line for line and point for point, on the same *horizontal* center line. In some of the plates, it has been found necessary to readjust the different views to accommodate them to the small size plate, in violation of the rules of *third angle projection*. The student should make allowance for these discrepancies.

Meaning of Projection. To understand thoroughly what the term "projection" means, it is well to study the action of light as we view an object. Take as an example a man walking along the street. Our view of that man is made possible by the fact that light is *reflected* from his body into our eyes. This is true of all objects which we view with our eyes and we say that we *see* the man or the object. In other words, the light which is reflected, or thrown back, from the man or from the object into our eyes gives us a view of the man or the object. If the man or the object faces toward us, we get a front view, if away from us, a rear view. While the object itself is not a source of light, it is so treated in viewing it and the light is said to be projected from the object viewed. When a view drawing is made, it is often known as a *projection*.

Projection of House. As an example of *ordinary* projection, suppose we select a house and view it from its several sides, at a distance of not less than 100 feet from the several sides. Taking the front end first, the viewer will note that it appears as a flat wall having a rectangular outline with its top line in the shape of an inverted V. A side view gives a bottom line where the house rests on the foundation; two vertical, or upright, lines at each end of the side; a horizontal, or level, line to show the eaves; and a second horizontal line above this to represent the ridgepole. If these two views have been penciled out on a sheet of paper to some exact size, they will show what the *outline* of the house is. We can also show on these views the several doors, windows, etc., as we see them when viewing the front end and when viewing one side of the house, and if the rear end and the opposite side have the same doors, windows, etc., in exactly the same positions, the workman would be able from these two views to construct walls which would be as desired. If, however, the rear end had the doors or the windows placed differently from those on the front end or if they were not of the same size even though placed in the same manner, the workman would need a rear view to show him this fact. The same thing would hold true in respect to the sides of the house. Also,

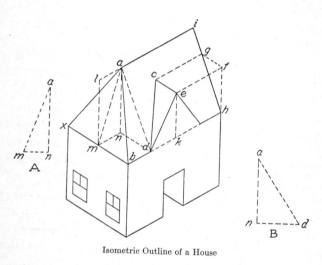

Isometric Outline of a House

if the roof itself were broken up by windows, a top view showing their size and layout would be necessary for the workman. For convenience in making and reading the drawing, the several views are universally arranged for shop use exactly opposite the surfaces which they represent, as noted in the use of the box with transparent sides.

Lines. *Working Lines.* A study of the views in the several blueprints in this book shows at once that each view is made up of straight lines and curved lines. The straight lines, or right lines (as they are often termed by draftsmen), are used to represent the edges of plane surfaces. In the example just used, two upright straight lines a certain distance apart would be used to show the corners of the house. A circle line may show the edges of a cylinder or a hole in any surface, for example, a bolt hole or, in a house, a circular window. By using a combination of straight lines and part of a circle, the rounded end of a straight-sided bolt, for example, can be shown. Where the edges are neither straight lines nor parts of a circle, they are drawn with a special tool having an irregularly curved edge, which can be fitted to the desired line shape. A view, then, may consist entirely of straight lines, entirely of curved lines or of circles, or of a combination of all these. It must in any case be clearly noted that any *working* line, straight or curved, is used to show where a surface on the work changes its direction, in other words, to show the *edge of a surface*. If the object viewed is a solid piece, for example, a bolt, all the working lines in the several views are solid and continuous straight or curved lines. If the work has holes through it or has hollow places hidden inside it, the lines which show the hidden edges are drawn as dots and the line is termed a dotted line.

In studying a blueprint it will be understood that the dotted lines in a view represent surfaces and edges which are hidden from the viewer's sight when the object is viewed from the side shown. In the case of the bolt, Fig. 1, a view of the head end would show the body of the bolt as a dotted circle. In a blueprint of the house, the wall timbers, partitions, etc., which are not seen from the outside, would be shown as dotted lines.

Dimension Lines. While the house outlines as they now stand give a general idea of how its exterior would look, they do not show its size or the sizes of the several doors, windows, trim, etc. To give this information, use is made of *dimension* lines drawn between points on the lines which make up the several views. To indicate the place where the measurement is to start and the point where it must stop, each end of a dimension line has a neat arrowhead, the point of which just touches the line at which the measurement starts or stops. Somewhere in the length of a dimension line are placed the numerals which give the exact measurement of the work as indicated by the arrow points. Dimension lines usually show on the blueprint much thinner than the lines which make up the views. This fact and the fact that at their ends are prominently placed neat arrowheads render it easy to avoid confusing them with the working lines of the blueprint.

In case a dimension line cannot readily be placed on the view, the working lines may be lengthened, or extended, a short distance from the view and the dimension line can then be drawn between the extended lines with the points of the arrowheads resting exactly against the extended lines. The end of an *extension* line, as it is called, should never quite touch the working line which it extends.

Section Lines. In addition to the working lines and the dimension lines on the blueprint views, the workman will, in some cases, find a series of parallel lines drawn closely together at an angle to the working lines of the view. These are known as *section* lines and are used by the draftsman to tell the workman that the part of the view covered by such lines is as if the work had been cut through and a portion removed.

Sections open up the interior of an object or a combination of working parts, for example, the headstock of a lathe, and give a clear view of the inside. To use a homely illustration, the draftsman seeks the same effect as the grocer does when he cuts a melon in halves for the customer's inspection. A view so drawn is said to be *sectioned;* hence the term section lines. In the case of the lathe headstock, some of its parts may be of cast iron, some of bronze, some of steel, etc. To show which parts are of cast iron, of steel, or of bronze, the draftsman makes use of various arrangements of section lines, each arrangement showing a different material.

Methods of Showing Large Work. *Reducing Scale of Drawing.* Several methods are used to make it possible to show a view of large work on a small sheet of paper. The view is often made a reduced size, which is usually spoken of as making it to a *reduced scale.* The term "scale" in such a case means that the length of the working lines in the blueprint views has a definite proportion to that of the actual lines of the work itself; for example, if the circles which represented the rim of a 24-inch pulley were drawn in a view as 12-inch circles, the view would be one-half size, or to one-half scale. If the circles were made 6 inches in diameter, the view would be to one-quarter scale. While in these cases the dimension lines would be, respectively, 12 inches or 6 inches in length from arrow point to arrow point, the dimension figures would read the exact size, 24 inches. For the reason that a blueprint view on a reduced scale does not give the average workman a good *size* picture of the work, it is customary to have the views show the work to exact, or full, size whenever it is practicable to do so. Such a view is known as a full-size view, or a full-scale view. The common machine shop *view scales* are one-eighth, one-quarter, one-half, three-quarters, and full size. Another way of expressing view scales is in inches to the foot; for example, a one-half scale is 6 inches to 1 foot and a full scale is 12 inches to 1 foot.

Showing Parts of Work. Another way of getting a view of a comparatively large piece of work into a small space on a blueprint is to show only a part of the work in the view. In the case of the pulley just mentioned, if the blueprint view showed one-quarter or one-half of the entire pulley, the average workman would be able to get all the directions necessary from the view to complete the work.

Breaking the Piece. Yet another way by which the space utilized to represent a piece of work in blueprint views can be lessened is what is known as breaking the piece. To illustrate, use is made of the front view of a long bolt or shaft of relatively small diameter. If such a piece were shown full scale, its working length lines might reach the entire length of the blueprint or even farther. If the body of the bolt or shaft is of uniform size and shape, it is sufficient to show a portion of the body near the head and a portion near the threaded, or opposite, end, and the portions shown may be brought close up to each other and thus little space used for the view.

Shade Lines. It must be admitted that the average blueprint view of a piece of work is a rather flat and dead thing and that some imagination on the part of the workman is needed to give it life and to make it lift up from the paper and really have form and substance. Fortunately for the machine shop workman who is just learning to read blueprints, much of his work comes to him roughly in the form in which he is to finish it. This is especially so when he is finishing ordinary castings. There are several methods used at times to give the blueprint views more "life". One much used method is to make certain of the working lines of increased thickness to represent a shaded portion. These heavier working lines are known as *shade* lines and aid somewhat in making the view stand, or lift, up from the paper. Such shade lines are used to a lesser extent now than formerly, as the workman is supposed to use his imagination when reading blueprint views.

Line Shading. The term *shade lines* should never be confused with the term *line shading* which refers to a decidedly different use of lines. Line shading as commonly used consists of a series of lines placed on the view within its working lines and arranged in such a manner as to give a picture effect to the view.

Finish Lines. Another line used in blueprint views is sometimes termed a *finish* line. Such a line is usually broken up into dashes and dots and is then known as a *dashed* line. It is placed on the view close to a working line to indicate that the surface represented by the working line is to be finished. Dashed lines are now little used for this purpose because of the chance of their being confused with dotted lines used to represent hidden surfaces and edges, and other methods of indicating finished surfaces are popular. Brown & Sharpe practice is to use a red pencil to draw a full red line on the blueprint views close beside all working lines which represent finished surfaces. A common method of indicating finish is to place a letter *f* across all working lines which represent finished surfaces.

Symbols Used. There are a number of words which often appear on blueprint views, each conveying certain information, and the workman must be familiar with the more commonly used ones to read his blueprint readily.

Special notes neatly lettered are often placed on the blueprint and these notes should always be read carefully. Each and every dimension line should have in clear distinct figures, either on the line or in a break in the line, the exact dimension which the dimension line represents. Dimension figures should be clear, distinct and easily found and read.

Certain working variations in dimensions are allowable in all work. These are termed *tolerances* and should be given on the blueprint. They are usually preceded by the sign $\pm$ and are placed near or follow the given dimension. If the tolerances are not to be found, the workman must learn what the practice of the shop is in regard to this point.

The terms which the workman is most likely to find on his blueprint views are ream, tap, grind, polish, scrape, frost, taper, crown, and drill. He will also often note the letters *F.A.O.* near certain views; when so found, they denote that the piece of work is to be finished all over and the letter f is left off the working lines. It is also common machine shop practice to place on the blueprint the name of the piece of work, the number wanted, and the material to be used, all neatly lettered. The several materials used in the construction of machinery are usually indicated by their initials, for example, *M. S.* for machinery steel. To read blueprints easily and accurately, the workman should learn the symbols used, the more common of which are given and defined in the following tabulation:

F.A.O. . . . . finished all over
f. . . . . finished surface
RAD . . . . radius
DIAM . . . . diameter
R.H. . . . . right hand
L.H. . . . . left hand
P.R. . . . . piston rod
P. Tap . . . . pipe tap
CTRS. . . . . centers
C.I. . . . . cast iron
S.C. . . . . steel casting
Bz. . . . . bronze
C.R.S. . . . . : . . . cold rolled steel
T.S. . . . . tool steel
O.H.S. . . . . open-hearth steel
W.I. . . . . wrought iron
M.S. . . . . machinery steel

Conventions Used. Certain conventions, as they are called, are often to be found on blueprints. Take screw threads as an example; they are seldom shown on a blueprint as actual threads but are *indicated* by an arrangement of parallel lines across the surface meant to be threaded, Fig. 1, page 3, and a note is usually lettered on or near the threaded surface giving the number of threads per inch and the form of the threads. Gear teeth are seldom shown on a blueprint; a lettered note is used instead to state the number of teeth in the gear and whether they are involute, cycloidal, or otherwise.

Intersections and Irregular Surfaces. While, in most cases, the workman can get the needed information from a sufficient number of views of the ordinary method of projection, this is not always true where two surfaces meet at an angle, especially if they meet or intersect at other than a right angle. As an example of such a case, take the spout of an ordinary tin coffee pot where it joins the body of the pot. In uniting the two, it is necessary to know just what the shape of the hole should be and its size; also, in making up the pot body and the spout body, each of which is usually tapered, it is necessary to know the exact shapes and sizes to which the sheet tin must be cut. All sheet-metal work is full of such problems, as well as work in leather, for example, shoe tops, bags, etc. To obtain the desired forms of the holes and the body of a sheet-metal object, it is in effect cut open and flattened out as if it were a sheet of paper. While the workman's blueprint should show the already developed surface, or pattern, he will better understand his job if he knows how such a pattern is made.

Single Picture Views. The practice in some shops is to furnish the workman with a small blueprint which has a single view of the piece he is to work on. These sketches can be made by the use of the regular draftsman's tools, or, given sufficient artist's skill, may be made free hand. Picture sketches showing thickness as well as outlines drawn in perspective or isometric projection are used for this work. Where one view is sufficient to show an object in its true shape, it must show the object tipped and turned into such a position as to give a picture view. The sketch artist views the object from a variety of angles, finally decides which view best shows the piece, and makes that the blueprint view for the workman.

Importance of Careful Study. The careful reader of the preceding text must now be impressed with the need of *knowing* things. The way to know a thing is to study it, just as a child studies his book when learning to read. The child first learns the simpler words, how they look, what letters of the alphabet are used in spelling them, how the words are pronounced, etc. Any one who is willing to study this text carefully, can learn how to read ordinary blueprints readily. To assist the reader of this text in doing this, a variety of simple blueprints have been selected for analysis. Although they by no means cover all classes of work, nevertheless, they have been selected from a large number as being the more typical of their kind. Carefully study each blueprint as well as the text, for, in the first place, you will become acquainted with good practice as carried out by several well-known firms and, in the second place, you will, by this thorough analysis, train yourself to see in any blueprint everything that was intended to be brought out.

ANALYSIS OF TYPICAL BLUEPRINTS

PLATE I

SADDLE NUT

It is evident that Plate I shows three views of a saddle nut. Before starting to read the views, the workman should read the lettered data at the top of the blueprint. From this he gets the name of the piece he is to make, "saddle nut," the number required, "one, on a single machine," the name of the machine to which the piece belongs, "5-foot boring mill," and the piece number, "14049." He next reads the lettered data at the lower edge of the blueprint and learns what material he has to work on, in this case, bronze. If this plan has been followed out, the workman now knows that he is to make a certain number of bronze saddle nuts, each of which is a part of a 5-foot boring mill.

The several views are a front view, a right end view, and a bottom view. The front view shows the piece as it would look when set on its flat base on the bench, with its long side toward the viewer. The right end view shows the piece as it would appear if set on the bench as before, but so placed that the right end would face the viewer as he stood at the bench. The remaining view shows the bottom, or base, of the piece as it would appear if the workman picked the piece up from its first position on the bench, held it above his head, and looked up at its bottom side. As both ends of the saddle nut are alike, no left end view is necessary; and as nothing is to be done to its upper, or top, surface or to its rear side, neither a top nor a rear view is necessary.

The dotted lines through the front and the bottom views show that there is a hole through the length of the work and the right end view shows that the hole is circular in shape. As the dotted lines through the front and the bottom are double lines exactly centered with the center lines of these two views and as the right end view shows a full-line circle and a dotted-line circle, something more than these lines are needed to tell us just what this hole is. Between the front view and the right end view are certain notes nicely lettered. They state that the hole has a left-hand square thread, four threads to the inch through its length, make everything clear as to what the hole is, and explain the name "nut" given to the piece in the title.

Near the base of the front and the right end views are certain other dotted lines which, of course, represent hidden surfaces or holes. When we look at the bottom view, it is easily seen that these are round holes. By reading the notes placed at the right of this view and by following the arrows, we learn that two of these holes are to be made to fit a No. 5 taper pin and that the two larger ones are to be drilled and tapped for a $\frac{3}{4}$-inch screw. This view also shows that there is a screw hole and a pin hole in each end of the piece and that the screw and the pin holes are placed in corners diagonally across from each other. It can also be seen by reference to the several views that the screw holes and the pin holes are placed on the same center lines. If the workman is used to general machine construction, he will know that the screw holes are for the bolts which are to hold the saddle nut to the saddle and that the pin holes are for the taper pins which locate and hold the nut to an exact position. The bottom view shows by dimension lines placed just above the view that the holes are to be placed 3 inches from each other along the length of the piece and $\frac{3}{4}$ inch in from the edges of the base. The end view shows by dimension lines placed just below the view that along the width of the piece the holes are 2 inches apart and $\frac{3}{4}$ inch in from the sides. The workman should understand that when the dimension lines are shown in this manner, the *center-to-center* distance is the more important one. In this case, the 2-inch and the 3-inch dimensions are of more importance that the $\frac{3}{4}$-inch dimensions, these latter being probably given to inform the workman that the holes must be symmetrical with the base of the nut.

Attention is called to the placing of the dimension lines between or at the side of the views and to the fact that the arrow points touch extension lines drawn to nearly touch the surface lines. Dimension lines placed between the front view and the bottom view show that the saddle nut is $4\frac{3}{4}$ inches long over all and that the over-all length of the base is $4\frac{1}{2}$ inches. Dimension lines placed just below the right end view show that the base of the nut is $3\frac{1}{2}$ inches wide over all. A dimension line placed just above the end view shows that the rounded part of the nut is 3 inches. While reading the over-all dimensions, for example, the 4¾-inch, the 3½-inch, and the 3-inch dimensions, the workman should at the same time see whether or not his castings measure up fairly close to these dimensions with finish allowances.

Attention is called to the fact that all the dimensions are given either in whole numbers or in whole numbers and common fractions, with the exception of the dimension for the bore of the hole, which has added to it the decimal 0.003. This would indicate that the various dimensions given, with this one exception, are not of exceptional importance, or that the workman will be furnished with a special gage, or that the work will be jigged.

In this blueprint, it will be noted that the surfaces to be finished are indicated by the letter f placed on the working surface lines. As thus indicated, the base of the nut, the right-hand end, and the hole through the nut are to be finished.

PLATE II
BACK CLUTCH PINION

The lettered data at the upper edge of Plate II informs us that the piece is a back clutch pinion for a 5-foot boring mill and that one is required on each boring mill. Lettered data also tells us that the material is machinery steel and that the rough stock is 5⅛ inches in diameter and 4⅛ inches long.

The views given are a front view and a left end view. As the work is round with a plain squared-up right end, two views, as shown, are sufficient for the workman to understand what the piece is as well as to get all his dimensions. As an aid in reading the blueprint, the front view shows the piece as if it had been cut in halves through its length. The parts of this view which show where the cutting is made in solid stock are cross-lined at an angle of 45 degrees with the working lines.

As the first machine operation on this piece of work is that of getting a hole chucked through its axis, or length, the workman will naturally read his drawing for the size of the hole. At the right hand of the front view we find a dimension line with the arrow points touching the diameter lines of the hole extended, as explained in "General Directions for Reading Blueprints." The figures placed in the dimension line inform us that the hole is to be made $2\frac{3}{4}$ inches, and as the left end view shows a central circle, the hole is a round one. The word "ream" placed on the dimension line to the right of the dimension figures shows that the hole is to be drilled sufficiently small to permit it being reamed to its exact figured size. This dimension, as well as all the other dimensions, in the original blueprint, read two times the actual distance between the arrow points as shown on the views. The views in the original blueprint are then one-half the size of the actual piece of work and are drawn to one-half scale, in other words, 6 inches on a view represents 12 inches on the actual work.

The next two machine operations on this piece are to square the ends to the over-all length and to turn and finish it to the exact diameter. By following the end extension lines upward, we find at their upper ends a single dimension line having arrowheads with their points touching the extension lines. By reading the numeral placed in the line, it is found that the over-all length is 4 inches. Thus far this blueprint is very easily read.

Before starting work on the diameter, the views and the lettered text must be more carefully read. The name of the piece, "back clutch pinion," and a study of the views show it to be a gear with a clutch on its left-hand end.

Following out the extension lines to the left and to the right of the front view, which represent the several working diameters, we learn that the surface where the gear teeth of the pinion are to be cut is 5 inches in diameter. By following the upward extension lines, it is seen that the right-hand ends of the teeth do not start at the exact end of the stock but $\frac{1}{4}$ inch to the left of this. The extension lines also show by proper dimension lines that the faces of the teeth are to be $2\frac{1}{4}$ inches long. In this same view, the upward extension lines and dimension lines show that the remaining length of the piece from the left-hand end of the pinion teeth is $1\frac{1}{2}$ inches. Following the diameter extension lines to the left, we learn that the diameter of this part of the work is $4\frac{3}{4}$ inches.

A further study of the *left* end of the *front view* and of the *left end view* will show that the inner diameters of the clutch teeth are counterbored out to $3\frac{1}{8}$ inches with a depth of $\frac{1}{2}$ inch. The right-hand end of the work is turned into the form of a hub having, according to the dimension line near that end, a small diameter of $3\frac{7}{8}$ inches but curving up into a fillet. Both views show that there is a tapped hole through one side of the piece, and the lettered data placed just below the front view tells us that the hole is to be drilled with a $\frac{5}{16}$-inch drill and tapped with a $\frac{3}{8}$-inch tap. Both views show the clutch teeth.

In the left end of the front view, extension lines carried upward have dimension arrowheads and numerals which show that the clutch teeth are to be cut $\frac{1}{2}$ inch deep. The left end view shows the general form of the clutch teeth. A lettered note just below this view states that there are to be five teeth and that the spaces between the teeth are to be $\frac{1}{8}$ inch wider than the teeth themselves. This indicates that the teeth in the mating part of the clutch and the teeth in the piece shown in this blueprint will, when in mesh, clear each other by a distance of $\frac{1}{8}$ inch. A lettered note placed just below the front view informs us that the gear teeth are twenty-three in number and that a five-pitch cutter is to be used in cutting them.

No finish f marks are placed on the various working lines in either view, but a lettered note $F.A.O.$ tells us that the piece is to be finished all over. Two dotted lines on the front view indicate that there are hidden surfaces—in this case, the right-hand and the left-hand ends of the gear teeth of the pinion. If this text has been carefully studied, the reader will readily understand that Plate II really represents two pieces of work made solid in one piece of stock, namely, a toothed clutch and a pinion gear.

PLATE III

DOWN=FEED WORM WHEEL

In reading Plates I and II, it will have been noted that in Plate I three views were needed to show the workman all he needed, while in Plate II two views were sufficient. In Plate III a single view shows all that is needed to build this piece of work completely. The data on the upper edge of the blueprint states that the piece represented is a down-feed worm wheel for the right-hand head of a 5-foot boring mill and that one is required. The data on the lower edge tells us that the material is bronze, which is also indicated by the arrangement of lines in the cross-sectioning of the view.

A worm wheel is a toothed gear with the gear teeth cut at an angle with the sides of its rim. This angle is such as will make its teeth readily mesh, or fit, into the screw threads of the worm which is used to drive it. While the driving worm is not shown on this blueprint, a dimension line at the right of the view, with one of its arrow points touching the center line of the worm wheel and the other touching another center line drawn near the lower edge of the blueprint, shows that the center-to-center distance of the worm and the worm wheel is $3\frac{3}{4}$ inches. Lettered data near the lower center lines states that the worm wheel is to have thirty-two teeth of $\frac{1}{2}$-inch circular pitch and that the worm will have a left-hand thread, two threads to the inch.

In reading Plate III, let us first study the view itself. We will see that it is the view seen by a viewer facing the central axis of the piece and is, therefore, a front view. Lines drawn on the view at an angle with the working lines show that it is a sectional view, the piece having been cut along the center of its length precisely as a watermelon is sliced along the center of its length. Since the view is shown in this way, it is somewhat easier to read. The fact that one view only is given to work from indicates: (a) that if the work were viewed from its ends, the views would show on the blueprint as circles; and (b) that the ends of the work are plain and squared up—hub and rim. The lettered data, as already noted, states that the piece is a toothed gear wheel. Altogether, the piece is shown to consist of a hub, a rim, and a connecting web.

Following the upward extension lines and the dimension lines which they carry, it is seen that the over-all length of the piece is $2\frac{3}{8}$ inches and that the rim width is $1\frac{5}{8}$ inches. The upward extension lines and their dimension lines also show that the worm wheel hub extends, or projects, to the left of the rim a distance of $\frac{3}{4}$ inch. Dimension lines on the body of the view show: (a) that the wheel hub is $1\frac{15}{16}$ inches long; (b) that the rim overhangs the right end of the hub $\frac{7}{16}$ inch; (c) that the right end of the hub projects $\frac{1}{8}$ inch beyond the web; and (d) that the web is $\frac{1}{2}$ inch thick. Following the extension lines to the left of the view, we learn that the hub is 3 inches in diameter and that the chucked hole in the hub must ream $1\frac{5}{8}$ inches. These extension lines also show that the over-all diameter of the toothed rim is $5\frac{1}{2}$ inches.

The curved diameter on the rim, as shown, is known as the throat diameter, to distinguish it from the over-all diameter. Following the extension lines to the left of the view, it is seen that the throat diameter is 5.4114 inches. The dimension line placed just over the rim with its arrow point touching the throat curve is drawn from the point where the short center line crosses the center line of the wheel rim. This dimension line indicates that the workman should machine the curved part, or throat, of the rim with a cutting tool having its cutting end formed to an arc of a circle of 1.0443 inches radius. The remaining radius dimension line has its arrow point resting on the curved working line which represents the inner surface of the wheel rim.

The teeth in worm wheel rims are invariably cut or machined by the use of a special tool known in shops as a *hob*, or a *hobbing cutter*. In using a hob to cut the gear teeth, the workman has to know to what depth the cutting teeth are to be sunk into the rim of the wheel. The sketch in the upper right-hand corner of Plate III indicates in outline the teeth, or threads, on the worm and on the hobbing cutter. This sketch shows: (a) the angle of the sides of the threads; (b) the center-to-center distance, $\frac{1}{2}$ inch; (c) the total depth of the hob thread, 0.3433 inch; and (d) the narrowest width of the hob thread and the space, 0.155 inch. The short note at the right of the view tells us that a keyway is to be cut in the surface of the hub hole $\frac{3}{8}$ inch wide and $\frac{3}{16}$ inch deep.

The f marks placed on the working lines of the view show that the sides and the outer surface of the rim and both ends and the hole through the hub are to be finished.

PLATE IV

INTERMEDIATE SHAFT CLUTCH

The piece shown in Plate IV is very nearly the same as that shown in Plate III. The practice is, however, that of another firm and the piece is represented by three views: a front view, a right end view, and a left end view. Reading the lettered data shows the piece to be an intermediate shaft clutch. The cross-section front view shows that the material is steel, and a further reading of the lettered note tells us that the company knows this steel as Carpenter No. 5–317 steel. The left end view shows the *general* form of the clutch teeth. A line drawn across this view near a single tooth shows that a section has been sliced off at this point. The line is lettered *A–B* at its opposite ends to enable the workman to find the view of the part sliced off.

Directly above the left end view is a small view named "section *A–B*". This shows a single clutch tooth viewed as if looked at from the inner, or small, end of the tooth. Extension lines projecting upward from the working lines of the tooth show that the tooth sides incline 5 degrees from the vertical. No other view shown tells us this, and therefore it is necessary for the workman to have this small section.

The right end view shows that the clutch teeth are slanted along their sides at an angle of 20 degrees, or, expressed another way, the sides of the clutch teeth make an angle of 20 degrees with each other. From a further study of this view, we learn that the inner surfaces of two adjacent teeth make an angle of 52 degrees. The lettered note at the right and the arrowhead tell us that the inner ends of the clutch teeth are counterbored $\frac{29}{32}$ inch in diameter and $\frac{1}{8}$ inch deep. Just above the front view at each end arrow points have the numerals 0.124–0.126. The decimal fraction for $\frac{1}{8}$ inch is 0.125; the numerals 0.124–0.126 then show that the $\frac{1}{8}$-inch depth must be cut to a tolerance of not more than 0.001 inch above or below the figured depth, $\frac{1}{8}$ inch. The right end view clearly shows that this shaft clutch has gear teeth in its outer surface, and data under the front view states that there are to be fifteen teeth, ten pitch. The only other note for the workman's use is that giving the size of the keyway.

PLATE V

DETAILS OF FOUR MACHINE PIECES

General Data. In the study of Plate V and of all succeeding plates, it will be assumed that the workman has thoroughly studied all that has gone before and understands what is meant by front, top, bottom, and end views, by sections, and by extension and dimension lines, and that he can find and read the dimensions.

Plate V is made up of four blueprints of small details and illustrates the way in which the Taft-Pierce Company send such into their shops. The number placed in the circle located in the upper right-hand corner of each small print is the part number of the piece and will be referred to in this text as the blueprint number. It will be noted that blueprints Nos. 63, 440, and 113 are all blueprints of bolts.

Swivel Table Stud. The piece shown in blueprint No. 63 is a swivel table stud for a semiuniversal grinding machine. A note placed just beneath the view states that the material is cold rolled steel, cyanide hardened. Only one view, a front view, is given, which indicates that the end views would show as circles. From this single view the workman can get all length dimensions and all diameter dimensions. Among the things to be noted in this blueprint are that the right end of the stud is to be threaded ten threads per inch and that some of the dimensions are given in pairs, for example, those of the body of the stud. This means that the length of the body and the diameter of the body, respectively, must lie within the given pair of figures for that dimension. Take the case of the body diameter; it must not be greater than 0.999 inch nor smaller than 0.998 inch, a tolerance of one-half of one-thousandth inch above or below a central dimension.

Wheel Guard T Bolt. Blueprint No. 440 is a wheel guard T bolt, and the note tells us that two are required and that the material is cold rolled steel. A front and a right end view are given. If a single front view of this piece were shown, the workman would infer that the bolt head was a circle; the end view shows that the bolt head is square. A left end view instead of a right end view would indicate this equally well, but in that case the circles which represent the body of the bolt would be dotted circles instead of showing as they do in the right end view. There are no finish f marks in either view because the piece, as noted, is made from cold rolled steel bar stock, which has a finished surface, and when the bolt is turned to size, the outer surfaces of the head have the original finish of the bar. Moreover, to construct the rest of the bolt naturally finishes those parts.

Diamond Tool Post T Bolt. Blueprint No. 113 is a diamond tool post T bolt, and the lettered note states that one is required and that the material is cold rolled steel, cyanide treated. Two views of this piece are necessary. The views differ from those shown in blueprint No. 440, since the view showing the bolt head is a left end view. Placed in this way, the circles which represent the body part of the bolt show as dotted circles. Another interesting thing is that the body dimension of the bolt is given by the dimension figures as $\frac{5}{8}$ inch, while a lettered note with an arrowhead tells us that the body of the bolt is turned to a diameter of $\frac{39}{64}$ inch and that the threaded part is $\frac{5}{8}$ inch in diameter and has eleven threads per inch. The end view shows that the bolt head inclines at an angle of 60 degrees with the base line.

Cross=Feed Connecting Link. Blueprint No. 345 shows a front view and a top view of a cross-feed connecting link. One only is required and both the lettered note and the arrangement of cross-section lines inform us that the material is cast iron. Where the shape of the cross-section is simple, as shown, it is usual to place it directly on one of the views rather than make an additional view. The cross-sections of pulley arms, connecting rods, and links are generally shown by this method. The workman in reading this blueprint should note that the reamed holes have limiting dimensions given and also that the thickness of the hubs is held to a small tolerance. The finish f marks clearly show what surfaces are to be machined.

PLATE VI

CENTER REST TOP

The lettered data states that Plate VI is a blueprint of a center rest top. One is required and the material is cast iron. A short study will show the machinist that many of the dimensions are given to or from horizontal or vertical center lines; also that some of the dimensions are plain distances, in which case the dimension line has an arrow point at each end, while others are from a center point and give the radius from that point of the working line which represents the surface. When a radius dimension is given, it is usual to place the initial letter $R.$ or the letters $Rad.$ after the dimension figures.

In the front view, the workman should especially note that the hole through the length of the upper part of the piece is to be drilled and reamed a part of the way and drilled and tapped eighteen threads per inch for the rest of its length. Another important item is that, while the radius of the hub is given as $\frac{9}{16}$ inch, the frame back of the hub is machined back to a radius of $\frac{5}{8}$ inch.

In the right end view, the things which the machinist should especially note are that one end of the lower hub is marked f, while the opposite end is marked "disc grind", indicating that the f end is to be carefully finished to an accurate bearing, while it is not necessary to be so particular with the opposite end. The end view also shows that the hole in the hub is to be drilled and reamed. The hole just above the hub is to be drilled and tapped for a $\frac{5}{16}$-inch screw, eighteen threads per inch.

PLATE VII

CENTER REST BASE

A reader of this text who is familiar with machine work knows that a center rest is a fixture used in turning or grinding to give support and steadiness to long or slender work. Plate VIII gives a complete view of a center rest and indicates its use and, before taking up a study of Plate VII, it will be well to glance at Plate VIII.

The lettered title of Plate VII states that it is the blueprint of the center rest base. One is required and it is made of cast iron. The piece of work shown is then the mate of that shown in Plate VI and some of its features and dimensions are the same. A complete front view and a complete right end view are given as well as a portion of a top view, which is placed directly above the left upper corner of the front view.

The working lines of the bottom of the front view and the end view show that the base is provided with a squared projection used to locate the center rest on the bed of the machine. Aside from this, the machinist should notice the data which relates to finishing the small hub at the top of the end view and at the upper right corner of the front view. The term "spot face $\frac{7}{8}''$" indicates that the surface touched by the arrow point is to be finished, by using a counterbore $\frac{7}{8}$ inch in diameter, to the limiting thickness given just above the end view. It should be noted that certain of the holes are drilled and reamed while others are drilled and threaded with a tap. The machinist should carefully observe on which of the working lines of the views the f mark is placed. He should also note in Plate VII, as in Plate VI, that many of the dimensions are given to or from horizontal or vertical center lines and that all dimensions bear a certain relation to a common center, or axis, A. In reading the dimension figures, the machinist will find that several of them have a limiting error tolerance telling him that he must be especially accurate in those dimensions.

PLATE VIII

CENTER REST ASSEMBLY

Plate VIII shows two views, and the lettered title placed just below the views states that the piece is a center rest assembly. The two views furnish a line picture of the completed center rest and show all its separate parts as they are when *assembled* or, as it is often termed, *set up*. It will be noted that each and every part is given a number. These numbers are known as the piece, or part, numbers.

PLATE IX

WORK SPINDLE SLIDE

Compared with many of the blueprints shown, Plate IX, showing the work spindle slide, is difficult to read and it has been selected to illustrate a fairly complicated and irregularly shaped piece. As an aid in reading this blueprint, a short study should be made of the general form and shape of the piece as shown in outline in the front, right end, and top views. An examination of the views shows that the piece consists in general of two hubs, or cylinders, with holes through their length. The cylinders are placed with the smaller above the larger and are connected by a short web running their entire length. When the reader clearly sees this and has the picture clearly in his mind, he can then study the various small hubs, bosses, and other pieces attached to the two long hubs and their connecting flange.

In tracing the location and shape of the several parts, holes, etc., it should be kept clearly in mind that each part in the front view, if shown in the top or in the end view, will be squarely above or squarely to the right of its position in the front view.

Another thing which aids the reader in getting a picture of the piece in mind is its name, "work spindle slide." The note just over the name plate, "Scale Half Size," of course applies to the original blueprint only and not to the reproduction in this text.

Several helps in the form of lettered notes are on this blueprint. As an example, attention is called to a note at one end of the front view which tells us that the dotted lines on which the arrow points touch represent oil grooves $\frac{1}{4}$ inch wide and $\frac{3}{32}$ inch deep. From a study of the upper part of the front view and of the end view we learn at which points the oil grooves start and also that they are drilled at an angle of 45 degrees to reach the surfaces of the slide bearings.

Among the specially important things to be noted is that, while the hole through the length of the smaller of the two long hubs is a straight plain cylindrical hole, the hole through the larger is tapered at its right-hand end $\frac{3}{4}$ inch to the foot for a distance of $5\frac{1}{2}$ inches. Attention is also called to the two slide bearings on the rear side of the work, one slide bearing having right-angle sides and the other a 60-degree side. Threads per inch on blueprints at the shops of the Brown & Sharpe Manufacturing Company are invariably given by Roman numerals. For example, as may be noted on the blueprint, a hole threaded fourteen threads per inch is marked *XIV*. Also, each surface which is to be finished is indicated by drawing a brilliant red line close beside the working line which represents the surface. On this plate and on Plates XII and XIII these lines are shown dotted and are drawn close to the finished surface lines. Lettered notes placed on this blueprint state what special tools should be got from the tool room before starting the work.

PLATE X

DRAWING=IN BOLT

Plate X shows a drawing-in bolt, and the lettered note just below the name tells us that one is required, that the material is cold rolled steel, that it is a forging, that it is forged on a heading machine, and that it is to be casehardened as shown. The fact that the forging is done on a heading machine indicates that the head end only is upset to its rough shape. The letters *C. H.*

placed just below the threaded end and just below the $\frac{3}{4}$-inch hexagon end show that the bolt is to be casehardened at these places, according to the lettered notes. One view only is given, which indicates that an end view would show circles unless otherwise specified. A note at the extreme left end of the view states that the end is made a $\frac{3}{4}$-inch hexagon.

All length dimensions are easily read with one exception, that of the over-all length, which is represented by the capital letter A. Notes lettered on the blueprint at the lower right-hand corner inform us that, when this bolt is made for and used on C2, A is $25\frac{7}{8}$ inches in length, and when it is made for and used on C3, A is $29\frac{15}{16}$ inches. While all the diameter dimensions are easily read, the machinist should surely note that several of them have lettered notes giving additional information. For example, we read that the $\frac{13}{16}$-inch diameter is to be ground 0.001 or 0.002 inch small, "Gr. $\left\{\begin{matrix} .001 \\ .002 \end{matrix}\right\}$ S." In this blueprint, the letters *Rad.* are used instead of the capital letter R. to denote a radius.

PLATE XI

KNEE SHAFT CLUTCH

The title plate at the lower right of Plate XI tells us that the piece of work shown is a knee shaft clutch. Further information given on the title plate indicates that this clutch is used on A3, AA3, BBH2, etc. A lettered note placed on the blueprint just below the two views states that the knee shaft clutch is to be made of machinery steel, that the rough stock is a piece measuring $2\frac{1}{16}'' \times 2\frac{9}{16}''$, and that a certain formed tool is used by the machinist. All the length and all the diameter dimensions are easily found and read, while a copious use of notes gives the machinist much special information. For example, a lettered note placed just below the front view tells us that a certain hole is drilled in position after the piece is taken from stock. This indicates that when finished by the machinist to be placed in stock, this hole is left off and that when the setting-up man gets the piece from the stockroom, he places it in position and then drills it in place. Before starting work on this piece, the machinist should read all notes. The front view is a complete section.

In this blueprint, the information concerning the clutch teeth is contained in a small view placed somewhat above the front view and named a "development of clutch teeth." This view represents the outer surface of the clutch teeth rolled out on a flat surface.

The note tells us that the spaces between the teeth are 0.005 inch wider than the teeth. The view also shows that the sides of the teeth slant to an angle of 5 degrees. The end view is sufficiently complete to show the form of the clutch teeth only, a lettered note placed just below the view giving the number of clutch teeth as eleven. As both views show that the piece of work is by construction finished all over inside and out, no finish needs to be indicated.

PLATE XII

BACK TOOL POST

The title plate informs us that the piece shown in Plate XII is the back tool post and that there are a set of tool posts. A lettered note placed at the upper right tells us that the tool post material is M.I. and that it is to be casehardened to have a mottled surface. This plate, like Plate IX, lists up the special tool-room tools for the job. The views given are front, top, and end views supplemented by a small section view, placed just above the right end view, showing a section on line A–B.

This small A–B section shows that the bottom of the large slot running through the tool post is at an angle of 5 degrees with the back surface of the slot. The working lines of this slot, as shown in the front and the end views, indicate that the top surface of the slot is parallel to the top surface of the tool post and that the lower, or bottom, surface of the slot makes an angle of 20 degrees with a center line drawn parallel to the upper surface of the slot. Working lines, drawn as full lines in the front and the end views but dotted in the top view, show a projecting feather on the under side of the tool post base. Clearly defined dimension lines and figures give the width, depth, and length of the piece. The machinist should note that the width is to be made standard 0.001 inch small; also that certain base surfaces are to be surface ground.

PLATE XIII

CENTER ARM HEAD

Plate XIII is in some respects similar to Plate IX. In reading this plate, the machinist should first strive to get a general picture of the piece well fixed in his mind. As an aid to this, he will first note that the work, a center arm head, consists of two principal hubs separated by a web or shank to give a center-to-center distance of $7\frac{1}{4}$ inches. The upper hub is simple, having as it does a plain hole through its length and a binder boss on its upper side to be drilled, tapped, and counterbored for a binder bolt. The lower hub, however, is well surrounded by projecting parts which, as they carry several holes and other finished surfaces, decidedly present difficulties to the reader. He will do well to take up each hole as shown in the end view and study each as a single hole, getting its position located in each view.

The larger hole, it will be noted, passes entirely through the main lower hub. The hole placed slightly above this hole and to the right hand of the end view can, by studying the front view, be seen to pass entirely through its hub from end to end. The upper hole of the three shown to the left of the main lower hole will be found to be placed on a center line with the one just noted. A small cross-section view just above, lettered "section A-B," aids the reader in clearing up the details of this hole and the two similar lower holes; he should carefully note where the section line A-B is drawn on the end view. A study of the front view and of the section view shows that the upper of the three holes passes entirely through the casting from end to end. A study of the two lower holes in the end view shows that they break into each other. Their location in the front view and in the small section view indicates that, while the hole farthest to the left passes entirely through the casting, the other, which cuts into it, is only $1\frac{1}{4}$ inches deep. Extensions of the centers of these two holes show by dimension figures that their center-to-center distance is $\frac{23}{32}$ inch, and a radius line just below the end view shows that the center of the outer hole is $2\frac{7}{8}$-inch radius from the center of the hole in the main lower hub.

Diagonally drawn dotted lines in the end view represent a hole coming in from the front of the casting at an angle of 22 degrees 35 minutes.   In the front view this hole and its boss show at the side as a series of full and dotted circles.   A lettered note placed on the end view at the right of the vertical center line of the view states that an oil hole is to be drilled.   Following carefully the lines which represent the oil hole, the reader will find that it is to be drilled at an angle of $17\frac{1}{2}$ degrees with the center line of a similar $\frac{3}{16}$-inch hole showing through the lower side of the main hub hole.   Further examination of the end view draws attention to two small circles at the sides of one of the $\frac{7}{8}$-inch holes.   A study of the small section view shows these circles to represent holes drilled, tapped, and counterbored for screws *II* having a $\frac{3}{8}$-inch filister head.   A radius arc drawn from the hole beside which these screw holes are placed shows that their centers are placed at $\frac{9}{16}$-inch radius.   Other screw holes, oil holes, and pin holes can easily be located by a study of the views.   In reading a blueprint such as this, especial care must be used in locating all center lines, radius lines, extension lines, dimension lines, and lines showing angles.

PLATE XIV

BRASS GLOBE VALVE

Plate XIV shows a $1\frac{1}{2}$-inch brass globe valve and the original blueprint is made to full-size scale.   Two views only are given. The front view shows the valve sectioned as if cut down through and on the center line, thus clearly giving an inside view of the valve.   The end view gives an outline of the valve and is in a sense a picture of the valve.   The arrangement of the cross-section lines in the front view indicates that the sectioned metal parts of the valve are, with the exception of the cast-iron handwheel, brass throughout.   By means of the outline view and the section, the draftsman has not only shown all the necessary dimensions of the valve as an assembly but has also shown those of each detail so well that the machinist can work it out.   While it is not general practice in shops to have the workman work from assembly blueprints, it may well be done when a shop is building a standard article.   As there are no finish lines nor *f* marks, the workman would have to decide for himself what surfaces should be finished, if given this drawing to work from.

The several parts of the valve as shown on the blueprint are the valve body, consisting of a globular shaped casting with threaded hexagon ends into which, on its upper side, is screwed the valve cover casting with a threaded bearing for the long spindle; and an upper part, consisting of a stuffing box for the wick packing. At the extreme upper end of the stuffing box are a small circular gland and a gland nut to force it along the valve spindle to compress the wick packing into the stuffing chamber. The valve spindle has on its top end a squared taper end to fit the cast-iron handwheel and a threaded hexagon nut to hold the hand-wheel in place. Toward its lower end an enlarged part of the valve spindle is threaded with a rather coarse-pitch Acme thread to fit the threaded bearing in the valve cap. The extreme lower end of the valve spindle is enlarged and finished to carry the valve disc which seats itself on the valve body seat to close the flow through the valve body from end to end. The disc, or upper, seat moves up and down in narrow guides, as shown in the front section view, and a lettered note placed just below this view states that these guides are to be bored $2\frac{3}{32}$ inches in diameter. The disc has in its lower, or seat, side a circular recess, $1\frac{15}{16}$ inches outside diameter by $1\frac{3}{16}$ inches inside diameter, for a fiber, leather, asbestos, or other seat ring. Two dotted lines about $\frac{3}{16}$ inch apart drawn diagonally across the inside of the valve body, as shown in the front view, represent a diaphragm rib. This is an interesting blueprint to read, as it is necessary to locate carefully all the *extension* lines to learn which *working* lines they extend. Care must also be taken to determine which lines many of the arrow points exactly touch.

PLATE XV

ASSEMBLED CONE GEARS

Plate XV illustrates a method of using an assembly drawing for shop purposes. The view shows a cone of four gears in section on a shaft. The arrangement of the cross-section lines indicates that the gears are made of machinery steel. As shown, the whole cone of gears is mounted on a steel sleeve which, in turn, runs on a composition sleeve. The whole combination is held in position on the shaft by steel collars having hexagon-head set screws. As is customary in such section views, the shaft is not shown sectioned.

Its ends, however, are shown as if broken off and the arrangement of the section lines at the break indicates that the shaft is of steel.

Immediately below each gear, as shown in the view, are placed the letters *A–B–C–D*. The first column of a lettered table placed in the upper right-hand corner shows that similar cones of gears are used on machines, size 2, 3, 4, and 5. The next column gives the number of teeth and the pitch of the teeth required in the gears *A–B–C–D* for the various sizes of machines. The remaining columns of the table give the outside diameter of each gear and its width of face. From this single section view, supplemented by the lettered table, the machinist should be able to get all the essential information for making these gears, with the exception of the hole diameter, which is not given. The two smaller cone gears are shown as if made from a plain steel blank, while the two larger gears plainly show that they have a distinct hub and rim with a thin web connection.

PLATE XVI

FACE GEAR

The two views of a special face gear shown in Plate XVI are half size in the original blueprint. The term "face gear" indicates that the piece represented is the large driving gear on the main spindle of the machine. While no finish *f* marks are found on the working lines of this blueprint, the average machinist would know that the outer diameter, the ends of the hubs, the holes through the gear, and the sides of the rim should be carefully and well finished. In addition to this, a lettered note at the upper right of the front view states that the surfaces indicated by the arrow points are rough turned. The title plate informs us that one is required and that the material is cast iron, which is also indicated by the arrangement of the cross-section lines in the front view.

The view looking toward the end of the gear hub shows that the upper small hub has a short supporting flange and that on its lower edge the upper hub is counterweighted. A lettered note placed just at the left of the front view tells us that the hole in the hub is keyseated $\frac{13}{32}$ inch deep and $\frac{5}{8}$ inch wide and that the key is dovetailed and drives into place. Both views show the key in place. Another important lettered note states that there are eighty-seven teeth milled into the outer face of the piece and that they are to be six pitch. The workman should especially note that the over-all diameter is to be held to definite limits of tolerance.

PLATE XVII

DOWN=FEED WORM

The upper title plate states that the piece shown in Plate XVII is a down-feed worm for a 5-foot boring mill. One is required and the lower title plate gives the material as machinery steel cut from $3\frac{3}{4}$-inch rod $13\frac{1}{8}$ inches long, rough dimensions. Two views are given, with the front view sectioned to indicate steel. All dimensions are given on the front view. The end view is sufficient to show that in general the piece has circular outlines. The end view also shows the shape of the two keyways and, while no direct dimensions are given, this view shows the general position of the holes mentioned in the lettered note, "$\frac{1}{4}$" drill–$\frac{1}{4}$" deep– 2 holes–drill in position".

In considering this piece of work, the machinist is, of course, first concerned with the reamed $1\frac{1}{2}$-inch hole through its length. After this hole is finished ready for the mandrel, he should carefully read all the notes and other lettered directions before beginning to square up and turn the piece. He should especially observe what surfaces are to be ground and give careful attention to the finished dimensions. He will note that certain dimensions have a small limiting tolerance given in thousandths of an inch. He should also note that, while the fine-pitch thread shown on the right end of the front view is a *right-handed* thread cut to suit a certain nut, the coarse-pitch 29-degree worm thread is to be cut *left-handed*. All dimension lines, figures, and extension lines are very clear and are easily located in reference to their working lines. The lettered notes have clearly defined arrow points to indicate the surfaces to which they refer. Attention is called to the diameter dimension reading "$2\frac{19}{64}$ inches neck". This shows that the piece is to be necked in to this diameter previous to grinding the $2\frac{5}{16}$-inch diameter as a protection to the corner of the grinding wheel. No finish f marks are shown, as the piece is finished all over, and this fact has been indicated by the initial letters

F.A.O. placed just below the front view. The $\frac{5}{16}$-inch hole showing just to the left of the flange collar should be drilled before cutting the keyway to give a clearance for the cutting point of the keyseating tool.

PLATE XVIII

SADDLE ADJUSTING LEVER

Plate XVIII, an assembly blueprint, is for the use of the setting-up machinist and clearly indicates how the group of parts which make up the saddle adjusting lever are assembled. It will be noted that each pin, cap screw, set screw, spring, lever arm, sleeve, etc., is given a part number and that an arrow point clearly indicates the part referred to. The arrangement of the cross-sectioning lines in the top view clearly indicates the material of each part; for example, they show that the lever arm #14249 and its hub are cast iron, while the handle screwed into its upper end is of steel. While the shape and position of each part of this mechanism are clearly shown in this blueprint, no dimensions are given, which shows us that, as previously stated, the print is to be used in the shop only by the assembler. The reader in studying this blueprint should consider that he is to assemble the various parts and endeavor to decide in what order they should be assembled: for example, it is clear that #20197, 02268, and 20180 must be placed in position in #14249 previous to screwing #20196 into it; also that #14249 must be placed in position on #14248 previous to attaching cover plate #14246.

PLATE XIX

TOP PULLEY BRACKET

The top title plate informs us that the several views shown in Plate XIX are of a top pulley bracket for a 5-foot boring mill and that two are required. The lower title plate states that the material is cast iron. The views are a front view, a right side view, and a top view, which is in this case projected and positioned just above the right side view. The arrangement of full and dotted lines indicates that the piece consists of a hollow base, or pedestal, having at its upper end a shaft-carrying box, or bearing, which, in turn, has a large grease, or oil, pocket on its upper side.

In reading this blueprint, the machinist should observe that many of the dimensions given are for the use of the pattern maker and are of no especial concern to him. The pattern maker, on the other hand, is concerned with all the dimensions as he must add sufficient stock to every surface marked with an f to allow excess metal for the machinist's purposes. As an instance of this, take some of the dimensions as given on the front view and the right side view. We observe that at the extreme right hand of the side view a dimension of 14 inches is given from the lower line, or base, of the pedestal bracket to the center line of the box. While this is a dimension for the machinist in particular, the pattern maker must also note that the base surface is to be finished and make the dimension enough longer than 14 inches so that the machinist will have metal stock sufficient to allow him to finish the base surface and still have the correct dimension. Also, in considering the shaft hole given as $3\frac{1}{8}$ inches ream, the pattern maker must make his core prints and core boxes enough less than $3\frac{1}{8}$ inches in diameter to allow stock for machining the hole to the specified size. The pattern maker only is concerned with the dimension $\frac{1}{2}$ inch given for the wall thickness of the hollow pedestal and that of $9\frac{1}{4}$ inches given at the bottom of the side view for the width of the pedestal. These and many other dimensions are not subjected to any machining. The pattern maker, then, in reading this blueprint will carefully consider each and every working line, whether drawn full to represent a visible outside surface or drawn dotted to represent an invisible inside surface, in order to give himself a clear mental picture of the construction not only of the outer outlines of the piece but also of all the interior outlines. When the pattern maker has this clear mental picture of the piece, he can then readily trace the dimensions of all parts of his construction by following the extension lines.

If the pattern maker has fully understood the views up to this point he clearly sees: (a) that they represent a ring oiling pedestal bracket with the base cored out to leave walls $\frac{1}{2}$ inch thick, the cored portion to extend up from the base line of the bracket to within $\frac{1}{2}$ inch of the bottom surface of the cored oil chamber; (b) that the cored oil chamber is $4\frac{1}{4}$ inches in length in a direction across the shaft bearing and $1\frac{1}{2}$ inches in width along the shaft hole, and that the oil chamber extends out toward the front of the bracket into a rounded-end projection, or lug; (c) that he must provide a loose pad on the front of the pedestal, as shown, "for belt drive only"; and (d) that the bottom surface of the bracket, the entire hole through the bracket box, the upper surfaces of the oil pocket, and the front face of the bracket pad are to be machined as indicated by finish f marks, and that excess stock for machining off must be allowed on such surfaces.

The machinist in reading the views should carefully note which surfaces are marked with the finish mark for machining. Starting at the pedestal base, as shown in the front and the side views, he will observe that its lower surface is to be machined and that certain holes are to pass through it. A study of the top view and its lettered notes shows that there are to be three holes through the base in each of its ends. Two of each three are drilled for holding-down bolts and one for No. 8 locating taper pins. The holding-down bolt holes are to be spot faced for the heads of the bolts.

Returning to a study of the front and side views, the machinist notes that the front surface of the pad is to be machined. This surface, as shown in the side view, is $4\frac{3}{8}$ inches from the vertical center line. Four $\frac{5}{8}$-inch tapped holes are to be drilled into the face of the pad $3\frac{3}{4}$ inches apart along the horizontal distance and $2\frac{1}{2}$ inches apart in the vertical dimension. Before machining the shaft bearing shown at the upper part of the front and the side views, the machinist should note: (a) that the bearing proper extends in length from the inner edge of a narrow circular oil-collecting pocket to the inner edge of a similar opposite circular oil-collecting pocket and that this bearing surface is bored and reamed to a diameter of $3\frac{1}{8}$ inches; (b) that outside of the circular oil-collecting pockets, the hole diameter is increased to $3\frac{5}{32}$ inches; (c) that while the circular oil-collecting pockets are marked f and are therefore to be machined, no dimensions are given, this indicating that they are simply machined to remove the original scale and to make them truly circular; and (d) that a large central oil-containing chamber is provided for an oil-conveying ring and that two oil-return holes are drilled from the edges of the two circular oil-collecting pockets at an angle which allows them to enter the central oil-containing chamber, the lettered note stating that these oil holes are $\frac{1}{4}$ inch in diameter. Two threaded holes are shown through the upper shell of the shaft-bearing box and a note attached by a line and an arrow point to the upper view explains that they are to be drilled $\frac{13}{32}$ inch for a $\frac{1}{2}$-inch tap. Finally, the upper surfaces of the oil box are marked f to be machined.

PLATE XX

SHAFT=BEARING PEDESTAL

Plate XX shows a shaft-bearing pedestal in which the shaft-bearing box is a separate unit (not shown) which may be supported inside the pedestal. As the shaft-bearing box would be held exactly central with the frame of the pedestal, many of the working lines of the left side view are drawn around the center line, or axis, and several of the dimensions are figured as a radius from a common center. The views consist of a front, or edge, view, a left side view, and two smaller views, one of which is a section on line $A-B$ and the other is placed just below the side view and shows a bottom view of the feet of the pedestal.

Very little machine work is to be done on this piece, merely machining the base supports on their under surface, drilling holes in the feet for four holding-down bolts, and drilling, tapping, and spot facing the three prominent bosses. It will be noted by the machinist that the latter holes are at an angle of 120 degrees with one another. The machinist should also observe that the base supports are to be finished to give their under surface a distance of $9\frac{1}{2}$ inches from the center line, or axis, of the views. Practically all the remaining dimensions are given for the pattern maker's use and are easily located and read.

PLATE XXI

END SHIELD

In reading the front view, the small view, and the right end view of Plate XXI, the reader should clearly see that when he looks at the right end view, he is in fact viewing this *end shield* at its large open end. A study of the front section view shows that the casting essentially consists of a large cup-shaped portion at the right with only a rim bottom. A half rim is attached and projects to the left and carries a circular hub having a circular hole of two diameters. In this blueprint the machinist, to understand the views, must carefully follow each working line of the drawing, locate each extension line, and note each arrow-pointed line.

All the important finished dimensions are given a limiting tolerance in thousandths of an inch. The rim edge of the large cup shown at the right of the front section view is finished to a 5.250-inch diameter and 0.094-inch depth; and three holes through the rim bottom are also finished. Two of these holes, $4\frac{15}{16}$ inches center to center, are counterbored for fillister-head cap screws, while the third hole, showing at the top of both views $2\frac{1}{4}$ inches up from the center line, is countersunk for riveting. A detail of this is given on the lower side of the blueprint. The circular hub which shows at the left of the front section view is machined on its outer end and a double-diameter hole is finished through it. Four holes are drilled and tapped into the outer face of the hub. A lettered note placed slightly to the left and above the hub gives the necessary information for these holes.

PLATE XXII

ARMATURE HEAD

Plate XXII is a combined assembly and detail blueprint and according to the title plate is made up of ① armature head assembly, ② armature head, and ③ stud (fan-supporting), the whole being given the title plate name armature head. The numbers 1, 2, and 3 are clearly shown in the blueprint placed near or on the views. The material of the stud is given in the title plate as cold rolled steel and that of the armature head as soft steel casting. The front view is shown in section on line $A-B-C$. The careful reader will note that section line $A-B-C$ follows the vertical center line of the right side view from A at its lower edge to B at the center axis and then slants to the right and upward, following the center line of one of the three ribs to C.

Stud. A study of the front and the end views shows that the studs ③ (also shown at the upper right of the blueprint) are screwed into the three ribs just mentioned, and a lettered note placed on the sectioned front view states that they are machined to a bevel after assembling.

A small detail section $A–A$ placed just over the center of the side view shows the form of the slot on the section line $A–A$ drawn across the upper edge of the side view. These slots, twelve in number, are shown by dotted working lines in the side view and are spaced evenly completely around the armature head at its extreme left end as the piece is shown in the front view.

Careful study of the views shows that the armature head casting is a circular cup having three narrow shallow ribs cast onto the inner side of its rim. It is into the outer ends of these ribs that the cold rolled steel studs are screwed, as shown. At the opposite, or base, end of the casting is located the outer flange for the slots shown in the detail section $A–A$. Extension lines drawn from the working lines of the flange carry a dimension line and arrow points which show that the flange diameter is $4\frac{3}{4}$ inches. The body rim of the casting is to be finished to an outside diameter of $4\frac{1}{8}$ inches. The hole through the hub of the casting, it should be noted, is finished to a diameter of 1.375 inches, with a tolerance of but one-half of one-thousandth inch above size and no tolerance below the figured diameter. The keyway is figured in the side view as being $\frac{1}{4}$ inch wide and $\frac{9}{64}$ inch deep. It must be noted that the keyway is located in the hub hole on the center line of a rib and not in the thinner part of the hub. The reader should observe that the radius of the rim side of the $4\frac{3}{4}$-inch flange is curved to a $\frac{5}{8}$-inch radius as shown at the upper left of the front view and that a corresponding radius of $\frac{1}{2}$ inch for the flange slots is shown at the lower left of the front view. The centers for these radius lines are shown as 2 inches from the center line of the piece and $\frac{1}{4}$ inch from the edge of the piece. A lettered note placed just below the side view gives the tapped stud holes as 14-24 tap–3 holes. The hole in the outer end of the stud is given as 10-32 tap–$\frac{5}{8}$ inch deep.

PLATE XXIII, Nos. 1 AND 2

DETAILS OF TYPICAL ARMATURE PUNCHINGS

General Data. Plate XXIII is made up of two **D**-size prints, each giving the details of a separate piece. For convenience in referring to them they have been given the numbers 1 and 2. Two other illustrations of a like construction are shown in Plate

XXIV. The pieces represented are punchings from sheet steel or sheet copper. The reader will note that a single complete view of each piece is shown supplemented by section details. The complete views, with the exception of blueprint No. 2 on Plate XXIV, are drawn to one-half scale in the original blueprint and the detail section views, in the original, are made to an enlarged scale about double size. These enlarged details show the form, size, and kind of holes to be made near the outer edge of the punching, as shown at the right of the complete views. A lettered note resting on an arrow states that there are to be eighty-three holes equally spaced around the punching.

Armature End Ring. The title plate gives blueprint No. 1 as an armature end ring punched from hard sheet copper 0.125 inch thick. The holes and the entire punching are made by using what is known as a perforating and shearing punch and die. The metal punched out of the hole, in this case, is turned, or bent, inward as shown in the enlarged details. A note with two arrow pointers tells us that this punching has two $\frac{1}{16}$-inch saw cuts.

Armature Punching. Blueprint No. 2 is an armature punching punched from standard quality soft sheet steel 0.014 inch thick. A single view shows the complete punching. It has a 7-inch hole of a maximum tolerance of 0.001 inch above size and the outside diameter is 10.960 inches with a minimum tolerance of 0.006 inch. The punching is provided with a keyway $\frac{1}{2}$ inch wide and $\frac{17}{64}$ inch deep. The outer rim is provided with eighty-three slotted holes equally spaced around the circumference. An enlarged view of these slots is placed just to the right of the complete view. Lettered notes with arrowhead pointers give all the slot dimensions.

PLATE XXIV, Nos. 1 AND 2

DETAILS OF TYPICAL FIELD PUNCHINGS

Field Punching. In Plate XXIV are shown two blueprints of which No. 1 is a field punching punched from soft sheet steel, standard quality, 0.014 inch thick. One complete view only is given but, as in the blueprints shown in Plate XXIII, there is an enlarged view of the slots. This enlarged view gives complete details of the slots and the exact dimensions with all limiting tolerances. A note placed below the complete view tells us that the slots are thirty-six in number. The punching has four lugs on its rim placed 90 degrees apart. The outer contour of each lug, the careful reader will observe, is made up of arcs of circles connected by short straight lines drawn tangent to the arcs. This gives an irregular outline to the lugs. The die maker will, of course, note that many of the dimensions for this punching are exact to quite small limiting tolerances.

Pole Piece Lamination. Blueprint No. 2 is a pole piece lamination, and the upper note informs us that it is punched from sheet steel, common quality, 0.0625 inch thick. When the reader considers the thickness dimensions of the punchings shown in Plates XXIII and XXIV, he will readily see why an edge view is not given except at an enlarged scale, as in the several detail views. Plate XXIV, No. 2, is drawn full scale in the original blueprint. Only two dimensions show limiting tolerances. Most of the radius lines are from a common center placed somewhat above the view and on its center line. Centers for the other radius lines are clearly defined by small circles inclosing the center points. Radius lines are clearly drawn and dimensioned with the arrow points touching the working lines of the view. The die maker should carefully locate that part of the working line to which each radius line refers.

PLATE XXV

GEARS USED ON 12=INCH MERCHANT MILL

The title plate tells us that Plate XXV shows gears used on a 12-inch merchant mill. The bill of material states that one of these is made from steel casting thoroughly annealed and the other from an open-hearth steel forging. In the original blueprint the views are drawn to a scale of 6 inches to 1 foot. Where two gears are shown and one is larger than the other, the smaller of the two is the pinion and the larger is the gear, and in reading this blueprint they will be referred to in this way.

The pinion is shown in two views, with the front view in section as if sliced through the center of its length. The end view at the left of the front view clearly shows the hole and its keyway through the pinion; other than this, it consists of three concentric circles representing the outside diameter, the pitch diameter, and the root diameter of the pinion teeth. A lettered note placed just beneath the views tells the machinist that the pinion is to be hobbed and has twenty-four teeth of the regular 14½-degree involute form, five diameter pitch. The term diameter pitch refers the pitch of the teeth to the pitch diameter of the gear. Finish f marks show that the pinion is to be finished all over.

The views of the gear are arranged similarly to those of the pinion. Finish f marks show that the ends of the hub, the sides of the rim, the outer diameter of the rim, and the hole through the center are to be machined and that the inside of the gear rim on both its ends is chamfered as shown. The machinist should carefully note that the hole through the hub is bored 3½ inches in diameter and that the gear is to be forced onto its shaft with a pressure of 18 tons. The machinist should also observe that there are forty-eight 14½-degree involute teeth in the gear and that they are to be cut on a gear-hobbing machine. The pattern maker should especially note that there are six holes cored through the web of the gear. All dimensions and extension lines are clearly and plainly defined and so placed as to be easily read.

PLATE XXVI

BEVEL GEARS FOR ROLLS ON SHEET BAR AND SLAB=MILL STEAM FLYING SHEAR TABLE

The title plate of Plate XXVI informs us that the views shown represent a pair of bevel gears used on a 21-inch sheet bar and slab mill steam flying shear table. The bill of material shows them to be open-hearth steel castings thoroughly annealed. The front view of the gears is sectioned by a plane along their axes and shows the gear and the pinion with their teeth engaging, or in *mesh* as it is called. A pair of bevel gears are usually shown thus, and the reader should make himself familiar with this fact and should study every detail. The end view of the pinion and the end view of the gear are just sufficiently complete to show the hubs and the holes and keyways through the hubs.

A lettered note A states the number of teeth in the pinion, the form of the teeth, the pitch of the teeth, and how they are to be machined. A lettered note B gives like information for the gear. When reading these lettered notes, the machinist should not fail to observe that the gear teeth are 20 degrees involute instead of the ordinary 14½ degrees, also that the pitch of the teeth is given as circular pitch instead of the more common diameter pitch. Circular pitch is the distance from the center line of a tooth to the center line of the next tooth and is measured along the pitch circle. In bevel gearing, it is measured at the largest pitch diameter.

The machinist, after carefully reading the lettered notes, is next concerned with the holes through the hubs of the gear and of the pinion. He will note that the gear is to be forced onto its shaft with a pressure of 15 tons and that in the pinion the hole should be a tight fit on the shaft. He will also observe that each keyway is to taper at the rate of ⅛ inch per foot. The machinist's next concern is the outside diameters of the gear and of the pinion. By following the extension lines to their dimension lines he learns that the gear is 14.725 inches and the pinion 9.705 inches outside diameter. He then locates the angles which give him the cone form of the pinion and the gear blank and notes that they are given in degrees and minutes. By using a bevel protractor in his measurements he can readily machine the cone sides and edges to the required angles as given on the blueprint. Making the length of the tooth an even 3 inches as given completes the pinion and the gear blanks (so far as the tooth rims are concerned) ready for cutting the teeth. The back end of each hub is faced up and its end circumference is machined into a circular groove of definite dimensions which are easily found and noted.

Previous to planing the teeth, the machinist should locate the angle marking the bottom of the tooth space. This angle is known as the *cutting angle*, and in this blueprint the reader will find it for both gear and pinion near where the center lines of the gear and the pinion cross each other. For the gear, the cutting angle is 54 degrees 37 minutes and for the pinion it is 29 degrees 19 minutes. The total depth measured at the outer end of the teeth should be noted. This is given as ⅜ inch+0.45 inch. As such gears as these are usually planed on a special gear-tooth planer, no further directions need to be given. The pattern maker will find in this blueprint all the necessary dimension lines, radius lines, and figured angles for a complete pattern for each gear.

PLATE XXVII

MOTOR COUPLING FOR ROD MILL DRIVE

Plate XXVII shows the parts of a motor coupling for a rod mill drive. The bill of material notes six parts A–B–C–D–E–F and gives the material from which each part is made and the number of each required. In the original blueprint all the views are one-quarter size, 3 inches to 1 foot. Lettered note 1 gives special shipping directions, and a most important note placed in the center of the end view gives explicit directions regarding the size of the hole and states that it is to be shrunk on the motor shaft. The front view of the coupling body A is sectioned through the center of its length. For the pattern maker, this is a simple job and he can make no mistakes in finding his dimension lines and figures.

The machinist who carefully reads the views will note that many of his dimensions are given to a special fixed gage. The note on the end view states that the hole is to be bored 0.007 inch small to allow a shrink fit. The keyway in the side of the hole is to be tapered $\frac{1}{8}$ inch per foot. A note at the hub end of the front view shows that this end of the hole is to be chamfered. There are two hole keyways $\frac{15}{32}$ inch deep at the deeper end and a broad shallow keyway across the face of the flange part of the coupling, $1\frac{1}{8}$ inches deep and $3\frac{1}{2}$ inches wide to gage. Finish f marks on the working lines of both views indicate that the piece is machined all over. The smaller details of the coupling B–C–F are given near the right end of the blueprint. F shows two views of the key which fits the broad keyway machined across the face of the coupling flange; one end of the key is curved, as shown, to a radius of $10\frac{7}{8}$ inches. A $1\frac{9}{16}$-inch hole is shown drilled near the curved end and this helps us to understand that a flange bolt B passes through this end of the key when it is fitted in place in the face of the flange. The width dimension shows that it is to gage. The flange coupling bolts B with their nuts C are shown by a front and an end view. The front view shows the nut C in place, which is a common way of showing bolts and nuts. A hole is shown drilled through the body of the bolt near its threaded point for a $\frac{5}{16}$-inch cotter pin. The end view gives the shape of the bolt head and nut and shows it is chamfered at its outer corners.

PLATE XXVIII
BINDER ARM FOR ROPE TAKE=UP

The title plate shows that the views in Plate XXVIII are of a binder arm for rope take-up used on the cooling beds of a 21-inch sheet bar and slab mill. A long bill of materials is given. The title also tells us that in the original blueprint the views are drawn to a scale of 3 inches to 1 foot.

The views are complete and this is a very interesting blueprint for either a pattern maker or a machinist. For example, the reader will note that at the right-hand upper part of the front view the bearing cap is shown in place on its bearing by a series of dash and dot lines known as *broken lines*. This gives a sort of *skeleton* view of the cap. At the same place is a skeleton view of a bushing marked *A18059F*. Looking this number up in the bill of materials, the reader finds that the bushing is made of lumen bronze and that eight are required for four binder arms. Directly below this part of the view and at its extreme lower edge, similar skeleton views are shown of a cap *A18059C* and a bushing *A18059D*. In looking for these numbers in the bill of materials, the reader finds the names of the parts, the material used, and the number required for four binder arms. When the reader has carefully located each part in the bill of materials, he should consider its name, the number required, and the material used. The bill of materials shows that the binder arm is marked *A*, that it is made from a steel casting, and that four are required.

Another interesting matter relating to this blueprint is the method used in sectioning various parts of the views to open up the bearings clearly to the reader. A bottom view of the lower bearing is shown placed just below the side view and a similar top view of the upper bearing is placed just above the left side of the front view. The machinist must finish the four bearings to fit the caps and the lumen bronze bushings and drill a pin hole $3\frac{29}{64}$ inches in diameter for *A18070G* through the length of two circular hubs plainly showing in the lower half of the front and the side views. In addition, he must drill a $\frac{1}{2}$-inch oil hole in the upper part of the lower bearing and a hole just below each of the upper bearing and tap for a $\frac{1}{2}$-inch pipe plug. The machinist will also note that both ends of all four bearings and the inner ends of the pin hubs are finished and that a spring brass wiper is riveted into each of the upper boxes near its inner end.

The pattern maker will note that the framework of the piece is a simple rib construction for supporting the several bearings and hubs and that the working lines are well dimensioned.

The upper bearings are complicated by having to be cored for an oil well, or chamber. The oil in this chamber is distributed to the shaft by means of a tinned steel universal chain *A18059Y* hung on the shaft into the enlarged part of the center of the oil chamber. The pattern maker should also note the special cored holes through the outer and the inner ribs showing just below the long pin hubs. Finish *f* marks placed across certain working lines of the view show the pattern maker for which surfaces he must allow an excess of metal for the machinist's needs. The bolt holes in the upper bearings for *A18059W* are cored, while those in the lower bearings for *A18059V* are drilled by the machinist.

PLATE XXIX

PARTS OF SHUTTLE MECHANISM FOR LOOM

Plates XXIX, XXX, and XXXI are each made up of four small blueprints originally $4\frac{1}{2}''\times5\frac{1}{2}''$ and show the practice of the Crompton-Knowles Loom Company. The small $4\frac{1}{2}''\times5\frac{1}{2}''$ blueprints are those used in their shops as working blueprints. Each small blueprint is from a *free-hand* sketch of some part of one of their machines and contains all that the workman needs to know when machining the piece. Blueprints made like those which we have been studying are used by the pattern maker.

A number placed in a circle has been added to each small blueprint to make it easy to refer to and each is provided with a title plate which contains certain information useful to the workman. For example, the title plate of the small blueprint No. 1 tells us that the piece is a rocker iron for a shuttle change motion on a medium duck loom and that the material is cast iron. Blueprint No. 2 shows the lower part of a shuttle carrier; No. 3, a stand for a lifter; and No. 4, the top part of a shuttle carrier. In many of these blueprints no over-all dimensions are given, and as they are not made to any particular scale of sizes, in such cases the sketch artist places the over-all length of the piece in the upper left-hand corner in small numerals over or on a short line; for example, the piece in blueprint No. 1 is 21 inches long. While this dimension is of no value to the machinist, it does aid the stores keeper in handling the castings, for, while each sketch is a picture of the piece in so far as its outlines are concerned, unless the small numerals are read, there is nothing in the view to indicate whether the piece is inches or feet in length. While such working blueprints are not commonly used, it is worth the reader's while to study them, as they show very clearly the use of free-hand sketches.

It must be borne in mind that in certain lines of machine building, while a given machine may consist of a great many parts, each part may be a very simple piece requiring but little or no machining; for example, blueprint No. 1 shows a piece of work that is to have four drilled holes, two of which are tapped; No. 2 shows a piece with one drilled hole; No. 3 is marked "no labor" and shows a piece of work in which the holes are made in the foundry by the use of properly shaped cores; and No. 4 is a little more complicated, having two $\frac{5}{16}$-inch tapped holes $3\frac{1}{4}$ inches apart and one $\frac{1}{4}$-inch tapped hole with the end of the hole boss, faced.

PLATE XXX

DETAILS OF GEARED MECHANISM USED ON CROMPTON=KNOWLES LOOM

In Plate XXX, blueprint No. 1, which represents a stand for a gear guard, is shown in the same manner as the blueprints in Plate XXIX. When pieces are sketched in this way, they are said to be shown in *perspective;* they are also termed picture sketches, as they are shown tipped and swung around from the regular squarely viewed position of the ordinary blueprint. Blueprints Nos. 2, 3, and 4, Plate XXX, representing a spur gear on the crankshaft, a hub for a pulley, and a spur gear on the bottom shaft, respectively, are shown viewed squarely from the front, and the real difference between them and most of the blueprints which we have studied lies in their being made by free-hand pen methods rather than by the use of drawing instruments. An end view of blueprint No. 2, 3, or 4 would show a series of concentric circles. Finish f marks indicate the working surfaces which are to be finished by some method of machining.

In Nos. 2 and 4 two dotted working lines and a lettered note tell us that a $\frac{5}{16}$-inch keyway is to be machined in the surface of the holes through the central hubs of these gears. In the case of No. 2, a lettered note states that four $\frac{9}{16}$-inch holes on a $6\frac{7}{8}$-inch circle are to be drilled through the web of the gear, and the sketch shows that these are placed in slightly raised hubs, or bosses.

It will be noted by the careful reader that, while in most instances the finish f marks are placed in the usual manner on the working lines of the views, in some cases they are given with the dimension figures. As a case in point, take the diameter of the longer hub in No. 2. Here the finish f mark follows the dimension figures thus, $2\frac{3}{4}''$ f. Several similar cases will be noted in these sketches by the interested reader. While most machine gears have "cut" teeth, this is not universally so on certain lines of machinery and lettered notes at the top of No. 2 and No. 4 state that these gears have "cut" teeth.

PLATE XXXI

MISCELLANEOUS MECHANISMS USED ON CROMPTON-KNOWLES LOOMS

Plate XXXI, like the two preceding plates, is made up of four blueprints originally $4\frac{1}{2} \times 5\frac{1}{2}''$. Reading the title plate, we learn what each piece is and the material used. Blueprints Nos. 1, 2, and 4 show, respectively, a stand for a shipper and lock lever, an angle iron post, and a guide for a lifter rod, and they are picture, or perspective, views. No. 3 is the ordinary type of freehand sketch and shows a front and an end view of a ratchet and pinion.

While no special directions are needed in reading, attention is called in No. 1 to the $\frac{5}{8}$-inch hole near the lower part of the piece. While this shows the stud #4757 in place, the stud is evidently a separate piece. In No. 2, the long shank has no finish f marks but is marked $\frac{3}{4}''$ f. In No. 3 two views are necessary to show that one set of teeth is on a slender hub.

PLATE XXXII

BRASS CHECK VALVE

First=Angle Projection. While "Mechanical Drawing," Parts I, II, and III, does not anlayze in detail the method of projection used in Plate XXXII, readers of blueprints often have such placed in their hands. The blueprints of machine parts shown in this text are, with this one exception, drawn in what is known as third-angle projection. In other words, instead of placing the object we are viewing on the far side of some material like plain glass and viewing it through the glass and then making on the glass a sketch of what we see, the object is placed in front of the glass and we make the sketch on the glass as if we sighted along its edges and drew lines on the glass in line with the edges we were sighting. Looking at an object in this manner places the right end view in the blueprint at the left side of the front view instead of at the right side as in previous blueprints, and the surface lines seen in looking down on the top of the object are shown below the front view.

Placing of Views. If this method is clear in the reader's mind, let him return to Plate XXXII. He will observe that the front view of this 1½-inch brass check valve has been placed at the upper left-hand corner of the sheet. Just below the front view and centered with it is the view one would get of this valve if he were viewing it on its top side, or upper surface. By the regular third-angle system of placing views, the top view would be shown above the front view. The end view, as the careful reader will note, represents the view one would get if looking at the left end of the front view. While it is, then, a view of the left end of the valve and would, in ordinary view arrangement, be placed at the left of the front view, it is by the first-angle arrangement of views placed at the right of the front view. In tracing the location of a line from one view to another, the blueprint reader will need to use care if he is not accustomed to this method of showing views.

Details of Blueprint. Other than the arrangement of views, this blueprint is easily read, having, as it does, a hollow spherical body with hexagon ends and a circular hole in its upper side, a hexagon cap screwed into the top side hole, and an internal swing hinged valve flapper. A tapped hole in the upper right corner of the body is made at an angle of 40 degrees with the axis of the valve body and into this is screwed a special plug as shown. The flapper is hinged on a small diameter spindle which is centered and held in place by two bearing plugs placed opposite each other in the body of the valve. The flapper consists of a hinged frame, a circular disc having a ring of leather or asbestos in its under side groove, a bolt, a nut, and a washer to hold the ring in the disc groove and the ring and disc onto the hinged frame.

PLATE XXXIII

SPINDLE

When interpreting Plate XXXIII, the reader will note from the title plate that the spindle is made from 15-point machine steel. Fifteen point when used in this manner means that the carbon content in the steel is fifteen-hundredths of one per cent. The shop man and the mill man shorten this by saying or writing it 15 point. A front view only is needed to show all the necessary outlines of the spindle and to give all the necessary dimensions for the workman as an end view would consist of a series of concentric circles except for the keys and their seatings.

Dotted lines centered with the center line of the work and drawn from end to end of the view show a hole through the length of the spindle. A lettered note tells us that in the right-hand, or nose, end of the spindle this hole is No. 12 taper to a plug depth of 6 inches. In producing the hole, the workman would first drill a hole $7\frac{5}{8}$ inches deep plus or minus $\frac{1}{8}$ inch, using a $1\frac{3}{16}$-inch drill, and then he would continue the hole completely through the length of the spindle, using a 1-inch drill. A lettered note with an indicating arrowhead informs us that the rear end of the hole is to be chamfered $\frac{1}{8}$ inch for center. Another lettered note states that the spindle bearings are to be pack hardened at least $\frac{1}{16}$ inch deep. A lettered note placed near the nose of the spindle tells us that the $3\frac{1}{4}$-inch and the $3\frac{1}{2}$-inch diameters are to be a forced fit in part #4470. Some makers of working blueprints use the term press fit instead of force fit. Either term would indicate that part #4470 is to be pressed onto the spindle at the places indicated by the arrow points. The lettered note placed at the left end of the spindle refers to a wringing fit. A wringing fit is one in which the parts are so fitted in dimensions as to have to be wrung, or twisted, together; some workmen interpret this to mean a fitting so snug that the pieces go together by lightly rapping them. In any case, it means a fit so snug that a little forcing is needed to slip the pieces together. The reader's attention is called to the limiting tolerances as expressed by the plus and minus signs and to the printed directions placed at the lower edge of the sheet which state that "unless otherwise specified, limits on this drawing are $\pm 0.005''$; dimensions of angles $\pm 1°$; and reamed or bored holes standard to $0.001''$ small". The term Woodruff key refers to the Whitney system of using Woodruff keys.

PLATE XXXIV

ROOF TRUSS

Plates XXXIV and XXXV are shown for the reason that the average shop man may be at times called upon to use such. Plate XXXIV shows a piece of structural work known as a roof truss. The word "truss" is shortened to *Tr.* on the blueprint. Steel structural work such as trusses, beams, girders, and columns is usually made up of angles, I beams, channels, plates, etc., riveted in such a manner as to get the desired construction. The various angles, channels, etc., are known as shapes and are hot rolled at the steel mills, straightened, and sold in open market.

The truss shown in Plate XXXIV is built up of angles of varying lengths riveted together and to flat pieces of plate known as gussets, or sometimes gusset plates. The several pieces of angles are given a letter symbol. In the roof truss shown the short pieces of angle steel used to tie the upper and lower parts together are symbolized by *D* and show on the blueprint as *D–1*, *D–2*, etc. The gusset plates are symbolized by *G* and appear on the blueprint as *G–1*, *G–2*, etc. In many cases a truss is too long to ship complete and has to be partly completed at the place used, or, as it is termed, in the field, and rivets driven after the truss leaves the shop are known as field rivets. The rivets which are to be driven while the truss is being built in the shop are indicated in the blueprint by small full circles, while the position of field rivets is shown on the angles by small white circular spots.

Noting what has been said relative to riveting, it will be observed that the blueprint shows that this truss is to be shipped in three sections and field riveted at the place where it is to be used.

A steel angle as rolled has the form shown in Fig. 2. The upright and the horizontal parts are known as the legs of the angle. In the truss shown, two of these angles about 30 feet 10 inches long are placed back to back to form the left half of the upper slant of the truss. In the same manner, two angles about 29 feet $11\frac{3}{16}$ inches long are placed back to

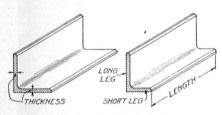

Fig. 2.   Details of Angle Sections

back to form the right upper half of the truss. Previous to riveting the angles together for making each top slant, gusset plates as shown at G–1, G–2, G–4, G–5, and G–7 are slipped between the angles and the whole is riveted together. In a like manner, the lower chord of the truss is riveted up. It will be noted that the gusset plates G are trimmed to come flush at the outer surfaces of the truss, but that they project into the inside of the truss a distance sufficient to allow the several short angles to be riveted to them. It will also be observed that when the angles are riveted together back to back with gusset plates, the surfaces of the legs of the angles are separated by an amount equal to the thickness of the gusset G. Any rivets driven through the angle plates at space points held apart by the gussets have small washers slipped into the crack, or space, between the angles, and the rivets are then set up through the washer. This is shown on the blueprint by means of a dotted circle around the space rivets. It must be noted that the bottom chord of the truss is not made up of single-length angles but is spliced at points about 15 feet $4\frac{1}{8}$ inches from each end of the truss. Where a splice such as this occurs in the bottom chord of a truss, it is strengthened by riveting a splice plate onto the bottom of the angles, covering and tying the splice.

Instead of giving in degrees and minutes the angle one piece makes with another, as is done in machine shop drawings, a small triangle is placed on the piece, as shown at the upper end of angle D–3 and on its lower side. This means that the line on the gusset plate along which the rivet holes are to be placed rises from a base line $8\frac{11}{16}$ inches in 12 inches. The layout man accordingly measures off a base line on the gusset 12 inches in length and erects a perpendicular line on one end $8\frac{11}{16}$ inches in height. From this height he may scribe a line to the other end of the 12-inch base line and this is the gage line for the rivet holes. In all structural steel work the rivet holes are spaced along lines located a given distance from the back of the angle. These lines are termed *gage* lines and are not center lines in the usual sense. For example, in the view shown the reader will note that in the top member of the truss in the front view there are two gage lines and therefore two lines of rivets.

It will be observed that, while the top view of the truss is placed above the front view as in previous blueprints which we have studied, it parallels the slant of the truss. If a bottom view were given of this truss, it would show as if viewed from inside the truss; such a view is distinctly different from the bottom views already studied, and this point should be carefully noted in reading structural drawings.

PLATE XXXV

PLAN OF FOUNDRY BUILDING

Plate XXXV shows the plan of a foundry building. While the blueprint is more than ordinarily complete, it fairly represents such plans. The walls of the building are of brick and the windows are the prominent features of the walls. The reader should observe that the outside dimensions of the building, the door sizes, and the thickness of the walls are given; the columns, posts, interior walls, and partitions are located; the center-to-center distances are given; the foundry equipment is given and its position located on the plan; all stairways are indicated; and room measurements are given. Attention is called to the method of representing the windows by means of two parallel lines placed across the openings in the brick wall and to the method of showing the doors swung partly open. The plan shows a gallery floor along one side of the building. On this floor are located the office of the foreman, the charging floor for the cupolas, the motor room, etc.; the gallery floor is supported partly by the 9-inch latticed channel columns and partly by a series of 6-inch round cast-iron columns. Three sets of doors are shown opening into the air and one opening into a tunnel to the shop. As a means of carrying off roof water and drainage from the pickling bed and cleaning room, a soil pipe line is shown. As most of this line of pipe is placed beneath the floor, it appears in the blueprint as a double dotted line. Two tile-lined chimneys are shown; one of these is for the brass furnace and one for the core oven. The core room is partly inclosed by means of a low wall capped with cast plates. The 8-foot door opens onto a driveway as do the two 5-foot 8-inch doors. These driveways and the street along the front of the building are not shown in the plan, but the street location could be assumed by the fact that the soil pipes, the clay drain, and the water pipes extend beyond the wall in a certain direction.

PLATE XXXVI

TYPICAL FIRE INSURANCE MAP

In fire insurance work the graphic description of a property has an important function; the custom is to show a plan or simple diagram of the insured properties, Plate XXXVI, adding certain simple devices for indicating such features of the building as may conveniently be described in this manner.

The map of a fire insurance risk gives the general location of the risk and its position relative to other risks. It also shows a scale drawing of the ground plan of the building, giving the dimensions, area, and, at the same time, a perfect idea of its general contour and the relation of the subdivisions of the building. By varying the thickness of the wall lines they are made to represent different kinds of walls. Unfinished or incomplete walls are represented by dotted lines; open spaces in the line indicate where the wall is interrupted or where a window opening occurs. Color is used to a large extent to indicate the different forms of construction; certain symbols, which follow in a measure the shapes of the things they represent, are used to shorten the description; and of course the use of initial letters is too well known to be more than mentioned. These symbols, it must be understood, are purely arbitrary but, having become established and recognized, they form the *symbol* language of the inspector and must be studied in a practical way in order to be recognized when presented. A few of these symbols and their description are given to convey some idea of the manner in which the map may be interpreted.

A solid thick line ▬▬▬▬ represents an independent wall. A solid thin line represents a party wall. A distinct break in the line representing a division or side wall —— —— indicates an opening made by a doorway or arch. A small curved line ⌐⌐⌐ or a short line at right angles indicates the presence of a fire door, the auxiliary line being placed on the side of the wall the door is on. An auxiliary line on each side indicates a fire door on each side of the walls. A double curved line ——⌐ is used to represent a standard fire door. ☐ A little black dot on the inside end of a window line indicates a window opening on that side of two adjoining walls. If the black dot is missing, it means that there is no window on this floor. A single curve over the end of the window line represents a non-standard fire shutter. A straight line indicates the presence of wire glass. The initial H within a hollow square is used to represent a hoistway or hatch. ☐S☐ ▥ The letter S within a hollow square is used to represent a stairway. A stairway is also represented by a rectangular outline crossed by straight lines supposed to represent the stair steps. A solid black oblong figure represents a horizontal boiler, while a solid black circle represents a vertical boiler. A thin line around the solid black oblong figure ▬◯ *60 H.P.* and the margin colored in red represents a horizontal steam boiler which is bricked in. A small thin-lined circle with diagonals and a black dot at their intersection ⊗*A.S.* indicates an automatic sprinkler riser. A sprinkler pressure tank is represented thus ⌐▭◯.

Plate XXXVI is a copy of a map issued in connection with the adoption of these symbols by the Fire Underwriters Uniformity Association and brings into use practically all the symbols needed in maps of this character. While this type of blueprint is special, the ability to read it is of value.

PLANER USED FOR PLANING HOWITZER GUN FORGING

Courtesy of Cincinnati Planer Company, Cincinnati, Ohio

PRACTICAL MATHEMATICS

PART I

INTRODUCTION

No one who is at all acquainted with the demands of the Engineering profession will deny the need of a good foundation in elementary mathematics any more than he will deny the need of a solid underpinning on which to rest the walls of a big business block.

The simplest problems of the contractor and workman, such as the number of feet of lumber required for a house, the number of cubic yards of excavation for a ditch or cellar, the proper understanding of plans and specifications, and the laying off of measurements according to these plans, all require a knowledge of this important subject. The size of a concrete retaining wall, the dimensions of a girder for a steel structure, the amount of iron in the field of a dynamo, or the capacity of the cylinders of an engine, is certainly not left to the arbitrary judgment of a foreman but is carefully worked out by mathematics and by a knowledge of the properties of the materials used.

Mathematics might be likened to a kit of tools which the workman carries; the master workman carries more than the apprentice and the more tools each man has in his kit and knows how to use, the more things he can do and the greater is his earning power. Each mathematical process is a tool to be used as the occasion demands. Some of them are used in every problem which comes up, others less frequently, but the more advanced the work the greater the number of tools required.

It is with this keen demand in mind, therefore, that we are requiring of each student at the outset of his course this work or its equivalent in Practical Mathematics. We want him to fill his kit with enough tools to meet the steady demands of the work ahead of him, and we feel sure that, once provided with this equipment, his progress will be assured.

In the preparation of this work the authors have intentionally lost sight of the material usually found in the school books on this subject, and have kept in mind only the particular parts which are of special importance to the engineering student. Not only the topics discussed but all of the problems have been made exceptionally practical, and the aim has been at all times to give the student the satisfaction of knowing that whatever he is learning will be of use in his work and will also count for his advancement.

DEFINITIONS AND MATHEMATICAL SIGNS

1. Definitions. *Mathematics* is the science which treats of quantity; its fundamental branches are Arithmetic, Algebra, and Geometry.

Quantity is anything which can be increased, diminished, or measured; as numbers, lines, space, motion, time, volume, and weight.

A *unit* is a single thing, or *one*.

A *number*, or quantity, is a unit or a collection of units and is either *concrete* or *abstract*.

A *concrete* number, or quantity, is one whose units refer to particular things, as, for example, 5 rivets, 7 bolts.

An *abstract* number, or quantity, does not refer to any particular thing. For example, 5, 23, etc., used without designating any particular objects, are abstract numbers.

Like quantities refer to the same thing, as 7 saws, 2 saws; *unlike* quantities refer to different things, as 2 trunks, 4 tables, 3 chairs.

2. Mathematical Signs. For the sake of brevity, signs are used in mathematics to indicate processes. Those signs most used in Arithmetic are $+$, $-$, $\times$, $\div$, $=$, ( ), and $\overline{}$.

The sign $+$ is read "plus" and is the sign of addition. It shows that the quantities between which it is placed are to be added together. If 2 and 2 are to be added, it is expressed, thus: $2+2$ are four.

The sign $-$ is read "minus" and is the sign of subtraction. It means that the quantity which follows this sign is to be subtracted or taken away from the quantity which precedes it, thus: $6-4$ are 2.

The sign $\times$ is read "times" and is the sign of multiplication. It means that the quantity which precedes this sign is to be multiplied by the quantity which follows it, thus: 2×5 are 10.

The sign ÷ is read "divided by" and is the sign of division. It means that the quantity which precedes this sign is to be divided by the quantity which follows it, thus: 4 ÷ 2 are 2.

The sign = is read "equals" or "is equal to" and is the sign of equality. It means that the expressions between which it is placed are identical in value, thus: $4 + 3 = 10 - 3$. This sign is very often misused. Great care should be taken at all times to make sure that the quantities connected by it are *equal*. For example, it would be absurd to say that $5 + 9 = 14 ÷ 2 = 7$, because $5 + 9$ does not equal 7.

The *parenthesis* ( ) and *vinculum* ‾‾‾ are used to show that two or more quantities are to be treated as one; or in other words, that the operations indicated within the parenthesis or under the vinculum are to be carried out first, thus: $- (20+5)$ is equal to -25, not $-20+5$; similarly, $-\overline{2+3}$ is equal to -5.

NOTATION

3. *Notation* is the art of writing numbers in words, in figures, and in letters.

There are two methods of notation in common use; the *Roman* and the *Arabic*.

4. Roman Notation. In the *Roman notation*, 7 capital letters are used, as follows:

I is used to express one.
V " " " " five.
X " " " " ten.
L " " " " fifty.
C " " " " one hundred.
D " " " " five hundred.
M " " " " one thousand.

All other numbers are expressed by repetitions or by combinations of these seven letters according to the following rules:

By repeating a letter the value denoted by the letter is doubled; thus: XX means twenty; CC means two hundred.

By placing a letter denoting a less value before a letter denoting a greater, their difference of value is represented; thus: IV denotes four or one less than five; XL denotes forty or ten less than fifty.

By placing a letter denoting a less value after a letter denoting a greater value, their sum is represented; thus: VII denotes seven or two more than five.　XV denotes fifteen or five more than ten.

A line ‾‾ *placed over a letter increases the value denoted by the letter a thousand times;* thus: $\overline{X}$ means ten thousand.　$\overline{IV}$ means four thousand.

The use of the Roman notation is now confined mainly to the writing of dates, and the numbering of chapters in books, and the hours on the dials of clocks.

Table I shows some of the combinations of the 7 letters used.

TABLE I
Roman Notation

I.	one	LXXX.	eighty
II.	two	XC.	ninety
III.	three	C.	one hundred
IV.	four	CC.	two hundred
V.	five	CCC.	three hundred
VI.	six	D.	five hundred
VII.	seven	DC.	six hundred
VIII.	eight	DCC.	seven hundred
IX.	nine	CM.	nine hundred
X.	ten	M.	one thousand
XX.	twenty	MD.	fifteen hundred
XXX.	thirty	MM.	two thousand
XL.	forty	$\overline{X}$.	ten thousand
L.	fifty	$\overline{M}$.	one million
LX.	sixty	MCMX.	1910
LXX.	seventy		

5. Arabic Notation.　The *Arabic notation* employs ten characters or figures in expressing numbers.　They are

1,	2,	3,	4,	5,	6,	7,	8,	9,	0
one	two	three	four	five	six	seven	eight	nine	cipher

The first nine are sometimes called *digits;* the cipher is also called *naught* or *zero* because it expresses *nothing* or the absence of a number.

The digits (1, 2, 3, 4, 5, 6, 7, 8, 9) have been termed *significant figures* because each has of itself a definite value, always representing so many units or *ones* as its name indicates.　However, the value of the units represented by a figure depends upon the particular position which that figure occupies with regard to other figures.　This position is called its *place* or *order.*

For example, if three figures are written together to represent a number, as 444, each of these figures, without regard to its **place,** expresses four units, but when considered as part of the number these fours differ in value. The 4 in the first place to the right represents *4 units;* the 4 in the second place, represents *4 tens* or 4 units each ten times the size or value of a unit of the first place; and the 4 in the third place, represents *4 hundreds,* or 4 units each one hundred times the size or value of a unit of the first place. It is readily seen that the value of any figure is increased ten-fold by removing it one place to the left.

$$
\begin{array}{r}
\text{hundreds} \\
\text{tens} \\
\text{units} \\
4 = 4 \text{ units} \\
4\ 0 = 4 \text{ tens} \\
4\ 0\ 0 = 4 \text{ hundreds} \\
\hline
4\ 4\ 4 = \text{total}
\end{array}
$$

The cipher becomes significant when connected with other figures by filling a place that otherwise would be vacant, as in 10 (ten) it gives a ten-fold value to the 1. In 130 (one hundred thirty) it gives a ten-fold value to the 13. A cipher between two or more figures produces the same effect. In 405 the cipher which fills the intervening place between 4 and 5 causes the 4 to represent four *hundreds,* not four **tens.**

$$
\begin{array}{r}
\text{hundreds} \\
\text{tens} \\
\text{units} \\
5 = 5 \text{ units} \\
0\ 0 = 0 \text{ tens} \\
4\ 0\ 0 = 4 \text{ hundreds} \\
\hline
4\ 0\ 5 = \text{total}
\end{array}
$$

The following principles should be firmly fixed in mind:

All numbers are expressed by the nine digits and zero.

Zero has no value; it is used to fill vacant places only.

A figure has different values according to the place it occupies.

The base of the system of notation is ten; ten units of any order making one unit of the next higher order.

NUMERATION

6. *Numeration* is the art of reading numbers when expressed by letters or figures.

This is accomplished by first enumerating the *orders* from right to left, as shown in Table II, and then reading these orders in the reverse direction in groups of three, called *periods.* The first three orders, *Units, Tens, Hundreds,* constitute the *first* or *unit period.* The second three orders form the *second* or *thousand period;* the third three orders, the *third* or *million period;* and so on.*

---

* Commas are used to separate the different periods of figures. In reading **numbers** never use "and" to connect the periods, or orders.

The system of periods is shown clearly in Table III. Such a number as 534 consists of one period and is read—five hundred thirty-four. The number shown below the orders in Table II is read—two million, seven hundred fifteen thousand, six hundred thirty-nine.

TABLE II
The Orders

7th	6th	5th	4th	3rd	2nd	1st
Millions	Hundreds of Thousands	Tens of Thousands	Thousands	Hundreds	Tens	Units
2	7	1	5	6	3	9

The number in Table III, which is 987654321987654, is divided into the periods 987, 654, 321, 987, 654, and is read—nine hundred eighty-seven trillion, six hundred fifty-four billion, three hundred twenty-one million, nine hundred eighty-seven thousand, six hundred fifty-four.

TABLE III
The Periods

Hundreds Tens Units } of Trillions	Hundreds Tens Units } of Billions	Hundreds Tens Units } of Millions	Hundreds Tens Units } of Thousands	Hundreds Tens Units } of Units
9 8 7	6 5 4	3 2 1	9 8 7	6 5 4
5th Period	4th Period	3rd Period	2nd Period	1st Period

PROBLEMS FOR PRACTICE

Write in words:

1. 18,765,972.
2. 834,769,780.
3. 3,576,879,421.
4. 10,805,056. Ans. Ten million, eight hundred five thousand, fifty-six.

Write in figures:

5. Seventy-eight million, forty-one thousand, seven.
6. One thousand three. Ans. 1,003.
7. Five hundred six thousand.
8. Ninety million, two thousand, three hundred twenty-seven.
9. Three hundred five thousand, seventy-nine.
10. Eight hundred sixty-four million, four thousand, twenty.

ADDITION

7. *Adding* is the process of finding a number which is equal to the combined values of two or more given numbers. The result thus obtained is called the *sum*. Hence, it may be said that the sum of two or more numbers is a number containing as many units as all the numbers taken together. Thus the sum of 5 rivets and 7 rivets is 12 rivets, since 12 contains as many units as 5 and 7 together.

Letters of the alphabet are also used to represent quantities. A letter may stand for any number, but the same letter must have one value throughout a given problem, although it may have different values in different problems. For example, a may equal 3 in one problem, and 7 or 13 in another; b may equal 2 in one problem, and 5 in another; c may equal 2, 3, 9 or 25; and so on with other letters. The sum of a, b, and c will be equal to $a+b+c$, just as the sum of 2, 5, and 7 will be equal to $2+5+7$. Now, if $a=2$, $b=5$, and $c=7$, the sum of a, b, and c is found by simply adding together 2, 5, and 7, obtaining 14; on the other hand, if the values of a, b, and c are not known, their sum can only be indicated. If a and b represent the horse-powers of two different engines or of two weights lying in a scale-pan, then $a+b$ equals the total horse-power or the total weight.

8. Since a number is a collection of units of the same kind, two or more numbers may be united into one sum only when they are like quantities; thus: 2 bolts $+ 4$ bolts $= 6$ bolts, but 4 rivets and 3 bolts cannot be united into one quantity, either of bolts or of rivets. On the other hand, if quantities of different kinds are represented by letters, they may be added together in order to help solve the problem. For example, if a represents a car, and b an engine, their sum may be indicated $(a + b)$. It must be remembered, however, that the car and the engine have not actually been added together, because they represent unlike quantities. The use of letters makes the solution of certain kinds of problems much simpler, and later will be taken up more fully.

Rules for Addition. *Write the numbers under each other, placing them so that units are under units, tens under tens, hundreds under hundreds, and so on.*

Add up the column of units; and put the right-hand figure of this sum under the unit column, carrying the remaining figure or figures to the column of tens; add up the tens column, including the carried figures, put down the right-hand figure and carry as before. Continue in this way until the last column is reached, putting down the total of the last column to give the final sum.

Examples.   1. Find the sum of 567; 141; and 93.

SOLUTION. Write these numbers under one another, so that the units of each shall be in the same vertical column. Then add up as follows: 3 and 1 are 4, and 7 are 11. Place the right-hand figure 1 under the units column and carry 1 ten to the next column. Adding the tens column, 1 (carried) $+ 9$ are 10 and 4 are 14 and 6 are 20. Put down the right-hand figure, which is zero, and carry 2 to the next column; then 2 (carried) and 1 are 3 and 5 are 8. Putting down the 8, the total sum is found to be 801.

$$\begin{array}{r} 567 \\ 141 \\ 93 \\ \hline 801 \end{array}$$

2. Find the sum of 6,321; 2,576; 9,702; and 257.

SOLUTION. Write these numbers one under the other as before. Add up the unit column as follows: 7 and 2 are 9, and 6 are 15, and 1 are 16. Put down the 6 and carry the 1; then adding the tens column, 1 (carried) and 5 are 6, and 7 are 13, and 2 are 15. Put down the 5 and carry the 1; then adding the hundreds column, 1 (carried) and 2 are 3, and 7 are 10, and 5 are 15, and 3 are 18; put down the 8 and carry the 1. Then adding the thousands column, 1 (carried) and 9 are 10, and 2 are 12, and 6 are 18. Putting down the whole amount, 18, gives the total sum of the numbers as 18,856.

$$\begin{array}{r} 6321 \\ 2576 \\ 9702 \\ 257 \\ \hline 18856 \end{array}$$

3. Add the following quantities: $a + 2b + c$, $3b + 2c$, $6a + b + c$, and $10b$.

SOLUTION. Write the quantities in columns, keeping the like terms under each other; that is, keep the a's in the first vertical column, the b's in the second, the c's in the third. The sum of the a's is $a + 6a$ or $7a$.* $2b + 3b + b + 10b$ are $16b$. $c + 2c + c$ are $4c$. Connecting the sums by the sign of addition the total is found to be $7a + 16b + 4c$. When the number showing how many times the letter is taken is omitted, the letter is to be taken once. Thus: $a = 1a$, $b = 1b$, $c = 1c$.

$$\begin{array}{r} a + 2b + c \\ 3b + 2c \\ 6a + b + c \\ 10b \\ \hline 7a + 16b + 4c \end{array}$$

9. Proof. To prove that a sum is correct, begin at the top and add the columns *downward* in the same manner as they were added upward; if the two sums agree, the work is presumably correct, for adding downward inverts the order of the figures, and therefore any error made in the first addition would probably be detected in the second.

PROBLEMS FOR PRACTICE

Find the sum of

1. $56 + 49 + 17 + 36 + 21$. Ans. 179
2. $42 + 46 + 43 + 58 + 91$.
3. $467 + 536 + 84 + 705$. Ans. 1,792
4. $2,008, + 1,400 + 706 + 300 + 77$.
5. $8,950 + 15,765 + 7,732$. Ans. 32,447
6. $26,661 + 8,735 + 6,877 + 33,413$.
7. $8,792 + 980 + 5,607 + 89$.
8. $346 + 4,682 + 64 + 798 + 21$.
9. $26 + 425,902 + 3,006 + 490 + 36,221$. Ans. 465,645
10. $3a + 11b + a + 7a + 5b$. Ans. $11a + 16b$
11. $c + 2a + 5c + 4a + 3c$.
12. $6a + b + 5d + 2d$. Ans. $6a + b + 7d$
13. $4a + 2b + 3a + 7c + 3c$.

10. It has now been shown how to add numbers correctly when the process is indicated. It often happens, however, that problems will be met in which only the statement of the relations between quantities are given. The following illustrative example will show the method of solving problems of this nature.

---

* 7 is called the *coefficient* of a and indicates that a is to be taken seven times. See §14, p. 15.

Example. An electric light plant, capable of furnishing current for 200 16-candle-power lamps cost as follows:

$$16 \text{ Horse-power engine.} \ldots \ldots \ldots 350 \text{ dollars}$$
$$\text{Dynamo.} \ldots \ldots \ldots \ldots 275 \quad \text{``}$$
$$\text{Driving belt.} \ldots \ldots \ldots 50 \quad \text{``}$$
$$\text{Installation.} \ldots \ldots \ldots 35 \quad \text{``}$$

What was the total cost?

SOLUTION. In an example of this kind the problem should be read several times until it is thoroughly understood. If the numbers to be used in computation are fixed in mind the student will not be misled by the wording. For example, it can readily be seen that 200 will not be used in the computation. Find the total cost of the equipment as shown in the margin.

$$\begin{array}{r} 350 \\ 275 \\ 50 \\ 35 \\ \hline 710 \end{array}$$

PROBLEMS FOR PRACTICE

1. A marine engine during a 3 hours' run makes 9,187 revolutions the first hour, 9,062 the second, and 9,233 the third. How many does it make in the 3 hours?

2. Coal is fed to a furnace as follows: Monday, 376 pounds; Tuesday, 307 pounds; Wednesday, 438 pounds; Thursday, 425 pounds; Friday, 399 pounds; Saturday, 301 pounds. Find the total for the week.

3. The items for lumber called for in a contract were—frame, 3,896 feet; flooring, 6,796 feet; finish, 2,739 feet. How many feet were used?

4. A surveying party works six weeks. The first week they survey 151 miles; the second week, 111 miles; the third week, 162 miles; the fourth week, 159 miles; the fifth week, 96 miles; the sixth week, 48 miles. How many miles did they survey?

5. There are five water wheels installed in a water power plant. The power furnished by the first wheel is 2,225 horse-power, and the others furnish, 3,150, 4,275, 5,650, and 8,275 horse-power. What is the total capacity of the five wheels?

6. The weekly capacity of 4 lathes is as follows: 2,500 castings, 4,175 nuts, 3,420 brass boxings, and 2,185 finished trimmings. How many pieces do the four lathes turn out per week?

7. When purchasing an 85 dollar indicator, the following extras were bought:

1 Spring.........................	5	dollars
1 Elbow.........................	3	"
Pantograph.......................	10	"
Speed Counter....................	2	"
Planimeter.......................	20	"

What was the total cost of the outfit including the indicator?

8. If a 10-inch belt will transmit 17 horse-power at a speed of 1,800 feet per minute, and a 16-inch belt will transmit 36 horse-power at the same speed, how much power will be transmitted by the two belts?

SUBTRACTION

11. *Subtraction* is the process of finding the difference between two quantities; this difference when added to the smaller will give a result equal to the greater.

For example, the difference between 16 and 7 is 9, since 7 added to 9 makes 16. The greater of the two quantities whose difference is to be found, is called the *minuend;* the smaller is called the *subtrahend.* The quantity left after taking the subtrahend from the minuend is called the *difference* or *remainder.*

Only like quantities and units of the same order can be subtracted, and the remainder is always like the minuend and subtrahend.

It can readily be seen that subtraction is the reverse of addition, and this fact is made use of to prove subtraction as shown in the following:

Example. Subtract 114 from 237 and prove the result.

SOLUTION. Beginning with the units column, 4 (units) are subtracted from 7 (units) leaving 3 (units), which is set down directly under the column in units place. Proceeding to the next column 1 (ten) is subtracted from 3 (tens) leaving 2 (tens), which is set down in tens place. Proceeding as before, the final remainder is found to be 123.

$$\begin{array}{cc} & \text{Proof} \\ 237 & 114 \\ \underline{114} & \underline{123} \\ \overline{123} & \overline{237} \end{array}$$

12. Rules for Subtraction. *Write the subtrahend under the minuend so that units of the same order will be in the same column.*

Begin with the units of the lowest order to subtract, and proceed to the highest, writing each remainder under the line in its proper place.

*If any digit of the minuend is less than the corresponding digit
of the subtrahend, add ten to it and then subtract; but consider that the
next digit of the minuend has been diminished by one.*

Examples.   1.   From 6,784 subtract 3,776.

SOLUTION. In order to subtract 6 in the units
place in the subtrahend from 4 in the units place in the
minuend, the 4 must first be increased by 10 giving 14;
then 6 subtracted from 14 leaves 8 in the units place of
the remainder.   But the 10 added to the 4, has been obtained by diminishing the 8 in the tens place of the
minuend by 1, leaving 7.   The 7 in the tens place of the
subtrahend subtracted from this leaves zero in the tens
place of the remainder.   The 7 in the hundreds place of
the subtrahend subtracted from the 7 in the hundreds
place of the minuend leaves zero in the hundreds place
of the remainder, and the 3 in the thousands place
of the subtrahend subtracted from the 6 in the
thousands place of the minuend leaves 3 in the thousands place of the remainder, giving 3,008.

6784 minuend
3776 subtrahend
3008 remainder

2.   From 1,000 subtract 621.

SOLUTION.   The 0 in the units place of the minuend must first be increased by 10; then 1 subtracted
from 10 leaves 9 in the units place of the remainder.   In
adding 10 to the 0, 1 has been taken from the tens place,
but as it was itself 0, it had to borrow from the next place
and continue borrowing until a numerical place was
reached.   Proceeding in this way the total remainder
379 is obtained.

1000 minuend
 621 subtrahend
 379 remainder

13.   Letters may be used in subtraction just as in addition.
For instance, if a quantity represented by b is to be subtracted from
a quantity represented by a, the difference will be represented by
the quantity $(a-b)$; or if c is to be subtracted from b, the difference
will be represented by the quantity $(b-c)$.   If the quantity consists
of a letter or letters with a coefficient, as $8ab$, and another term containing the same letters, as $3ab$, is to be subtracted from it, the subtraction may be performed in the usual way.   It must be remembered, however, that $8ab$ means that ab is taken eight times, while
$3ab$ means that ab is to be taken three times.   Therefore, if $3ab$
is taken from $8ab$, $5ab$ remains.   In other words, $8ab-3ab$ equals
$5ab$.

Examples.   1.   From $7ab + 9b + 4c$ subtract $3ab + b + 2c$.

SOLUTION. Arrange the terms as in addition of letters, subtracting the coefficients only and bringing down the letter or letters after each result. Thus: $7ab-3ab=4ab$; $9b-b=9b-1b=8b$; $4c-2c=2c$. The separate results of the subtraction may now be connected by the plus sign, giving as the final answer the quantity $4ab+8b+2c$.

$$7ab + 9b + 4c$$
$$3ab + b + 2c$$
$$\overline{4ab + 8b + 2c}$$

2.   From $6a + 2d$ subtract $5a + 2d$.

SOLUTION. Subtracting we have $6a-5a=1a=a$; $2d - 2d = 0d = 0$. When the difference between the coefficients is 0, the term is 0. Therefore, the second term of the remainder disappears, giving as the final result the quantity a.

$$6a + 2d$$
$$5a + 2d$$
$$\overline{a}$$

PROBLEMS FOR PRACTICE

1.   From 7,282 subtract 4,815   Ans.   2,467
2.   From 64,037 subtract 5,908.
3.   From 6,231 subtract 3,084.   Ans.   3,147
4.   From 1,740,932 subtract 807,605.
5.   From 71,287 subtract 40,089.   Ans.   31,198
6.   From 1,000,000 subtract 999,999.
7.   From the sum of 2,465,321 and 975,803
  subtract 739,034.   Ans.   2,702,090
8.   From $9b + 7c$ subtract $4b + c$.
9.   From $12a + 15b + 6c$ subtract $8a + 14b + 6c$.
10.   From $5a + 2b$ subtract $3a + b$.   Ans. $2a + b$
11.   From $a + 5b + 2d$ subtract $a + 4b + 2d$.   Ans. b

12.   From a tank containing 935 gallons of water, 648 gallons were drawn off. Then 247 gallons ran in. How many gallons were then in the tank? (Suggestion: Subtract 648 from 935 and add 247.)

13.   A man purchased 8,983 bricks, but used only 5,363. How many had he left?

14.   A coal shed contains 8,579 tons. 3,243 tons are taken from it. It then receives 4,112 tons more. After that 1,602 tons are taken out of it. How many tons remain?

15.   An electric power plant can generate 2,000 horse-power. Of this, 1,910 horse-power is used. The manager then agrees to

furnish another firm with 784 horse-power.   How much more power will he need?   (Suggestion: Add 784 to 1,910 and subtract 2,000.)

Ans.   694 horse-power.

16.   An engine develops 147 horse-power.   16 horse-power is used in running the engine itself.   How much power is available for running machinery?

17.   1,200 gallons are pumped from a tank.   Of this, 32 gallons are lost in leakage, etc.   How much is discharged by the pump?

18.   A 75 horse-power boiler evaporates 2,140 pounds of water into steam per hour.   One engine uses 1,310 pounds, another uses 417 pounds, and a pump requires the remainder.   How much steam is used by the pump?   (Suggestion: Add 417 to 1,310 and subtract from 2,140.)

Ans.   413 pounds.

19.   An engine makes 54,000 revolutions in a day of 12 hours. A motor makes 720,000 revolutions in the same time.   By how many revolutions per day does the speed of the motor exceed that of the engine?

20.   It takes 3,880 pounds of steam per hour to run a certain 160 horse-power engine.   If it takes 1,940 pounds to run a 60 horse-power engine and 2,140 pounds to run a 72 horse-power engine, does the largest engine require as much steam as the two small ones? (Suggestion: Add 1,940 to 2,140 and compare with 3,880.)

MULTIPLICATION

14.   *Multiplication* is a short method of adding a quantity to itself a certain number of times; or, it is the process of taking one quantity as many times as there are units in another.

It is known that $2 + 2 + 2 + 2 + 2 = 10$; but this same process may be expressed more briefly by the aid of multiplication, thus: $5 \times 2 = 10$.   The 5 shows how many twos are used in adding. This last expression is read, "five times two equals ten."

In multiplication three terms are employed—the multiplicand, the multiplier, and the product.

The *multiplicand* is the quantity to be multiplied or taken.

The *multiplier* denotes the number of times the multiplicand is to be taken.

The *product* is the result or quantity obtained by the multiplication.

Another term, called the *coefficient*, is used to indicate the numerical part of a quantity which consists of numbers and letters multiplied together. Thus in the expression $3ab$, 3 is the coefficient of ab, and denotes that ab is taken 3 times. Sometimes it is convenient to consider any part of the product as the coefficient of the remaining part. Thus in $3ab$, $3a$ might be considered the coefficient of b, or $3b$ the coefficient of a. A coefficient is, therefore, called *numerical* or *literal* according as it is a number or one or more letters. When no numerical coefficient is expressed, 1 is always understood,

TABLE IV
Multiplication Table

1	2	3	4	5	6	7	8	9	10	11	12	13	14	15	16	17	18	19	20	21	22	23	24	25
2	4	6	8	10	12	14	16	18	20	22	24	26	28	30	32	34	36	38	40	42	44	46	48	50
3	6	9	12	15	18	21	24	27	30	33	36	39	42	45	48	51	54	57	60	63	66	69	72	75
4	8	12	16	20	24	28	32	36	40	44	48	52	56	60	64	68	72	76	80	84	88	92	96	100
5	10	15	20	25	30	35	40	45	50	55	60	65	70	75	80	85	90	95	100	105	110	115	120	125
6	12	18	24	30	36	42	48	54	60	66	72	78	84	90	96	102	108	114	120	126	132	138	144	150
7	14	21	28	35	42	49	56	63	70	77	84	91	98	105	112	119	126	133	140	147	154	161	168	175
8	16	24	32	40	48	56	64	72	80	88	96	104	112	120	128	136	144	152	160	168	176	184	192	200
9	18	27	36	45	54	63	72	81	90	99	108	117	126	135	144	153	162	171	180	189	198	207	216	225
10	20	30	40	50	60	70	80	90	100	110	120	130	140	150	160	170	180	190	200	210	220	230	240	250
11	22	33	44	55	66	77	88	99	110	121	132	143	154	165	176	187	198	209	220	231	242	253	264	275
12	24	36	48	60	72	84	96	108	120	132	144	156	168	180	192	204	216	228	240	252	264	276	288	300
13	26	39	52	65	78	91	104	117	130	143	156	169	182	195	208	221	234	247	260	273	286	299	312	325
14	28	42	56	70	84	98	112	126	140	154	168	182	196	210	224	238	252	266	280	294	308	322	336	350
15	30	45	60	75	90	105	120	135	150	165	180	195	210	225	240	255	270	285	300	315	330	345	360	375
16	32	48	64	80	96	112	128	144	160	176	192	208	224	240	256	272	288	304	320	336	352	368	384	400
17	34	51	68	85	102	119	136	153	170	187	204	221	238	255	272	289	306	323	340	357	374	391	408	425
18	36	54	72	90	108	126	144	162	180	198	216	234	252	270	288	306	324	342	360	378	396	414	432	450
19	38	57	76	95	114	133	152	171	190	209	228	247	266	285	304	323	342	361	380	399	418	437	456	475
20	40	60	80	100	120	140	160	180	200	220	240	260	280	300	320	340	360	380	400	420	440	460	480	500
21	42	63	84	105	126	147	168	189	210	231	252	273	294	315	336	357	378	399	420	441	462	483	504	525
22	44	66	88	110	132	154	176	198	220	242	264	286	308	330	352	374	396	418	440	462	484	506	528	550
23	46	69	92	115	138	161	184	207	230	253	276	299	322	345	368	391	414	437	460	483	506	529	552	575
24	48	72	96	120	144	168	192	216	240	264	288	312	336	360	384	408	432	456	480	504	528	552	576	600
25	50	75	100	125	150	175	200	225	250	275	300	325	350	375	400	425	450	475	500	525	550	575	600	625
1	2	3	4	5	6	7	8	9	10	11	12	13	14	15	16	17	18	19	20	21	22	23	24	25

as a is the same as $1a$. When a coefficient occurs just before a parenthesis, it indicates that every term within the parenthesis is to be multiplied by that coefficient.

To multiply with accuracy and rapidity, the product of any two quantities, at least from 2 to 12, must be known at sight. The combinations of these should be practiced until they can be given correctly and without hesitation.

The following points should also be fixed firmly in mind: Zero times any quantity or any quantity times zero is zero. For example,

$0 \times 0 = 0$; $0 \times 8 = 0$; $942 \times 0 = 0$, $b \times 0 = 0$, etc. One times any quantity or any quantity times one gives that quantity as a product. For example, $1 \times 7 = 7$, $85 \times 1 = 85$, $1 \times 1 = 1$, $a \times 1 = a$.

Table IV gives the product of any two numbers up to 25×25. To use this table, find one of the two numbers in the upper row and the other in the left-hand column. The product of the two will be found at the intersection of two imaginary lines drawn parallel to the heavy lines shown in the table at 12×12 and 20×20. For example under the 9 and opposite the 8 is found the product, 72. That is, $9 \times 8 = 72$.

15. Rules for Multiplication. (a) *In performing multiplication, treat both terms as abstract quantities, always using the larger quantity as the multiplicand. After the result is obtained, determine from the nature of the problem in what units the result should be expressed.*

(b) *Place right-hand digit of multiplier directly under right-hand digit of multiplicand* (with one exception—See Case 2, p. 17).

(c) *Each figure of the multiplicand is multiplied by each significant figure of the multiplier, and the right-hand figure of each product is placed under the figure of the multiplier used to obtain it. The sum of the several products will be the entire product. When there is a zero in the multiplier, multiply by the significant figures only, taking care to place the right-hand figure of each separate product under the figure used in obtaining it.*

Examples. 1.

SOLUTION. Having written the multiplier under the unit of the multiplicand, multiply the 5 units by 7, obtaining 35. Then set down the 5 units directly under the 7 and carry the 3; in other words, reserve the 3 tens for the tens column. Next multiply the seven tens by 7, obtaining 49, and add the 3 which is carried, and obtain 52 tens (which is the same as 5 hundreds and 2 tens). Set down 2 tens and carry the 5 hundreds; multiply 1 and 7 and add the 5 which was carried, making 12, which can be written down in full.
The product then reads, 1,225.

$$\begin{array}{r} 175 \text{ multiplicand} \\ 7 \text{ multiplier} \\ \hline 1225 \text{ product} \end{array}$$

2. Find the product of 145 and 13.

SOLUTION *a*. It can be seen that $13 = 10 + 3$, hence the product of 13×145 will be the same as $(10 \times 145) + (3 \times 145)$. Adding the products gives 1,885 as a result.

$$\begin{array}{r} 145 \times 3 = 435 \\ 145 \times 10 = 1450 \\ \hline 1885 \end{array}$$

Solution b. The same result is obtained, however, if the numbers are arranged as follows:

Commence with 3, multiply through and write the product 435. Under this write the product 1,450 obtained by multiplying by 10. In this latter product the 0 may be discarded but it must be remembered to write the 5 under second place. Adding these two products, called *partial products*, gives the final product 1,885.

```
 145
  13
 435
 145
1885
```

3. Multiply 1246 by 235.

Solution. Note that the three partial products are the results of multiplying by 5, 3, and 2 where each successive partial product is set one place further to the left than the preceding one. Note that 0 is under 5, 8 is under 3, and 2 is under 2; in other words, the first figure of each partial product is placed under the digit used to obtain it.

```
  1246
   235
  6230
  3738
  2492
292810
```

Two special cases not covered by the general rules given above should be here considered.

Case 1. *When digits of multiplier are separated by ciphers:*

Example. Find the product of 13,456 and 2,004.

Solution. Although the multiplier contains four digits, in the short method only two partial products appear.

The first figures obtained by multiplying by 4 and 2 appear under these respective digits, the zeros simply marking the absence of any other characters in the product.

Regular method

```
   13456
    2004
   53824
   00000
   00000
   26912
26965824
```

Short method

```
   13456
    2004
   53824
   26912
26965824
```

Case 2. *When ciphers are at right of multiplier or multiplicand:*

Example. Multiply 5,760 by 3,000.

Solution. In this case it is necessary only to multiply 576 by 3 giving 1,728; then annex the total number of ciphers found at the right of both multiplier and multiplicand, in this case four, giving as the final result, 17,280,000.

```
    5760
    3000
17280000
```

16. Short Methods. *To multiply by ten and *powers of ten.* This method is only a slight variation of that given in the previous paragraph.

---

* A power of ten is the product obtained by using ten as a factor a certain number of times. Thus, 1,000 and 10,000 are, respectively, the third and fourth powers of 10.

Annexing a cipher to a whole number multiplies that number by ten, etc. Thus, to multiply 378 by 1,000 write at once 378,000.

To multiply by a number a little less than 10, 100, or 1000 the process may be shortened as shown in the following:

Examples. 1.   Multiply 254 by 99.

SOLUTION.   99 is 100 diminished by 1; hence, multiply 254 first by 100 and then by 1 and subtract the results.

$$\begin{array}{r} 25400 \\ 254 \\ \hline 25146 \end{array}$$

2.   Multiply 196 by 997.

SOLUTION.   997 is 1,000 diminished by 3, hence, multiply 196 first by 1,000 and then by 3 and subtract the results.

$$\begin{array}{r} 196000 \\ 588 \\ \hline 195412 \end{array}$$

To multiply by 25 annex two ciphers to the multiplicand and divide by 4.

To multiply by 11:

(a) *When the multiplicand contains two figures,* place their sum between them. If this sum is greater than 10, carry 1 to the third place.

Example.   Multiply 47 by 11.

SOLUTION.   Place 7 in units place.   Add 4 and 7.   Putting 1 in tens place and carrying 1.   Place (4 + 1) in hundreds place.   Result 517.

(b) *When the multiplicand is any number,* write the right-hand figure in units place; then add the first and second, second and third, and so on, finally setting down the left-hand figure.   Carry as usual.

Example.   Multiply 365 by 11.

SOLUTION.   Write 5; 5 + 6 = 11; write 1 and carry 1; 1 carried + 6 + 3 = 10; write 0; 1 carried + 3 = 4; write 4, making the result, 4,015.

$$\begin{array}{r} 365 \\ 11 \\ \hline 4015 \end{array}$$

17.   A Method of Checking Multiplication.   *Add separately the figures of the multiplicand and multiplier until they are reduced to one figure each; then multiply these together and again reduce this product by addition to one figure.   If the multiplication is correct, the final result will usually check with the successive additions of the figures of the product.*

Example.   Multiply 6,547 by 301 and check.

SOLUTION. The solution is shown in the margin.   To check proceed as follows: Taking the multiplicand, $6 + 5 + 4 + 7 = 22$; $2 + 2 = 4$. Again for the multiplier, $3 + 1 = 4$. Their product, $4 \times 4 = 16$; $1 + 6 = 7$.

Treating the product in the same manner; $1 + 9 + 7 + 6 + 4 + 7 = 34$; $3 + 4 = 7$.   The multiplication is correct.

$$
\begin{array}{rr}
6547 & -\ \mathbf{4} \\
301 & -\ 4 \\
\hline
6547 & 16-7 \\
19641 & \\
\hline
1970647 & -\ 7
\end{array}
$$

18.   Letters may be used in multiplication as follows: **The** product of a and b is $a \times b$, and the product of a, b, and c is $a \times b \times c$. If $a = 6$, $b = 4$, and $c = 1$, the product of a, b, and c is $6 \times 4 \times 1$ or 24.   The common practice is to omit the multiplication sign when letters are multiplied by letters or numbers thus: $2 \times x$ is written $2x$; $2a \times 3b$ is written $6ab$; $3a \times 4b \times 5c$ is written $60abc$.   The order in which the letters are placed is immaterial although the alphabetical order is usually followed.   For example, $60\ cab$ is the same as $60abc$.

PROBLEMS FOR PRACTICE

Multiply:

1.   2,928 by 364.   Ans.   1,065,792
2.   7,319 by 394.
3.   5,698 by 792.   Ans.   4,512,816
4. $9a$ by $2b$.   Ans. $18ab$
5. $3ab$ by $4cd$.   Ans. $12abcd$
6.   3,186 by 839.   Ans.   2,673,054
7.   42,308 by 692.
8.   876 by itself.   Ans.   767,376
9. $4ab$ by $14c$.
10.   57 by 1,000.
11.   52 by 99.
12.   16 by 25.
13.   92 by 11.
14.   103 by 25.

15.   There are 746 watts in a horse-power.   How many watts are there in 20 horse-power?   (Suggestion: Multiply 746 by 20.)

16.   A piston has an area of approximately 113 square inches. If the steam pressure is 47 pounds per square inch, what is the total pressure upon it?   Ans.   5,311 pounds.

17. The head of a boiler has an area of 11,310 square inches. If the pressure per square inch is 40 pounds, what is the total pressure on the head?   Ans. 452,400 pounds.

18. A concrete mixer delivers 14 cubic yards per hour. A gang of men takes away 12 cubic yards per hour. How many cubic yards will remain unmoved at the end of 4 hours? At the end of 8 hours?

19. If there are 12 threads per inch on a screw, how many threads are there in 4 inches?

20. If a piston moves through 468 feet in one minute, how far does it travel in 45 minutes?   Ans. 21,060 feet.

21. If a boiler evaporates 1,945 pounds of water in one hour, how many pounds will it evaporate in 9 hours?

22. A certain girder supports 136,925 pounds. How much will 65 such girders support?   Ans. 8,900,125 pounds.

23. An engine in a certain power plant requires 18 pounds of steam per horse-power per hour. If the engine is developing 640 horse-power, what is the total steam consumption?

DIVISION

19. *Division* is a process of finding how many times one quantity contains another. In division there are three principal terms, the dividend, the divisor, and the quotient or answer.

The *dividend* is the quantity to be divided.

The *divisor* is the quantity which is divided into the dividend.

The *quotient* is the number of times the divisor is contained in the dividend.

When the dividend does not contain the divisor an exact number of times, the excess is called the *remainder*. The remainder being a part of the dividend will always be of the same kind as the dividend and must necessarily be less than the divisor.

Division may be indicated in any of the following ways: $24 \div 2$; $\frac{24}{2}$; $2\overline{)24}$

Division is the reverse of multiplication, as shown by the following:

$6 \times 7 = 42$	$42 \div 6 = 7$	$42 \div 7 = 6$
$5 \times 8 = 40$	$40 \div 8 = 5$	$40 \div 5 = 8$

20. There are two distinct methods used, viz, *long division* and *short division;* in the former all the work is written out but in the latter the process is performed mentally and the result only is written. Short division is generally used when the divisor does not exceed 12.

The following examples illustrate the two processes.

Examples.   1.   Divide 720 by 5.

Long Division

144 quotient

5)720
  5
  ‾‾
  22
  20
  ‾‾
   20
   20
   ‾‾

SOLUTION.   In long division it is found that 5 is contained in 7 once. Write 1 as the first figure of the quotient, and subtract, giving a remainder of 2. To the remainder *annex the next figure of the dividend, and divide as before, obtaining 4 as the second figure of the quotient. Annex 0 which is the next figure of the dividend, and divide again by 5, obtaining 4 as the last figure of the quotient with no remainder. The division is now complete.

Short Division

5)720
 ‾‾‾‾
 144 quotient

It often happens, after bringing down a figure from the dividend, that the *number is too small to contain the divisor.* In this case *place a zero in the quotient, and continue bringing down the figures from the dividend until the number thus formed will contain the divisor.* The following example illustrates this point:

2.   Divide 10,426 by 13.

SOLUTION.   It is seen that the first two places in the dividend are less than the divisor; therefore, three places must be taken. 13 is contained in 104 exactly 8 times, giving 8 as the first figure in the quotient. There being no remainder, the next figure of the dividend, when brought down, stands alone and is, of course, less than 13. Place a zero as the second figure of the quotient and annex the next figure 6 of the dividend making 26, into which 13 goes exactly twice. This makes the complete quotient 802 without a remainder.

$$\begin{array}{r} 802 \\ 13\overline{)10426} \\ 104 \\ \hline 26 \\ 26 \\ \hline \end{array}$$

21.   Rules for Long Division.   (a)   *Write the divisor and dividend in the order named, and draw a curved line between them.*

(b)   *Find how many times the divisor is contained in the left-hand*

---

*In the above solution the term "annex", meaning *to place after*, is used. The opposite term "prefix", meaning, *to place before*, is also often used. Be careful to make a distinction between "annex" and "add".

figure or figures of the dividend, and write the number in the quotient over the dividend.

(c) *Multiply the divisor by this figure of the quotient, writing the product under that part of the dividend from which it was obtained; subtract, and to the remainder annex the next figure of the dividend.*

(d) *Find how many times the divisor is contained in the number thus formed, and write the figure denoting it at the right hand of the last figure of the quotient.*

(e) *Proceed in this manner until all the figures of the dividend are divided. If there is a remainder after dividing all the figures of the dividend, place the remainder over the divisor with a line between them, and annex to the quotient.*

(f) *The proper remainder is, in all cases, less than the divisor. If, in the course of the operation, it is found to be larger than the divisor, this indicates that there is an error in the work and that the figure in the quotient should be increased.*

Example. Divide 5,441 by 26.

SOLUTION:

$$209\tfrac{7}{26}$$
$$26)\overline{5441}$$
$$\underline{52}$$
$$241$$
$$\underline{234}$$
$$7 \text{ remainder}$$

Proof. In order to prove division, multiply the quotient by the divisor, and add the remainder, if there is any. If the quantity thus obtained gives the dividend, the work is correct.

22. ***Short Methods.** *To divide by ten and powers of ten.* From the right in the dividend point off as many places as the divisor contains ciphers. The figures so cut off represent the remainder, to be written over the divisor and annexed to the quotient.

To divide by multiples of ten.

Example. Find the quotient of 18,653 ÷ 3,000.

SOLUTION. Mark off as many figures in the dividend as there are ciphers in the divisor, thus dividing by 1,000. This leaves 18 to the left of the mark to be divided by 3, giving a quotient of 6 with a remainder of 653. Place this remainder over the divisor and annex it to the 6, giving, finally, $6\tfrac{653}{3000}$.

$$6\,\tfrac{653}{3000}$$
$$3|000)\overline{18|653}$$
$$\underline{18}$$
$$653$$

*These methods may be made more comprehensive and valuable after the subject of Decimals has been discussed.

To divide by 25.

Multiply the dividend by 4 and divide the product by 100, by cutting off two figures to the right.

23. Letters may be used in division as follows: a divided by b may be expressed as $a \div b$ or $\dfrac{a}{b}$; a divided by c, as $a \div c$, or $\dfrac{a}{c}$.

If $a = 6$ and $b = 3$, a divided by b will equal $6 \div 3 = 2$. If $a = 6$ and $c = 2$, a divided by c will equal $6 \div 2$ or 3. In dividing terms containing letters, it is useful to remember the statement on page 20, that *division is the reverse of multiplication*. For example, $4abc$ divided by $2c$ equals $2ab$, for $2c \times 2ab$ equals $4abc$.

Examples. 1. Divide $16abcd$ by $4ad$.

SOLUTION. The coefficient of the divisor is contained in the coefficient of the dividend 4 times. Place a 4 in the quotient. Again a and d of the divisor are contained in a and d of the dividend exactly once but ad is contained in $abcd$, bc times for $ad \times bc$ equals $abcd$. The complete quotient is, therefore, $4bc$ without a remainder.

$$4ad \overline{)\begin{array}{l} 4bc \\ 16abcd \\ \underline{16abcd} \end{array}}$$

2. Divide $(15abc + 6ab)$ by $3b$.

SOLUTION. In this problem the two terms of the dividend are divided separately and the two quotients connected by the proper sign. $15abc$ divided by $3b$ gives a quotient of $5ac$; $6ab$ divided by $3b$ gives $2a$ as a quotient. The final quotient is, therefore, $5ac + 2a$.

$$3b \overline{)\begin{array}{l} 5ac + 2a \\ 15abc + 6ab \\ \underline{15abc + 6ab} \end{array}}$$

PROBLEMS FOR PRACTICE

Divide:

1. 65,814 by 6.   Ans. 10,969
2. $6ab$ by $3b$.   Ans. $2a$
3. 3,870 by 10.
4. $24abcd$ by $6d$.   Ans. $4abc$
5. 9,473 by 100.   Ans. $94\frac{73}{100}$
6. 13,987 by 1000.
7. $30abcd$ by $5ac$.
8. $(18abc + 12abd)$ by $3b$.
9. If coal costs 5 dollars per ton, how many tons may be bought for 275 dollars? (Suggestion: Divide 275 by 5.)

10. A steamer runs 276 miles in 23 hours. What is her average speed per hour? (Suggestion: Divide 276 by 23.)

11. How many 30-foot rails are there in a double track (four rails) two miles long? There are 5,280 feet in one mile. (Suggestion: Divide 2 × 4 × 5,280 by 30.)

12. If 9 days' work will pay for 6 tons of coal at 6 dollars per ton, what is the price of a day's labor?

13. A company furnishes equal power to 26 establishments. The total horse-power is 8,450. How much does each receive?

14. If a locomotive goes to shop for inspection after every average run of 283 miles, how many times would it be in shop during runs aggregating 10,188 miles?   Ans. 36 times.

15. A certain boiler supplies steam for heating. If there are 180 square feet of heating surface in the boiler and each radiator requires 12 square feet of heating surface of the boiler, how many radiators can be supplied by the boiler?   Ans. 15 radiators.

16. If 800 cubic feet of air are required for each person, how many people can occupy a room that contains 21,600 cubic feet?

17. If 1 foot of 1 inch pipe is allowed for every 90 cubic feet of space in heating a factory, how many feet of the same pipe will be required to heat 225,000 cubic feet of space?

FACTORING

24. An *integer* is a whole number, as 1, 8, 15.

All numbers are either odd or even. An *odd* number is a number that cannot be divided by 2 without a remainder, as 3, 9, 13, etc. An *even* number is one that can be divided by 2 without a remainder, as 4, 6, 8, etc.

A *prime* number is a number which can be exactly divided only by itself or 1, as 1, 3, 5, 7, etc.

A *factor* of an integer is a number which is contained an exact number of times in the given integer.

A *prime factor* is a factor which is a prime number.

Numbers are prime to each other when they have no factor in common. Thus 7 and 11 are prime to each other; also 18 and 25, etc.

In speaking of the factors of a number it is not customary to include the number itself or 1. For this reason a prime number is said to have no factors.

Example. What are the prime factors of 16?

SOLUTION. Divide 16 by 2 which is the least prime number greater than 1, and obtain 8 as the quotient. Since 8 may again be divided by 2, the division is carried out giving 4 as the next quotient. Next divide 4 by 2 giving a quotient of 2, which is a prime number and cannot be further divided. Now the several divisors and the last quotient, all of which are prime, are the prime factors of 16.

$$\begin{array}{r} 2)\overline{16} \\ 2)\overline{\ 8} \\ 2)\overline{\ 4} \\ 2 \end{array}$$

The rule for finding prime factors may be expressed as follows:
Divide the given number by the least prime number (greater than 1) that will divide it; and divide each quotient, in the same manner. Continue dividing until a prime number is obtained as the quotient. The several divisors and the last quotient will be the prime factors desired.

Example. What are the prime factors of 78?

SOLUTION.

$$\begin{array}{r} 2)\overline{78} \\ 3)\overline{39} \\ \overline{13} \end{array}$$ Ans. 2, 3, and 13

25. Factoring by Observation. Certain numbers have such characteristics that some of their factors may be found without the trouble of an actual operation in division. The simplest of these rules for factoring by observation are as follows:

2 is a factor of all even numbers.

3 is a factor of all numbers the sum of whose digits is divisible by 3.

4 is a factor of all numbers whose last two places are divisible by 4.

5 is a factor of all numbers ending in 5 or 0.

10 is a factor of all numbers whose last figure is 0.

Examples. 1. Factor the number 56.

SOLUTION. By inspection it is seen that 56 is divisible by 4, and although 4 is not a prime factor, its use saves one division. The resulting factors are 4, 2, and 7

$$\begin{array}{r} 4)\overline{56} \\ 2)\overline{14} \\ 7 \end{array}$$ Ans. 4, 2, and 7

2. Factor the number 720.

SOLUTION. According to the rule in §25 this number is divisible by 10 and, although 10 is not a prime number, the process of factoring is shortened by its use. The quotient 72 is divisible by 4, which should be used instead of dividing twice by the factor 2. The remaining factors are 2, 3, and 3. 720 may also be divided into the factors 10, 8, and 9, the two latter being equal, respectively, to 4 × 2 and 3 × 3.

$$\begin{array}{r} 10)\overline{720} \\ 4)\overline{72} \\ 2)\overline{18} \\ 3)\overline{\ 9} \\ 3 \end{array}$$ Ans. 10, 4, 2, 3, and 3

3. Factor the number 426.

SOLUTION.

$$\frac{2)426}{3)\overline{213}}$$

71 Ans. 2, 3, and 71

Find the prime factors of the following:

1. 36   Ans. 2, 2, 3, and 3
2. 30
3. 68
4. 148
5. 189   Ans. 3, 3, 3, and 7
6. 1,264
7. 2,552
8. 1,932
9. 91
10. 2,508   Ans. 2, 2, 3, 11, 19

CANCELLATION

26. Cancellation Methods. When a series of multiplied factors is to be divided by a second series, the operation may be shortened by a process called "Cancellation". The first series is placed above and the second below a horizontal line and divisions are performed between the factors on opposite sides of the line. Any number on one side which is exactly divisible by a number on the other side of the line may be so divided.

Examples. 1. Divide 18 × 5 by 10 × 3.

SOLUTION: Arranging the first series above and the second series below the line we have

$$\frac{18 \times 5}{10 \times 3} = \frac{\overset{6}{\cancel{18}} \times 5}{10 \times \underset{1}{\cancel{3}}} = \frac{\overset{6}{\cancel{18}} \times \overset{1}{\cancel{5}}}{\underset{2}{\cancel{10}} \times \underset{1}{\cancel{3}}}$$

It will be seen that 18, the first term above, and 3, the second term below the line, are divisible by 3. The 18 is, therefore, crossed out or "cancelled out" and a 6 placed above it; the 3 below is also cancelled and a 1 placed below it. Similarly 5 is contained in 5 and 10, the remaining factors, and these should also be cancelled out as indicated, a 1 being placed above the 5 and a 2 below the 10.

Further inspection shows that the 6 which remains above the line is divisible by the 2 which remains below the line and this cancellation gives a final result of 3. The complete process is

$$\frac{\overset{3}{\cancel{6}} \times \overset{1}{\cancel{5}}}{\underset{2}{\cancel{10}} \times \underset{1}{\cancel{3}}} = \frac{3}{1} = 3$$

2. $$\frac{6 \times 8 \times 12 \times 18 \times 24}{2 \times 3 \times 2 \times 4 \times 6} = ?$$

SOLUTION. To cancel, select any two numbers one above and one below the line, and find some number that will divide each of them without a remainder. For instance, it is seen that 2 will be contained an exact number of times in both 6 and 2. Then perform the division, crossing out both numbers and placing the results directly over and below, the numbers crossed out. Proceed in this manner until there is no longer a number below the line that can be cancelled with one above the line. Then multiply together all the numbers above the line and use as a dividend; and multiply together those below the line, and use as a divisor.

$$\frac{\overset{3}{\cancel{6}} \times \overset{4}{\cancel{8}} \times \overset{4}{\cancel{12}} \times \overset{3}{\cancel{18}} \times \overset{6}{\cancel{24}}}{\underset{1}{\cancel{2}} \times \underset{1}{\cancel{3}} \times \underset{1}{\cancel{2}} \times \underset{1}{\cancel{4}} \times \underset{1}{\cancel{6}}} =$$

$$\frac{3 \times 4 \times 4 \times 3 \times 6}{1} = 864$$

3. $$\frac{16 \times 2 \times 15 \times 4}{32 \times 6 \times 8 \times 22} = ?$$

SOLUTION. In an example where the product above the line, after cancelling, is less than the product below the line, the result is allowed to stand as obtained, thus: Since 5 and 22 do not cancel into any of the other numbers the result is the product of the quantities in the numerator divided by the product of the quantities in the denominator.

$$\frac{\overset{1}{\cancel{16}} \times \overset{1}{\cancel{2}} \times \overset{5}{\cancel{15}} \times \overset{1}{\cancel{4}}}{\underset{2}{\cancel{32}} \times \underset{3}{\cancel{6}} \times \underset{2}{\cancel{8}} \times 22} = \frac{5}{88}$$

4. Four men have the task of sorting 24 boxes of castings, each box containing 720 pieces. If each man can handle 12 pieces per minute, how many hours will it take the men to sort the castings?

SOLUTION. A little examination of this problem will show that the total number of pieces to be handled will form the quantity above the line, that is, 24 times 720. As there are 4 men and each can handle 12 pieces per minute, the number handled per minute will be 4×12 and the number per hour will be $4 \times 12 \times 60$. This quantity is placed below the line as the total number of pieces divided by the number handled per hour will give the required result. Carrying on the cancellation as before, the final result is 6, that is, it will take the men 6 hours to sort the castings.

$$\frac{\overset{1}{\cancel{2}}\overset{6}{\cancel{4}} \times 7\cancel{20}}{\underset{1}{\cancel{4}} \times \underset{1}{1\cancel{2}} \times \underset{1}{\cancel{60}}} = 6$$

Rules. *Cancel the common factors from both dividend and divisor.*

Next, divide the product of the remaining factors of the dividend by the product of the remaining factors of the divisor.

It is seen, therefore, that cancellation is merely a combination of the processes of factoring and division.

PROBLEMS FOR PRACTICE

Divide:

1. $2 \times 3 \times 8 \times 12 \times 24$ by $6 \times 4 \times 36 \times 4$.   Ans.   4
2. $18 \times 24 \times 32 \times 36$ by $9 \times 48 \times 4 \times 18$.
3. $15 \times 20 \times 25 \times 27$ by $15 \times 18 \times 25 \times 10$.   Ans.   3
4. $40 \times 48 \times 54 \times 60$ by $30 \times 24 \times 72 \times 3$.
5. $12 \times 60 \times 36 \times 70$ by $28 \times 5 \times 48 \times 6$.   Ans.   45
6. $32 \times 36 \times 33 \times 45$ by $24 \times 30 \times 44 \times 9$.
7. 18 piers, each consisting of 5 piles, were set by 10 men in 3 days. What is the cost of driving each pile if each of the men receive 3 dollars a day?
8. Each of 40 teamsters hauls 9 yards of sand per day for 4 days at 1 dollar per yard. How many men with wheelbarrows will earn the same amount in two days wheeling 3 yards per day at 1 dollar per yard?   Ans.   240 men.

REVIEW PROBLEMS

1. A steam plant has two engines of 934 horse-power each The starboard engine of a steamship develops 3,218 horse-power and the port engine 3,232 horse-power. How much greater power is developed in the ship than in the steam plant? Ans. 4,582 H. P.

2. A pump delivers 33,720 cubic feet of water in two hours (60 minutes each). How many cubic feet are delivered per minute? Ans. 281 cu. ft.

3. A nine-foot blower makes 175 revolutions per minute. How many revolutions will it make in 29 minutes? Ans. 5,075 rev.

4. There are 360 rivets in a hundred pounds. How many

pounds will be required to afford 64,800 rivets.   Ans.   18,000 pounds.

5.   The heating surface in a locomotive is 88 square feet in the fire box and 792 square feet in the tubes.   What is the total heating surface?   How many times as much surface is there in the tubes than in the fire box?   Ans. $\begin{cases} 880 \text{ square feet} \\ 9 \text{ times} \end{cases}$

6.   The weight of a battery of eight marine boilers and their equipments is as follows:

Boilers complete with mountings.........295 tons
Water in boilers....................... 73 "
Funnels............................. 50 "
Stoke-hole plates, floors, etc............ 23 "
Feed pumps .... 7 "
Fans and fan engines .... 8 "
Feed regulators .... 2 "
Tools and fittings .... 2 "
Spare gear........................... 10 "

What is the weight of two such batteries?

7.   At 100 degrees Fahrenheit a cubic foot of water weighs 62 pounds.   At 205 degrees a cubic foot weighs 60 pounds.   What is the difference in weight between 173 cubic feet of water at 100 degrees and 189 cubic feet at 205 degrees?   Ans.   614 pounds.

8.   A roof is composed of 11 frames.   The weight of one frame in detail is as follows:

2 rafters each weighing........................875 lbs.
5 rods, each weighing..........................176 "
16 bolts, each weighing......................... 5 "
8 bridle-straps, each weighing................. 15 "
2 piers supporting rafters at ridge, average each. .. 11 "
6 pieces at foot of struts, average each........... 11 lbs.
4 pieces uniting rafters at junction in strut, with bolts and nuts, each........................ 44 "
2 rafter shoes, each...........................144 "
2 cast-iron struts, each. ....154 "

What is the total weight of the roof?   Ans.   40,590 pounds.

9.   A double mine ventilating fan runs at the rate of 84 revolutions per minute.   It gives 2,818 cubic feet of air per revolution.

How many cubic feet should it give per minute?

Ans.   236,712 cubic feet.

10.   If oak-tanned leather belting costs 2 dollars per foot, and four-ply stitched canvas belting costs 1 dollar per foot, what is the difference in the cost of 40 feet?   Ans.   40 dollars.

11.   If there are 9,326 heat units in a pound of lignite coal, how many heat units in 287 pounds?

12.   If 23 square feet of No. 30 sheet iron weighs 11 pounds, how much will 23 square feet weigh if three times as thick?

13.   The weight of the masonry of a bridge and an engine passing over it is 1,698,575 pounds.   The engine weighs 198,560 pounds. What is the weight of the masonry?

14.   A pound of Pennsylvania petroleum will theoretically evaporate about 22 pounds of water.   How many pounds are necessary to evaporate 4,378 pounds of water?

15.   A cubic foot of hemlock weighs 25 pounds.   A cubic foot of iron weighs 450 pounds.   Find the difference between the weight of 230 cubic feet of hemlock and 87 cubic feet of iron.

16.   Three guy ropes are fastened to a stake.   The pull on one rope is 560,800 pounds; the pull on the second is 118,421 pounds; and on the third is 104,863 pounds.   What is the total pull?

17.* Divide $(20ac \times 4bd)$ by $16b$.   Ans. $5acd$

18.* Divide the product of $7a$ and $6bcd$ by $3ad$.

19.   Let a, b, and c have, respectively, the values 4, 7, and 2. Subtract a from the sum of b and c and give the numerical result.

Ans. 5

20.   Give values of 5, 9, 6, and 12 to a, b, c, and d, respectively; find the numerical result of adding $3a$, $7c$, and $5d$, and subtracting $8b$ from this sum.

21.   The record of a pieceworker in a shop for one week was as follows: for Monday 122 pieces, Tuesday 140, Wednesday 114, Thursday 154, Friday 132, and Saturday 142.   What is his average day's work.   (Suggestion: An average is found by dividing the sum of the various items by the number of items.)

Ans. 134 pieces per day.

---

* Work this problem by cancellation.

PRACTICAL MATHEMATICS

PART II

FRACTIONS

27. A *fraction* is an expression denoting one or more equal parts of a unit, and may be regarded as indicating division. The fraction is written, *i. e.,** the division is indicated, by placing the dividend over the divisor with a line between.

Thus, $\frac{5}{12}$ denotes that 5 of the 12 equal parts of a unit are to be taken. $\frac{5}{12}$ is merely a different way of writing $5 \div 12$, and the fraction is used because the dividend is less than the divisor.

To say $\frac{1}{4}$ of a 100 pound keg of bolts indicates, that the keg of bolts is to be divided into 4 equal parts, and 1 of these parts taken. In this use, the unit may be considered as made up of a number of equal parts, but when used separately and without reference to any certain thing, it is convenient to consider the fraction merely as an unperformed division; thus, $\frac{1}{4} = 1 \div 4$; $\frac{3}{4} = 3 \div 4$; $\frac{875}{361} = 875 \div 361$.

The quantity below the line is called the *denominator*. It shows into how many equal parts the unit is divided.

The quantity above the line is called the *numerator*. It shows how many of these equal parts are taken. Thus, in the fraction $\frac{1}{12}$, the 12 shows that the unit has been divided into 12 equal parts, and the 1 shows that one of the 12 parts is taken. In the fraction $\frac{a}{b}$ the unit is divided into b parts and a of these parts are taken.

The numerator and denominator are called the *terms* of a fraction.

---

* The letters "*i. e.*" are used to represent the expression "that is".

A *fractional unit* is one of the equal parts into which the unit in question is divided. Thus, if the unit is divided into fourths, $\frac{1}{4}$ is the fractional unit; if divided into b parts, $\frac{1}{b}$ is the fractional unit.

Since any number divided by 1 gives a quotient equal to the dividend, any whole number may be expressed as a fraction by writing 1 for the denominator. Thus, 4 may be written $\frac{4}{1}$, as $\frac{4}{1} = 4 \div 1 = 4$.

The *value* of a fraction depends upon the value of the fractional units and the number of these units taken, or simply upon the division of the numerator by the denominator. Thus, in $\frac{4}{2}$, the quotient of $4 \div 2$ is 2, and the value of the fraction can be expressed as 2.

If the numerator and the denominator are equal, the value of the fraction is 1. Thus, $\frac{8}{8}$ may be expressed as $8 \div 8$ and is equal to 1. This shows that one unit is divided into eight parts, each part being an eighth and that 8 of these are taken, making a unit or 1.

Strictly speaking a fraction is less than a unit; hence if the numerator is less than the denominator, the value is less than 1, and it is known as a *proper fraction*. For example, the expression $\frac{8}{9}$ means that a unit has been divided into nine parts, each part forming a fractional unit having a value of $\frac{1}{9}$, and that eight of these parts are taken. This is one less than the nine parts necessary to make a unit, and therefore $\frac{8}{9}$ is less than 1.

If the numerator is greater than the denominator, the value of the fraction is greater than 1, and it is called an *improper fraction*. Thus, the fraction $\frac{8}{7}$ is an improper fraction, because 7 is contained once in 8 with a remainder, or, expressing it in another way, because eight parts, each one being a seventh of a unit, have been taken, forming a unit and one seventh

REDUCTION OF FRACTIONS

28. *To reduce a fraction* is to change its form without changing its value.

To reduce a fraction to higher terms multiply both numerator and denominator by the same quantity. Thus, $\frac{3}{4} = \frac{3 \times 3}{4 \times 3} = \frac{9}{12}$. The value of the fraction has been increased three times by multiplying the numerator by 3, and then decreased just as many times by multiplying the denominator by 3. If in the fraction $\frac{b}{d}$ both the numerator and denominator are multiplied by c, the value of the fraction is not changed but the form is changed to $\frac{bc}{dc}$. Thus, multiplying both numerator and denominator by the same quantity does not change the value of the fraction.

To reduce a fraction to lower terms divide both numerator and denominator by the same number. Thus, $\frac{4 \div 2}{6 \div 2} = \frac{2}{3}$. In this case dividing the denominator by 2 changes the fractional parts from sixths to thirds, which are twice as large as sixths and this much of the operation has doubled the value of the fraction. Dividing the numerator by 2 decreases the number of parts to one-half of the original number. Therefore dividing both numerator and denominator by the same quantity does not change the value of the fraction. In the same way $\frac{mp}{mn}$ may be reduced to $\frac{p}{n}$ by dividing both numerator and denominator by m.

A fraction is reduced to its lowest terms when its numerator and denominator have no common factor other than 1; that is when the terms are prime to each other. Thus, $\frac{1}{2}$, $\frac{2}{3}$, $\frac{15}{16}$, $\frac{a}{b}$, are reduced to their lowest terms, but $\frac{4}{6}$ is not, as 4 and 6 may both be divided by 2, reducing the fraction to $\frac{2}{3}$, and $\frac{ad}{ac}$ is not, as ad and ac may both be divided by a, reducing the fraction to $\frac{d}{c}$.

An *entire quantity* is one which has no fractional part as 3, **11,** or b. An entire quantity, which is also a number, is called an *integer*. For example, 3 and 11 are integers.

A *mixed quantity* consists of an entire quantity and a fraction. Thus, $5\frac{1}{6}$, $3\frac{7}{8}$, and $a + \frac{b}{d}$ are mixed quantities. To reduce a mixed quantity to an improper fraction, multiply the entire quantity by the denominator of the fraction, add to this product the numerator of the fraction and place their sum over the denominator. To reduce $3\frac{7}{8}$ to an improper fraction, reduce 3 units to eighths by multiplying 3 by 8 obtaining 24; add this to 7 and the result, 31, is the numerator of the fraction. $3\frac{7}{8} = \frac{31}{8}$. In the same way $a + \frac{b}{d} = \frac{ad + b}{d}$.

To reduce an improper fraction to a mixed quantity divide the numerator by the denominator, write the quotient as the entire quantity of the mixed quantity and place the remainder over the divisor (denominator of improper fraction) as the fraction.

Examples.   1.   Change $\frac{31}{21}$ to a mixed number.

SOLUTION.   Divide the numerator 31 by the denominator 21, and place the remainder 10 over the divisor 21 as the fraction of the mixed quantity. As 21 twenty-firsts constitute one unit, 31 twenty-firsts constitute one unit and ten more twenty-firsts.

$$1\frac{10}{21} \text{ quotient}$$
$$21\overline{)31}$$
$$\underline{21}$$
$$10 \text{ remainder}$$

2.   Reduce $\frac{35ab}{16a}$ to a mixed number.

SOLUTION.   Following the process already given $\frac{35ab}{16a} = 2b + \frac{3b}{16}$, for by cancellation $\frac{3ab}{16a}$ becomes $\frac{3b}{16}$, giving the final form $2b + \frac{3b}{16}^*$. This quantity $2b +$ $\frac{3b}{16}$ can be changed to the original quantity thus: Following the rule given above, $16 \times 2b$ equals $32b$ and adding to this $3b$ and placing 16 as the denominator we have $\frac{35b}{16}$. Multiplying both numerator and denominator by the same quantity a does not change its value and gives $\frac{35ab}{16a}$, the original fraction.

$$2b + \tfrac{3\,b}{1\,6} \text{ quotient}$$
$$16a\overline{)35ab}$$
$$\underline{32ab}$$
$$3ab \text{ remainder}$$

───────────

*This must not be expressed as $2b\frac{3b}{16}$, as this would   mean $2b \times \frac{3b}{16}$. Page 15, Part I.

PROBLEMS FOR PRACTICE

Reduce to mixed quantities:

1. $\dfrac{25679}{4}$

2. $\dfrac{13}{7}$

3. $\dfrac{117}{5}$ Ans. $23\dfrac{2}{5}$

Change to improper fractions:

4. $3\dfrac{3}{5}$

5. $90\dfrac{3}{9}$

6. $21\dfrac{7}{20}$

Reduce to lowest terms:

7. $\dfrac{369}{936}$

8. $\dfrac{288}{360}$

Find the proper numerators:

9. $\dfrac{1}{16} = \dfrac{?}{96}$ 10. $\dfrac{3}{5} = \dfrac{?}{525}$ 11. $\dfrac{21}{22} = \dfrac{?}{462}$ Ans. $\dfrac{441}{462}$

SUGGESTION: Problem 9. $96 \div 16 = 6$. Hence, 6 is the multiplying factor for numerator and denominator of fraction. See § 28, second paragraph.

Reduce to mixed quantities:

12. $\dfrac{14abc}{5bc}$ Ans. $2a + \dfrac{4a}{5}$ 13. $\dfrac{16a}{6}$

Reduce to lowest terms:

14. $\dfrac{8a}{12}$ Ans. $\dfrac{2a}{3}$ 15. $\dfrac{16bc}{32c}$

Change to improper fractions:

16. $4 + \dfrac{6}{7p}$ Ans. $\dfrac{28p + 6}{7p}$ 17. $7a + \dfrac{3a}{5}$

Find the proper numerators:

18. $\dfrac{1}{5a} = \dfrac{?}{25a}$ 19. $\dfrac{5}{6b} = \dfrac{?}{12b}$ Ans. $\dfrac{10}{12b}$

LEAST COMMON DENOMINATOR

29. The product of a number of factors is called a *multiple* of any one of them. Thus, 6 is a multiple of 3; 21 is a multiple of 7; and ab is a multiple of b.

Now the denominators of any group of fractions must be reduced to some common multiple, called a *common denominator*, before the fractions may be added, subtracted, or compared in value. This common denominator may be obtained by multiplying together the denominators of the fractions. Suppose, for example, it is desired to reduce $\frac{1}{3}$ and $\frac{1}{4}$ of a foot to fractional parts of a foot, having a common denominator. Let the common denominator be $3 \times 4 = 12$.

To reduce $\frac{1}{3}$ to higher terms, i. e., to a fraction having the given denominator 12, multiply both numerator and denominator by the factor 4; thus, $\frac{1}{3} = \frac{4}{12}$. In a similar manner $\frac{1}{4}$ is found to be $\frac{3}{12}$.

The least common denominator of several fractions is the least quantity which may be divided by each denominator without a remainder. Thus, 24 is the least common denominator of the fractions $\frac{5}{6}$, $\frac{3}{8}$, and $\frac{7}{12}$, and ab is the least common denominator of the fractions $\frac{1}{a}$ and $\frac{1}{b}$.

The least common denominator of several fractions contains all of the prime factors of the given denominators. Thus, either 96 or 192 is a common denominator of the fractions $\frac{5}{12}$ and $\frac{7}{16}$, and contains all their prime factors, 2, 2, 3, and 2, 2, 2, 2. The *least* common denominator, however, is neither 96 nor 192, but 48, because 48 is the least quantity which contains the prime factors of both 12 and 16 the greatest number of times that they appear in either one of these quantities.

$$12 = 2 \times 2 \times 3$$
$$16 = 2 \times 2 \times 2 \times 2$$
$$48 = 2 \times 2 \times 2 \times 2 \times 3$$

Since 2 is a common factor of 12 and 16 and appears four times in the latter, it is taken four times. There are no other common factors and therefore, the four 2's and the remaining factor 3, are all the factors which make up the least common denominator, and their product is 48.

Therefore, to find the least common denominator, separate the denominators into their prime factors and take each factor as many times as it appears in the denominator containing it the greatest number of times.

Examples. 1. Find the least common denominator of the fractions, $\frac{1}{3}$, $\frac{3}{4}$, $\frac{2}{9}$, and $\frac{7}{12}$.

SOLUTION. First, write the denominators in a row, as shown in the margin. Now the least quantity to contain 3, 4, 9, and 12 must be the smallest quantity that will contain the factors of each of them, but no other factors. Then all the prime factors that the common denominator contains must be found. 2 is a prime factor of 4 and 12. Therefore, it must be a factor of any quantity that contains 4 and 12 without a remainder. Divide the 4 and 12 by 2, writing the quotients below, carrying down the 3 and 9 which are not divisible by 2. Again it is seen that 2 is a factor of 2 and 6, and the operation is repeated, obtaining 3, 1, 9, and 3. Next dividing by 3, the result is 1, 1, 3, and 1. Now these final quotients have no common factor, and must be factors of the least common denominator just as 2, 2, and 3 are. Disregarding the 1's, $2 \times 2 \times 3 \times 3 = 36$. The result 36 is the least common denominator. Whenever 1's appear, they may be disregarded, as multiplying by the factor 1 produces no change in the quantity.

$$
\begin{array}{r}
2)\overline{3;\ 4;\ 9;\ 12} \\
2)\overline{3;\ 2;\ 9;\ \ 6} \\
3)\overline{3;\ 1;\ 9;\ \ 3} \\
\overline{1;\ 1;\ 3;\ \ 1}
\end{array}
$$

2. Find the least common denominator of the fractions $\frac{5}{12ax}$, $\frac{7}{48by}$, and $\frac{5}{42bx}$.

SOLUTION. Dividing through by the successive factors, remainders are a, $4y$, and 7. Therefore, $x \times 2 \times 3 \times 2 \times b \times a \times 4y \times 7 = 336abxy$. The work can sometimes be shortened by dividing out any factor common to all the denominators even though it is not prime. It may be observed that 6 is such a common factor, and could have been used as a divisor in place of 2 and 3.

$$
\begin{array}{r}
x)\overline{12ax;\ 48by;\ 42bx} \\
2)\overline{12a;\ \ 48by;\ \ 42b} \\
3)\overline{\ 6a;\ \ 24by;\ \ 21b} \\
2)\overline{\ 2a;\ \ \ 8by;\ \ \ 7b} \\
b)\overline{\ 1a;\ \ \ 4by;\ \ \ 7b} \\
\overline{\ a;\ \ \ 4y;\ \ \ 7}
\end{array}
$$

Sometimes the least common denominator may be found by inspecting the fractions. In $\frac{1}{6}$, $\frac{5}{12}$, and $\frac{4}{7}$, since 12 is a multiple of 6, and any quantity which has 12 as a factor must contain 6, it is only necessary to find the least common denominator of the denominators 12 and 7, which is 84.

To reduce fractions to their least common denominator, first reduce each fraction to its lowest terms, and then find the least common denominator of these fractions.   Each fraction must now be changed to a fraction whose denominator is the least common denominator, which operation, it is readily seen, is merely the reducing of the fractions to higher terms.   For example, in the preceding paragraph, the least common denominator of the fractions $\frac{1}{6}$, $\frac{5}{12}$, and $\frac{4}{7}$, is found to be 84; when the reduction is accomplished, $\frac{1}{6}$ becomes $\frac{14}{84}$; $\frac{5}{12}$ becomes $\frac{35}{84}$; and $\frac{4}{7}$ becomes $\frac{48}{84}$.

Examples.   1.   Let $\frac{6}{18}$, $\frac{3}{4}$, $\frac{2}{9}$, and $\frac{7}{12}$, be reduced to equivalent fractions with a least common denominator.

SOLUTION. $\frac{6}{18}$ must be reduced to lower terms by dividing both numerator and denominator by 6, which changes the form to $\frac{1}{3}$.   The least common denominator of $\frac{1}{3}$, $\frac{3}{4}$, $\frac{2}{9}$, and $\frac{7}{12}$ has just been found to be 36.

$36 \div 3 = 12$	$12 \times 1 = 12$	$\frac{1}{3} = \frac{12}{36}$
$36 \div 4 = 9$	$9 \times 3 = 27$	$\frac{3}{4} = \frac{27}{36}$
$36 \div 9 = 4$	$4 \times 2 = 8$	$\frac{2}{9} = \frac{8}{36}$
$36 \div 12 = 3$	$3 \times 7 = 21$	$\frac{7}{12} = \frac{21}{36}$

2.   Reduce $\frac{15}{36ax}$, $\frac{7}{48by}$, and $\frac{5}{42bx}$ to equivalent fractions with a least common denominator.

SOLUTION.   The fraction $\frac{15}{36ax}$ may be reduced by dividing both numerator and denominator by 3. $\frac{15}{36ax} = \frac{5}{12ax}$.   The least common denominator of $\frac{5}{12ax}$, $\frac{7}{48by}$, and $\frac{5}{42bx}$ was found on Page 37 to be $336abxy$.

$336abxy \div 12ax = 28by$	$28by \times 5 = 140by$	$\frac{5}{12ax} = \frac{140by}{336abxy}$
$336abxy \div 48by = 7ax$	$7ax \times 7 = 49ax$	$\frac{7}{48by} = \frac{49ax}{336abxy}$
$336abxy \div 42bx = 8ay$	$8ay \times 5 = 40ay$	$\frac{5}{42bx} = \frac{40ay}{336abxy}$

PROBLEMS FOR PRACTICE

1. Change $\dfrac{5}{6}$ and $\dfrac{3}{10}$ to fractions having a common denominator.

2. Change $\dfrac{4}{5}$, $\dfrac{7}{12}$, and $\dfrac{5}{6}$ to fractions having a common denominator.

3. Change $\dfrac{3}{7}$, $\dfrac{5}{8}$, $\dfrac{2}{3}$, and $\dfrac{1}{2}$ to fractions having a common denominator.

Change to proper or improper fractions using the least common denominator:

4. $\frac{2}{25}$, $\frac{3}{10}$, $\frac{47}{50}$, and $\frac{4}{75}$.

5. $5\frac{1}{2}$, $2\frac{1}{4}$, and $1\frac{3}{8}$.

6. $\frac{4}{5}$, $\frac{7}{15}$, $3\frac{2}{3}$, and 7.

7. $\frac{5}{6}$, $\frac{1}{2}$, $\frac{3}{4}$, and $\frac{6}{7}$.

8. $\frac{1}{3}$, $\frac{7}{20}$, and $\frac{4}{15}$.

9. $\frac{9}{16}$, $\frac{1}{3}$, $\frac{3}{8}$, and $\frac{5}{6}$.

10. $\frac{3}{7}$, $\frac{2}{10}$, and $\frac{1}{2}$.

11. $\dfrac{5}{b}$ and $\dfrac{b}{c}$

12. $\dfrac{c}{ad}$, $\dfrac{b}{d}$, and $\dfrac{g}{de}$.

13. $\dfrac{1}{m}$, $\dfrac{a}{n}$, $\dfrac{b}{mp}$, and $\dfrac{c}{np}$.

14. $\dfrac{a}{xy}$, $\dfrac{b}{xz}$, and $\dfrac{c}{yz}$.

15. $\dfrac{2a}{yz}$, $\dfrac{3b}{xy}$, and $\dfrac{4c}{y}$.

ADDITION OF FRACTIONS

30. To add together two or more fractions, the fractional **units** must be of the same size; in other words, they must be reduced to a common denominator before the addition can be accomplished. For example, suppose it is desired to add the fractions $\dfrac{1}{4}$ and $\dfrac{1}{3}$. These may for convenience represent $\dfrac{1}{4}$ and $\dfrac{1}{3}$ of a foot. Now, it is well known that a foot contains 12 inches, and the $\dfrac{1}{4}$ may be considered as 3 inches or $\dfrac{3}{12}$ of a foot, the $\dfrac{1}{3}$ as 4 inches, or $\dfrac{4}{12}$ of a foot.

The required sum is then $3 + 4 = 7$ inches, or $\dfrac{3}{12} + \dfrac{4}{12} = \dfrac{7}{12}$ feet. This process is graphically illustrated in Fig. 1.

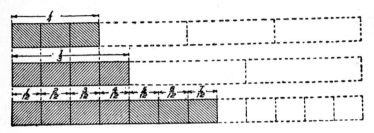

Fig. 1. Graphical Representation of Addition of Fractions

Now if an example be taken in which there are more than **two** fractions, it will be noted that the procedure is the same. $\dfrac{5}{8} + \dfrac{7}{12} + \dfrac{11}{24} + \dfrac{3}{4} = ?$ It may be seen by inspection or by the process already given that 24 is the least common denominator of the several fractions. The next step is to change the numerators of the fractions so that they will express the same value with the common denominator 24 as they now express with their respective denominators. $\dfrac{5}{8} = \dfrac{15}{24}$; $\dfrac{7}{12} = \dfrac{14}{24}$; $\dfrac{11}{24}$ will stand as written; $\dfrac{3}{4} = \dfrac{18}{24}$. Adding the several numerators and placing the sum over the common denominator the required sum is found to be $\dfrac{58}{24}$, which is an improper fraction. Reducing the improper fraction to a mixed quantity gives $2\frac{10}{24}$, or finally $2\frac{5}{12}$.

Again, to add $\dfrac{d}{2p}$, $\dfrac{d}{5p}$, and $\dfrac{d}{3p}$, first find the least common denominator, which is $30p$. Then $\dfrac{d}{2p} = \dfrac{15d}{30p}$; $\dfrac{d}{5p} = \dfrac{6d}{30p}$; $\dfrac{d}{3p} = \dfrac{10d}{30p}$; and $\dfrac{d}{2p} + \dfrac{d}{5p} + \dfrac{d}{3p} = \dfrac{15d}{30p} + \dfrac{6d}{30p} + \dfrac{10d}{30p} = \dfrac{31d}{30p}$.

If the problem involves letters only, the process is essentially the same. If $\dfrac{a}{n}$ and $\dfrac{b}{p}$ are to be added, they must first be reduced to their common denominator, np. $\dfrac{a}{n} = \dfrac{ap}{np}$; $\dfrac{b}{p} = \dfrac{bn}{np}$; $\dfrac{a}{n} + \dfrac{b}{p}$ $= \dfrac{ap}{np} + \dfrac{bn}{np}$. As the relation between ap and bn is not known, the sum of the numerators can only be represented by the expression $ap + bn$, giving the final sum $\dfrac{ap + bn}{np}$.

To add mixed quantities, add the entire quantities and the fractions separately, and if the fractional result of this addition is an improper fraction, reduce it to a mixed quantity and add the entire part to the sum of the entire quantities already obtained.

Examples. 1. $20\frac{2}{3} + 13\frac{1}{2} + 7\frac{1}{8} = ?$

SOLUTION. Adding the entire quantities together gives $20 + 13 + 7 = 40$. Reduce the fractions to higher terms having a common denominator and add, obtaining $\dfrac{16}{24} + \dfrac{12}{24} + \dfrac{3}{24} = \dfrac{31}{24} = 1\frac{7}{24}$. $40 + 1\frac{7}{24} = 41\frac{7}{24}$ as the final result.

$$20\tfrac{2}{3} = 20\tfrac{16}{24}$$
$$13\tfrac{1}{2} = 13\tfrac{12}{24}$$
$$7\tfrac{1}{8} = 7\tfrac{3}{24}$$
$$\overline{40\tfrac{31}{24}}$$
$$= 40 + 1\tfrac{7}{24} = 41\tfrac{7}{24}$$

2. Add $ab + \dfrac{b}{2}$ and $2ab + \dfrac{b}{3}$.

SOLUTION. The sum of the entire quantities is $3ab$. The least common denominator for $\dfrac{b}{2}$ and $\dfrac{b}{3}$ is 6, and the new forms of the fractions become $\dfrac{3b}{6}$ and $\dfrac{2b}{6}$ giving $\dfrac{5b}{6}$ as their sum. As $\dfrac{5b}{6}$ cannot be reduced to lower terms, the result is complete as shown in the margin.

$$ab + \dfrac{b}{2} = ab + \dfrac{3b}{6}$$
$$2ab + \dfrac{b}{3} = 2ab + \dfrac{2b}{6}$$
$$\overline{3ab + \dfrac{5b}{6}}$$

PROBLEMS FOR PRACTICE

Find the sum of

1. $\frac{5}{8}$, $\frac{7}{12}$, and $\frac{11}{24}$. Ans. $1\frac{2}{3}$

2. $\frac{3}{20}$, $\frac{7}{12}$, and $\frac{5}{15}$.

3. $6\frac{2}{3}$, $2\frac{2}{7}$, and $4\frac{4}{15}$. Ans. $13\frac{23}{105}$

4. $\dfrac{T}{2}$ and $\dfrac{T}{3}$.

5. $\dfrac{R}{N}$ and $\dfrac{M}{P}$. Ans. $\dfrac{PR + MN}{NP}$

6. $d + \dfrac{4d}{6}$ and $4d + \dfrac{d}{2}$.   Ans. $6d + \dfrac{d}{6}$

7. $a + \dfrac{c}{3}$ and $b + \dfrac{c}{4}$.

8. A room is $32\frac{2}{3}$ feet long and $29\frac{7}{8}$ feet wide. What is the distance around the room?

9. Three castings weigh respectively $225\frac{3}{8}$, $232\frac{5}{16}$, and $240\frac{1}{2}$ pounds. What is their total weight?

10. A steel rod is to be cut into five pieces; the first to be $4\frac{5}{8}$ inches long, the second $3\frac{3}{4}$ inches, the third $5\frac{3}{16}$ inches, the fourth $4\frac{5}{32}$ inches, and the fifth $1\frac{15}{16}$ inches. Find the length of the rod required.

11. A casting weighing $18\frac{3}{8}$ pounds has had $2\frac{1}{8}$ pounds of metal removed by the planer. How much did the original casting weigh?

SUBTRACTION OF FRACTIONS

31. *Fractions may be subtracted* only when they have a common denominator, and express quantities of like units.

Hence *to subtract proper fractions* reduce the given fractions to their equivalents, having a least common denominator, and write the difference of the numerators over the common denominator.

Examples. 1. Find the difference between $\dfrac{5}{6}$ and $\dfrac{8}{15}$.

SOLUTION. The fractions, when reduced to the least common denominator, become $\dfrac{25}{30}$ and $\dfrac{16}{30}$; their difference is, therefore, $\dfrac{9}{30}$, or reduced to lowest terms $\dfrac{3}{10}$.

$$\frac{5}{6} = \frac{25}{30}$$
$$\frac{8}{15} = \frac{16}{30}$$
$$\frac{9}{30} = \frac{3}{10}$$

2. Find the difference between $\dfrac{a}{p}$ and $\dfrac{a}{2p}$.

SOLUTION. The fraction $\dfrac{a}{p}$ may be reduced to $\dfrac{2a}{2p}$. Then, subtracting, $\dfrac{2a}{2p} - \dfrac{a}{2p} = \dfrac{2a}{2p} - \dfrac{1a}{2p} = \dfrac{1a}{2p}$ or $\dfrac{a}{2p}$.

$$\frac{a}{p} = \frac{2a}{2p}$$
$$\frac{2a}{2p} - \frac{a}{2p} = \frac{a}{2p}$$

To subtract mixed quantities, subtract the fractional and entire parts separately, and add the remainders. If the mixed quantities are small, they may be reduced to improper fractions and subtracted.

Examples. **1.** From $27\frac{5}{6}$ subtract $14\frac{5}{8}$.

SOLUTION. Subtracting the entire quantities, 27 $- 14 = 13$. Reduce the fractions to higher terms having a common denominator and subtract, obtaining $\frac{20}{24} - \frac{15}{24} = \frac{5}{24}$.

$$27\frac{5}{6} = 27\frac{20}{24}$$
$$14\frac{5}{8} = 14\frac{15}{24}$$
$$\overline{\hphantom{14\frac{5}{8} = }13\frac{5}{24}}$$

2. From $2\frac{11}{14}$ subtract $1\frac{2}{7}$.

SOLUTION. The common denominator is **14,** hence $2\frac{11}{14} = \frac{39}{14}$, and $1\frac{2}{7} = \frac{9}{7} = \frac{18}{14}$. The difference is $\frac{21}{14}$, which may be reduced to the lowest terms by dividing both numerator and

$$2\frac{11}{14} = \frac{39}{14}$$
$$1\frac{2}{7} = \frac{18}{14}$$
$$\overline{\hphantom{1\frac{2}{7} = }\frac{21}{14} = \frac{3}{2} = 1\frac{1}{2}}$$

denominator by 7 giving $\frac{3}{2} = 1\frac{1}{2}$.

To subtract a fraction or mixed quantity from an entire quantity, or from a mixed quantity in which the fraction of the minuend is less than the fraction of the subtrahend, one unit of the integer in the minuend must be written as a fraction. This is shown by the following example.

3. From 17 take $\frac{9}{11}$.

SOLUTION. First write one of the 17 units as a fraction having 11 parts. Thus, $17 = 16 + \frac{11}{11}$. Now the subtraction may be accomplished without difficulty, giving $16\frac{2}{11}$.

$$17 = 16\frac{11}{11} \text{ minuend}$$
$$\frac{9}{11} \text{ subtrahend}$$
$$\overline{16\frac{2}{11}}$$

In the case of letters, subtraction may be made after writing the entire quantity, as shown in the margin.

4. From m take $\frac{a}{p}$.

SOLUTION. The entire quantity m may be written in fractional form having the desired denominator by multiplying and dividing m by p, thus giving $\frac{mp}{p}$. The subtraction is then indicated as shown.

$$m = \frac{mp}{p}$$
$$\frac{mp}{p} - \frac{a}{p} = \frac{mp - a}{p}$$

PROBLEMS FOR PRACTICE

1. From $1\frac{2}{6}$ subtract $\frac{5}{7}$.

2. From $\frac{5}{7}$ subtract $\frac{3}{5}$.   Ans. $\frac{4}{35}$

3. From $\frac{5a}{16}$ subtract $\frac{3a}{24}$.   Ans. $\frac{9a}{16}$

4. From $\frac{10}{3}\frac{9}{8}$ subtract $\frac{8}{4\,6}$
5. From $\frac{12}{3\,1\,p}$ subtract $\frac{6}{4\,9\,r}$ Ans. $\frac{22}{4\,9\,p}$
6. From $\frac{17}{1\,8}$ subtract $\frac{11}{2\,7}$
7. From $2\frac{5}{9}$ subtract $1\frac{1}{7}$
8. From $\frac{27}{3\,2}$ subtract $\frac{9}{3\,4}$ Ans. $\frac{315}{5\,4\,4}$

9. A flagstaff $50\frac{3}{10}$ feet high was broken off in a storm so that $43\frac{7}{10}$ feet remained standing. How much was broken off?

10. A box and its contents weighed $75\frac{3}{8}$ pounds. The box alone weighed $3\frac{5}{16}$ pounds. What was the weight of its contents?

MULTIPLICATION OF FRACTIONS

32. *Multiplication of fractions* requires no such reduction of the fractions as was found necessary in addition and subtraction. Multiplying the numerator of a fraction multiplies the number of fractional units, their *size* remaining the same, and dividing the denominator multiplies the size of the fractional units, the *number* remaining the same. In many solutions cancellation will be found useful.

To multiply a fraction by an entire quantity, multiply the numerator of the fraction by the whole number, and write the product over the denominator, or divide the denominator of the fraction by the entire quantity, when it can be done without a remainder, and write the quotient as the denominator. Then reduce to lowest terms, and if necessary to a mixed quantity.

Examples. 1. Multiply $\dfrac{7}{8}$ by 4.

SOLUTION *a.* Multiplying the numerator by 4 increases the number of fractional units from 7 to 28, giving $\dfrac{28}{8}$, which, reduced to lower terms, becomes $\dfrac{7}{2}$ and finally as a mixed number $3\frac{1}{2}$.

$$\frac{7}{8} \times 4 = \frac{28}{8} = \frac{7}{2} = 3\frac{1}{2}$$

SOLUTION *b.* Dividing the denominator by the divisor is equivalent to cancellation. 4 divided into 8 is 2. The denominator is then 2, making the fractional unit 4 times as large. By the usual process $\dfrac{7}{2}$ is changed to $3\frac{1}{2}$.

$$\frac{7}{\underset{2}{\cancel{8}}} \times \cancel{4}^{\,1} = \frac{7}{2}$$

$$\frac{7}{2} = 3\frac{1}{2}$$

2. Multiply $\dfrac{7}{6p}$ by $3p$.

SOLUTION a. Multiply the numerator of the fraction by $3p$, and place over the denominator $6p$. $\dfrac{21p}{6p}$ may be reduced by dividing out p in the numerator and denominator.

$$\frac{7}{6p} \times 3p = \frac{7 \times 3p}{6p} = \frac{21p}{6p}$$

$$\frac{21p}{6p} = \frac{21}{6} = 3\frac{3}{6} = 3\frac{1}{2}$$

SOLUTION b. The same result would have been obtained more briefly by dividing the denominator of the fraction by $3p$. By cancellation the result $\dfrac{7}{2}$ is immediately obtained.

$$\frac{7}{\cancel{6p}_{2}} \times \cancel{3p}^{1} = \frac{7}{2}$$

$$\frac{7}{2} = 3\tfrac{1}{2}$$

To multiply one fraction by another, multiply together the two numerators and place this product over the product of the two denominators, or indicate the multiplication, and cancel wherever possible.

3. Multiply $\dfrac{5}{8}$ by $\dfrac{2}{5}$.

SOLUTION a. The 2 of the multiplier makes the product larger, and therefore, the numerator of the multiplicand is multiplied by 2. The 5 of the multiplier makes the product smaller, and hence, the denominator is multiplied by 5.

$$\frac{5}{8} \times \frac{2}{5} = \frac{5 \times 2}{8 \times 5} = \frac{10}{40} = \frac{1}{4}$$

SOLUTION b. The solution in the margin shows how the multiplication may be more briefly performed by cancellation.

$$\frac{\cancel{5}^{1}}{\cancel{8}_{4}} \times \frac{\cancel{2}^{1}}{\cancel{5}_{1}} = \frac{1}{4}$$

4. Multiply $\dfrac{d}{4}$ by $\dfrac{2a}{b}$.

SOLUTION. By the usual method the numerator is equal to the product of d and $2a$, or $2ad$, and the denominator is $4b$.

$$\frac{d}{4} \times \frac{2a}{b} = \frac{d \times 2a}{4 \times b} = \frac{2ad}{4b}$$

$$\frac{2ad}{4b} = \frac{ad}{2b}$$

To multiply mixed quantities, change them to improper fractions and multiply as before.

5. Multiply $2\dfrac{2}{7}$ by $5\dfrac{1}{4}$.

SOLUTION. Write these as improper fractions. $\dfrac{16}{7}$ and $\dfrac{21}{4}$ is obtained. Cancellation gives 12 at once.

$$\frac{\cancel{16}^{4}}{\cancel{7}_{1}} \times \frac{\cancel{21}^{3}}{\cancel{4}_{1}} = 12$$

To multiply mixed quantities and whole numbers or fractions, change the mixed quantities and whole numbers to improper fractions and multiply.

6. Find the product of $2\frac{2}{7}$, $2\frac{5}{8}$, $\frac{7}{3p}$, and $6p$.

SOLUTION: $\frac{\overset{2}{\cancel{16}}}{7} \times \frac{21}{\cancel{8}} \times \frac{7}{\cancel{3p}} \times \frac{\overset{2}{\cancel{6p}}}{1} = 84$

PROBLEMS FOR PRACTICE

Find the product of

1. $\frac{5}{8}$ and $\frac{4}{7}$.   Ans. $\frac{5}{14}$
2. $\frac{8m}{9}$ and $\frac{36n}{37}$.
3. $\frac{12a}{17}$ and $\frac{10}{13b}$.
4. $12\frac{3}{4}$ and $11\frac{5}{9}$.
5. $11\frac{2}{7}$ and $8\frac{4}{5}$.   Ans. $99\frac{11}{35}$
6. $12\frac{3}{5}$ and 7.
7. $6\frac{5}{6}$; $\frac{4}{5}$; and $4\frac{4}{5}$.
8. $\frac{3}{5}$; $\frac{4}{9}$; $\frac{10}{13}$; and $\frac{12}{21}$.
9. A water-tube boiler has a grate surface of $27\frac{9}{10}$ square feet. It burns $15\frac{3}{4}$ pounds of coal per square foot per hour. How much does it burn in $1\frac{1}{2}$ hours?
10. What will 142 yards of curbing cost at $\$6\frac{5}{9}$ per yd.?
11. What will $17\frac{1}{2}$ tons of coal cost at $\$4\frac{7}{10}$ per ton?
12. A point on the fly wheel of an engine travels $16\frac{3}{4}$ feet per revolution. How far does it travel in $29\frac{5}{9}$ revolutions? How long would it take if the wheel made one revolution in $2\frac{3}{7}$ seconds?

DIVISION OF FRACTIONS

33. *Division of fractions* is the reverse of multiplication. Dividing the numerator of a fraction divides the number of fractional units, their size remaining the same, and multiplying the denominator also divides the size of the fractional units, the number remaining the same. This latter process is equivalent to inverting the divisor and multiplying. Thus $\frac{7}{8} \div \frac{3}{4}$ and $\frac{7}{8} \times \frac{4}{3}$ are equivalent expressions. The fraction after inverting is called the *reciprocal* of the original fraction.

To divide a fraction by an entire quantity, change the entire quantity to a fractional form with one as a denominator; invert the fractional form and multiply; or, divide the numerator of the fraction by the entire quantity.

Examples. 1. Divide $\dfrac{8}{9}$ by 4.

SOLUTION. The reciprocal of 4 is $\dfrac{1}{4}$. This multiplied by $\dfrac{8}{9}$, using, cancellation gives the quotient $\dfrac{2}{9}$.

$$\frac{8}{9} \div 4 = \frac{\overset{2}{\cancel{8}}}{9} \times \frac{1}{\cancel{4}_{1}} = \frac{2}{9}$$

2. Divide $\dfrac{a}{b}$ by a.

SOLUTION. The reciprocal of a is multiplied by the fraction, and by cancellation the result is obtained.

$$\frac{a}{b} \div a = \frac{\overset{1}{\cancel{a}}}{b} \times \frac{1}{\cancel{a}_{1}} = \frac{1}{b}$$

3. Divide 13 by $\dfrac{3}{7}$.

SOLUTION. Invert the fraction and multiply. Multiplying 13 by the reciprocal of $\dfrac{3}{7}$ gives at once $\dfrac{91}{3}$ or $30\dfrac{1}{3}$.

$$13 \div \frac{3}{7} = 13 \times \frac{7}{3} = \frac{91}{3} = 30\frac{1}{3}$$

4. Divide d by $\dfrac{d}{c}$.

SOLUTION. The reciprocal of the fraction is multiplied by d, and cancellation is used.

$$d \div \frac{d}{c} = \frac{\overset{1}{\cancel{d}} \times c}{\cancel{d}_{1}} = c$$

To divide a fraction by a fraction, invert the divisor, that is, the second fraction, and then proceed as in multiplication of fractions.

5. Divide $\dfrac{3}{4}$ by $\dfrac{7}{8}$.

SOLUTION. The multiplication is accomplished by multiplying $\dfrac{3}{4}$ by the reciprocal of $\dfrac{7}{8}$, using cancellation. The result $\dfrac{6}{7}$ is obtained at once.

$$\frac{3}{4} \div \frac{7}{8} = \frac{3}{\cancel{4}_{1}} \times \frac{\overset{2}{\cancel{8}}}{7} = \frac{6}{7}$$

6. Divide $\dfrac{d}{p}$ by $\dfrac{a}{c}$.

SOLUTION. The process is exactly the same as used in the preceding examples.

$$\frac{d}{p} \div \frac{a}{c} = \frac{d}{p} \times \frac{c}{a} = \frac{cd}{ap}$$

When division involves a mixed number, the mixed number may be reduced to an improper fraction and one of the preceding methods used.

7. Divide $2\frac{1}{2}$ by $1\frac{7}{8}$.

SOLUTION.

$$2\frac{1}{2} \div 1\frac{7}{8} = \frac{5}{2} \div \frac{15}{8} = \overset{1}{\underset{1}{\cancel{5}}} \times \frac{\overset{4}{\cancel{8}}}{\underset{3}{\cancel{15}}} = \frac{4}{3} = 1\frac{1}{3}$$

When a fraction takes the form called a *complex fraction*, that is, having a fraction in numerator or denominator or both, as $\dfrac{\frac{7}{8}}{4}$, the division is handled as in the examples just discussed. That is, $\dfrac{7}{8} \div 4 = \dfrac{7}{8} \times \dfrac{1}{4} = \dfrac{7}{8 \times 4} = \dfrac{7}{32}$.

8. Divide $\dfrac{\frac{9}{11}}{\frac{2}{5}}$ by $\frac{3}{4}$.

SOLUTION. The complex fraction is first reduced to a simple fraction; the division by the second fraction is then indicated, and this second fraction inverted so as to allow multiplication. Cancellation reduces the fractions to the final result.

$$\frac{9}{11} \div \frac{2}{5} = \frac{9}{11} \times \frac{5}{2}$$

$$\left(\frac{9}{11} \times \frac{5}{2} \right) \div \frac{3}{4} = \frac{9}{11} \times \frac{5}{2} \times \frac{4}{3}$$

$$= \frac{\overset{3}{\cancel{9}}}{11} \times \frac{5}{\underset{1}{\cancel{2}}} \times \frac{\overset{2}{\cancel{4}}}{\underset{1}{\cancel{3}}} = \frac{30}{11} = 2\frac{8}{11}$$

PROBLEMS FOR PRACTICE

Divide:

1. $\frac{7}{9}$ by $\frac{4}{7}$. Ans. $1\frac{13}{36}$
2. $\frac{7}{8}$ by $\frac{1}{4}$.
3. $\frac{9}{13}$ by $\frac{3}{26}$.
4. $\frac{19}{20}$ by $\frac{7}{20}$.
5. $7\frac{3}{8}$ by $4\frac{1}{2}$. Ans. $1\frac{23}{36}$

6. $\dfrac{ft}{s}$ by $\dfrac{f}{b}$. Ans. $\dfrac{bt}{s}$

7. $\dfrac{mt}{a}$ by $\dfrac{b}{a}$.

8. A railroad $16\frac{1}{2}$ miles long cost \$66,937; find cost per mile.

9. A steam pump delivers $2\frac{3}{4}$ gallons per stroke. It delivers

330 gallons in $2\frac{1}{2}$ minutes. How many strokes does it make per minute? SUGGESTION: First find gallons delivered per minute.

DECIMALS

34. Decimal Fractions. It has been shown that common fractions may be reduced to higher or lower terms, *i. e.*, to fractions having any desired denominator. For example, the fraction $\frac{3}{4}$ may be reduced to one having a denominator of 12 by multiplying both terms by a number which will change the denominator to 12, viz, by 3. Thus $\frac{3}{4} \times \frac{3}{3} = \frac{9}{12}$, which is the desired fraction. The same fraction may have the denominators, 20, 32, 40, 60, and 80 by multiplying both terms successively by 5, 8, 10, 15, and 20, giving the fractions $\frac{15}{20}$, $\frac{24}{32}$, $\frac{30}{40}$, $\frac{45}{60}$, and $\frac{60}{80}$; all of these fractions are *of equal value* with the original fraction.

Now, suppose it is desirable to reduce all fractions to a *standard denominator of* 10, 100, 1,000, etc. Under this system the fraction $\frac{3}{4}$ will have successively the forms $\frac{7\frac{1}{2}}{10}$, $\frac{75}{100}$, $\frac{750}{1000}$, etc., while another fraction like $\frac{7}{8}$ will have the forms $\frac{8\frac{3}{4}}{10}$, $\frac{87\frac{1}{2}}{100}$, and $\frac{875}{1000}$. Notice that the first form for $\frac{3}{4}$ and the first and second for $\frac{7}{8}$ have fractions in the numerators. This makes an awkward combination which may always be avoided in dealing with such fractions by using the higher forms which contain no fraction in the numerator, as $\frac{75}{100}$ and $\frac{875}{1000}$.

However, it will be evident that if all fractions are so reduced, many of them will have fractional numerators, even though the denominators are made higher powers of 10, and hence, in cutting off the extra fractions certain errors will be made. It will be learned in the section on Per Cent that such errors, if they are small, are usually neglected. The fraction $\frac{1}{13}$, for example, may be given a denominator of 10,000, making a fraction $\dfrac{769\frac{3}{13}}{10000}$, which may be considered equal to $\dfrac{769}{10000}$ or even $\dfrac{77}{1000}$ without any appreciable difference.

Such fractions, as $\dfrac{75}{100}$, $\dfrac{875}{1000}$, and $\dfrac{77}{1000}$, etc., having 10, 100, 1000, etc., as denominators are called *decimal fractions*. In order to simplify this system and thus avoid writing the denominator, decimal fractions are expressed in another form which consists in writing only the numerator and placing a point (.) so that the number of places on the right of it shall be equal to the number of ciphers in the denominator. The decimal fractions given above, when expressed in this way, become .75, .875, .077, and when so used they are called *decimals*.

The point (.) is called the *decimal point* and its office is to mark the beginning of the decimal or separate it from a whole number.

A pure decimal has only decimal places, as, .93678.

A mixed decimal consists of a whole number and a decimal, as 364.23.

The *decimal* system is merely an extension of the ordinary number system to the *right* of units place, with a decimal point to indicate the boundary line. This is clearly shown in Table V.

TABLE V

Thousands	Hundreds	Tens	Units	Decimal Point	Tenths	Hundredths	Thousandths	Ten-Thousandths	Hundred-Thousandths	Millionths	Ten-Millionths	Hundred-Millionths
6	4	3	9	.	3	6	5	7	9	8	2	3

In reading the decimals, use the names just given to represent the places, omitting the word *and* except at the decimal point. The following examples give the proper reading and the corresponding figures for a few cases:

1. Nine tenths 0.9
2. Ninety-five hundredths...................... 0.95
3. Nine hundred fifty-four thousandths.......... 0.954
4. Six thousand one ten-thousandths. 0.6001
5. Six and one ten-thousandth. 6.0001

The number shown in Table V is read thus: Six thousand, four hundred thirty-nine, and thirty-six million, five hundred seventy-nine thousand, eight hundred twenty-three hundred-millionths.

The United States and some other countries use the decimal system in money. For instance, take the sum of $13.74. This may be considered to be made up of 1 ten dollar bill (tens position), 3 one dollar bills (units place, dollars being considered units), 7 dimes or tenths of a dollar (tenths position), and 4 cents or hundredths of a dollar (hundredths position). It is read thirteen dollars and seventy-four cents, and means thirteen dollars and seventy-four hundredths of a dollar. It is, of course, better to say seventy-four hundredths than seven tenths plus four hundredths, just as it is better to say seventy-four cents than to say seven dimes and four cents.

PROBLEMS FOR PRACTICE

Write in words:

1.	.965	4.	.10792
2.	3.8506	5.	.010952
3.	5.0061	6.	.4563

Write in figures:

7. Seven thousand eight hundred forty-nine hundred-thousandths.

8. Sixteen thousandths.

9. One hundred thirteen ten-thousandths.

10. Six hundred and thirty-three thousand seven hundred fifty-eight millionths. Ans. 600.033758

11. Twenty-nine hundredths.

12. Twelve and twenty-seven hundredths.

13. Four hundred seventy-two and four hundred eighty-seven ten-thousandths.

ADDITION OF DECIMALS

35. In *addition of decimals*, place the numbers so that the decimal points will be directly under each other, regardless of the number of figures. Having done this, add the figures as in addition of whole numbers. The last step is to place a decimal point in the sum directly under the column of decimal points.

Example. Add 1.75; 62.625; and 3.937.

SOLUTION. Following the process given above and placing the decimal point in the sum directly under the column of decimal points, 68.312 is obtained.

$$\begin{array}{r} 1.75 \\ 62.625 \\ 3.937 \\ \hline 68.312 \end{array}$$

The greatest accuracy must be exercised in using decimals. A decimal point is more important than any figure, because a misplaced decimal point increases the error at least ten times.

SUBTRACTION OF DECIMALS

36. In *subtraction of decimals*, the process is exactly the same as in the case of whole numbers.

Place the subtrahend under the minuend with the decimal points directly under each other. Subtract as in whole numbers. In the remainder, place the decimal point in the same column and directly under the other decimal points.

Examples. 1. From 5.17 subtract .01.

SOLUTION. Subtract as in whole numbers paying careful attention to the decimal point.

$$\begin{array}{r} 5.17 \\ .01 \\ \hline 5.16 \end{array}$$

2. From 128 subtract 96.307.

SOLUTION. This is an example in which the minuend is a whole number, which necessitates placing a decimal point to the right of the whole number, and annexing ciphers. In doing this the integer is changed to a mixed decimal. Adding ciphers to the right of the decimal point multiplies both the numerator and denominator of the decimal fraction by the same number, which, although changing its form, does not change its value. Carrying out the subtraction as in whole numbers, the remainder 31.693 is obtained.

$$\begin{array}{r} 128.000 \\ 96.307 \\ \hline 31.693 \end{array}$$

3. From 134.089 subtract 93.

SOLUTION. Placing a decimal point at the right of 93, subtract as before.

$$\begin{array}{r} 134.089 \\ 93. \\ \hline 41.089 \end{array}$$

PROBLEMS FOR PRACTICE

1. From 25.38 take 14.05
2. From 39.85 take 29.755   Ans. 10.095
3. From 72.189 take 35.976   Ans. 36.213
4. From 78.896 take 53.5987
5. From 21.12 take 12.31
6. From 6.325 take 1.0345
7. From 6.45 take 2.3375
8. From 81.35 take 11.679   Ans. 69.671

9. From a cistern that contained 30.5 barrels of water, 25.75 barrels were drawn off. How much water remained in the cistern?

10. A hundred pounds of coke were found to contain 5.79 pounds of ash and .597 pounds of sulphur. The rest was combined carbon. How much combined carbon was there?

11. In 1 pound of brazing metal there are .5 pound of copper and .125 pound of tin. The remainder is zinc. How much zinc is there?

12. An iron casting weighed in the rough 22.75 pounds, and when finished, it weighed only 16.875 pounds. How much had been taken off in the process?

MULTIPLICATION OF DECIMALS

37. In *multiplying decimals* proceed as with whole numbers, paying no attention to the decimal point until all the figures in the product are obtained. Then point off as many places in this product as the total number of places in both multiplicand and multiplier, prefixing ciphers if necessary.

Examples. 1. Multiply .397 by 41.

$$
\begin{array}{r}
.397 \\
41 \\
\hline
397 \\
1588 \\
\hline
16.277
\end{array}
$$

SOLUTION. Since there are three decimal places in the multiplicand and none in the multiplier, point off 3 + 0 places in the product.

2. Multiply .027 by .05.

$$
\begin{array}{r}
.027 \\
.05 \\
\hline
.00135
\end{array}
$$

SOLUTION. First write the decimals so that the multiplication may be most readily performed. 27 is multiplied by 5 as if both were integers. Ciphers are then prefixed to 135 until the product contains 3 + 2 = 5 decimal places.

To multiply a decimal or a mixed number expressed as a decimal by 10, 100, 1,000, etc., move the decimal point as many places to the right as there are ciphers in the multiplier. If there are not figures enough for this, annex sufficient ciphers.

Observe the following:

.046×1 = .046   .046×100 = 4.6
.046×10 = .46   .046×10000 = 460.

In the last two multiplications the product contains whole numbers. The reason for this is that after the decimal point has been moved the required number of places to the right, the cipher which comes before is dropped since it has no effect on the value. In the last case it is necessary to annex a cipher to the 46 to give the number of places required by the four ciphers in the multiplier.

After a multiplication is completed, if ciphers occur at the right of the decimal point with no figures following, the ciphers may be dropped. Thus 12.4×10.5 = 130.20. The result should, therefore, be written 130.2.

PROBLEMS FOR PRACTICE

Find the product of

1. .876 and .375   Ans. .3285
2. 72.2 and .055
3. 3.62 and .0037
4. 15.8 and .0855
5. 2.53 and .00635   Ans. .0160655
6. .765 and .067
7. 18.46 and 1.007   Ans. 18.58922
8. .00076 and .0015
9. Thirty-four million and twenty-six millionths.
10. Eight hundred and forty-two thousandths and five hundred thousand.
11. A U. S. gallon of water weighs 8.335 pounds. What is the weight of 17.3 gallons?   Ans. 144.1955 lbs.
12. A steamship sailed at an average speed of 325.75 miles per day. If another steamer sailed from the same port at the same time and in the same direction at the rate of 395.25 miles per day, how far apart were they in 5.5 days?   Ans. 382.25 miles.

13. A cubic foot of water weighs 62.3 pounds. How much will 177.3 cubic feet of water weigh? Ans. 11,045.79 lbs.

14. A steam pump delivers 26.4 gallons per stroke. A gallon weighs 8.335 pounds. What weight of water will be delivered in 117 strokes?

15. In one pound of phosphor bronze, .925 is copper, .07 is tin, and .005 is phosphorus. How much of each (copper, tin, and phosphorus) is there in 369.5 pounds?

16. A round bar of rolled iron $2\frac{1}{16}$ inches in diameter weighs 11.1 pounds per foot. What is the weight of a bar of the same diameter and material which is 9.33 feet long?

17. A train made an average speed of 1.33 miles per minute. How many miles did it cover in 17.5 minutes?

DIVISION OF DECIMALS

38. In division of decimals proceed as with whole numbers paying no attention to the decimal point until the quotient is obtained. Then point off in the quotient as many decimal places as those in the dividend exceed those in the divisor. This, it will be noted, is the reverse of the process just given in multiplication of decimals.

It should be remembered that *while the dividend may contain more decimal places than the divisor, it must contain at least as many.* To bring this about, annex as many ciphers as necessary to the right of the decimal point in the dividend.

When the division does not come out evenly, annex ciphers to the dividend and continue the division so as to give at least two decimal places in the quotient.

Examples. 1. Divide 36.744 by 24.

$$\begin{array}{r} 1.531 \\ 24\overline{)36.744} \\ \underline{24} \\ 127 \\ 120 \\ \hline 74 \\ 72 \\ \hline 24 \\ 24 \\ \hline \end{array}$$

SOLUTION. No attention is paid to the decimal point until all the figures of the quotient are obtained. As there are no decimal places in the divisor and three in the dividend, the number of decimal places in the quotient is three.

2. Divide .196 by .004.

SOLUTION. There are three decimal places in the
divisor and three in the dividend. Therefore, none will be
found in the quotient. The decimal point is placed to the
right of the result.

.004) .196
49.

3. Divide .0027 by 1.35.

SOLUTION. It is seen that 135 is not contained in
27. Therefore, annex a cipher to the dividend making
270, and the divisor 135 is contained twice without a
remainder. Since a cipher was added to the dividend,
it contains five decimal places, the divisor contains two,
and hence, in the quotient there must be five minus two,
or three decimal places. In order to have three decimal
places, two ciphers must be prefixed to the quotient,
and the decimal point placed before them.

.002
1.35).00270
270
0

4. Divide 7 by 8.

SOLUTION. As 8 is not contained in 7 an integral
number of times it is necessary to annex ciphers, the
decimal point being placed to the right of 7. The
division is then carried out as with whole numbers and
the number of decimal places in the quotient is equal to
the number in the dividend.

8)7.000
.875

By performing the division which the fraction only expresses, a
common fraction becomes a *decimal*. Thus, $\frac{3}{8}$, $\frac{5}{24}$, $\frac{7}{16}$, and $\frac{15}{32}$, may
be expressed as decimals by dividing 3 by 8, 5 by 24, 7 by 16, and 15
by 32, giving respectively .375, .208+*, .437+, and .469−.

PROBLEMS FOR PRACTICE

Divide:

1. 183.375 by 489   Ans. .375
2. 67.8632 by 32.8
3. 67.56785 by .035
4. .567891 by 8.2   Ans. .06925+
5. .1728 by 100   Ans. .001728
6. 13.50192 by 1.38
7. 783.5 by 6.25
8. 983 by 6.6   Ans. 148.93+

---

* The + and − signs after the decimals indicate that the true values are slightly
more or less than the values given.

9. 3 by 8   Ans. .375

10. 1.95 by .45

11. How much gas at $1.25 per thousand cubic feet can be bought for $17.50?

12. The distance between two places is 167.75 miles. How long will it take a steamer to run the distance if she makes, on the average, 12.5 miles per hour?

13. If a freight train runs at the rate of 15.75 miles per hour, how long will it take it to run 189 miles?

14. A lot of 22,840 railroad ties cost $39,867.22. What was the cost per hundred?

15. Seven readings of a dynamometer gave the following horse-powers: 17.31, 17.95, 18.13, 17.79, 17.87, 17.63, and 17.47. What was the average reading?

Reduce to decimals:

16. $\dfrac{5}{8}$ 18. $\dfrac{32}{64}$

17. $\dfrac{3}{4}$ 19. $\dfrac{5}{16}$

20. Change .756 to the nearest 12th.   Ans. $\frac{9}{12}$

21. Change .564 to the nearest 64th.

PERCENTAGE

39. The idea of a fraction of anything, whether it be a common fraction like $\dfrac{1}{15}$ or a decimal fraction like .001, should now be quite clear. The fraction $\dfrac{1}{15}$ merely serves to show that something has been divided into 15 parts and one of these parts has been taken. If $\dfrac{1}{1000}$ of the same thing were taken, this portion would evidently be smaller than the $\dfrac{1}{15}$. Again, a given quantity is a bigger part of a small group than it is of a large group. The results of one day's excavating may be $\dfrac{1}{30}$ of all the work to be done on one section of a tunnel, but only $\dfrac{1}{3000}$ of the total work if there are 100 sections.

The coin which a man with a bank account gives to a boy in exchange for a small service is an insignificant part of the man's money, but becomes at once in the boy's hands a large and important portion of his capital.

Evidently, therefore, there must be some standard number by which to determine the importance of quantities which are to be measured or compared. *This standard group number is 100* and all changes in numbers can be so reduced as to be expressed in terms of 100 parts; when so reduced the result is called the *per cent* of change in that number (written % and meaning *by the hundred*). For example, a change of 2 parts in 200, that is, a change from 200 to 198, may be reduced by dividing by 2, to equal 1 part in 100, or 1%; a change of 10 parts in 500 when divided by 5 is found to be the same as 2 parts in 100, or 2%. A man who has one hundred $1 bills and spends one of them, has decreased his capital by 1 part in 100 or 1%; if he spends $3, $5, or $15, his capital has been diminished by 3%, 5%, and 15%, respectively. Again, a man who buys corn at 33c and sells at 35c makes 2c on every 33c, 4c on 66c, or 6c on 99c, say $1; that is, his gain is 6%.

Fractions may be expressed in terms of per cent. $\frac{1}{15}$ may be expressed as 1 part in 15 or $6\frac{2}{3}$ parts in 100, roughly 7%. This means that $\frac{1}{15}$ of any thing, as the weight of a casting, is about 7% of it. The fraction $\frac{1}{1000}$ means 1 part in 1000, or .1 part in 100, or .1%. Similarly $\frac{1}{8} = 12\frac{1}{2}\%$; $\frac{1}{3} = 33\frac{1}{3}\%$; $\frac{1}{10} = 10\%$, etc.

Examples. 1. What per cent of error is allowed in a shop if a steel shaft 2 inches in diameter must be true to the third decimal place?

SOLUTION. Accuracy to the third decimal place means that the shaft can have a diameter of 2.001 inches or 1.999 inches. This is 1 part in 2000, .5 part in 1000, or .05 part in 100. The permissible error is, therefore, .05%.

2. A base line 500 feet long was measured by a party of surveyors. The total error in this measurement proved to be 2 inches. What is the per cent of error?

Solution. 500 feet = 500 × 12 inches = 6000 inches. An error of 2 inches is, therefore, an error of 2 parts in 6000, or 1 part in 3000. This is $\frac{1}{3}$ of a part in 1000 or $\frac{1}{30}$ in 100—that is, $\frac{1}{30}$ of 1% or approximately .03%.

3. A contractor figured the cost of a certain piece of work at $6750; he added 10% for delays and accidents and 20% for profit. What was his profit and what was the amount of his bid?

Solution. The cost price of the work is $6750. 10% added for accidents is 6750 × .10 or $675. 20% added for profit will be 2 × 675 = $1350. The amount of his bid should be, therefore, $6750 + $675 + $1350 = $8775.

4. What error is made in using the reducing factor 2.5 centimeters to the inch instead of the actual value 2.540 centimeters?

Solution. 2.540 − 2.5 = .04, the error. This is an error of 4 hundredths in 254 hundredths or 4 parts in 254 or about 1 in 64. Increasing 64 by $\frac{1}{2}$ = 96, approximately 100, and increasing 1 by $\frac{1}{2}$ = 1$\frac{1}{2}$. Therefore, 1 part in 64 equals 1$\frac{1}{2}$ parts in 100 or 1$\frac{1}{2}$%. The error is 1$\frac{1}{2}$%.

To put the matter in rule form it is necessary to give names to the different quantities as follows:

The quantity of which the per cent is taken is called the *base*.

The number of hundredths or % of the base to be taken is called the *rate*.

The result obtained by taking the required per cent of the base is called the *percentage*.

Rules. (a) *The product of the rate and the base equals the percentage.*

(b) *The percentage divided by the base equals the rate.*

(c) *The percentage divided by the rate equals the base.*

(d) *To change a number to the per cent form multiply by 100 and annex the sign %.*

(e) *To change a number indicating per cent back to the original figures, drop the % sign and divide by 100.* For example $\frac{1}{4} = .25$ and this expressed as a per cent equals .25×100 or 25%. Conversely 20% $= \frac{20}{100} = \frac{1}{5} = .2$.

These rules will help in many cases, but for applications to shop work or calculations in general, the more informal method given above is strongly recommended.

Examples. 1. Find the per cent of error made by a machinist who took a dimension from a drawing as 4.72 inches and finished his piece with a dimension of 4.79 inches.

SOLUTION a. The difference between the two dimensions is .07 and as there are approximately 470 hundredths in the dimension, the error is 7 parts in 470, about 1 in 65, or 1.5 in 100, *i. e.*, 1.5% error. Ans.

SOLUTION b. The base is 4.72, the percentage is .07, to find the rate. .07 ÷ 4.72 = .0148+ or 1.48+%.

NOTE. In solution a, approximate values are taken so as to arrive at the conclusion without labored calculation. In this way it is easy to calculate % of error mentally with sufficient accuracy. In solution b it is necessary to move the decimal point of the quotient two places to the right in order to obtain the %.

2. In a town of 8,000 inhabitants, during an epidemic of typhoid fever, there were 114 deaths from the disease. Find the per cent of deaths.

SOLUTION. 114 deaths in every 8,000 equals about 14 in 1,000 or 1.4 in 100, *i. e.*, 1.4% Ans.

3. A business firm has a factory stock valued at $28,000. At inventory time the firm allows a depreciation of 8%. What is the loss?

SOLUTION a. 8% depreciation means $8 loss on every $100, and as there are 280 of these $100, the loss is $8 × 280 = $2240. Ans.

SOLUTION b. The base is $28,000, the rate 8%. The percentage will be the loss. $28000 × .08 = $2240. Ans.

NOTE. In such problems as No. 3, solution b is the better method.

4. The total weight of a freight car when loaded is 148,600 pounds, and the weight of the empty car is 41,700 pounds; what per cent of the entire weight is the weight of the empty car? What per cent of the entire weight is the freight carried?

SOLUTION. 41,700 ÷ 148,600 = .28+ or 28+%. Ans.

Evidently the weight of the freight is (100 − 28) or 72% of the total weight.

The method of *per cent* may be used also in determining how far to carry the calculations in various problems. The multiplication of the two numbers 4.75 and 65.4 gives 310.65. If it is asked whether it is necessary to carry the second decimal place (.05) in this product, this could be determined at once by finding what per cent .05 is of the whole number. .05 in 310.65 is roughly 5 in 31,000 or 1 in 6,000, which is $\frac{1}{60}$ in 100 or $\frac{1}{60}$%, a very small error. The slide rule, by which engineers often make important calculations, does not give an accuracy of more than $\frac{1}{2}$% to $\frac{1}{10}$%. Consequently in all of the problem calculations, the carrying of the results to four or five *numerical* places (this means the actual figures and does not count the ciphers) is usually sufficient. It is with this probable error in view that reports on elections, census, etc., are given *in round numbers*. The population of the U. S. in 1900 may have been 84,755,643, but for all practical purposes 85 million is sufficient. A contractor might figure that a piece of work would be worth $12,743.22 but his bid probably would be $12,750.

PROBLEMS FOR PRACTICE

Express in two other ways:

1. $\frac{1}{4}, \frac{1}{8}, \frac{1}{25}, \frac{3}{8}$.   3. $3\%, 5\%, 70\%$.   5. $20\%, 66\frac{2}{3}\%, 125\%$.

2. $.25, .12\frac{1}{2}, .75$.   4. $\frac{1}{12}, \frac{1}{10}, \frac{1}{20}$.   6. $.06\frac{1}{4}, .62\frac{1}{2}, .33\frac{1}{3}$.

7. What per cent is $25 of $75? $107.03 of $1,946? $7,894 of $11,841?   Ans. $33\frac{1}{3}\%; 5\frac{1}{2}\%; 66\frac{2}{3}\%$.

8. A merchant lost $3,000 of his capital and had $21,000 remaining. What per cent of his capital did he lose?   Ans. $12\frac{1}{2}\%$.

9. The value of the ratio of the circumference to the diameter of a circle (usually designated by the Greek letter π, pi) is 3.1416, with an approximate value of $\frac{22}{7}$. What per cent of error is made in this approximation?   Ans. $.04+\%$

10. A steam engine furnishes 350 horse-power to a dynamo, which transforms this into electrical energy with a loss of 8%. Find the horse-power supplied by the dynamo.

11. If gunpowder consists of 15% charcoal, how much charcoal is required to make up 250 pounds of gunpowder?

12. Plaster is made from a mixture of 5 bushels of lime and 7 bushels of screen sand. What proportion of the mixture is sand?

13. If $6.00 is 20% of a man's money, how much has he?

14. A train of gears transmits 64% of the power supplied at one end. If 14.3 H. P. is furnished to the train, how much will be delivered to the machinery at the other end?   Ans. 9.152 H.P.

15. A certain 200 H. P. steam engine uses only 18.5% of the energy of the coal. What would be its horse-power if it turned all of the energy into useful work?   Ans. 1081.08+H.P

25-INCH AUTOMATIC BEVEL GEAR PLANER
Courtesy of Gleason Works, Rochester, New York

PRACTICAL MATHEMATICS

PART III

DENOMINATE NUMBERS

40. A *denominate number* is one in which the unit of value is established by law or custom. For example, 7 pounds, 6 feet, 10 kilograms.

When a denominate number is composed of units of but one denomination, as, for example, 3 gallons, it is called a *simple number*. If it contains units of more than one denomination that are related to each other, as 6 feet 10 inches, or 7 pounds 5 ounces, it is called a *compound number*.

The *reduction* of denominate numbers is the process of changing them from one denomination to another without changing their value. The reduction may be from a higher to a lower denomination, or from a lower to a higher denomination.

NOTE. In a decimal system like the *Metric System*, the units increase and decrease by a uniform scale of 10, but in the *English System* the scale varies.

MEASURES

41. A *unit of measure* is a standard by which a quantity—such as length, area, capacity, or weight—is measured. For example, the length of a piece of cloth is ascertained by applying the *yard* or the *meter* measure; the capacity of a cask by the use of the *gallon* or the *liter* measure; the weight of a body by the use of the *pound* or the *kilogram*, etc.

There are two systems of measurement which are legalized in the United States, the *English System* and the *Metric System*. The former is in common use in the United States and England, the latter in all other countries and in our own governmental departments. The metric system is introduced here for general information and for those who hold government positions or who are in foreign trade. The student is referred to the Appendix for a complete list of tables in the English and Metric systems.

MEASURES OF EXTENSION

42. *Extension* is that property of a body by virtue of which it occupies space and has one or more of the dimensions—length, breadth, and thickness.

A *line* has a single dimension—length—and its measurement is accomplished by *linear measure*.

A *surface* or *area* has two dimensions—length and breadth—and its measurement is accomplished by *square measure*.

A *solid* has three dimensions—length, breadth, and thickness— and its volume or capacity is obtained by *cubic measure*.

The *standard units of extension* in the United States are the *yard* and the *meter*. The yard is 36 inches, the meter 39.37 inches.

43. Linear Measure. The English measure for length or distance, called *long measure*, makes use of the *yard* as its fundamental unit, with subdivisions for convenience into *feet* and *inches*. For instance, a merchant sells cloth by the yard; a person measures his height in feet, and the length of his arm in inches. Larger units, the rod and the mile, are used when distances to be measured become so great that the small units are not convenient. A complete table of long measure is given in the Appendix. For ordinary calculations it is sufficient to remember the following:

$$12 \text{ inches (in.)} = 1 \text{ foot (ft.)}$$
$$3 \text{ ft. or } 36 \text{ in.} = 1 \text{ yard (yd.)}$$
$$5280 \text{ ft.} = 1 \text{ mile (mi.)}$$

The *metric system* is founded on the *meter* as the fundamental unit, and as it is a decimal system, the smaller and larger units are all decimal divisions or multiples of the meter. For example, the centimeter, which is about $2\frac{1}{2}$ times smaller than the inch, is, as its name indicates, $\frac{1}{100}$ of a meter; while the kilometer, which is about .6 miles is 1,000 meters. Remember the following units:

$$10 \text{ millimeters (mm.)} = 1 \text{ centimeter (cm.)}$$
$$100 \text{ centimeters (cm.)} = 1 \text{ meter (m.)}$$
$$1000 \text{ meters (m.)} = 1 \text{ kilometer (km.)}$$

It is also useful to remember the following approximate values: 25 mm. or 2.5 cm. = 1 inch, Fig. 2; 30 cm. = 1 ft.; 1 kilometer = .6 mi.

Engineers have adopted the *decimal* plan in connection with the English system by using scales and steel tapes with feet divided

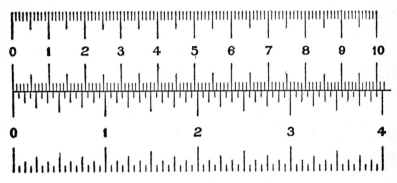

Fig. 2. Comparison between Centimeter and Inch Scales.

into tenths. They also use Surveyors' long measure in making land surveys. (See Appendix.)

44. Square Measure. A surface has two dimensions, length and breadth.

The *area* of a surface is defined as the number of units of surface it contains, and is equal to the product of its two dimensions expressed in the same linear units. The *unit of surface* is a square, which is a plane figure bounded by four equal sides and having four right angles, Fig. 3. A square, each side of which is one inch in length, is called a square inch. Squares formed with sides of 1 foot, 1 meter, 1 mile, etc., are called respectively, 1 square foot, 1 square meter, 1 square mile, etc.

Fig. 3.
A Foot
Square.

A distinction should be clearly made between the terms *square foot* and *foot square* or between *square mile* and *mile square*. If Fig. 3 may be supposed to represent a square 1 foot on a side, it may be called either 1 sq. ft. or 1 ft. square. On the other hand, Fig. 4 measures two feet on a side and hence it is 2 ft. square, but, as may readily be seen, it has not 2 sq. ft. but 4 sq. ft. of area. Therefore a cattle ranch covering an area 3 miles square has really 9 square miles of surface.

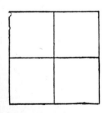

Fig. 4. A 2-Foot
Square.

Square measure, therefore, involves units whose names are the same as those used in linear measure with the term *square* in front of each. The English system has an extra unit used in measurements of land, which is called the *acre*, equal to the area of a square about 209 ft. on a side.

In the metric system, the *square centimeter* and *square meter*— the latter being about 20% larger than the English *square yard*— are used for small areas. The larger surfaces are measured in *ares* and *hectares*, the former being 10 meters square ($\frac{1}{40}$ acre) and the latter equal to 100 ares or $2\frac{1}{2}$ acres.

45. Cubic Measure. The volume of any solid is obtained by *cubic measure*. The unit of volume is a cube, Fig. 5, each edge of which is some unit of length; for example, the cubic inch, cubic centimeter, cubic foot are common units of volume.

Fig. 5. A 1-Foot Cube.

The volume of a body of rectangular figure is equal to the product of its three dimensions, each expressed in the same linear unit.

In the case of an irregular body, however, the volume although still expressed in cubic measure, must be measured by displacement of water. Liquids are classed as irregular bodies but in the English system are measured by a different unit, giving rise to the classification as given in Sec. 46.

In Sec. 44 it was proved that the area of a square surface increases as the second power of the side of the square; *i. e.*, a surface 2 feet square was found to cover 2×2 or 4 sq. ft. of area. In the same manner, Figs. 5 and 6 show that a 2-foot cube has $2 \times 2 \times 2$ or 8 cubic feet of volume; *i. e.*, the volume of a cube increases as the third power of the length of the side.

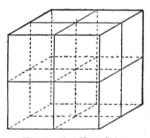

Fig. 6. A 2-Foot Cube.

NOTE. The use of the multiplication sign in finding the volume has given rise to its use in indicating the dimensions of surfaces and solids. Thus a 2×12 joist means a joist 2 inches thick and 12 inches wide; or a room $15' \times 12' \times 10'$ means a room 15 feet long, 12 feet wide, and 10 feet high.

The units of cubic measure in the English system are the same as those in long measure with the prefix *cubic;* for example, cubic inch, cubic yard. The *cord* (128 cu. ft.) for wood and the *perch* (24¾ cu. ft.) for stone or masonry are also used.

In the metric system, the *cubic centimeter* and *cubic meter* are common, the latter being 30% larger than the *cubic yard* and used in place of it in measuring earth and rock excavations, as well as in measuring timber, stone, etc., where the English *cord* and *perch* are used.

MEASURES OF CAPACITY

46. *Capacity* signifies the extent of volume or space. In the English system a lack of unity exists in the measurement of capacity because of the use of several kinds of measure. For example, the common *liquid measure* and the *apothecaries' fluid measure* are used for liquids, and still another kind called *dry measure* for grains, vegetables, etc.

This complication is avoided in the metric system by having the same units for all measurements of capacity.

47. Liquid Measure. Liquid measure is used in measuring liquids and in estimating the capacity of cisterns, reservoirs, etc. In the English system, the most common liquid measure makes use of the gallon, barrel, etc. The following units should be remembered:

$$2 \text{ pints (pt.)} = 1 \text{ quart (qt.)}$$
$$4 \text{ quarts} = 1 \text{ gallon (gal.)}$$
$$31\tfrac{1}{2} \text{ gallons} = 1 \text{ barrel (bbl.)}$$

In the metric system the unit is the *liter,* which is 5% larger than the liquid quart and 10% smaller than the dry quart, Fig. 7.

Fig. 7. Comparison of Liter, Dry Quart, and Liquid Quart. (¼ actual size)

Note the following:

$$1000 \text{ cubic centimeters (c.c.)} = 1 \text{ liter (l.)}$$
$$100 \text{ liters} = 1 \text{ hectoliter.}$$

48. Dry Measure. Dry measure is used in measuring **dry** substances such as grain, vegetables, salt, etc. In the English system the quart, peck, and bushel are used. In the metric system the *hectoliter* serves the same purpose as the United States *bushel* and is equal to about 3 bushels.

The common units in dry measure are:

$$8 \text{ quarts* } = 1 \text{ peck (pk.)}$$
$$4 \text{ pecks } = 1 \text{ bushel (bu.)}$$

MEASURES OF WEIGHT

49. *Weight* is a measure of the force of the earth's attraction **for** a body.

In the English system several units of weight are used, viz, the standard *Troy weight*, which is used in weighing gold, silver, and jewels; the more common *avoirdupois weight*, used in general trade; and the *apothecaries' weight*, used by druggists and physicians. The student is referred to the Appendix for the Troy and apothecaries' measure.

50. Avoirdupois Weight. Avoirdupois weight is used to measure the weight of objects in general trade. The most useful units are as follows:

$$16 \text{ ounces (oz.)} = 1 \text{ pound (lb.)}$$
$$2000 \text{ pounds} = 1 \text{ ton (t. or T.)}$$

The ton just given is the *short ton* and is more generally used than the *gross ton* which is equal to 2,240 lbs. This latter unit is now mainly used in the United States custom house and in weighing coarser articles, such as coal at the mines.

51. Metric Weight. In the metric system the unit of weight is the *gram* which is equal to the weight of 1 cubic centimeter of pure water at a temperature of 38° F. The following are the most important units:

$$1000 \text{ grams (g.)} = 1 \text{ kilogram (kg.)}$$
$$1000 \text{ kilograms} = 1 \text{ metric ton.}$$

*The dry quart is about 15% larger than the liquid quart. Fig. 7.

30 grams approximately equal one ounce, and one kilogram equals 2.2 pounds, hence the gram is used wherever the ounce, pennyweight, etc., would be used, while the *kilo* and *half kilo* replace the pound. The *metric ton* serves the same purpose as the *short* or *gross tons*.

MEASURE OF TIME

52. *Time* is measured in the same manner and by the same unit throughout the civilized world, the unit being the *mean solar day*.

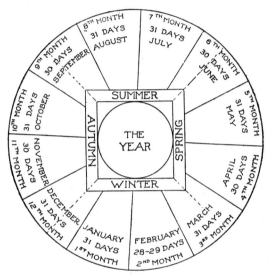

Fig. 8. Chart of the Calendar Year.

This *mean solar day* is obtained by taking the average of all of the days of the year, a day being measured from noon of one day to noon of the next day. This process is necessary because the position of the earth relative to the sun changes as the year advances, and, therefore, no one day can be taken as the true day. Evidently the time when it is *noon*, *i. e.*, the instant the sun is passing the north and south line, will be different as we pass from east to west. For example, London has her noon five hours earlier than New York. This has led to the adoption in the United States of *four standard times*, the *Eastern*, *Central*, *Western*, and *Pacific*, each one hour later than the preceding. Therefore, when it is noon in Washington it is 11 o'clock in Chicago, 10 o'clock in Denver, and 9 o'clock in San Francisco. All cities or towns falling in one of the four regions adopt the standard time of that section. The divisions of the calendar year are shown graphically in Fig. 8.

MISCELLANEOUS MEASURES

53. The *English money system* has for its principal units the *pound sterling* (£.) equal roughly to $5.00, and the shilling, equal to 25 cents. The *French money system* has for its unit the *franc*, equal roughly to 20 cents. The German money system makes use of the *mark*, equal to about 25 cents, for its principal unit.

A useful table of *enumeration* is given briefly as follows:

$$12 \text{ units } = 1 \text{ dozen (doz.)}$$
$$12 \text{ dozen } = 1 \text{ gross (gro.)}$$

Another table much used by stationers is as follows:

$$24 \text{ sheets } = 1 \text{ quire}$$
$$20 \text{ quires } = 1 \text{ ream}$$

The student is referred to the Appendix for the complete tables to which references have already been made together with others which are in more or less common use. It is well to have these tables fairly well memorized, and problems are given in the following sections on the assumption that the required familiarity has been attained.

REDUCTION OF DENOMINATE NUMBERS

54. *The reduction of denominate numbers* in the English system is accomplished according to the following rules:

To change a compound denominate number to a simple number of lower denomination: *Multiply the integer of the highest denomination by the number of units of the next lower denomination in one unit of the higher denomination, and add to this product the given number of the lower denomination. Proceed into lower terms in this manner until the required denomination is reached.*

To change a simple denominate number to a compound number of higher denominations: *Divide the given number by the number of units contained in one unit of the next higher denomination. Set aside the remainder; then in the same manner divide the quotient thus obtained, and proceed in this way until the required denomination is reached. The last quotient and the several remainders will be the result sought.*

Examples. 1. Reduce 6 mi. 116 yds. 24 ft. to feet.

SOLUTION. Since 1 mile = 1760 yds., 6 mi. = 6 × 1760 yds. = 10,560 yds.; and with 116 yds. added this becomes 10,676 yds. Since 1 yd. = 3 ft., 10,676 yds. = 32,028 ft., and with 24 ft. added, this becomes 32,052 feet, Ans.

2. Reduce 765 liquid pints to higher denominations.

SOLUTION. Dividing 765 pints by 2 gives 382 qts. 1 pt. Dividing by 4 to reduce to gallons gives 95 gal. 2 qts. 1 pt. Dividing by 31.5 to reduce to bbl. gives 3 bbl. $\frac{1}{2}$ gal. 2 qts. 1 pt. As 2 qts. = $\frac{1}{2}$ gal. this added to the $\frac{1}{2}$ gal. already obtained gives as a final result 3 bbl. 1 gal. 1 pt.

$$2)\underline{765 \text{ pts.}}$$
$$4)\underline{382 \text{ qts.} + 1 \text{ pt.}}$$
$$31.5)\underline{95 \text{ gal.} + 2 \text{ qts.}}$$
$$3 \text{ bbl.} + \tfrac{1}{2} \text{ gal.}$$

55. Reduction in the metric system is accomplished *by moving the decimal point.*

Example. Reduce 10,450 millimeters, 276 centimeters, and 600 meters to kilometers.

SOLUTION. Reduce 10,450 mm. to meters by moving the decimal point three places to the left = 10.45 meters. Similarly reduce 276 cm. to m. by moving the decimal point two places to the left = 2.76 m. 600 + 2.76 + 10.45 = 613.21 m. This result may be changed to kilometers by moving three points to the left = 0.6132 km.

When quantities expressed in the English system are to be reduced to their equivalents in the metric system, or the reverse, the comparative tables, p. 105, are used. For example, if 34 meters should be changed to yards, the table shows that 1 meter equals 1.1 yards; 34 meters equal 34×1.1 yards or 37.4 yards.

Examples. 1. Change 172 feet to centimeters.

SOLUTION. From the table, 1 foot equals .3 m. 172 feet equals 172 × .3 or 51.6 m. 51.6 m. equals 51.6 × 100 = 5160 cm.

2. Change 12.4 pounds to grams.

SOLUTION. From the table, 1 pound equals .45 kilograms. 12.4 pounds equals 12.4 × .45 or 5.58 kilograms. 5.58 kilograms equals 5.58 × 1000 or 5580 grams.

PROBLEMS FOR PRACTICE

1. Change 2560 lbs to ounces; to tons.
2. Change 42 meters to centimeters; to millimeters.

3.   Reduce 76 yds. to inches; to feet.

4.   Change 35 ft. to centimeters (approx.).

Reduce

5.   18 lbs. 12 oz. to ounces.   9.   3 A. 78 sq. ft. to square feet.

6.   £ 8 12 *s* to shillings.   10.   5 bbl. 12 gal. to gallons.

7.   75 m. 86 cm. to centimeters.   11. $2\frac{1}{4}$ T. to pounds.

8.   8 bu. 4 pks. to pecks.   12. $746.50 to dimes.

Reduce to higher denominations

13.   1560 ft.   16.   1640 dry pints.   19.   7562 oz., avoir.

14.   15,760 mm.   17.   685 doz.   20.   375 pints.

15.   86,400 sec.   18.   659 shillings.   21.   2500 sq. in.

Using approximate values, change

22.   120 yds. to meters.   25.   4750 francs to dollars.

23.   15 s. to dollars.   26.   65 cm. to inches.

24.   56 kilos to pounds.   27.   450 liters to pints.

OPERATIONS WITH DENOMINATE NUMBERS

56.   There are two methods of *adding, subtracting, multiplying,* or *dividing* denominate numbers.   One is to reduce the given numbers to the lowest denomination mentioned in the example, then perform the required process and reduce the result to higher denominations.   The other is to perform the process on the numbers as they stand, making the necessary reductions during the operations.

57.   Addition and Subtraction.   Examples.   1.   Find the sum of 3 mi. 182 rd. 4 yds. 2 ft.; 304 rd. 1 ft.; and 5 mi. 76 rd. 4 yds. 2 ft.

SOLUTION *a*.

3 mi. 182 rd. 4 yds. 2 ft. = 15,840 + 3,003 + 12 + 2 = 18,857 ft

       304 rd. 0 yds. 1 ft. =   5,016 + 1   =   5,017 ft.

5 mi.   76 rd. 4 yds. 2 ft. = 26,400 + 1,254 + 12 + 2 = 27,668 ft.

                                                     51,542 ft.

51,542 = 9 mi. 243 rd. 4 yds. 0 ft. 6 in. Ans.

SOLUTION. *b*.   The sum of the right-hand column = 5 ft. = 1 yd. 2 ft.; write down the 2 ft. and add 1 to the yds. column.   The sum of the yds. column and 1 carried = 9 yds.; $9 \div 5\frac{1}{2} = 1$ rd. $+ 3\frac{1}{2}$ yds., the 1 rd. to be added to the rds. column.   The sum of the rds. column + 1 carried = 563 rds. $563 \div 320 = 243$ rds. + 1 to be added

mi.	rd.	yds.	ft.
3	182	4	2
0	304	0	1
5	76	4	2
9	243	4	$\frac{1}{2}$

to the mi. column, making it 9 miles. The result is therefore 9 mi. 243 rds.
3½ yds. 2 ft. = 9 mi. 243 rds. 4 yds. 0 ft. 6 in.

2. Subtract 3 pks. 1 qt. 1 pt. from 1 bu. 2 pks. 4 qts.

SOLUTION. Mentally take 1 qt. (2 pts.) from the
second column and place it in the first; 2 − 1 = 1 pt.
(4 − 1 borrowed) − 1 = 2 qts. 1 bu (4 pks.) + 2 pks.
= 6; 6 − 3 = 3 pks. The result is therefore 3 pks. 2 qts.
1 pt.

bu.	pks.	qts.	pts.
1	2	4	0
0	3	1	1
	3	2	1

PROBLEMS FOR PRACTICE

Find the sum of

1. 10 yds. 2 ft. 10 in.; 15 yds. 1 ft. 9 in.; 8 yds. 2 ft. 7 in.;
18 yds. 1 ft. 11 in.; 16 yds. 2 ft. 8 in. Ans. 12 rd. 4 yds. 2 ft. 9 in.

2. 12 A. 35 sq. rd.; 14 A. 110 sq. rd.; 15 A. 132 sq. rd.; 11 A.
96 sq. rd.; 25 A. 100 sq. rd.   Ans. 79 A. 153 sq. rd.

3. 5 t. 6 cwt. 14 lbs. 10 oz.; 7 t. 15 cwt. 36 lbs. 15 oz.; 17 t.
5 cwt. 84 lbs. 12 oz.; 70 t. 9 cwt. 94 lbs. 11 oz.

Ans. 100 t. 17 cwt. 31 lbs.

From

4. 12 gal. 2 qts. 1 pt. 2 gi. take 6 gal. 3 qts. 1 pt. 3 gi.

Ans. 5 gal. 2 qts. 1 pt. 3 gi.

5. 15 yds. 2 ft. 7 in. take 4 yds. 2 ft. 10 in.

Ans. 10 yds. 2 ft. 9 in.

6. 25 t. 8 cwt. 75 lbs. 10 oz. take 10 t. 11 cwt. 35 lbs. 15 oz.

Ans. 14 t. 17 cwt. 39 lbs. 11 oz.

58. Multiplication and Division. Examples. 1. Multiply 14
gals. 3 qts. 1 pt. by 7.

Solution *a.*

14 gal. 3 qts. 1 pt.   = 112 + 6 + 1 = 119 pts.

119 pts. × 7 = 833 pts. = 416 qts. 1 pt. = 104 gal. 1 pt. Ans.

SOLUTION *b.* (14 gal. 3 qt. 1 pt.) × 7 = 98 gal.
21 qts. 7 pts. = 98 gal. 24 qts. 1 pt. = 104 gal. 0 qts.
1 pt. Ans.

14 gal. 3 qts. 1 pt.
           7
——————————————
104 gal. 0 qts. 1 pt.

2. Divide 14 gal. 3 qts. 1 pt. by 4.

Solution *a.*

14 gal. 3 qts. 1 pt. = 119 pts.

4)119 pts.
29¾ pts. = 14 qts. 1¾ pts. = 3 gal. 2 qts. 1¾ pts. **Ans.**

PROBLEMS FOR PRACTICE

Multiply

1. 3 hrs. 20 min. 35 sec. by 5. Ans. 16 hrs. 42 min. 55 sec.
2. 2 t. 5 cwt. 48 lbs. 15 oz. by 8. Ans. 18 t. 3 cwt. 91 lbs. 8 oz.
3. 12 cu. yds. 15 cu. ft. by 6. Ans. 75 cu. yds. 9 cu. ft.

Divide

4. 15 bu. 3 pks. 5 qts. by 4. Ans. 3 bu. 3 pks. 7 qts. $\frac{1}{2}$ pt.
5. 23 cwt. 68 lbs. 10 oz. by 5. Ans. 4 cwt. 73 lbs. $11\frac{3}{5}$ oz.
6. 15 rd. 4 yds. 2 ft. 8 in. by 5. Ans. 3 rd. 2 ft. $11\frac{1}{5}$ in.

POWERS AND ROOTS

59. Powers. A *power* of a quantity is the product of factors, each of which is equal to that number. This quantity may be simply a number, as 1, 2, 3, or 4, or it may be any letter, as *a, b, c,* or *d,* which may have any numerical value whatsoever.

In order to show how many times the quantity is to be used as a factor, a small figure is placed to the right and a little above the quantity; as 3^4 or a^4. This small number is called an *exponent,* and shows to what power the quantity is to be raised. Thus, 3^4 means the fourth power of 3, or $3 \times 3 \times 3 \times 3 = 81$; *i. e.,* 3 is taken 4 times as a factor. If the letter *a* is substituted for the figure 3 and this letter is raised to the fourth power, the result is $a \times a \times a \times a$ or a^4. Since no definite value for *a* has been given, the result of raising the letter to the power can only be indicated; thus, a^4.

The *second* power of the quantity is called its *square.* For example, 4 is the square of 2, for $2 \times 2 = 4$; again, a^2 is the square of *a,* for $a \times a = a^2$. The third power of a quantity is called its *cube;* thus, 8 is the cube of 2, for $2 \times 2 \times 2 = 8$; or a^3 is the cube of *a.*

Suppose now it is required to find the square of a^2. $a^2 \times a^2 = a^4$, for $a^2 \times a^2 = (a \times a) \times (a \times a) = a^4$; or, in other words, *when two like quantities are multiplied together, the exponent of the product is equal to the sum of the exponents of the quantities.*

The power of a fraction is obtained by multiplying the numerator by itself and the denominator by itself the required number of times. Thus, the second power of $\frac{2}{4} = \frac{2 \times 2}{4 \times 4} = \frac{4}{16}$; the third power of $\frac{1}{7} = \frac{1 \times 1 \times 1}{7 \times 7 \times 7} = \frac{1}{343}$.

Examples.   1. What is the cube, or third power of 21?

$$21^3 = 21 \times 21 \times 21$$

SOLUTION.   Here it is readily seen that raising 21 to the third power is the same as using 21 three times as a factor.

$$
\begin{array}{r}
21 \\
21 \\
\hline
21 \\
42 \\
\hline
441 \\
21 \\
\hline
441 \\
882 \\
\hline
9261 \quad \text{Ans.}
\end{array}
$$

2. What is the cube, or third power of $2a$?

$$(2a)^3 = 2a \times 2a \times 2a.$$

SOLUTION.   Note here, that when raising a quantity like $2a$ to a power, the coefficient 2 and the letter a are each raised separately to the required power.

$$
\begin{array}{r}
2a \\
2a \\
\hline
4a^2 \\
2a \\
\hline
8a^3 \quad \text{Ans.}
\end{array}
$$

3. What is the cube of .71?

$$.71^3 = .71 \times .71 \times .71$$

SOLUTION.   When raising a decimal like .71 to a power, care should be taken to correctly place the decimal point.   In the answer to this problem there will be six places to be pointed off, thus bringing the decimal point before the 3.

$$
\begin{array}{r}
.71 \\
.71 \\
\hline
71 \\
497 \\
\hline
.5041 \\
.71 \\
\hline
5041 \\
35287 \\
\hline
.357911 \quad \text{Ans.}
\end{array}
$$

4. What is the fourth power of $\dfrac{3}{5}$?

$$\frac{3}{5} \times \frac{3}{5} \times \frac{3}{5} \times \frac{3}{5} = \frac{3 \times 3 \times 3 \times 3}{5 \times 5 \times 5 \times 5} = \frac{81}{625}. \qquad \textbf{Ans.}$$

PROBLEMS FOR PRACTICE

Raise the following quantities to the power indicated:

1. 47   to the second   Ans. 2,209
2. $6m$ "   "   second

3. 71 to the second   Ans. 5,041

4. 2.61 " " second   Ans. 6.8121

5. .13 " " third

6. c^2 " " third

7. r " " fifth

8. k " " fourth

9. $6k$ " " fourth   Ans. $1296k^4$

60. Roots. A *root* of a quantity is one of the equal factors which, when multiplied together, give the quantity. Thus, if a certain quantity is used twice in order to produce another quantity, then the quantity first mentioned is the *square root* of the second. Thus, 2 is the square root of 4, for $2 \times 2 = 4$. If the first quantity must be used three times as a factor, it is the cube root of the second quantity; thus, the cube root of 8 is 2, for $2 \times 2 \times 2 = 8$; the cube root of 27 is 3, for $3 \times 3 \times 3 = 27$. This also applies to any root as the 4th, 5th, etc. Thus, the 5th root of $a^5 = a$, for $a \times a \times a \times a \times a = a^5$.

This process of finding the root is merely the reverse of finding the power, and is termed *extracting the root*.

The *radical sign* $\sqrt{}$ when placed before a quantity shows that some root of it is to be taken. The root is indicated by a small figure called the *index* placed above the radical sign; thus, $\sqrt[3]{}$. When no index is written, the square root is always understood.

The following **examples** show the meaning of the sign **and** index:

$$\sqrt{81} = 9, \text{ for } 9 \times 9 = 81.$$

$$\sqrt[3]{27} = 3, \text{ for } 3 \times 3 \times 3 = 27.$$

$$\sqrt[4]{81} = 3, \text{ for } 3 \times 3 \times 3 \times 3 = 81.$$

$$\sqrt[5]{32} = 2, \text{ for } 2 \times 2 \times 2 \times 2 \times 2 = 32.$$

$$\sqrt{b^2} = b, \text{ for } b \times b = b^2.$$

$$\sqrt[3]{8b^3} = 2b, \text{ for } 2b \times 2b \times 2b = 8b^3.$$

$$\sqrt[5]{32b^{10}} = 2b^2, \text{ for } 2b^2 \times 2b^2 \times 2b^2 \times 2b^2 \times 2b^2 = 32b^{10}.$$

61. Square Root. In the above illustrations the required root may be readily determined by inspection, but in most cases, this method cannot be followed. When the root desired is the *square root* the method illustrated below should be used.

Examples. 1. Find the square root of 185,761.

SOLUTION. First point off the number into periods of two figures each commencing at the right of the number. Then find the largest number whose square is equal to or less than 18. This is found to be 4. Set down the square of 4 or 16 under 18, and place 4 as the first figure of the root.

Subtract 16 from 18 and to the remainder annex the next period, obtaining 257 as the new dividend. The new divisor is twice the root already found with a cipher annexed, that is $2 \times 40 = 80$. By trial 80 is found to be contained 3 times in 257, so 3 is placed as the second figure of the root. Add 3 to 80 and multiply this sum 83 by 3. Place this product, 249, under 257 and subtract. Annex to the remainder the last period obtaining 861 as the new dividend.

The next divisor is twice 430 or 860. This is contained in 861 once. Place the 1 as the third figure of the root, add 1 to 860, thus making the complete divisor 861. As there is no remainder, the number 185761 is a perfect power, and its square root is **431.**

$$
\begin{array}{r}
431 \\
\overline{18\ 57\ 61} \\
\end{array}
$$

$2 \times 40 = 80$

$$
\begin{array}{r}
3\ 16 \\
\hline
83)257 \\
\end{array}
$$

$2 \times 430 = 860$

$$
\begin{array}{r}
1\ 249 \\
\hline
861)\ 861 \\
861 \\
\end{array}
$$

2. Find the square root of 18,763.8910.

SOLUTION. Point off the periods to the left and right of the decimal point, obtaining for the whole number the periods, $\overline{1}$, $\overline{87}$, and $\overline{63}$, and for the decimal the periods, $\overline{89}$ and $\overline{10}$. The root must have three numerical places to the left of the decimal point to correspond to the three periods in the whole number; hence, the final value of the root is 136.98.

$$
\begin{array}{r}
1\ 36.98+ \\
\overline{1\ 87\ 63.89\ 10} \\
\end{array}
$$

$2 \times 10 = 20$

$$
\begin{array}{r}
3\ 1 \\
\hline
23)87 \\
\end{array}
$$

$2 \times 130 = 260$

$$
\begin{array}{r}
6\ 69 \\
\hline
266)1863 \\
\end{array}
$$

$2 \times 1360 = 2720$

$$
\begin{array}{r}
9\ 1596 \\
\hline
2729)26789 \\
\end{array}
$$

$2 \times 13690 = 27380$

$$
\begin{array}{r}
8\ 24561 \\
\hline
27388)222810 \\
219104 \\
\end{array}
$$

3. Find the square root of .001225.

SOLUTION.   In finding the square root of a decimal
like the above, it is seen that the first period contains
only zeros; consequently the first figure of the root will
be a zero.   Begin by finding the square next smaller
than 12, and proceed as in previous examples.   Point
off three places in the root to correspond to the three
periods in the decimal.

$$
\begin{array}{r}
.035 \\ \hline
.00\ 12\ 25 \\
9 \\ \hline
65)\overline{325} \\
325 \\ \hline
\end{array}
$$

4. Find the square root of 3 to three decimal places.

SOLUTION.   Annex ciphers at the right of the
decimal point and separate into periods as usual.

$$
\begin{array}{r}
1.732+ \\ \hline
3.\overline{00}\ \overline{00}\ \overline{00} \\
1 \\ \hline
27)\overline{200} \\
189 \\ \hline
343)\overline{1100} \\
1029 \\ \hline
3462)\overline{7100} \\
\end{array}
$$

Rules.   (a) *Point off the given number into periods of two figures,
beginning at the decimal point.   If the number contains a whole number and a decimal, point off periods to the left of the decimal point
for the whole number, and to the right for the decimal, annexing a
cipher to the last figure of the decimal if necessary.*

(b) *Find the greatest number whose square is contained in the left-
hand period.   This figure will be the first figure in the root.   Subtract
the square of this number from the left-hand period and annex the
next period to the remainder to form the new dividend.*

(c) *After annexing a cipher to that part of the root already found
and doubling the result, place the quantity thus obtained on the left for a
trial divisor.   Ascertain how many times this divisor is contained in the
new dividend, and write the quotient as the next figure of the root.   Then
add the number just placed in the root to the trial divisor, and multiply
the completed divisor by the last figure in the root.   Subtract this product from the dividend, and to the remainder annex the next period for
the new dividend.   Continue the operation until all the periods are used.*

(d) *To place the decimal point in the result, if the number is a
decimal number, point off in the root as many figures from the left as there
are periods from the left to the decimal point in the original number.*

(e) *If after the root is found there is a remainder, it should be
dropped and a + sign placed after the root.*

PROBLEMS FOR PRACTICE

1. Find the square root of 364,936   Ans. 604.09+
2. Find the square root of 825,487.69   Ans. 908.56+
3. Find the square root of .003864   Ans. .0621+
4. Find the square root of .0563   Ans. .2372+
5. Find the square root of 1,873
6. Find the square root of 6,432

62. Square Root of Fractions. When the square root of a common fraction is desired, first see if the numerator and denominator have perfect square roots. If so, write the root of the numerator over the root of the denominator. If this is not the case, reduce the common fraction to decimal form and find the required root as before. If the quantity is a mixed quantity change to decimal form before extracting the root.

The following solutions will illustrate these principles:

Examples. 1. Find the square root of $\dfrac{16}{49}$

$$\sqrt{\frac{16}{49}} = \frac{\sqrt{16}}{\sqrt{49}} = \frac{4}{7} \quad \text{Ans.}$$

2. Find the square root of $\dfrac{4a^2}{16b^2}$

$$\frac{\sqrt{4a^2}}{\sqrt{16b^2}} = \frac{2a}{4b} \quad \text{Ans.}$$

3. Find the square root of $\dfrac{169}{250}$ to three decimal places.

$$250)\overline{169.000}$$
$$.676$$

$$\begin{array}{l}
.822+ \\
.67\overline{)60\,00} \\
64 \\
162\overline{)360} \\
324 \\
1642\overline{)3600} \\
3284
\end{array}$$

Hence, $\sqrt{\dfrac{169}{250}} = \sqrt{.676} = .822+$ **Ans.**

4. Find the square root of $\dfrac{64k^2}{81m^2}$

$$\dfrac{\sqrt{64k^2}}{\sqrt{81m^2}} = \dfrac{8k}{9m} \quad \text{Ans.}$$

5. Find the square root of $\dfrac{3}{8}$ to two decimal places.

$$
\begin{array}{r}
.61+ \\
\hline
.37\,\overline{50} \\
36 \\
\hline
121)\overline{150} \\
121 \\
\hline
29
\end{array}
$$

$$
\begin{array}{r}
8)3.000 \\
\hline
.375
\end{array}
$$

Hence, $\sqrt{\dfrac{3}{8}} = \sqrt{.375} = .61+ \quad$ Ans.

PROBLEMS FOR PRACTICE

Find the square root of

1. $\dfrac{49}{169}$

2. $\dfrac{27}{15625}$ Ans.   .041+

3. $\dfrac{64}{81}$

4. $\dfrac{5}{8}$ Ans.   .79 +

5. $\dfrac{4}{9}$

6. $\dfrac{81a^6}{121b^4}$

RATIO AND PROPORTION

63. Ratio. Ratio is the relation which one quantity bears to another quantity of the same kind; or, in other words, it is the quotient obtained by dividing the one by the other. The ratio of 15 to 3 is 5, because 15 contains 3, five times. The ratio of 3 to 15 is $\dfrac{1}{5}$, because 3 is $\dfrac{1}{5}$ of 15.

The two quantities given are called the *terms* of the ratio. The first term is called the *antecedent;* the succeeding one, the *consequent.* The antecedent is the dividend, the consequent is the divisor, and the value of the ratio is the quotient resulting from the division. The symbol used to express a ratio is two dots (:), which is merely an abbreviated form of the sign of division ($\div$) For example, the ratios 7 to 11, and a to b, are written thus, $7 : 11$, and $a : b$. The same ratios may also be expressed in fractional form thus, $\frac{7}{11}$ or $\frac{a}{b}$.

A ratio like the above is called a *direct ratio;* that is, one in which the antecedent is divided by the consequent. An *inverse* ratio is a direct ratio inverted. Thus, if $\frac{7}{11}$ and $\frac{a}{b}$ are the direct ratios, the inverse ratios of the same quantities are $\frac{11}{7}$ and $\frac{b}{a}$.

As a ratio is always an abstract number, it is possible to have a ratio *between similar quantities only*. For example, it is possible to establish a ratio between 75 rivets and 16 rivets, but no ratio between 75 rivets and 10 horses. If the ratio $\frac{a}{b}$ is given, and a represents 5 horses and b, 10 horses, it can be seen that, although this ratio has been expressed in letters, each letter is a quantity of the same kind.

The value of a ratio is not changed by either dividing or multiplying both terms of the ratio by the same number. Thus, for example, if $16 : 32$ is divided by 2, the ratio becomes $8 : 16$; likewise, each term may be multiplied by 2, obtaining $32 : 64$. From the above it is seen that the values of the ratios have not been changed for $\frac{16}{32} = \frac{8}{16} \times \frac{2}{2} = \frac{32}{64} \div \frac{2}{2}$. Consider the ratio $5a : 10b$. Dividing each term by 5, the ratio $a : 2b$ is obtained. Again multiplying each term of the first ratio by 2, it becomes $10a : 20b$, which has the same value as before because $\frac{a}{2b} \times \frac{10}{10} = \frac{10a}{20b}$.

PROBLEMS FOR PRACTICE

What is the value of each of the following?

1. $51 : 17$ Ans. 3

2. $20c : 40d$ Ans. $\frac{c}{2d}$

3. $16 : 48$

4. $6k : 8m$ Ans. $\frac{3k}{4m}$

5. What is the inverse ratio of 9 : 81? Ans. $\dfrac{81}{9} = 9$

6. What is the inverse ratio of $a : b$?

7. What is the inverse ratio of $10k : 20r$?

64. Proportion. (a) A *proportion* is an expression of equality between ratios and is indicated by the sign :: or by the equality sign =. For example, the proportion $3 : 9 :: 6 : 18$ is read 3 is to 9 as 6 is to 18. The same proportion may be stated thus: 3 over 9 equals 6 over 18; that is, $\dfrac{3}{9} = \dfrac{6}{18}$. Any proportion whatever existing between letters is expressed in a similar manner; thus, $a : b :: c : d$ may also be written $\dfrac{a}{b} = \dfrac{c}{d}$.

(b) The *terms* of a proportion are made up of the antecedents and consequents of two ratios. Thus, in the proportion $\dfrac{a}{b} = \dfrac{c}{d}$, a, b, c, d, are called the *terms* and are numbered—first, second, third, and fourth. This may be illustrated as follows:

	First		Second		Third		Fourth
	3	:	9	::	6	:	18
or	a	:	b	::	c	:	d

The first and fourth terms are called the *extremes;* the second and third terms, the *means;* thus, 3, 18, and a, d, are the extremes, while 9, 6, and b, c are the means.

(c) In all proportions the *product of the means is equal to the product of the extremes.* Thus, in the proportion $3 : 9 = 6 : 18$, the product of the means is $9 \times 6 = 54$ and the product of the extremes is $3 \times 18 = 54$. If the proportion is expressed in fractional form, that is, $\dfrac{3}{9} = \dfrac{6}{18}$, it is seen that the law just stated means that the product of the numerator of the first fraction with the denominator of the second is equal to the product of the numerator of the second fraction with the denominator of the first. Therefore, in the proportion $\dfrac{3}{9} = \dfrac{6}{18}$, $3 \times 18 = 9 \times 6$ and, in the proportion $\dfrac{a}{b} = \dfrac{c}{d}$, $ad = bc$. When taken by themselves the letters, a, b, c, d, may have any values whatsoever, but as soon as they are placed in the proportion, their relation to each other becomes fixed. If the proportion has an unknown term to be found, this latter form $\dfrac{a}{b} = \dfrac{c}{d}$ is perhaps the simpler form in which to arrange the ratios for finding the missing term.

Rules. (d) *The product of the means divided by either extreme gives the other extreme; or the product of the numerator of the second fraction with the denominator of the first fraction divided by the numerator of the first fraction gives the denominator of the second fraction.*

(e) *The product of the extremes divided by either mean gives the other mean; or the product of the numerator of the first fraction with the denominator of the second fraction divided by the denominator of the first fraction gives the numerator of the second fraction.*

In stating a proportion in which one term is unknown, let x represent the unknown term and solve for x.

Examples. 1. Solve for x in the proportion, $18 : 6 = 9 : x$, or $\dfrac{18}{6} = \dfrac{9}{x}$.

SOLUTION. Product of extremes, $18 \times x = 9 \times 6$, product of means

Dividing each side by 18 $x = \dfrac{54}{18} = 3$ Ans.

Hence the missing term is 3.

2. Solve the proportion, $6 : 18 = x : 3$.
SOLUTION. $18 \times x = 6 \times 3$ $x = 1$ Ans.

3. Solve the proportion, $9 : 3 = 18 : x$

SOLUTION. $x = \dfrac{18 \times 3}{9} = 6$ Ans.

4. Solve the proportion, $3 : 9 = 6 : x$

SOLUTION. $x = \dfrac{6 \times 9}{3} = 18$ Ans.

5. Solve for x in the proportion $a : b :: c : x$

SOLUTION. This may be written in this form, $ax = bc$, from which $x = \dfrac{bc}{a}$. In this case the answer can only be indicated, but if a, b, and c, had the respective values, 5, 6, and 10, their substitution would give to x a value of 12, since $x = \dfrac{6 \times 10}{5} = 12$.

$$ax = bc$$
$$x = \dfrac{bc}{a}$$

Find the value of x in the following proportions:

6. $k : m : : x : n.$

SOLUTION. $\dfrac{k}{m} = \dfrac{x}{n}$ $mx = kn$ $x = \dfrac{kn}{m}$ **Ans.**

7. $s : r : : x : p.$

SOLUTION. $\dfrac{s}{r} = \dfrac{x}{p}$ $rx = sp$ $x = \dfrac{sp}{r}$ **Ans.**

8. $e : f : : x : h.$

SOLUTION. $\dfrac{e}{f} = \dfrac{x}{h}$ $fx = eh$ $x = \dfrac{eh}{f}$ **Ans.**

PROBLEMS FOR PRACTICE

Solve for the unknown value of x in the following proportions:

1. $6 : 3 : : m : x$ Ans. $\dfrac{m}{2}$ 6. $21m : 3 : : x : 7$

2. $8 : 9 : : x : 9$ 7. $x : 4 : : 3r : s$ Ans. $\dfrac{12r}{3}$

3. $9 : 81 : : 2 : x$ 8. $384 : 64 : : x : m$

4. $4 : x : : 10 : 5$ 9. $480 : x : : 10 : 48$

5. $r : s : : 2 : x$ 10. $90 : x : : 9 : k$ Ans. $10k$

65.   Any root of both sides of a proportion may be extracted, or any power of both sides may be taken, without destroying the proportion.

Examples.   1.   Extract the square root of both sides of the following proportion: $1 : 9 = 49 : 441.$

SOLUTION.   Extracting the square root of each term

$$1 : 3 = 7 : 21$$

or

$$\frac{1}{3} = \frac{7}{21}$$

which equation, by clearing of fractions, shows that the equality of the proportion has not been destroyed.

2.   Extract the square root of both sides of the following proportion: $a^2 : b^2 = c^2 : d^2.$

SOLUTION.   This proportion may be stated thus:

$$\frac{a^2}{b^2} = \frac{c^2}{d^2}$$

Extracting the square root $\dfrac{a}{b} = \dfrac{c}{d}$

3. Find the cube of the proportion, $1 : 2 = 2 : 4$

SOLUTION. Changing its form $\dfrac{1}{2} = \dfrac{2}{4}$

Cubing each term $\qquad \dfrac{1}{8} = \dfrac{8}{64}$

Thus it is seen that the proportion is not destroyed.

4. Cube the proportion, $\dfrac{a}{b} = \dfrac{c^2}{d^2}$

SOLUTION. Cubing each term $\dfrac{a^3}{b^3} = \dfrac{c^6}{d^6}$

Thus it is seen the rules are true for both letters and numbers.

66. Two numbers or quantities are *directly proportional* when they increase or decrease together; in which case their *ratio* is always the same.

Two numbers are *inversely proportional* when one increases as the other decreases; in which case their *product* is always the same.

For example, if 8 men perform 10 units of work per hour, they will perform 40 units in 4 hours and 100 units in 10 hours; that is, as the time increases the amount of work done increases. This is a *direct ratio*. Now, on the other hand, if there are say 800 units of work to be done on a job, 8 men will finish this work in 10 hours, 16 men will finish it in 5 hours, 40 men in 2 hours. Here the time varies inversely, or oppositely, as the number of men employed, and such a ratio is called an *inverse ratio*.

67. The following rule will solve any problem in simple proportion whether it be direct or inverse:

Rule. *Place for the third term of the proportion the number whose units are like the answer sought* (80 rivets in Example 1 below; 7 hours in Example 2). *From the conditions of the problem determine if the answer* (x) *is to be greater or less than the third term; if greater, place the larger of the two remaining numbers for the second term; if less, place it for the first term. Then solve according to the rules given for finding the missing term.*

Examples. 1. If a joint 16 feet long requires 80 rivets, what number will a joint 11 feet long require?

SOLUTION. Let x equal the number of rivets required.
Then 16 : 11 = 80 : x

or

$$\frac{16}{11} = \frac{80}{x}$$

$$x = \frac{80 \times 11}{16}$$

$$x = 55 \text{ rivets. Ans.}$$

The result shows that the shorter joint requires fewer rivets; hence, this is called a *direct proportion*.

2. A train running 27 miles per hour covers a certain distance in 7 hours. How long does it take a train running at 32 miles per hour to cover the same distance?

SOLUTION. It is evident that the train running 32 miles per hour will require less time to cover the same distance than the train running 27 miles per hour. Thus, the faster train requires less time, and the slower train more time; or, in other words, the speed varies inversely as the time.

$$32 : 27 : : 7 : x$$
$$32\,x = 27 \times 7$$
$$x = \frac{189}{32}$$
$$x = 5.9 + \text{hrs. Ans.}$$

It can readily be seen that the proportion 32: 27: : 7: x is an inverse one. If the speed varied as the time, the proportion would be direct and stated as follows: 32: 27 : : x : 7. It will be noted in the direct form of this proportion just given, that the second and fourth terms refer to the first train and its time, while the first and third terms refer to the other train and the unknown time. In the inverse proportion the time of the first train is found as the third term.

PROBLEMS FOR PRACTICE

1. If the earth moves through 360 degrees in $365\frac{1}{4}$ days, how far will it move in a lunar month of $29\frac{1}{2}$ days?   Ans. 29.07+

2. How long will it take a gang of 50 workmen to erect the walls of an 8 story building, if it requires 4 days for 100 workmen to erect one story?

3. If 15 men can build a wall 12 feet high in one week, how many men will it require to raise it 20 feet in the same time?

4. If it requires 18 hours to saw 10,000 feet of lumber, using a 20 h.p. engine, what horsepower will be required to saw the same amount in 10 hours?

68. Negative Quantities. If an ordinary thermometer is consulted it will be found that the scale divisions have opposite them numbers which increase both upwards and downwards from 0.

All values below the zero point are considered negative and all values above are considered positive; thus a temperature of −6 degrees means that the mercury reads 6 degrees below zero; similarly 6 degrees means that the reading is 6 degrees above zero.

The boiling point of water on the Fahrenheit thermometer scale is 212 degrees. On the other hand, the temperature of liquid air, which is a very cold body, is −292 degrees Fahrenheit. Thus it is seen that the 0 point is merely a point of reference. In the same manner, the 0 of the numerical system is considered as a figure of no value and all numbers with the + sign have positive values and all numbers with the − sign have negative values.

Suppose a man's money in the bank is 300 dollars and his debts amount to 350 dollars; here his money in the bank may be considered as positive and his debts as negative. Thus + 300 − 350 = −50 dollars. This −50 shows that the man is in debt 50 dollars, or has virtually 50 dollars less than nothing.

Again when a ship sails a miles to the north of the equator, it is sailing in a positive direction as compared with a course to the south of the equator. For example, if a ship travels 200 miles north it is said to have traversed + 200 miles; on the other hand if it turns about and sails in the reverse direction 250 miles, it then will have a position 50 miles to the south of the starting point, *i.e.*, its position will be −50 miles. Expressing this in equation form gives 200−250 = −50.

Examples. 1. What is the difference in longitude between two places where the longitudes are −80° and +30°?

SOLUTION. Since one position is 80° from the starting point in one direction and the other 30° in the opposite direction from the starting point, the difference between the two places will be represented by the equation:

$$80+30=110° \quad \text{Ans.}$$

2. A man has bills receivable to the amount of 500 dollars, and bills payable to the amount of 1,000 dollars; how much is he worth?

SOLUTION. Having bills receivable to the amount of $500, this is what he is worth; but having bills payable to the amount of $1,000, this is what he owes. He is actually worth then:

$$\$500-\$1000 = -\$500 \text{ Ans.}$$
or he is in debt $500

PROBLEMS FOR PRACTICE

1. The temperature at 6 P. M. is $+ 14°$ and during the evening it grows colder at the rate of $4°$ an hour. Required the temperature at 9 P. M., at 10 P. M., and at midnight.

2. What is the difference in latitude between two places where the latitudes are $+86°$ and $-14°$?

69. Parenthesis. The parenthesis has already been shown to indicate that the terms enclosed are to be considered as one quantity. The following rules indicate the proper use of the parenthesis.

Rules. (a) *When a parenthesis is preceded by the $+$ sign the parenthesis may be removed without making any change in the expression within the parenthesis.*

(b) *When a parenthesis is preceded by the $-$ sign the parenthesis may be removed if the sign of every term within the parenthesis be changed.*

(c) *When a number or letter immediately precedes or follows the parenthesis, with no sign between, the multiplication sign is understood.*

(d) *When the first term within a parenthesis has no sign before it, the $+$ sign is always understood.*

Examples. 1. Remove the parenthesis from the expression: $8 + (2 + 6)$.

$$8 + (8) = 8 + 8 = 16$$

In this problem, 2 is added to 6 before the parenthesis is removed, and the result is added to 8 to give the total sum of 16. It should be noted that the parenthesis has been removed without changing the signs within the parenthesis.

2. Remove the parenthesis from $a + (b + c - d)$.

$$a + (b + c - d) = a + b + c - d$$

3. Remove the parenthesis from $12 - (6 - 4)$

According to the rule, since the quantity $(6 - 4)$ is preceded by a minus sign the removal of the parenthesis makes it necessary to change the $+ 6$ to $- 6$, and the $- 4$ to $+ 4$. The expression then becomes $12 - 6 + 4$, or 10.

If the operation indicated had been performed before removing the parenthesis and the result subtracted from 12 the remainder would have been the same.

4. Remove the parentheses from $c + k - (m - 1) + (a + b)$.
The signs of m and 1 are changed to $-$ and $+$ respectively on the

removal of the parentheses and the final expression becomes $c+k-m+1+a+b$.

5. Remove the parentheses from $a-6(b+7c-e)$.

Removing the parentheses and changing the necessary signs the expression becomes $a-6(b+7c-e)=a-6b-42c+6e$.   Ans.

PROBLEMS FOR PRACTICE

Remove the parentheses in the following problems:

1. $6-(4+10)$
2. $a+b-(c-ax+5)$
3. $36-(14-8)+(3-10)$
4. $c-(a+b)+(c^2-m)$

EQUATIONS

70. An equation is an expression of equality between two quantities.   It has been proved that the proportion $\dfrac{a}{b}=\dfrac{x}{d}$ can be expressed in the form $ad=bx$, by the law of the means and extremes. Since the products ad and bx are equal the whole expression, $ad=bx$, is called an *equation*.   The quantities on the left side of the equality sign constitute the *first member;* those on the right side constitute the *second member.* Any quantity or group of quantities which is separated from others by the + or − sign is called a *term* of the equation.

The equation has the following properties:

(a)   *If letters occur in an equation, they must be given such numerical values that when substituted in the equation both members will be numerically equal.*   In the equation $2b=4k$, let $b=4$ and $k=2$.   Substituting these values, the equation becomes $2\times4=4\times2$, or $8=8$.

(b)   *The same quantity may be added to or subtracted from each member without destroying the equality.*   In the equation, $2b=4k$, let 8 be added to each member.   Thus, $2b+8=4k+8$.   Then substituting the values given in (a) in the above equation, it becomes

$$(2\times4)+8=(4\times2)+8$$
$$8+8=8+8$$
$$16=16$$

It is seen that the quantities within the parentheses, which represent the values of the members of the original equation, are equal and the final result shows that the equality has not been destroyed by adding the same quantity to both members.

Similarly it can be shown that the same quantity may be *subtracted* from both members without destroying the equality.

(c) *Each member of the equation may be multiplied or divided by the same quantity without destroying the equality.* For example, divide by 3 each side of the equation $3x + 6c = 9m + 15$.

$$\frac{3x + 6c}{3} = \frac{9m + 15}{3}$$

Let $x = 25$, $c = 5$, and $m = 10$. Substituting these values in the equation, it becomes $\dfrac{(3 \times 25) + (6 \times 5)}{3} = \dfrac{(9 \times 10) + 15}{3}$

$$\frac{75 + 30}{3} = \frac{90 + 15}{3}$$

$$\frac{105}{3} = \frac{105}{3}$$

It is seen that the equality has not been destroyed by the division. Similarly it may be shown that the same root of each member may be extracted, or that each member may be raised to the same power without destroying the equality.

(d) *When a term has no sign before it, the plus sign is understood.*

(e) *The order of the terms or of the letters within the terms is unimportant; the proper sign, however, must be given to each term.* For example $6abc + 4cy = 0$ is the same as $6cab + 4yc = 0$. [Again, $3a - 6bc - xy = 40$ is equivalent to $-xy + 3a - 6bc = 40$.

71. Transposition. (a) Suppose it is required to solve for the unknown value of x in the equation $4x + 2 = 6 + 3x$. In this equation the unknown quantity is found in both members. *In any equation containing the unknown quantity in both members it is common to arrange the unknown values on the left side of the equation, and the known values on the right. After combining the terms divide both sides of the equation by the coefficient of the unknown quantity.* The above operation may be accomplished by subtracting $3x$ and 2 from both members of the equation which results in the following:

$$4x + 2 - 3x - 2 = 6 + 3x - 3x - 2$$
combining terms $\qquad x + 0 = 4 + 0$

$$x = 4, \quad \text{Ans.}$$

Again, solve for x in the equation

$$8x + 4x + 6 = 2x + 8$$

Subtracting $2x$ and 6,
from both members, $\quad 8x + 4x + 6 - 2x - 6 = 2x + 8 - 2x - 6$
combining terms $\quad\quad\quad\quad\quad\quad\quad\quad 10x = 2$

$$\text{or} \quad x = .2 \quad \text{Ans.}$$

(b)   The above form of solution may be simplified by the use of a method known as *transposition. All terms containing the unknown quantity, which are found on the right side, are transposed to the left, at the same time changing their signs; likewise all known terms found on the left side are transposed to the right, at the same time changing signs.* If, when the terms have been combined, x is found to be $-$, change its sign to $+$ and at the same time change the sign of its numerical equivalent.   (See Examples 6 and 8 following.)

Examples. 1. Solve the equation, $4x + 2 = 6 + 3x$.

SOLUTION: Bring over the $3x$ to the left-hand side of the equation and change its sign from $+$ to $-$; also transpose the 2 to the right-hand side and change its sign to $-$; thus,

Transposing $\quad\quad\quad\quad 4x - 3x = 6 - 2$
Combining $\quad\quad\quad\quad\quad\quad\quad x = 4 \quad \text{Ans.}$

2. Solve the equation: $8x + 4x + 6 = 2x + 8$
Transposing $\quad\quad 8x + 4x - 2x = 8 - 6$
$$10x = 2$$
$$x = \frac{2}{10} \text{ or } .2 \quad \text{Ans.}$$

3. Solve for m in the equation, $10m + 12 - 2m = 24 - 2m$
Transposing $\quad 10m - 2m + 2m = 24 - 12$
Combining $\quad\quad\quad\quad\quad\quad 10m = 12$
$$m = \frac{12}{10} = 1.2 \quad \text{Ans.}$$

4. Solve the equation: $9x = 6x + 20$
Transposing $\quad\quad 9x - 6x = 20$
Combining $\quad\quad\quad\quad 3x = 20$
$$x = \frac{20}{3} \text{ or } 6\tfrac{2}{3} \quad \text{Ans.}$$

5. Solve the equation: $4x - 3 = 61$
Transposing $\qquad 4x = 61 + 3$
Combining $\qquad 4x = 64$

$$x = \frac{64}{4} \text{ or } 16 \quad \text{Ans.}$$

6. Solve the equation: $8x - 22 = 12x - 18$
Transposing $\qquad 8x - 12x = 22 - 18$
Combining $\qquad -4x = 4$
Dividing each side by 4 and changing signs,
$$x = -1 \quad \text{Ans.}$$

7. Solve the equation: $32x + 24 = 30 - 50x$
Transposing $\qquad 32x + 50x = 30 - 24$
Combining $\qquad 82x = 6$

$$x = \frac{6}{82} \text{ or } \frac{3}{41} \quad \text{Ans.}$$

8. Solve the equation: $12 - 13x = 5 - 10x$
Transposing $\qquad -13x + 10x = 5 - 12$
Combining $\qquad -3x = -7$
Changing signs $\qquad 3x = 7$

$$x = \frac{7}{3} \text{ or } 2\tfrac{1}{3} \quad \text{Ans.}$$

PROBLEMS FOR PRACTICE

Solve for x in the following equations:

1. $5x + 9 = 14 - 2x$
2. $6x - 28 = 15x - 16$ $\qquad\qquad$ Ans. $\quad -1\tfrac{1}{3}$
3. $20 - 14x = 26 - 18x$
4. $12x + 25 - 35 = 14x + 22x - 22$
5. $81 + 10 - 20x = 60 + 40x$

72. Equations Containing Fractions. The equations which have so far been given illustrate more simple algebraic forms. In practice, equations may often contain fractions and it will be well to study the method of handling such equations.

In the treatment of fractions, Part II, it was shown that a group of fractions could be added or subtracted only by reducing them all to a common denominator. This same process may be applied to an equation containing fractions. For example, let us take the equation

$$\frac{4x + 7}{7} + \frac{x}{6} = 13$$

By inspection the L. C. D. is seen to be 42. Reducing each term of the equation to the least common denominator, we have

$$\frac{(6 \times 4x) + (6 \times 7)}{6 \times 7} + \frac{(7 \times x)}{7 \times 6} = \frac{42 \times 13}{42}$$

or

$$\frac{24x + 42}{42} + \frac{7x}{42} = \frac{546}{42}$$

Combining

$$\frac{(24x + 42 + 7x)}{42} = \frac{546}{42}$$

It has just been learned in article 70 that each member of an equation may be multiplied by the same quantity without destroying the equality. Multiplying the above equation by 42, we have

$$\frac{\cancel{42}\,(24x + 42 + 7x)}{\cancel{42}} = \frac{\cancel{42} \times 546}{\cancel{42}}$$

Cancelling like terms in numerator and denominator of each fraction, we have

$$24x + 42 + 7x = 546$$
$$31x = 504$$
$$x = 16.2 +$$

An inspection of the last fractional equation shows that multiplying by 42 was unnecessary as the same result would have been obtained by simply dropping the common denominator from each term. This leads to the following rules:

Rules. (a) *To solve an equation containing fractions, reduce all terms of the equation to a common denominator in the usual manner and then drop the denominators* (This process is termed "clearing of fractions".) *The resulting equation is then solved for the unknown quantity by the usual process.*

(b) *If fractions occur in the numerator or denominator of any term, this term must be reduced to a simple fraction before finding the L. C. D.*

Examples. 1. Solve the equation $\dfrac{6x}{8} - (7+x) = \dfrac{2}{3}$

Reducing to L. C. D. $\dfrac{18x}{24} - \dfrac{24\ (7+x)}{24} = \dfrac{16}{24}$

Dropping denominator $18x - 168 - 24x = 16$

$$-6x = 184$$
$$6x = -184$$
$$x = -30.6 + \quad \text{Ans.}$$

2. Solve the equation $\dfrac{8x+3}{15} - \dfrac{(2-4x)}{5} = 3$

Clearing of fractions $8x + 3 - 6 + 12x = 45$
Combining $\qquad\qquad 20x = 48$
$$x = 2.4 \quad \text{Ans.}$$

PROBLEMS FOR PRACTICE

Solve for x in the following equations:

1. $\dfrac{x}{20} - \dfrac{2}{4} = \dfrac{4}{5}$

2. $\dfrac{(8x+3)}{12} + \dfrac{1}{2} = 8$ $\qquad\qquad$ Ans. $10\frac{7}{8}$

3. $\dfrac{42-x}{25} - \dfrac{(2x+14)}{10} = 20$ $\qquad\qquad$ Ans. $-82.16+$

73. General Application of Equations to Problems.
In the preceding problems the relation of the quantities has been expressed directly in equation form and solutions given for the value of the unknown quantity. However, the equation finds its greatest field of usefulness in problems in applied science and engineering where no equation is given directly but must be formed from conditions stated in the problem itself.

The solution of such a problem consists of two distinct parts: (1) The *statement* of the problem, and (2) the *solution* of the equation.

The statement of the problem is the process of expressing the conditions of the problem in the form of an equation. The statement of the problem is often more difficult to beginners than the solution of the equation. No rule can be given for the statement of every particular problem. Much must depend on the skill of the student, and practice will give him readiness in this process. The following is the general plan of finding the equation:

(a) *Study the problem, to ascertain what quantities in it are known and what are unknown, and to understand it fully, so as to be able to prove the correctness or incorrectness of any proposed answer.*

(b) *Represent the unknown quantity by x, and express in equation form the relations which hold between the known and unknown quantities; an equation will thus be obtained which can be solved by the methods already given, and from which the value of the unknown quantity may be found.*

The problems which follow the illustrative examples will test the ability of the student to state the problem in equation form, and solve for the unknown quantity.

Examples. 1. *A, B,* and *C* receive \$1285 among them; *A's* share is \$25 more than $\frac{5}{6}$ths of *B's*, and *C's* is $\frac{4}{15}$ths of *B's*. Find the share of each.

In this problem we must first determine what unknown quantity is to equal x. Since both *A's* and *C's* shares are compared with *B's*, (or depend upon *B's*), we may let x represent *B's* share. Now, *A's* share is \$25 more than $\frac{5}{6}$ths of *B's*, and as *B's* share is x, *A's* must be $(\frac{5}{6} \times x) + 25$, or $\frac{5x}{6} + 25$. As *C's* share is $\frac{4}{15}$ths of *B's*, it will be $\frac{4}{15} \times x$ or $\frac{4x}{15}$.

We now have a statement of all three shares, and since together the men have \$1285, the sum of their shares must equal \$1285. We, therefore, place the sum of the three shares as the first member of the equation, and the actual value of these three shares in dollars for the second member of the equation, as follows:

SOLUTION. Let x represent *B's* share

then $\qquad \frac{5x}{6} + 25$ represents *A's* share

and $\qquad \frac{4x}{15}\qquad$ represents *C's* share

Forming the equation, we have:

$$x + \left(\frac{5x}{6} + 25\right) + \frac{4x}{15} = 1285$$

Clearing equation of fractions:

$$30x+25x+750+8x=38{,}550$$

Transposing:

$$30x+25x+8x=38{,}550-750$$

Combining terms:

$$63x=37{,}800$$
$$x=\$600,\ B\text{'s share}$$

Since we have B's share, to find the other two shares, we substitute \$600 for x, as follows:

$$A\text{'s share} =\frac{5x}{6}+25=\frac{(5\times600)}{6}+25=\$525$$

$$C\text{'s share} =\frac{4x}{15}=\frac{4\times600}{15}=\$160$$

Answers $\begin{cases} A\text{'s share } \$525 \\ B\text{'s share } \$600 \\ C\text{'s share } \$160 \end{cases}$

2. Divide 19 into two parts such that 7 times the less shall exceed 6 times the greater by 3.

SOLUTION. Let x = the lesser part
$(19-x)$ = the greater part

then $7x$ = 7 times the lesser part and $6(19-x)$ = 6 times the greater part, but 7 times the lesser part must exceed 6 times the greater by 3.

Therefore, $\qquad 7x-6(19-x)=3$

Expanding, $\qquad 7x-114+6x=3$

Transposing, $\qquad\qquad 13x=114+3$
$$13x=117$$

Dividing by 13, $\qquad\qquad x=\frac{117}{13}=9$ Ans.

Therefore, $x=9$, the lesser part; $19-9=10$, the greater part. It can readily be seen that the conditions have been met, as 7 times the lesser, 63, exceeds 6 times the greater, 60, by 3.

3. In an ingot of brass weighing 105 lb., if the copper used weighed 20 lb. less and the tin 20 lb. more, the weight of the copper would still be 5 lb. more than the weight of the tin. What is the weight of each?

SOLUTION. Let x represent weight of copper and $(105-x)$ represent weight of tin.

Then by the conditions of the problem, the weight of the copper reduced by 20 lb., that is $(x-20)$, is 5 lb. more than the weight of tin increased by 20 lb., that is, $(105-x) + 20$. The equation is, therefore,

$$(x-20) - 5 = (105-x) + 20$$

Transposing $\quad x + x = 105 + 20 + 20 + 5$

$$2x = 150$$

$$x = 75 \text{ lb. weight of copper}$$
$$105 - 75 = 30 \text{ lb. weight of tin} \Bigg\} \text{Ans.}$$

PROBLEMS FOR PRACTICE

1. A bar of solder weighs 51 lb. It is composed of tin and lead. There are 9 lb. more tin in the bar than lead. How much lead is there? How much tin?

(Suggestion: Let x = the amount of lead. Then $51 - x$ = the amount of tin.)

Ans. 30 lb. tin. 21 lb. lead.

2. Divide a freight train of 76 cars into two trains so that twice the longer train shall be less by 16 than 4 times the shorter train.

(Suggestion: x = number of cars in longer train; $76 - x$ = number of cars in shorter train.)

Ans. 48, 28.

3. Two dynamos furnish 84 horsepower. One dynamo furnishes $\frac{3}{4}$ as much power as the other. What does each furnish?

(Suggestion: x = horsepower of one machine, $\frac{3x}{4}$ = horsepower of other machine.)

Ans. 48 h.p., 36 h.p.

4. In a ton of prepared mortar, the sand weighs 200 pounds more than the gypsum and the plaster of Paris one-fourth as much as the gypsum. What is the weight of each?

5. A tank can be filled by two pipes A and B, in 12 and 15 minutes respectively. A service pipe C will empty the tank in 10 minutes. How long will it take A and B to fill the tank when C is emptying it?

Ans. 20 minutes.

APPENDIX

MEASURES OF EXTENSION

Linear Measure

12 inches (in. or ") = 1 foot (ft. or ')
3 feet = 1 yard (yd.)
5½ yards or 16½ ft. = 1 rod (rd.), pole, or perch
320 rods or 5280 ft. = 1 mile (mi.)

A *knot*, used in navigation, is equal to 1.15 miles.
A *fathom* is equal to six feet.

Square Measure

144 square inches (sq. in.) = 1 square foot (sq. ft.)
9 square feet = 1 square yard (sq. yd.)
30¼ square yards = 1 square rod (sq. rd.)
160 square rods = 1 acre (A.)
640 acres = 1 square mile (sq. mi.)

Cubic Measure

1728 cubic inches (cu. in.) = 1 cubic foot (cu. ft.)
27 cubic feet = 1 cubic yard (cu. yd.)
128 cubic feet = 1 cord (cd.)
8 cord feet = 1 cord (cd.)

A *perch* of stone or masonry is 16½ feet (1 rod) long, 1½ feet wide, and 1 foot high, or 24¾ cu. ft. capacity. The perch sometimes has other values, viz, 22 cu. ft. and 18 cu. ft. The value first mentioned is used throughout this text.

16 cu. ft. = 1 cord foot (cd. ft.). A pile of wood 8 feet long, 4 feet wide, and 4 feet high contains a cord. The cord foot is 1 foot of the length of such a pile.

Surveyors' Linear Measure

7.92 inches (in.) = 1 link (l.)
25 links = 1 rod (rd.)
100 links
4 rods   each = 1 chain (ch.)
66 feet
80 chains = 1 mile (mi.)

Surveyors' Square Measure

16 square rods	= 1 square chain
10 square chains	= 1 acre (A.)
640 acres	= 1 square mile (sq. mi.)
1 square mile	= 1 section (sec.)
36 sections	= 1 township (Tp.)

Surveyors' measure was obtained by calling one tenth of an acre a *square chain*. A tenth of an acre is equal to 16 square rods, and is equivalent to a square each side of which measures 4 rods. Thus, since 16 square rods is equal to one square chain, a linear chain is 4 rods or 792 inches. The linear chain is divided into 100 equal parts called *links*.

MEASURES OF CAPACITY

Dry Measure

2 pints (pts.)	= 1 quart (qt.)
8 quarts	= 1 peck (pk.)
4 pecks	= 1 bushel (bu.)

The *Winchester bushel* contains 2,150.4 cubic inches and is used in measuring shelled grains. The *heaped bushel* of 2747.7 cubic inches is used for measuring apples, potatoes, corn in the ear, etc. The *dry gallon*, or half peck, contains 268.8 cubic inches.

Liquid Measure

4 gills (gi.)	= 1 pint (pt.)
2 pints	= 1 quart (qt.)
4 quarts	= 1 gallon (gal.)
$31\frac{1}{2}$ gallons	= 1 barrel (bbl.)
2 barrels, or 63 gallons	= 1 hogshead (hhd.)

One U. S. standard gallon contains 231 cubic inches, and one gallon of water weighs approximately $8\frac{1}{3}$ pounds.

One cubic foot of water contains approximately 7.5 U. S. standard gallons and weighs 62.3 pounds.

Apothecaries' Fluid Measure

60 minims	= 1 fluid drachm
8 fluid drachms .	= 1 fluid ounce
16 fluid ounces	= 1 pint

MEASURES OF WEIGHT

Troy Weight

24 grains (gr.)	= 1 pennyweight (dwt. or pwt.)
20 pennyweights	= 1 ounce (oz.)
12 ounces	= 1 pound (lb.)

The standard Troy pound contains 5,760 grains and is identical with the Troy pound of Great Britain. Troy weight is used in weighing gold, silver, and jewels.

The *carat* (car.), a weight of about 3.2 grains Troy, is used in weighing diamonds and other precious stones. The term carat is used also to express the fineness of gold, and means $\frac{1}{24}$ part. For example, gold is said to be 18 carats fine when it contains 18 parts of pure gold and 6 parts of alloy or baser metal.

Avoirdupois Weight

16 ounces (oz.)	= 1 pound (lb.)
100 pounds (lbs.)	= 1 hundredweight (cwt.)
20 hundredweight, or 2,000 lbs.	= 1 ton (t. or T.)

The Avoirdupois pound contains 7,000 grains Troy.
There are 7.3 Apothecary drams in an Avoirdupois ounce.
25 pounds are sometimes called a *quarter*.
The ton of 2,000 pounds is sometimes called the *short ton*.

Long Ton Weight

16 ounces	= 1 pound (lb.)
112 pounds (lbs.)	= 1 hundredweight (cwt.)
20 cwt. or 2,240 lbs	= 1 ton (T. or t.)

NOTE. The long ton table is not to be used unless specially designated.

Apothecaries Weight

20 grains	= 1 scruple (sc.)
3 scruples	= 1 dram (dr.)
8 drams	= 1 ounce (oz.)
12 ounces	= 1 pound (lb.)

The pound, ounce, and grain of this weight are identical with those of Troy weight.

Drugs and medicines are bought and sold at wholesale by Avoirdupois weight.

METRIC SYSTEM

The fundamental unit of the metric system is the *meter*—the unit of length. From this the units of capacity—*liter*—and of weight —*gram*—were derived. All other units are the decimal sub-divisions or multiples of these. These three units are simply related; *e. g.*, * for all practical purposes one *cubic decimeter* equals one *liter* and one *liter* of water weighs one *kilogram*. The metric tables are formed by combining the words *meter*, *gram*, and *liter* with the six numerical prefixes, as in the following tables:

PREFIXES	MEANING			UNITS
milli	= one thousandth	$\frac{1}{1000}$	.001	
centi-	= one hundredth	$\frac{1}{100}$	.01	*meter* for length
deci-	= one tenth	$\frac{1}{10}$	.1	
Unit	= one		1	*gram* for weight or mass
deka-	= ten	$\frac{10}{1}$	10	
hecto-	= one hundred	$\frac{100}{1}$	100	*liter* for capacity
kilo-	= one thousand	$\frac{1000}{1}$	1000	

Units of Length

milli-meter	= .001	meter
centi-meter	= .01	meter
deci-meter	= .1	meter
METER	= 1	meter
deka-meter	= 10	meter
hecto-meter	= 100	meter
kilo-meter	= 1,000	meter

Where *miles* are used in England and the United States for measuring distances, the *kilometer* (1,000 meters) is used in metric countries. It is about 5 furlongs. There are about 1,600 meters in a statute mile, 20 meters in a chain, and 5 meters in a rod.

The *meter* is used for dry goods, merchandise, engineering construction, building, and other purposes where the *yard* and *foot* are used. The meter is about a tenth longer than the yard.

The *centimeter* and *millimeter* are used instead of the *inch* and its fractions in machine construction and similar work. The centimeter, as its name shows, is the hundredth of a meter. It is used in cabinet

---

* The term "e. g." means "for example."

work, in expressing sizes of paper, books, and in many cases where the inch is used. The centimeter is about two-fifths of an inch and the millimeter about one twenty-fifth of an inch. The millimeter is divided for finer work into tenths, hundredths, and thousandths.

If a number of distances in millimeters, meters, and kilometers are to be added, reduction is unnecessary. They are added as dollars, dimes, and cents are now added. For example, "1,050.25 meters" is not read "1 kilometer, 5 dekameters, 2 decimeters, and 5 centimeters," but "one thousand fifty meters and twenty-five centimeters," just as "$1,050.25" is read "one thousand fifty dollars and twenty-five cents."

Area

The table of areas is formed by squaring the length measures, as in our common system. For land measure 10 meters square is called an *are* (meaning *area*). The side of one *are* is about 33 *feet*. The *hectare* is 100 meters square, and, as its name indicates, is 100 ares, or about $2\frac{1}{2}$ acres. An *acre* is about 0.4 hectare. A standard United States *quarter section* contains almost exactly 64 hectares. A *square kilometer* contains 100 hectares.

For smaller measures of surface the *square meter* is used. The square meter is about 20 per cent larger than the *square yard*. For still smaller surfaces the *square centimeter* is used. A *square inch* contains about $6\frac{1}{2}$ square centimeters.

Volume

The cubic measures are the cubes of the linear units. The *cubic meter* (sometimes called the *stere*, meaning *solid*) is the unit of volume. A *cubic meter* of water weighs a *metric ton* and is equal to 1 *kiloliter*. The cubic meter is used in place of the cubic yard and is about 30 per cent larger. This is used for "cuts and fills" in grading land, measuring timber, expressing contents of tanks and reservoirs, flow of rivers, dimensions of stone, tonnage of ships, and other places where the cubic yard and foot are used. The thousandth part of the cubic meter (1 cubic decimeter) is called the liter. (See table of capacity units.)

For very small volumes the *cubic centimeter* (c.c. or cm³.) is used. This volume of water weighs a *gram*, which is the unit of weight or mass. There are about 16 cubic centimeters in a cubic inch. The cubic centimeter is the unit of volume used by chemists as well as in pharmacy, medicine, surgery, and other technical work. One thousand cubic centimeters make 1 liter.

Units of Capacity

milli-liter	=	.001	liter
centi-liter	=	.01	liter
deci-liter	=	.1	liter
*LITER	=	1	liter
deka-liter	=	10	liter
hecto-liter	=	100	liter
kilo-liter	=	1,000	liter

The *hectoliter* (100 liters) serves the same purpose as the United States *bushel* (2,150.42 cubic inches), and is equal to about 3 bushels, or a barrel. A *peck* is about 9 liters. The liter is used for measurements commonly given in the *gallon*, the liquid and dry *quarts*, a liter being 5 per cent larger than our liquid quart and 10 per cent smaller than the dry quart. A *liter* of water weighs exactly a *kilogram*, i. e., 1,000 grams. A thousand liters of water weigh 1 metric ton.

Units of Weight (or Mass)

milli-gram	=	0.001	gram
centi-gram	=	.01	gram
deci-gram	=	.1	gram
GRAM	=	1	gram
deka-gram	=	10	gram
hecto-gram	=	100	gram
†kilo-gram	=	1,000	gram

Measurements commonly expressed in *gross tons* or *short tons* are stated in *metric tons* (1,000 kilograms). The metric ton comes between our long and short tons and serves the purpose of both. The *kilogram* and *half kilo* serve for everyday trade, the latter being 10 per cent larger than the pound. The kilogram is approximately 2.2 pounds. The *gram* and its multiples and divisions are used for the same purposes as ounces, pennyweights, drams, scruples, and grains. For foreign postage, 30 grams is the legal equivalent of the avoirdupois ounce.

*One liter equals 1.05668 liquid quarts or 0.9081 dry quarts.
†One kilogram equals 2.204622 avoirdupois pounds.

MEASURES OF TIME

60 seconds (sec.)	= 1 minute (min.)
60 minutes	= 1 hour (hr.)
24 hours	= 1 day (d.)
7 days	= 1 week (w. or wk.)
365 days or 52 wks.	= 1 year (yr.)
12 months (mos.)	= 1 year
366 days	= 1 leap year
100 years (yrs.)	= 1 century

In most business transactions 30 days are considered a month and 360 days a year.

The solar year is exactly 365 d. 5 hrs. 48 min. 49.7 sec.

A common year consists of 365 days for three successive years. Every fourth year, except as noted below, one day is added for the excess of the solar year over 365 days, and we have 366 days, which make what is called a *leap year*. The extra day is added to the month of February, which then has 29 days.

The following rule for leap year will make the calendar correct to within one day for a period of 4,000 years.

Every year exactly divisible by 4 is a leap year, the centennial years excepted; the other years are common years. Every centennial year exactly divisible by 400 is a leap year; the other centennial years are common years. Thus 1904 is a leap year, but 1905 is a common year; also, the year 2000 is a leap year, but 1800 and 1900 are common years.

MEASURES OF MONEY

United States Money

10 mills (mi.)	= 1 cent (¢)
10 cents	= 1 dime (d.)
10 dimes	= 1 dollar ($)
10 dollars	= 1 eagle

These values, with the exception of the eagle, apply also to Canadian money.

English Money

4 farthings (far.)	=	1 penny (d)
12 pence	=	1 shilling (s)
20 shillings	=	1 pound (£) or sovereign

The unit of English money is the pound sterling, the value of which in United States money is $4.8665.

French Money	**German Money**
1 franc = $0.193	100 pfennige = 1 mark (Rm.) = $0.238

MISCELLANEOUS MEASURES

Measures of Angles and Arcs

60 seconds (″)	=	1 minute (′)
60 minutes	=	1 degree (°)
90 degrees	=	1 right angle or quadrant
360 degrees	=	1 circle

Stationers' Table

24 sheets	=	1 quire (qr.)
20 quires	=	1 ream (rm.)
2 reams	=	1 bundle (bdl.)
5 bundles	=	1 bale (bl.)

Comparative table of Metric and English equivalents.*

Linear Measure

1 inch	=	2.5 cm.
1 foot	=	.3 meter
1 meter	=	39.37 inches
1 yard	=	.9 meter
1 meter	=	1.1 yards
1 rod	=	5. meters
1 mile	=	1.6 kilometers.
1 kilo	=	.62 miles

Solid Measure

1 cu. inch	=	16.4 cu. cm.
1 cu. cm.	=	.06 cu. in.
1 cu. foot	=	28.3 cu. dm.
1 cu. dm.	=	.035 cu. feet
1 cu. yard	=	.76 cu. meter
1 cu. meter	=	35.3 cu. feet
1 cord	=	3.6 stares

Square Measure

1 sq. inch	=	6.45 sq. cm.
1 sq. cm.	=	.155 sq. in.
1 sq. foot	=	.09 sq. meter
1 sq. meter	=	10.73 sq. feet
1 sq. yard	=	.84 sq. meter
1 sq. rod	=	25.3 sq. meters
1 acre	=	40.5 ares
1 are	=	.024 acres

Measure of Capacity

1 fl. ounce	=	.03 liter
1 liq. qt.	=	.95 liter
1 liter	=	1.05 liq. qt.
1 gallon	=	3.8 liters
1 dry qt.	=	1.1 liters
1 liter	=	.9 dry qts.
1 bushel	=	.35 hectoliter
1 hectoliter	=	2.84 bushels

Measures of Weight

1 grain Troy	=	.06 gram
1 gram	=	15.4 grains Troy
1 ounce Troy	=	31. grams
1 lb. Troy	=	.37 kilogram
1 kilo	=	2.7 lbs. Troy

1 ounce Avoir.	=	28.35 grams
1 gram	=	.035 oz. Avoir.
1 lb. Avoir.	=	.45 kilogram
1 kilo	=	2.2 lbs. Avoir
1 metric ton	=	2200. lbs. Avoir

* Values given in these tables are only approximate but are sufficiently accurate for all ordinary computations. These tables need not be memorized.

FIVE-KILOWATT GASOLINE ELECTRIC GENERATING SET

Courtesy of B. F. Sturtevant Company

Practical Mathematics

PART IV

INTRODUCTION

Mathematics has a language of its own and certain signs and symbols that belong to it. It is necessary for the student to know this language, and these signs and symbols and their uses, in order to understand his textbooks in mathematics. Failure to learn the exact meaning and use of the signs and symbols, and the definitions and terms used, keeps many students from mastering mathematical subjects.

It is sufficient at this time to call your attention briefly to those signs with which you are already familiar and bespeak a thorough mastery of the subject matter in this textbook.

Review of Signs. The following signs indicate operations to be performed:

Addition	$+$
Subtraction	$-$
Multiplication	$\times$
Division	$\div$

The signs denoting operations are used thus: $4+2=6$; $6-2=4$; $4\times2=8$; $8\div2=4$. They are not used when the numbers are written one below the other, arranged for addition, subtraction, or multiplication, or when the dividend is written with the divisor at the left, with a curved line between, arranged for division.

It will be remembered also that a coefficient (Part I, page 15) indicates multiplication, and that the line of a fraction indicates division. Thus, $7a$ means 7 times a, and $\frac{1}{2}(B\times A)$ means $\frac{1}{2}$ times B times A; $\frac{11}{3}$ means 11 divided by 3.

The equality sign $=$ is used to show that two quantities or expressions are equal. It is never used except when the quantities so joined *are* equal.

The parentheses ( ) and the vinculum ‾‾‾‾ are used to show that the quantities so tied together are to be treated as one.

Order of Signs. In a series of operations denoted by the signs of addition, subtraction, multiplication, and division, the multiplications must be performed first, the divisions next, and lastly the additions and subtractions.

If several additions or several multiplications occur together, they may be performed in any order.

If several subtractions or several divisions occur together, they *must* be performed in the order in which they come from left to right.

The work of solving problems may often be simplified by using cancellation. (See Part I, page 26.) It must be remembered that this method cannot be used when there are additions or subtractions indicated in the problem, because it is only common *factors* that are cancelled. When you cancel a factor, you have divided by that factor.

$$\frac{4\times9}{2}=\frac{\overset{2}{\cancel{4}}\times9}{\cancel{2}}=18$$

but

$$\frac{4+9}{2}=\frac{13}{2}\text{ or } 6\tfrac{1}{2}$$

and

$$\frac{12-3}{3}=\frac{9}{3}\text{ or } 3$$

The radical sign $\sqrt{}$ is used to indicate that a root is to be extracted. (See Part III, page 76.) The index shows what root is to be taken. $\sqrt[3]{}$ indicates the cube root. $\sqrt[2]{}$ indicates the square root. When no index appears the square root is understood.

A small number written at the right and slightly above a number indicates that a power of that number is to be found. (See Part III, page 74.) Thus 12^2 means that 12 is to be used twice as a factor, or that the second power is to be found. $12^2=12\times12=144$. The number indicating the power to be found is called the exponent.

MENSURATION

Mensuration is the process of computing the length of lines, the area of surfaces, and the volume of solids.

Lines are measured in linear units. Areas are measured in square units. Volume is measured in cubic units.

A *line* has length only.

A *surface* has length and breadth (or width).

A *solid* has length, breadth, and thickness (or heignt).

These facts may be expressed in another way:

A line extends in one direction only.

A surface extends in two directions.

A solid extends in three directions.

These *directions of extension* are spoken of as dimensions.

We think of a point as something that has position only, without length, breadth, or thickness. Thus, the end of a line is a point. The intersection of two lines is a point.

LINES

74. A *straight line* is one that has the same direction throughout its length. It is the shortest distance between two points.

A *curved line* is one that is continually changing its direction. It is sometimes called a *curve*.

A *broken line* is one made up of several straight lines.

A *plane surface* (or simply a plane) is a surface such that when a straight edge is applied to it, the straight edge will in every part touch the surface.

If two straight lines in the same plane are extended, they will meet or they will not meet. If they meet they form angles. If they do not meet they are parallel.

Parallel lines are lines that lie in the same plane and are equally distant from each other at all points.

Lines are lettered to distinguish them; thus, if one end is marked *A* and the other *B*, it is called "the line *A B*," or "the line *B A*."

| Straight Line | Curved Line | Broken Line | Parallel Lines |

ANGLES

75. An *angle* is the measure of the difference in direction of two straight lines that meet. The lines are called *sides*, and the point of meeting, the *vertex*.

If one straight line meets another so that the angles formed are equal, the lines are said to be *perpendicular* to each other and the angles are *right angles*, Fig. 9.

An *acute angle* is less than a right angle, Fig. 10.

An *obtuse angle* is greater than a right angle and less than two right angles, Fig. 11.

Angles are distinguished by placing letters at the ends of the lines forming the sides and at the vertex. For example, in Fig. 10 the angle would be read as "the angle *A B C*" or "the angle *C B A*." In writing, the sign ∠ is often used in place of the word "angle."

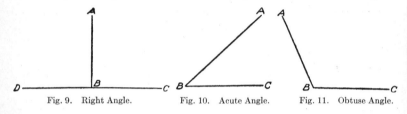

Fig. 9.   Right Angle.   Fig. 10.   Acute Angle.   Fig. 11.   Obtuse Angle.

As two right angles are formed when one line meets another perpendicularly, Fig. 9, it follows that:

(a)   *The sum of all the angles about a point on one side of a straight line is equal to two right angles.*

(b)   *The sum of all the angles about any point is equal to four right angles.*

When two lines intersect they form four angles, Fig. 12. The angles *A O C* and *A O D* are called *adjacent* angles because they have the same vertex *O* and the line *A O* is common to both as it forms a side of each angle. It has been proved that ∠*A O C* + ∠*A O D* = two

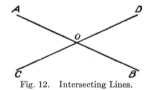

Fig. 12.   Intersecting Lines.

right angles and it may also be proved that the angles *A O C* and *D O B*, called *opposite* angles, are equal to each other. Therefore, *when two straight lines intersect, the opposite angles formed are equal to each other.*

Take two narrow strips of cardboard or stiff paper and lay them on the table crossing each other. Fasten at the point of crossing with a pin, so that the upper strip will turn freely. Set it first perpendicularly. You will see that you have made four right angles. Turn it in either direction. You will see that, no matter at what angle the one strip crosses the other, the sum of the angles formed will equal four right angles.

76. Measurement of Angles. It has been shown in Fig. 12 that the sum of the angles about the point of intersection of two lines is always four right angles. Evidently, other lines might be drawn through the same intersection, making the angles smaller and more in number, without changing the value of their sum. In measuring angles, therefore, it has been agreed to divide these four right angles about a point into 360 equal parts called *degrees*, indicated by the sign, °. In this case each of the four right angles would contain

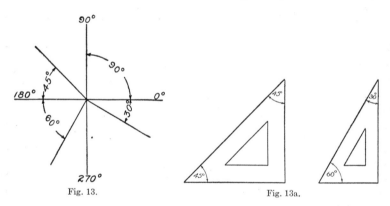

Fig. 13.   Fig. 13a.

90° while one-half, two-thirds, and one-third of a right angle would represent angles of respectively 45°, 60°, and 30°, as shown in Fig. 13. In drawing work, it will be found that the 45° triangle and the 30° —60° triangle, Fig. 13a, are useful articles of equipment, but when it comes to accurate values of angles, some device like a *protractor*, Fig. 14, showing degrees and fractions of degrees, is necessary. Each degree is divided into 60 equal parts called *minutes* ('), and each minute into 60 equal parts called *seconds* ("). Thus to represent an angle of 23 degrees, 47 minutes, and 9 seconds, write 23° 47′ 9″.

The relations of these units may be summarized as follows:

60 seconds (″) = 1 minute (′).
60 minutes   = 1 degree (°).
360 degrees   = 1 circle, or circumference.
90 degrees   = 1 right angle.
180 degrees   = 2 right angles.
360 degrees   = 4 right angles, or 1 circumference.

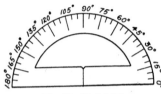

Fig. 14.   Protractor.

Two angles are *complementary* when their sum is equal to one right angle or 90°; they are *supplementary* when their sum is equal to two right angles or 180°. Thus, an angle of 33° is the complement of one of 57° because 33+57 = 90. Angles of 148° and 32° are supplementary because 148+32 = 180.

PROBLEMS FOR PRACTICE

1. How many seconds in 180 degrees?   Ans. 648,000
2. How many right angles in 202° 30′?   Ans. $2\frac{1}{4}$
3. What is the complement of 37°?
4. What is the complement of 11° 47′ 3″?   Ans. 78° 12′ 57″
5. What is the supplement of 131° 4′ 27″?   Ans. 48° 55′ 33″
6. Does an acute angle contain more or less than 90°? an obtuse angle?
7. In Fig. 12, the angle *A O C* is, say, 52°; find the value of the three other angles about the point *O*.
8. How many seconds in 30′?

PLANE FIGURES

A *plane figure* is a plane surface bounded by lines, either straight or curved.

The distance around a plane figure is called its *perimeter*.

The *area* of a plane figure is the number of square units it contains.

POLYGONS

77. A *polygon* is a plane figure bounded by straight lines. The boundary lines are called the *sides* and the sum of the sides is called the *perimeter*.

Fig. 15.   Pentagon.   Fig. 16.   Hexagon.   Fig. 17.   Octagon.

Polygons are classified according to the number of sides.

A *triangle* is a polygon of three sides.

A *quadrilateral* is a polygon of four sides.

A *pentagon* is a polygon of five sides, Fig. 15.

A *hexagon* is a polygon of six sides, Fig. 16.

An *octagon* is a polygon of eight sides, Fig. 17.

An *equilateral polygon* is one all of whose sides are equal.

An *equiangular polygon* is one all of whose angles are equal.

A *regular polygon* is one all of whose angles and all of whose sides are equal.

TRIANGLES

78. A *triangle* is a polygon enclosed by three straight lines called *sides*. The *angles* of a triangle are the angles formed by the sides.

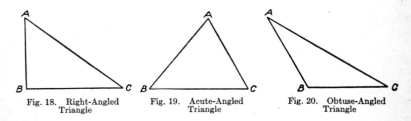

Fig. 18.   Right-Angled   Fig. 19.   Acute-Angled   Fig. 20.   Obtuse-Angled
     Triangle   Triangle   Triangle

A *right-angled* triangle, often called a *right* triangle, Fig. 18, is one that has a right angle. The longest side (the one opposite the right angle) is called the *hypotenuse* and the other sides are some-times called *legs*.

An *acute-angled* triangle, Fig. 19, is one that has all of its angles acute.

An *obtuse-angled* triangle, Fig. 20, is one that has an obtuse angle.

An *equilateral* triangle, Fig. 21, is one having all of its sides equal.

An *equiangular* triangle is one having all of its angles equal.

An *isosceles* triangle, Fig. 22, is one two of whose sides are equal.

A *scalene* triangle, Fig. 23, is one no two of whose sides are equal.

(a) The *base* of a triangle is the lowest side; it is the side upon which the triangle is supposed to stand. Any side may, however, be taken as the base. In an isosceles triangle, the side which is not one of the equal sides is usually considered as the base.

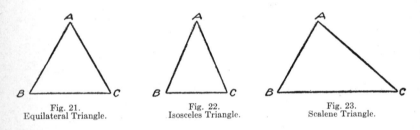

Fig. 21.
Equilateral Triangle.

Fig. 22.
Isosceles Triangle.

Fig. 23.
Scalene Triangle.

(b) The *altitude* of a triangle is the perpendicular drawn from the vertex to the base *A D*, Fig. 24. In some triangles, Fig. 25, it

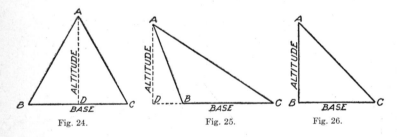

Fig. 24.

Fig. 25.

Fig. 26.

is necessary to produce the base so that the altitude may meet it. In a right triangle one leg may be considered as the base and the other as the altitude, Fig. 26.

Rule: *The sum of the angles of any triangle is equal to two right angles.*

Cut a triangle from a piece of paper or cardboard. Number the angles 1, 2, and 3. Cut off two points of the triangle. Fit the three angles together and you will see that they make the equivalent of two right angles, or 180°.

Keep this rule in mind, for you will find it useful.

Since you know that the sum of all the angles of a triangle is two right angles, or 180°, when you know two of the angles of a triangle you can readily compute the third angle.

Example. Given a right triangle with one of its angles 38° 40′, to find the third angle.

Solution. You know that one angle is 90°, since this is a right triangle, hence the sum of the other two angles must be 90°.

$$90° - 38° \ 40′ = 51° \ 20′$$
$$90° = 89° \ 60′$$
$$\underline{38° \ 40′}$$
$$51° \ 20′$$

PROBLEMS FOR PRACTICE

The following numbers in each case represent two angles of a triangle. Find the size of the third angle.

1.	90° and 45°	Ans. 45°
2.	90° and 60°	Ans. 30°
3.	120° and 40°	Ans. 20°
4.	100° 30′ and 30°	Ans. 49° 30′
5.	60° and 60°	Ans. 60°

How would you describe the triangle of Problem 5?

Ans. Equiangular and equilateral

(c) *Law of the right triangle.* If in the right triangle *A B C*, Fig. 27, the side *A B* is made 3 inches long, and the side *A C* is made 4 inches long, then the side *B C*, called the *hypotenuse*, is found to be 5 inches long.

The proof of this may be found by considering the accompanying figure. The square *A B E D* constructed on the side *A B* contains

9 squares; the square $L\,C\,A\,M$ constructed on the side $A\,C$ contains 16 squares, and the square $C\,F\,G\,B$ constructed on the hypotenuse $B\,C$ contains 25 squares. Now,

$$9 + \quad 16 = 25$$
$$3^2 + \quad 4^2 = 5^2$$
$$\overline{A\,B}^2 + \overline{A\,C}^2 = \overline{B\,C}^2$$

Rule: *The square of the hypotenuse is equal to the sum of the squares of the other two sides.* By means of this relation it is possible

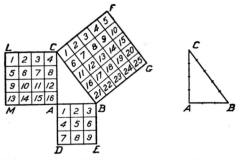

Fig. 27. Graphical Proof of the Law of the Right Triangle.

to find the length of one side of a right triangle if the other two are known.

Examples. 1. A right triangle has sides 6 inches and 10 inches long respectively; what is the length of the hypotenuse?

Solution. Let x represent the hypotenuse.
$$x^2 = 6^2 + 10^2$$
$$= 36 + 100 = 136$$
$$x = \sqrt{136} = 11.66 + \text{inches.} \quad \text{Ans.}$$

2. The hypotenuse of a right triangle is 24 feet long and one of the short sides is 9 feet. How long is the other side?

Solution. Let x represent the other side.
$$24^2 = 9^2 + x^2$$
$$x^2 = 24^2 - 9^2$$
$$= 576 - 81 = 495$$
$$x = \sqrt{495} = 22.248 + \text{feet.} \quad \text{Ans.}$$

3. A ladder 40 feet long when placed on the ground 24 feet from the bottom of a wall reaches to the top. Determine the height of the wall.

Solution. As the ladder is 40 feet long and the base is 24 feet from the wall, there is a right-angled triangle whose hypotenuse is 40 feet, one short side 24 feet, and the other short side to be determined. As in the previous example make use of the law of the right triangle and this will give $40^2 - 24^2 = 1024$. Taking the square root of 1024 will give 32 feet as the height of the wall.

If $H =$ the hypotenuse and a and b the other sides, we have the formula

$$H^2 = a^2 + b^2$$

NOTE. The square is found by multiplying a number by itself. Hence a square is the product of two equal factors, $5 \times 5 = 25$; $5^2 = 25$. One of the two equal factors of a number is called its *square root*. The square root of 25 is 5, written $\sqrt{25} = 5$.

You already know the squares of numbers up to 12. The following squares will be useful for reference and will soon be learned by using them:

$13^2 = 169$	$20^2 = 400$
$14^2 = 196$	$21^2 = 441$
$15^2 = 225$	$22^2 = 484$
$16^2 = 256$	$23^2 = 529$
$17^2 = 289$	$24^2 = 576$
$18^2 = 324$	$25^2 = 625$
$19^2 = 361$	

PROBLEMS FOR PRACTICE

Draw figures and find the unknown side in each of the four problems following:

	Base	Perpendicular	Hypotenuse
1.	12 ft.	9 ft.	?
2.	?	18 ft.	30 ft.
3.	5 ft.	12 ft.	?
4.	3 yd.	?	5 yd.

5. A park is 40 rods long and 30 rods wide. What is the length of a walk running through it from opposite corners in a straight line? Ans. 50 rods

6.　The base and the altitude of a right triangle are equal, and the hypotenuse is 10 feet.　Find the other two sides.

Ans. Each is 7.07+ft.

7.　The foot of a ladder is 15 feet from the base of a building, and the top reaches a window 36 feet above the base.　What is the length of the ladder?　　　　　　　　　　　Ans. 39 ft.

8.　If the gable end of a house 24 feet wide is 10 feet high, what is the length of the rafters?　　　　　Ans. 15.62+ft.

9.　A ladder 35 feet long touches a point in a wall 28 feet from the ground.　How far from the base of the wall is the foot of the ladder?　　　　　　　　　　　　　　　Ans. 21 ft.

79.　Areas of Triangles.　A triangle is a surface and as such has two dimensions, *base* and *altitude*.　Under *denominate numbers* the fact was brought out that surfaces or areas were measured by square measure, and that the area of the surface was proportional to the product of its two dimensions.　If the surface is a triangle it has been found that the *area is equal to one-half of the product of the base by the altitude*.　For example, in Fig. 24 and Fig. 25, the area of each triangle is $\frac{1}{2}(BC \times AD)$.　Other methods might be given but, by the above method, most cases which are met may be easily solved.

Examples.　1.　Find the area of the triangle $A\ B\ C$ shown in Fig. 26 if the base $B\ C$ is 10 inches and the altitude $A\ B$ is 10 inches.

Solution.　Area $=\frac{1}{2}(A\ B \times B\ C) = \frac{1}{2}(10 \times 10) = 50$ square inches.

2.　Find the area of a right triangle whose base is 50 feet and the hypotenuse 200 feet.

Solution.　To obtain the altitude, make use of the law of the right triangle, that is, take the square root of the difference in the squares of the hypotenuse and base of the triangle.

$$\overline{200}^2 - \overline{50}^2 = 40000 - 2500 = 37500$$
$$\sqrt{37500} = 193.64 + \text{ft. altitude of the triangle.}$$

Area of the triangle $=\frac{1}{2}(50 \times 193.64) = 4841$ sq. ft.

Since A = area, b = base, and a = altitude, we have the formula

$$A = \frac{b \times a}{2}$$

Knowing the rule for finding the area of a triangle it is easy to find one dimension when the area and one dimension are given.

Since
$$A = \frac{b \times a}{2}$$

$$2A = b \times a$$

Hence
$$\frac{2A}{b} = a$$

or
$$\frac{2A}{a} = b$$

Writing this out in full, you know that the area is one-half the product of the base and the altitude; therefore, base×altitude = 2×area; from this you easily deduce that 2×area, divided by either dimension will give the other dimension, because the product divided by either factor will give the other factor.

Examples. 1. The area of a triangle is 12 square feet; its altitude is 4 feet. Find its base.

$$A = \frac{(b \times a)}{2}$$

$$12 = \frac{(b \times 4)}{2}$$

$$2 \times 12 = b \times 4$$

$$\frac{24}{4} = b, \text{ or } b = 6$$

Hence the base is 6 feet.

Prove this by using the formula for area, and the values for base and altitude.

$$\text{Area} = \frac{1}{2} \ (6 \times 4) = 12 \text{ sq. ft.}$$

2. The area of a triangle is 56 square feet; its base is 14 feet. Find its altitude.

$$56 = \frac{1}{2}(14 \times a)$$
$$112 = 14 \times a$$
$$a = \frac{112}{14} = 8$$

Hence the altitude is 8 feet.

Proof:

$$\frac{1}{2}(8 \times 14) = 56$$

In finding the area of a right triangle, remember that the two short sides are perpendicular to each other and that, therefore, the area is equal to one-half the product of the two short sides.

PROBLEMS FOR PRACTICE

1. A piece of sheet metal in the form of a triangle weighs 18 pounds. If the height of the triangle is 8 feet and the base 3 feet, what is the weight of the metal per square foot? Ans. $1\frac{1}{2}$ lb.

2. In surveying a triangular piece of land it was found that two of the angles measured 44° 56′ 4″ and 31° 11′ 8″. Compute the value of the third angle. Ans. 103° 52′ 48″

3. An iron brace used in supporting a shelf is fastened to the wall 18 inches below the shelf and to the shelf 12 inches from the wall. Find the length of the brace. Ans. 21.63+in.

4. The area of a triangle is 24 square inches. If the altitude is 6 inches, find the length of the base. Ans. 8 in.

5. An iron chimney is supported by a guy wire which makes an angle of 63° 24′ with the ground. Determine the angle between the chimney and guy wire. Ans. 26° 36′

6. Find the altitude of a triangle whose area is 48 acres and whose base is 48 rods. Ans. 1 mi.

7. If one end of a ladder 50 feet long rests on the ground 10 feet from the base of a wall, how far from the ground does the top of the ladder touch the wall? Ans. 49−ft.

8. Find the area of the right triangle of Problem 7.

9. Find the area of a triangle whose base is 9 inches and altitude 6 inches. Ans. 27 sq. in.

QUADRILATERALS

80. A *quadrilateral* is a polygon bounded by four straight lines, as Fig. 28.

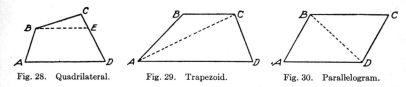

Fig. 28. Quadrilateral. Fig. 29. Trapezoid. Fig. 30. Parallelogram.

A *trapezoid* is a quadrilateral having two sides parallel, Fig. 29. The parallel sides are called the *bases* and the perpendicular distance between the bases is called the *altitude*.

A *parallelogram* is a quadrilateral whose opposite sides are parallel, Fig. 30.

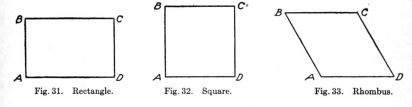

Fig. 31. Rectangle. Fig. 32. Square. Fig. 33. Rhombus.

The three important kinds of parallelograms are as follows: The *rectangle*, Fig. 31, whose angles are right angles.

The *square*, Fig. 32, all of whose sides are equal and whose angles are right angles.

The *rhombus*, Fig. 33, whose sides are equal but whose angles are not right angles.

81. Areas of Quadrilaterals. Considering first the *trapezoid*, it will be seen that in Fig. 29 the dotted line $A\,C$ (called a *diagonal*) divides the figure into two triangles, $A\,B\,C$ and $A\,C\,D$, whose altitudes are the same, namely, the altitude of the trapezoid. By a previous rule the areas of these triangles will be respectively

$$\frac{1}{2}\,(\text{altitude} \times B\,C) \text{ and } \frac{1}{2}\,(\text{altitude} \times A\,D)$$

Therefore Area of trapezoid $=$ altitude $\times \dfrac{B\ C + A\ D}{2}$

Rule: (a) *The area of a trapezoid is equal to the product of the altitude by one-half the sum of the bases.*

The area of a *quadrilateral* like that shown in Fig. 28 may be obtained by drawing a line, $B\ E$, parallel to the base $A\ D$. The figure will then be divided into a trapezoid and an extra triangle whose areas are measurable by the methods given.

The *parallelogram*, Fig. 30, may also be divided by means of a diagonal into two triangles whose areas are respectively $\dfrac{A\ D \times\ altitude}{2}$ and $\dfrac{B\ C \times\ altitude}{2}$. But $A\ D$ and $B\ C$ are equal and, consequently, the sum of these areas $= \dfrac{2(A\ D \times altitude)}{2} = A\ D \times altitude$.

Example. Find the area of a trapezoid whose parallel sides are 60 rods and 80 rods, and whose altitude is 30 rods.

Solution. Represent the two bases by b and b'. The formula may then be written

$$A = \frac{b + b'}{2} \times a$$

Substituting the values given for this problem

$$\text{Area} = \frac{60 + 80}{2} \times 30$$
$$\text{Area} = 70 \times 30 = 2100$$

Since   160 sq. rd. $= 1$ Acre
             2100 sq. rd. $= 13$ A. 20 sq. rd.

Rule: (b) *The area of a parallelogram is equal to the product of the base and the altitude.* This will be true of any parallelogram and hence true of the rectangle, Fig. 31, the square, Fig. 32, and the rhombus, Fig. 33. In the case of the first two, the fact that the angles are all right angles makes the length of the vertical side become the altitude.

$$A = b \times a$$

Find the area in acres of a parallelogram whose base is 80 rods and altitude 60 rods.

$$A = b \times a$$
$$A = 80 \times 60 = 4800$$
$$4800 \text{ sq. rd.} = 30 \text{ acres}$$

The complete solution may be written

$$A = \frac{80 \times 60}{160} = 30$$

Rule: (c) *The area of a rectangle is equal to the product of two adjacent sides.* This has already been learned in denominate numbers. The fact that all land measurements are made in the rectangular system makes the rectangle an extremely important figure.

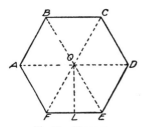

Fig. 34. Hexagon.

Areas of Other Polygons. In finding the areas of polygons, other than the triangle and quadrilateral, the system of dividing the figure into triangles is used. For example, the regular *hexagon*, Fig. 34, consists of six equal equilateral triangles, and consequently the area of the hexagon will be $\dfrac{6(F\,E \times O\,L)}{2} = 3(F\,E \times O\,L)$.

Rule: (d) *The area of a regular hexagon is equal to three times the product of one side (which is the same as $\frac{1}{2}$ the perimeter) by the perpendicular distance from the side to the center of the hexagon.*

The perpendicular distance from the center to one side of a regular polygon is called the *apothem*.

Example. The perimeter of a hexagon is 36 feet. Find the perpendicular distance and the area of the hexagon.

Solution. If the perimeter of the hexagon is given as 36 feet, one side (as *A B*) is ⅙ of 36, or 6 feet.

Since the triangles are equilateral, the distance from any point (*A, B, C, D, E. F*) to the center is equal to the length of one side, or 6 feet.

To find the perpendicular distance from the center to one side, consider one of the triangles, as *F O E*.

Note how the altitude, *O L*, divides the triangle into two equal right-angled triangles, and the base, *F E*, into two equal parts.

Find *O L* by the law of the right triangle, page 115. (See Example 2, page 116.)

$$6^2 - 3^2 = x^2$$
$$36 - 9 = x^2$$
$$x^2 = 27$$
$$x = \sqrt{27} = 5.196+$$

The perpendicular distance is 5.196+ feet.
The area of the hexagon is 3×6×5.196, or 93.528 sq. ft.

Answers: 5.196 ft.; 93.528 sq. ft.

PROBLEMS FOR PRACTICE

1. What is the area of the end of a regular hexagonal drain tile whose sides are 2 inches in length and whose perpendicular distance from the center to a side is 1.7 inches?   Ans. 10.2 sq. in.

2. How much would it cost to lay a concrete sidewalk 8 feet wide and 525 feet long at 20 cents per square foot?   Ans. $840

3. How many square yards of plastering are needed for walls and ceiling of a room 10×12 feet and 9 feet high; the room contains a door $3\frac{1}{2}$×7 feet and two windows $3\frac{1}{2}$×6 feet?   Ans. 50–sq. yd.

4. An irregular-shaped room has two parallel sides, one 14 ft. 8 in. long, the other 20 ft. 3 in. long. One end of the room is perpendicular to the two sides and is 12 ft. 5 in. long. What will it cost to paint the floor at 25 cents per square yard?   Ans. $6.02+

5. A trough 2 feet deep with equally sloping sides is constructed. One end is 5 feet across the top and 4 feet across the bottom. How many square feet of tin will be required for the end? Ans. 9 sq. ft.

CIRCLES

82. A *circle* is a plane figure bounded by a curved line called the *circumference*, every point of which is equally distant from a point within called the *center*, Fig. 35.

A *diameter* of a circle is a straight line drawn through the center, terminating at both ends in the circumference.

Fig. 35. Circle.

A *radius* of a circle is a straight line joining the center and the circumference. All radii of the same circle are equal and their length is always one-half that of the diameter.

An *arc* is any part of the circumference of a circle.

An arc equal to one-half the circumference is called a *semi-circumference*.

A *chord* is a straight line joining the extremities of an arc, Fig. 36. When a number of chords form the sides of a polygon, the polygon is said to be *inscribed in the circle*.

A *segment* of a circle, Fig. 37, is the area included between an arc and a chord.

A *sector* is the area included between an arc and two radii drawn to the extremities of the arc, Fig. 37.

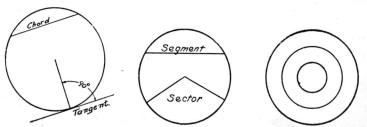

Fig. 36. Chord and Tangent.   Fig. 37. Segment and Sector.   Fig. 38. Concentric Circles.

A *tangent* is a straight line of unlimited length which touches the circumference at only one point, called the *point of tangency* or *point of contact*, Fig. 36. It may be proved that a tangent is perpendicular to a radius drawn to the point of tangency.

Concentric circles are circles having the same center, Fig. 38.

Relation of the circumference to the diameter. If the lengths of the circumference and the diameter of a circle are carefully measured, the ratio, $\dfrac{\text{circumference}}{\text{diameter}}$, will be found to have a fixed value, whatever circle may be selected. This constant ratio has been given the name π (Greek letter *pi*) and has a value of 3.1416 (approximately $\dfrac{22}{7}$).

Therefore, *the circumference of any circle is equal to π times the diameter*.

The formula may then be written

$$C = \pi \times d$$

When the circumference is given, the diameter may be found by dividing by π.

$$d = \frac{C}{\pi}$$

The value $\dfrac{22}{7}$, or $3\dfrac{1}{7}$, may be used for rough calculations, but 3.1416 is more nearly correct, and should be used when greater accuracy is desired. Sometimes the value 3.14159 is given and used. In many cases the value $\dfrac{22}{7}$ may be used with safety as the error is only about .04%. Then, to find the circumference when the diameter is known, *multiply the diameter by $\dfrac{22}{7}$.* Conversely, to find the diameter when the circumference is known, *divide the circumference by $\dfrac{22}{7}$.*

83. Areas of Circles. The circle may be divided into a number of equal sectors, Fig. 39, that are essentially triangles. The radius of the circle represents the altitude of these triangles, and the arc represents the base. Hence the area of all the sectors, Fig. 40 (which is the area of the circle), is one-half the radius multiplied by the sum of all the arcs, which is the circumference. From this explanation the rule is obtained.

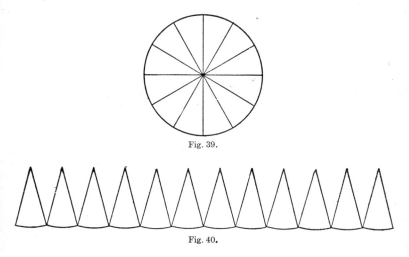

Fig. 39.

Fig. 40.

Rule: *The area of a circle is equal to the circumference multiplied by one-half the radius.*

$$\text{Area} = \frac{1}{2}(C \times r), \text{ or } C \times \frac{r}{2}$$

But you have already had the rule $C = \pi \times d$. Substituting this for C in the formula for area

$$\text{Area} = \pi \times d \times \frac{r}{2}$$

Since diameter
$$= 2r$$

$$\text{Area} = \pi \times 2r \times \frac{r}{2}$$

or
$$\text{Area} = \pi \times r \times r$$

This in turn gives the formula

$$A = \pi r^2$$

This is the most commonly used formula and for many the most easily remembered.

In terms of the diameter the formula becomes

$$\text{Area} = \pi \times d \times \frac{d}{4}$$

because

$$r = \frac{d}{2}, \frac{r}{2} = \frac{d}{4}$$

From this formula the rule is obtained that the area equals .7854 times the diameter squared, because

$$\pi \times d \times \frac{d}{4} = \frac{1}{4}(\pi \times d \times d)$$

$$\frac{1}{4} \text{ of } 3.1416 = .7854 \text{ and } d \times d = d^2$$

It is well to remember this rule also. The formula is

$$A = \frac{1}{4}\pi d^2$$

From the formula $A = \pi r^2$, the radius equals the square root of the quotient when the area is divided by π. Or, in formula

$$r = \sqrt{A \div \pi}$$

Likewise from the formula $A = \frac{1}{4}\pi d^2$ the value of the diameter may be found.

$$d = \sqrt{A \div \frac{1}{4}\pi} = \sqrt{A \div .7854}$$

Examples. 1. Find the radius of a circle whose area is 392.70 square rods. Ans. 11.18 rd.

$$r = \sqrt{392.7 \div 3.1416}$$
$$= \sqrt{125} = 11.18+$$

2. Find the diameter of a circle whose area is 78.54 square inches.

$$d = \sqrt{A \div \frac{1}{4}\pi} = \sqrt{78.54 \div .7854} = \sqrt{100} = 10$$

Ans. 10 in.

It has been shown that a line has but one dimension, and a surface or area, two. If this be true, then an expression representing a length contains *one* dimension and an expression representing area contains *two* dimensions. The circumference of a circle is πd, in which the diameter is the *dimension* and π is a ratio, or pure number. Again, the area of a circle is πr^2, in which $r \times r$ gives the *two* dimensions; similarly the formula for area of a triangle is $\frac{1}{2}(b \times a)$, in which b and a are the dimensions.

EXERCISES

Find the circumference if the diameter is:

1. 10 in.   3. 5 ft.
2. 12 ft.   4. 2 ft. 6 in.

Find the diameter when the circumference is:

1. 126.7112 ft.   Ans. 40 ft. 4 in.
2. 94.248 in.   Ans. 30 in.
3. 87.9648 yd.   Ans. 28 yd.
4. 39.27 ft.   Ans. 12 ft. 6 in.

When the circumference equals 125.664 feet, what is the radius?
                                           Ans. 20 ft.

Circumference $= C$; diameter $= d$; radius $= r$; area $= A$

Find the area if

1. $d = 10$ rd.   5. $C = 3.1416$ ft.
2. $r = 10$ rd.   6. $d = 25$ yd.
3. $d = 18$ ft.   7. $C = 94.248$ in.
4. $r = 60$ ft.   8. $r = 20$ yd.

The student is recommended to use the value for π, 3.1416. When π is written together with a figure or a letter, the multiplication sign is understood between them. Thus, 2π means 2×3.1416, and πr^2 means 3.1416 times the square of the radius.

PROBLEMS FOR PRACTICE

1. When the diameter of a circle is $7\frac{3}{4}$ inches, what is the radius?   Ans. $3\frac{7}{8}$ in.
2. What is the circumference of a 4-foot wheel? Ans. 12.5664 ft.

3.   How far will a 6-foot wheel go in making 110 revolutions?
Ans. 2073.456 ft.

4.   How many revolutions will the same wheel make in going 1 mile?   Ans. 280.112+

5.   The diameter of a pulley is 18 inches.   What is the circumference?   Ans. 56.5488 in.

6.   The bottom of a tank is circular and is 3 feet in diameter. What is the area of the bottom?   Ans. 7.0686 sq. ft.

7.   What is the area of one side of a flat circular ring whose outside diameter is 8 inches and inside diameter 4 inches?   Ans. 38-- sq. in.

8.   A carriage wheel 4 feet in diameter makes how many revolutions in traveling 1,000 feet?   Ans. 79.57+rev.

9.   The circumference of a circular chimney is 47.12 feet. What is its diameter?   Ans. 14.99+ ft.

10.   What will it cost to build a walk 5 feet wide around a circular flower bed 24 feet in diameter, at 35 cents per square yard?
Ans. $17.71

SOLIDS

84.   A *solid* has three dimensions—length, breadth, and thickness.   The most common forms of solids are *prisms, cylinders, pyramids, cones,* and *spheres.*

PRISMS

85.   A *prism* is a solid having two opposite faces, called *bases,* which are equal and parallel, and other faces, called *lateral faces,* which are parallelograms.   The *altitude* of a prism is the perpendicular distance between the bases.

Prisms are called *triangular, rectangular, hexagonal,* etc., according to the shape of the bases.   Further classifications are as follows:

Fig. 41.   Right Prism.

Fig. 42.   Parallelepiped.

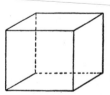

Fig. 43.   Rectangular Parallelepiped.

A *right* prism is one whose lateral faces are perpendicular to the bases, Fig. 41.

A *regular* prism is a right prism having regular polygons for bases.

A *parallelepiped* is a prism whose bases are parallelograms, Fig. 42. If all the edges are perpendicular to the bases, it is called a *right parallelepiped*.

A *rectangular parallelepiped* is a right parallelepiped whose bases and lateral faces are rectangles, Fig. 43. When these faces are all squares the prism is called a *cube*.

86. Areas of Prisms. The *area of the bases* of any given prism is to be found by the method already given for that particular shape of base. The *lateral area*, as each face is a parallelogram, will be the sum of the products of each base line by the altitude. This is equivalent to the product of the perimeter of the base by the altitude. The *total area* will evidently be the sum of the areas of the two bases and the lateral faces.

Example. Find the total area of a box 3 feet long, 2 feet wide, and 6 feet deep.

Solution. The area of one base is 2×3 or 6 sq. ft., and of two, 12 sq. ft.

The perimeter of the base $= 2+2+3+3 = 10$ ft.; the altitude $= 6$ ft.

The lateral area $= 10 \times 6 = 60$ sq. ft.

The total area $= 60+12 = 72$ sq. ft. Ans.

The total area of a cube is the sum of the six square surfaces that bound it. The line where any two of the surfaces meet is called the *edge* of the cube.

87. Volumes of Prisms. It has already been made clear in the discussion of *Cubic Measure* in denominate numbers that the measurement of volume involves the product of the three dimensions of the figure and is determined by the number of times the unit of cubic measure, such as the cubic inch, cubic centimeter, or cubic foot, is contained in the volume under consideration. If A, Fig. 44, represents a cubic foot, it will be noticed that A is contained four times in the bottom layer of B. As there are three layers, A is contained a total of twelve times in B, that is, the volume of B is 12 cubic feet.

But the area of the base of B is 4 sq. ft. and the altitude is 3 ft. The product of these two gives 12 cu. ft., the same as obtained by the use

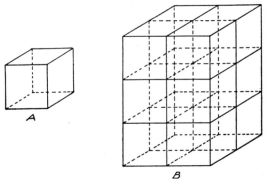

Fig. 44. Volume of a Rectangular Solid.

of the unit A. Rule: *The volume of any prism is equal to the product of the area of the base by the altitude.*

If V represents volume; l, length; w, width; and h, height, we have the formula

$$V = l \times w \times h$$

PROBLEMS FOR PRACTICE

1.   What is the weight of a cast-iron block 6 inches long, 5 inches wide, and 3 inches high? The block is a rectangular parallelepiped and weighs .26 pounds per cubic inch.   Ans. 23.4 lb.

2.   How many square feet of sheet copper will be required to make an open rectangular tank 7 feet long, 3 feet wide, and $1\frac{1}{2}$ feet deep, allowing 10% extra for waste?   Ans. 56.1 sq. ft.

3.   How many cubic feet of concrete will be required to construct a column 15 feet high having a hexagonal cross section. The cross section is $1\frac{1}{2}$ feet long on each side of the hexagon and the perpendicular distance from center to each side is 1.3 feet.   Ans. 87.75 cu. ft.

4.   What will it cost to paint the above column, exclusive of the base and top, at 35 cents per square yard?   Ans. $5.25

5.   Find the volume of a triangular prism whose altitude is 20 feet and each side of the base 4 feet.   Ans. 138.4 cu. ft.

6.   Find the total area of the prism given in Problem 5.

Ans. 253.84 sq. ft.

CYLINDERS

88. A *cylinder* is a solid having as bases two equal parallel plane surfaces and as its lateral face the continuous surface generated by a straight line connecting the bases and moving along their cir-

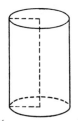

Fig. 45. Right Cylinder.

cumferences. The bases are usually circles and such a cylinder is called a *circular cylinder*.

A *right cylinder*, Fig. 45, is one whose side is perpendicular to the bases.

89. You may make a figure in the form of a cylinder by rolling a sheet of paper or a card until its opposite sides meet. Thus you see that the length of the card or paper is the altitude of the cylinder, and the width is the distance around, or the perimeter, of the cylinder. You can now see that the lateral area of the cylinder is equal to the product of the circumference of the base by the altitude.

$$\text{Lateral area} = C \times a, \text{ or } Ca$$

The total area is evidently equal to the sum of the areas of the bases and the lateral area.

Example. How much tin will be required to make a cylindrical can, 3 inches in diameter and 4 inches high, allowing nothing for seams and waste?

Solution. The can is a right cylinder the circumference of whose base is $\frac{22}{7} \times 3 = \frac{66}{7} = 9.43$ inches, nearly. Now, the radius of the base is $3 \div 2 = 1\frac{1}{2}$ inches, and the area of the base $\frac{22}{7} \times (1\frac{1}{2})^2 = 7.07$ sq. in.,

The lateral area is $9.43 \times 4 = 37.72$ sq. in.

The total area equals $37.72+(2\times7.07)=37.72+14.14=51.86$ square inches.

90.   Volumes of Cylinders.   *The volume of a cylinder is equal to the product of the area of one base by the altitude.*

$$V=a\times\pi r^2$$

Examples.   1.   Find the volume of a cylinder the diameter of whose base is 20 inches, and whose altitude is 30 inches.

Solution.   You have given the diameter of the base, 20 inches, and the altitude of the cylinder, 30 inches.   First find the area of the base.

$$\text{Area}=\pi r^2$$

When diameter$=20$ inches, $r=10$

$$\pi r^2=3.1416\times 100=314.16$$
$$V=314.16\times 30=9424.8 \text{ cu. in.}$$
$$9424.8\div1728=5.45+\text{cu. ft., or 5 cu. ft. 784.8 cu. in.}$$

2.   A piece of iron weighing 30 pounds has 4 holes 6 inches deep and 1 inch in diameter bored into it.   What is the weight of the piece after the boring has been completed, iron weighing .26 pounds per cubic inch?

Solution.   Each hole has a radius of $\dfrac{1}{2}$ inch and its volume is then $\dfrac{22}{7}\times(\tfrac{1}{2})^2\times6=4.7$ cu. in.

There are 4 holes making $4\times4.7=18.8$ cu. in.
The weight of the material cut out is $18.8\times.26=4.9$ lb.
Then the final weight is $30-4.9$ lb. $=25.1$ lb.

PROBLEMS FOR PRACTICE

1.   What is the capacity of a cylindrical tank 9 feet long and 5 feet in diameter, inside measurements?

2.   If a gallon contains 231 cubic inches, what must be the diameter of a cylindrical tank 10 feet high which will hold 1,000 gallons?   Ans. 4.1+ft.

3.   Find the number of square feet of material necessary for a straight piece of copper pipe 10 feet long and 12 inches in diameter.

PYRAMIDS

91. A *pyramid* is a solid whose base is a polygon and whose sides are triangles.

The vertices of the triangles meet to form the *vertex* of the pyramid.

The *altitude* of the pyramid is the perpendicular distance from the vertex to the base.

Pyramids are named according to the kind of polygon forming the base, namely, triangular, quadrangular, Fig. 46; pentagonal, Fig. 47; hexagonal, Fig. 48.

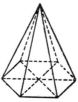

Fig. 46. Pyramid. Fig. 47. Regular Pyramid. [Fig. 48. Hexagonal Pyramid.

A *regular* pyramid is one whose base is a regular polygon and whose vertex lies in a perpendicular erected at the center of the base, Fig. 47, Fig. 48, Fig. 49.

The *slant height* of a regular pyramid is a line drawn from the vertex perpendicular to a side of the base. (See the line *O F*, Fig.

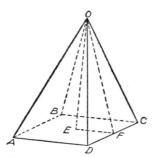

Fig. 49. Pyramid Showing Altitude and Slant Height.

49.) In other words, it is the altitude of one of the triangles which form the sides.

The *lateral edges* of a pyramid are the intersections of the triangular sides, called the *faces*.

92. Areas of Pyramids. (a) The *lateral area* is the combined area of all the triangles forming the sides.

The area of each triangle is equal to the product of the base by one-half the altitude. Therefore the lateral area of a pyramid is found by adding the products of each side of the base by one-half the same altitude; that is, it is equal to the perimeter of the base multiplied by one-half the slant height. If the slant height is not given it can usually be found by means of the law of the right triangle.

(b) The *total area* of a pyramid is equal to the sum of the lateral area and the area of the base.

Example. Find the lateral area and total area of the pyramid shown in Fig. 49, if it has an altitude $O\,E$ of 12 feet and each side of the square base is 8 feet.

Solution. $E\,F = 4$ feet. Since the angle $O\,E\,F$ is a right angle

$$\overline{OF}^2 = \overline{OE}^2 + \overline{EF}^2$$
$$= 144 + 16$$
$$= 160$$
$$OF = \sqrt{160} = 12.65 \text{ (nearly)}$$

$$\text{The lateral area} = \frac{12.65 \times 32}{2}$$

$$= 202.4 \text{ square feet.} \quad \text{Ans.}$$

The area of the base is $8 \times 8 = 64$ sq. ft., making the total area $64 + 202.4 = 266.4$ sq. ft. Ans.

93. Volumes of Pyramids. It may be shown that any triangular prism may be divided into three equivalent triangular pyramids, having bases and altitudes equal to those of the prism; and therefore the volume of each pyramid must be one-third of the volume of the prism. But the volume of a prism is equal to the product of the area of the base by the altitude; therefore, *the volume of a pyramid is equal to the product of the area of the base by one-third of the altitude.*

$$V = \text{Area of Base} \times \frac{1}{3} \text{ Altitude}$$

or

$$V = \frac{B \times h}{3}$$

Here $B =$ Area of base and $h =$ height or altitude of the pyramid.

Example. What is the volume of a triangular pyramid whose base is 3 feet on a side, and whose altitude is 9 feet?

Solution. The base is an equilateral triangle. Find the altitude.

$$3^2 - \left(\frac{3}{2}\right)^2 = 9 - \frac{9}{4} = \frac{27}{4}$$

$$\sqrt{\frac{27}{4}} = \frac{5.196}{2} + = 2.598 +$$

$$\text{Area of base} = \frac{3 \times 2.598}{2} = 3.897 +$$

$$\text{Volume} = 3.897 \times \frac{9}{3} = 11.691 + \text{cu. ft.} \quad \text{Ans.}$$

PROBLEMS FOR PRACTICE

1. A triangular pyramid is 9 inches in height and each side of the base is 4 inches long. Find the volume.　　Ans. 20.76 cu. in.

2. What is the volume of a square pyramid one side of whose base is 4 inches and whose height is 4 inches?　　Ans. $21\frac{1}{3}$ cu. in.

3. Find the total area of a square pyramid whose slant height is 28 inches and one side of whose base is 8 inches.　　Ans. 512 sq. in.

4. A regular hexagonal pyramid has an altitude of 18 inches, and each side of the hexagon is 6 inches long. Find total area and volume of pyramid.　　Answers: 430.84+sq. in.; 561.16+cu. in.

CONES

94. A *cone* is a solid bounded by a conical surface and a plane which cuts the conical surface. It may be considered as a pyramid with an infinite number of sides.

The conical surface is called the *lateral area*, and the plane is called the *base*. The conical surface tapers to a point called the *vertex*.

The *altitude* of a cone is the perpendicular distance from the vertex to the base.

An *element of the cone* is any straight line from the vertex to the perimeter of the base. Such a line is the *slant height* of the cone.

A *circular cone* is a cone whose base is a circle, Fig. 50.

A *right circular cone*, or *cone of revolution*, Fig. 51, is a cone whose axis is perpendicular to the base. It may be generated by the revolution of a right triangle about one of the sides as an axis.

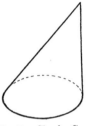

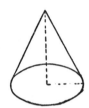

Fig. 50.   Circular Cone.
               Fig. 51.   Cone of Revolution.

Cut a right triangle of cardboard. Stand it upright on its base, and turn it once around, keeping the altitude in the same position. You will make a circle whose radius is the base of the right triangle.

The circle is the *base* of a cone of revolution, the hypotenuse of the triangle is the slant height of the cone, and the altitude of the triangle is the altitude of the cone. See Fig. 51.

95. Areas of Cones. The *lateral area* of a cone is found in the same way as in the case of a pyramid. *Multiply the perimeter of the base by one-half the slant height.*

Example. The base of a cone is 12 inches in diameter and the slant height is 16 inches. What is the total area?

$$\textit{Solution.} \quad \text{Perimeter of base} = 12 \times \frac{22}{7}$$

$$= 37.71 \text{ inches}$$

$$\text{Lateral area} = 37.71 \times \frac{16}{2}$$

$$= 301.68 \text{ square inches}$$

To find the *total area*, add to this the area of the base. In the above example, the area of the base is

$$\frac{22}{7} \times 36 = 113.14 \text{ sq. in.}$$

Total area $= 113.14 + 301.68 = 414.82$ square inches.

96. Volumes of Cones. As a cone may be considered a pyramid with an infinite number of sides, it follows from Section 93 that *the volume of a cone is equal to the product of the area of the base by one-third the altitude.*

Example. The altitude of a cone is 18 inches and the radius of the base is 2 inches. What is the volume?

$$\text{Area of base} = \frac{22}{7} \times 4 = 12.57$$

$$\text{Volume} = 12.57 \times 6 = 75.42 \text{ cubic inches}$$

In case the altitude is not known, it may be found if the slant height and the radius of the base are known.

PROBLEMS FOR PRACTICE

1. Find the volume of a cone whose altitude is 12 inches and the diameter of whose base is 6 inches.　　　　Ans. $113\frac{1}{7}$ cu. in.

2. Find the total area of a cone having an altitude of 21 feet and a base whose diameter is 15 feet.　　　　Ans. 702.4 sq. ft.

3. Find the lateral area of a cone whose diameter is 17 feet 6 inches, and the slant height 30 feet.　　　　Ans. 824.67 sq. ft.

4. Find the solid contents of a cone whose altitude is 24 feet, and the diameter of whose base is 30 inches.　　　Ans. 39.28+cu. ft.

SPHERES

97. A *sphere* is a solid bounded by a curved surface, every point of which is equally distant from a point within called the *center.*

The *diameter* is a straight line drawn through the center and having its extremities in the curved surface. The *radius* is the straight line from the center to a point on the surface; it is equal to one-half the diameter.

A *plane is tangent to a sphere* when it touches the sphere in only one point. A plane perpendicular to a radius at its outer extremity is tangent to the sphere.

98. Areas of Spheres. To find the *area* of the surface of a sphere, *multiply the square of the diameter by* $\frac{22}{7}$.

Example. Find the area of the surface of a sphere which is 9 inches in diameter.

$$9^2 = 81. \quad 81 \times \frac{22}{7} = 254.6 \text{ square inches}$$

To find the *diameter* when the surface is given, *divide the surface by* $\frac{22}{7}$ *and extract the square root of the quotient.*

Example. What is the diameter of a sphere whose area is 113.14 square feet?

$$113.14 \div \frac{22}{7} = 36 \text{ nearly.} \quad \sqrt{36} = 6 \text{ feet}$$

99. Volumes of Spheres. To find the *volume* of a sphere, multiply the cube of the diameter by $\frac{\pi}{6}$ (equal to $\frac{11}{21}$ nearly).

Examples. 1. A sphere is 10 inches in diameter; what is the volume?

$$10^3 = 1000. \quad 1000 \times \frac{11}{21} = 523.8 \text{ cubic inches}$$

2. Find the volume of a sphere having a diameter of 7 feet.

$$7^3 = 343; \quad 343 \times \frac{11}{21} = 179\tfrac{2}{3} \text{ cubic feet}$$

PROBLEMS FOR PRACTICE

1. The surface of a sphere contains 314.16 square inches. What is the diameter?   Ans. 10 in.

2. What will be the volume of an aluminum sphere which has a diameter of 15 inches?   Ans. 1.02 cu. ft.

3. How much will a sphere of cast iron weigh if it is 3 feet in diameter and iron weighs 450 pounds per cubic foot? Ans. 6364$\tfrac{2}{7}$ lb.

4. How much will it cost to paint the sphere in Problem 3 at 25 cents per square yard?   Ans. 78$\tfrac{4}{7}$¢.

5. How much less surface has a sphere which is 12 inches in diameter than a cube with an edge of 2 feet? Ans. 20.85+sq. ft.

6. A spherical balloon, when inflated, has a diameter of 50 feet. Find the surface and the number of cubic feet of gas contained in the bag.   Answers: 7857$\tfrac{1}{7}$ sq. ft.; 65,476$\tfrac{4}{21}$ cu. ft.

GRAPHS

The method of presenting the results of research, as well as the compiling of statistics and various tables of information, by pictorial means is familiar to all readers of newspapers and magazines. Some of the most common means of such presentation are the line, or bar, the sector, and the curve.

The following graph, Fig. 52, represents the yield of corn in several states: Kansas, 174,225,000; Nebraska, 182,616,000; Indiana, 174,600,000; Iowa, 432,021,000; Illinois, 426,320,000.

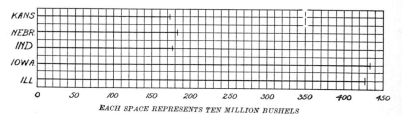

Fig. 52.   Graph Showing Yield of Corn in Five States.

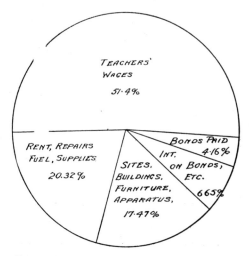

Fig. 53.   Graph Showing Distribution of School Funds.

The graph represented in Fig. 53 shows the distribution of $13,649,000 spent for school purposes in a western state.

By means of squared paper the results of experiments and observations of various kinds can be represented by lines and curves.

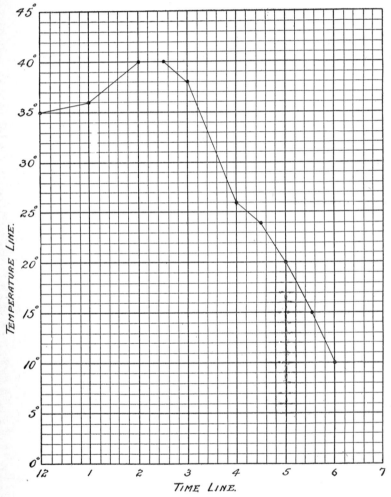

Fig. 54.   Curve Showing Temperature for Six Hours.

A curve showing the temperature for six hours, from noon to 6 P. M., is shown, Fig. 54. Notice that the hours are shown on a horizontal line, or axis, and the temperature on a vertical line, or axis.

Time	Temperature
12:00 noon	35°
1:00	36°
2:00	40°
2:30	40°
3:00	38°
4:00	26°
4:30	24°
5:00	20°
5:30	15°
6:00	10°

Curves can be drawn showing the cost of doing contract work or of operating a certain machine; the variation in temperature of a fever patient in a hospital; the fluctuations in the price of wheat; or the cost of living. The range of application is unlimited. The student can readily see that curves are valuable records for commercial and professional men, as well as for trained engineers, skilled machinists, and statisticians.

ILLUSTRATIVE CURVES

Curves for Squares and Square Roots. In Fig. 55 is shown a curve expressing the relation of numbers and the squares of those numbers. Curves of this kind are very practical, and, as can be readily seen, may be used to save time in all kinds of mathematical work. Compare, for example, the time required to find the *square* of 9.8 mathematically and the time to take the result directly from the above curve. To understand thoroughly the method of using such a curve, the following explanation will be helpful. Five divisions on the horizontal axis equal one unit and, therefore, each division equals $\frac{1}{5}$, or $\frac{2}{10}$, or .2. On the vertical axis there are five divisions to ten numbers and, therefore, each division equals $\frac{1}{5}$ of 10, or 2. First find on the horizontal axis the point whose value is 9.8. It will be between 9 and 10, just one line short of division 10. Follow this line upward until it meets the curve and from this point go horizontally to the left until the vertical axis is reached. On this line read the value. It is between 90 and 100, three divisions **above**

90. Each division represents 2, therefore three divisions equal 6. This must be added to 90, giving as a final result 96 approximately.

To find the *square root* of a number the above method would be reversed, using the same curve. Find the number on the vertical

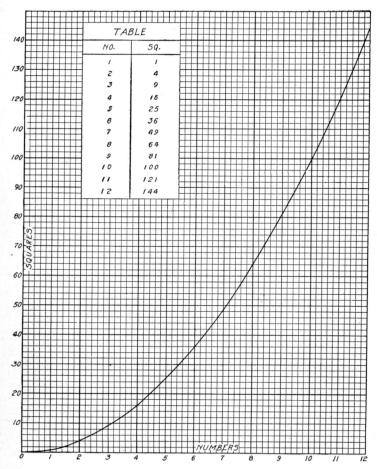

TABLE	
NO.	SQ.
1	1
2	4
3	9
4	16
5	25
6	36
7	49
8	64
9	81
10	100
11	121
12	144

Fig. 55. Curve of Squares and Square Roots.

axis whose root is to be extracted, then follow horizontally across the sheet to the point of intersection with the curve and then downward to the horizontal axis. The value found there will be the square root; for instance, the square root of 96 = 9.8 approximately.

CURVE PROBLEMS FOR PRACTICE

1. Plot the curve from the following data for the cost of high-speed compound engines, using thousands of dollars for vertical values and horsepower for horizontal values. What will be the cost of a 750-horsepower engine of this type?

Dollars	Horsepower
6400	400
9600	600
12800	800
16000	1000
24000	1500
32000	2000
40000	2500
48000	3000

2. Plot the curve from the following data for the increase of Chicago's population, using population in thousands as vertical values and years for horizontal values. Assuming the same increase in the next decade as in the last, find the population of Chicago in 1920.

Population	Years
109,206	1860
178,492	1865
306,605	1870
400,500	1875
503,185	1880
665,000	1885
1,099,850	1890
1,366,813	1895
1,698,575	1900
1,949,116	1905
2,195,551	1910

3. Plot the curve from the following data for the areas and diameters of circles, using areas for vertical values and diameters for horizontal values. What is the diameter of a circle having an area of 40 square inches?

Area Square Inches	Diameter Inches
.7854	1
3.1416	2
7.0686	3
12.566	4
19.635	5
28.274	6
38.485	7
50.265	8
63.617	9
78.540	10
95.033	11
113.097	12

4. The average monthly rainfall in inches at a certain station in Nebraska for 35 years ending 1909 was as follows:

Jan. .42	May 2.86	Sept. 1.47
Feb. .49	June 3.41	Oct. 1.10
Mar. .81	July 2.90	Nov. .46
April 2.04	Aug. 2.37	Dec. .49

Represent by means of squared paper.

EXERCISES

Look at these expressions and see how many of them you can define *accurately*, in mathematical language: diameter, acute, equation, ratio, obtuse, arc, radius, sector, altitude, circumference, cube root, hypotenuse, perimeter, slant height, right angle, plane, solid, dimension, area, volume, trapezoid, lateral area, prism, pyramid, cylinder, cone, sphere.

Write the formulas for the following areas: triangle, square, trapezoid, circle, hexagon, right triangle, parallelogram, lateral area of a cone.

Write the formulas for the following volumes: cube, rectangular prism, cylinder, pyramid, cone.

Write these exercises and then check your own answers by referring to the book.

GENERAL SUGGESTIONS FOR THE SOLUTION OF PROBLEMS

In considering a problem there are several points that are especially important:

1. Read the problem carefully, several times, to make sure that you understand the exact meaning of it.

2. Analyze the problem, separating the information given from the result that is required, and determining how the result is to be obtained from the conditions given in the problem.

It is not always necessary to set down a complete analysis, but enough should be shown to indicate that the student has *mentally* gone through all the steps necessary for the solution. A complete *statement* should be set down. The equation method is recommended. Do not write out an analysis in words.

3. The solution should involve no unnecessary work. Cancellation and other short methods should be used if possible.

4. All arithmetical work should be carefully checked. The student must realize that *accuracy* is of the highest importance, and that to insure accuracy his work must always be checked. Arithmetical work that has an error in it is of no practical value. The check also gives the student a means of knowing for himself whether his work is right or not. In the real business of life he is not furnished with answers to his problems.

Another way to check on your work is to examine your result from the standpoint of *reasonableness*. By this is meant to read the problem carefully and then think whether your result seems to you a reasonable result for the conditions given in the problem. Often an error is detected at once by applying this test. It may be a mistake in calculation, or in the placing of a decimal point. Such mistakes are found by checking, and by applying the rule for placing the decimal point. If your result still seems wrong, go over your methods and see if you have used the right one in each step of the work. Verify each rule you have used.

'5. It is often a good plan to state a problem in one step so as to shorten the work by cancelling.

Examples. 1. A canning factory can put up 300 cans of peas per hour. If an acre produces 640 cans of peas, how long will it take the factory to put up the product of 75 acres, if the men work 8 hours a day, 6 days in the week?　Give the answer in weeks.

$$\frac{75 \times 640}{300 \times 8 \times 6} = \frac{10}{3} \text{ or } 3\tfrac{1}{3} \qquad \text{Ans. } 3\tfrac{1}{3} \text{ wk.}$$

2.　What is the expense of covering a floor with plain matting 1 yard wide, the room being 21 by $23\tfrac{1}{2}$ feet, the matting worth 40 cents a yard, allowing 6 inches extra on each strip?

$$\frac{21 \times 24 \times .40}{9} = 22.40$$

or

$$7 \times 8 \times .40 = 22.40$$

A room 21 feet wide requires exactly 7 strips of matting.

Hence　　　　$23\tfrac{1}{2}$ ft. $+ 6$ in. $= 24$ ft., or 8 yd.
　　　　　　　$7 \times 8 \times .40 = $ cost of the matting.

The two steps of reasoning may be taken mentally and not set down.

In working with problems involving decimals, carry to as many places as the given quantities or the formulas show.　For example, any problem in which you use π should be accurate to at least four decimal places.

"Accurate to two decimal places" refers to the *final* result, and not to the intermediate steps of a problem.

Note: For ready reference, common tables used in solving problems will be found on page 152 preceding the examination.

MISCELLANEOUS PROBLEMS

NOTE: These problems are *not* to be sent to the School. They are given so that the student may test his knowledge and progress.

1. Simplify:

(a) $\dfrac{6\frac{3}{4}+(5\frac{1}{2}\times3\frac{1}{2})-7\frac{1}{2}}{6\frac{2}{5}+5-8\frac{1}{5}}$

(b) $(.26\times.3\times.02)\div(.5\times.01\times1.04)$

(c) $(2\frac{1}{15}+1\frac{5}{6})\div(8-5\frac{2}{5})$ Answers: (a) $5\frac{25}{32}$; (b) .3; (c) $1\frac{1}{2}$

2. If evaporation from a tank is estimated at $6\frac{1}{4}\%$ in a week, how many gallons will be lost from a tank that has a capacity of 6400 gallons but which is only 75% full at the beginning?

Ans. 300 gal.

3. Find the number of hours it will take a locomotive running at the rate of 36 miles per hour to make the distance passed over by another locomotive running 9 hours at the rate of 48 miles per hour.

Ans. 12 hr.

4. A steel rail 30 feet long weighs 720 pounds. What is its weight per yard of length?

5. What is the area of a square one side of which is $9\frac{1}{2}$ feet?

Ans. $90\frac{1}{4}$ sq. ft.

6. What is the side of a square whose area is 64 square inches?

7. How many square feet of floor area in a freight car whose inside dimensions are 33 feet 6 inches by 8 feet 3 inches?

Ans. $276\frac{3}{8}$ sq. ft.

8. How many square feet of glass in a window containing 4 panes, each 18 inches by 36 inches?   Ans. 18 sq. ft.

9. How many square feet in the walls of a room 30 feet long, 18 feet wide and 16 feet high?   Ans. 1536 sq. ft.

10. What is the area of the ceiling of the same room?

Ans. 540 sq. ft.

11. Which is larger, a triangle having a base of $6\frac{1}{2}$ inches and an altitude of $3\frac{1}{4}$ inches, or a parallelogram whose base is $4\frac{1}{4}$ inches and whose altitude is $2\frac{3}{8}$ inches? How much?

Ans. The triangle. $\frac{15}{32}$ sq. in.

12. Find the area of a trapezoid whose altitude is 8 inches and whose parallel sides are respectively 18 inches and 24 inches.

Ans. 168 sq. in.

13. Find the area of a triangle whose base is 26 inches and whose altitude is 15 inches.   Ans. 195 sq. in.

14. Find the base of a triangle whose altitude is 18 inches and whose area is 90 square inches.   Ans. 10 in.

15. If the area of an obtuse triangle is 34 square inches and the altitude is $4\frac{1}{4}$ inches, what is its base?   Ans. 16 in.

16. Find the area of a right triangle whose two legs are 5 inches and 12 inches and whose hypotenuse is 13 inches.

In finding the area of this triangle, which of the dimensions is unnecessary? Why?

17. How many pieces of zinc 4 inches ×6 inches can be cut from a sheet of zinc 3 feet×6 inches?   Ans. 9 pieces

(The sign × used as above means "by.")

18. If a sheet of copper 30 inches×60 inches weighs 25 pounds, what is the weight per square foot?   Ans. 2 lb.

19. What is the area of a parallelogram whose base is 14 feet and whose altitude is 8 feet?   Ans. 112 sq. ft.

20. What is the altitude of a parallelogram whose base is 16 feet and whose area is 80 square feet?   Ans. 5 ft.

21. Find the cost at 65 cents per square yard of a concrete platform rectangular in shape, 100 feet long and 25 feet wide.

Ans. $180\frac{5}{9}$

22. The sides of a right triangle are 16 and 30 inches, respectively. What is the hypotenuse?   Ans. 34 in.

23. A guy wire is fastened to the top of a wireless tower 454 feet high and is anchored to the ground 724 feet from the foot of the tower. Find the length of the wire.   Ans. 854.57+ft.

24. One side of a right triangle is 9 feet, and the hypotenuse is 41 feet. Find the length of the other side.   Ans. 40 ft.

25. A tree was broken off 10 feet from the ground and the top struck the ground 40 feet from the foot of the tree. What was the height of the tree?   Ans. 51.23+ft.

26. If the circumference is $3\frac{1}{7}$ times the diameter, and the drive wheel of a locomotive is 6 feet in diameter, how many revolutions will it make in going 140 miles?   Ans. 39,200 rev.

27. Soldiers marching quickstep take 120 steps per minute, averaging $2\frac{1}{2}$ feet each step. At this rate, how far will a company of soldiers march in an hour?   Ans. $3\frac{9}{22}$ mi.

28. The diameters of two concentric circles are 20 feet and 30 feet. Find the area of the ring.   Ans. 392.7 sq. ft.

29. Find the circumference and the area of the largest circle that can be drawn in an 8-foot square.

     Answers: 25.133— ft.; 50.266— sq. ft.

30. The diagonal of a square field is 40 rods. How many acres are in the field?   Ans. 5 A.

31. Find the cost, at 25 cents a rod, of building a fence around a 10-acre square field.   Ans. $40

32. How many cubic feet in a Portland cement pillar in the form of a right cylinder whose diameter is 12 inches and whose height is 15 feet?   Ans. 11.781 cu. ft.

33. If Portland cement weighs 10 pounds per cubic foot, what is the weight of the pillar?   Ans. 117.81 lb.

34. A cylindrical water tank 24 feet high has a capacity of 32,000 cubic feet. What is the diameter?   Ans. 41.2 ft.

35. How many cubic yards must be removed in digging a tunnel 468 feet long, 21 feet wide, and 18 feet 6 inches deep?

     Ans. 6734 cu. yd.

36. The volume of a rectangular parallelepiped is 100 cubic inches. The area of one end is 20 square inches. Find the length.

     Ans. 5 in.

37. How many cubic feet of air are in a room 12 feet 6 inches long, 10 feet 8 inches wide, and 9 feet high?   Ans. 1200 cu. ft.

38. Find the weight of a rectangular block of stone at 135 pounds per cubic foot, if the length is 10 feet and the other two dimensions are 2 feet and 5 feet.

39. How many tons of coal will a bin 10 feet by $6\frac{1}{2}$ feet by $7\frac{2}{3}$ feet hold, if one ton occupied 36 cubic feet?

     Ans. 13 T. 16 cwt. $85\frac{5}{27}$ lb.

If the student can solve these problems with ease, he is ready to write the examination. On the other hand, if the problems give him serious trouble, a careful review of the textbook is needed. With due care in the preparation of the work given for practice, every student will be able to do excellent work in his examination paper.

LINEAR MEASURE

12 inches (in. or ″) = 1 foot (ft. or ′)
3 feet   = 1 yard (yd.)
$5\frac{1}{2}$ yards or $16\frac{1}{2}$ ft. = 1 rod (rd.), pole, or perch
320 rods or 5280 ft. = 1 mile (mi.)

A *knot*, used in navigation, is equal to 1.15 miles.
A *fathom* is equal to six feet.

SQUARE MEASURE

144 square inches (sq. in.) = 1 square foot (sq. ft.)
9 square feet   = 1 square yard (sq. yd.)
$30\frac{1}{4}$ square yards   = 1 square rod (sq. rd.)
160 square rods   = 1 acre (A.)
640 acres   = 1 square mile (sq. mi.)

CUBIC MEASURE

1728 cubic inches (cu. in.) = 1 cubic foot (cu. ft.)
27 cubic feet   = 1 cubic yard (cu. yd.)
128 cubic feet   = 1 cord (cd.)
8 cord feet   = 1 cord (cd.)

LIQUID MEASURE

4 gills (gi.)   = 1 pint (pt.)
2 pints   = 1 quart (qt.)
4 quarts   = 1 gallon (gal.)
$31\frac{1}{2}$ gallons   = 1 barrel (bbl.)
2 barrels, or 63 gallons = 1 hogshead (hhd.)

One U. S. standard gallon contains 231 cubic inches, and one gallon of water weighs approximately $8\frac{1}{3}$ pounds.

One cubic foot of water contains approximately 7.5 U. S. standard gallons and weighs 62.3 pounds.

SQUARES AND SQUARE ROOTS OF NUMBERS

Number	Square	Square Root	Number	Square	Square Root
1	1	1	51	2601	7.141
2	4	1.414	52	2704	7.211
3	9	1.732	53	2809	7.280
4	16	2	54	2916	7.348
5	25	2.236	55	3025	7.416
6	36	2.449	56	3136	7.483
7	49	2.646	57	3249	7.550
8	64	2.828	58	3364	7.616
9	81	3	59	3481	7.681
10	100	3.162	60	3600	7.746
11	121	3.317	61	3721	7.810
12	144	3.464	62	3844	7.874
13	169	3.606	63	3969	7.937
14	196	3.742	64	4096	8
15	225	3.873	65	4225	8.062
16	256	4	66	4356	8.124
17	289	4.123	67	4489	8.185
18	324	4.243	68	4624	8.246
19	361	4.359	69	4761	8.307
20	400	4.472	70	4900	8.367
21	441	4.583	71	5041	8.426
22	484	4.690	72	5184	8.485
23	529	4.796	73	5329	8.544
24	576	4.899	74	5476	8.602
25	625	5	75	5625	8.660
26	676	5.099	76	5776	8.718
27	729	5.196	77	5929	8.775
28	784	5.291	78	6084	8.832
29	841	5.385	79	6241	8.888
30	900	5.477	80	6400	8.944
31	961	5.568	81	6561	9
32	1024	5.657	82	6724	9.055
33	1089	5.745	83	6889	9.110
34	1156	5.831	84	7056	9.165
35	1225	5.916	85	7225	9.220
36	1296	6	86	7396	9.274
37	1369	6.083	87	7569	9.327
38	1444	6.164	88	7744	9.381
39	1521	6.245	89	7921	9.434
40	1600	6.325	90	8100	9.487
41	1681	6.403	91	8281	9.539
42	1764	6.481	92	8464	9.592
43	1849	6.557	93	8649	9.644
44	1936	6.633	94	8836	9.695
45	2025	6.708	95	9025	9.747
46	2116	6.782	96	9216	9.798
47	2209	6.856	97	9409	9.849
48	2304	6.928	98	9604	9.899
49	2401	7	99	9801	9.950
50	2500	7.071	100	10000	10

ELECTRIC PASSENGER LOCOMOTIVE IN USE ON NEW YORK, NEW HAVEN, AND HARTFORD ROADS

Courtesy of Westinghouse Electric and Manufacturing Company

*PRACTICAL PHYSICS

PART I

INTRODUCTION

We are a careless and unobserving people; we ride day after day on the electric cars without a thought of the wonderful machines which make this ride possible; we are content idly to observe the many operations of nature all about us without an effort to find out *why* they operate as they do. And yet, the proper explanations of most of the phenomena whose occurrence and recurrence we witness day by day are so much along the line of the commonplace that Physics, the science which treats of these phenomena, has sometimes been called "the science of common sense."

In order to be effective, however, our common sense must be supported by actual knowledge of certain fundamental laws, upon which these various processes of nature are based. A proper appreciation of the law of Conservation of Energy will effectively prevent a man of inventive mind from wasting his mental and physical energy on a *perpetual-motion* device ; a consideration of the principles of heat engines may satisfy him at once that a certain form of engine which he has been developing will not revolutionize the engineering industry. Investigation of such familiar phenomena as the motion of bodies, the working of machines, the occurrence of the seasons, and of day and night, and the behavior of electricity will show that they are simple demonstrations of these laws, whose importance to one who is starting the broad subject of engineering should be self-evident, and a thorough knowledge of which will serve as a foundation upon which the study of the more advanced work may be based.

---

* The author wishes to acknowledge having freely consulted the following textbooks, particularly the first mentioned: Millikan and Gale's "First Course in Physics," Adams' "Physics," and Hoadley's "Elements of Physics".

FORCE AND MOTION

FORCE

§1. Definition of Force. Time was when the behavior of any peculiar device or even an illustration of nature's simplest laws was ascribed to some occult power. Today no one thinks it strange to see a trolley car moving along a track, an aëroplane flying through the air, or a complicated set of wheels going round and round in a glass case. That there is *motion* is considered sufficient proof that some *force* has been or is at work—so convincing, indeed, that the observer's curiosity will not be sufficiently aroused to make him investigate the cause of the motion. Those acquainted with the trolley car will consider it certain that under the car there is an electric motor through which a current of electricity must be flowing in order to produce the force to drive the car. The average observer will be sure that the man in the aëroplane, Fig. 1, has under his control an engine which is driving the bird-like object through the air. The wheels under the glass case may *appear* to be running without cause, but every one will be sure that a thorough investigation will reveal a hidden spring or electric motor. In short, all of the motions described will be thought of as perfectly natural and in each case as the result of the action of some force which is known and understood.

But does force always produce motion? A stone may lie for ages on the brink of a cañon, until a touch of the foot sends it crashing hundreds of feet below. Yet the force of attraction of the earth for the stone was just as properly in action during the long period of rest, as it was when the stone was in motion. The steam in the engine cylinder forces the piston back and forth, and makes the driving wheels go around, but it acts with equal force on the cylinder head without producing any motion. The engineer of a fast-moving train can, by opening the throttle wider, increase the speed of his train, or, by applying the force of the air-brakes to the moving wheels, can destroy the motion and bring the train to a stand-still.

Force may, therefore, be defined as *any cause which tends to produce, to change, or to destroy motion.*

Fig. 1. Claude Grahame-White Landing in the Streets of Washington

§2. Measurement of Forces. It is well known that different objects have different weights, a fact easily proved by our sensations in lifting these objects. The heavy ones take a greater muscular effort because the force exerted must counterbalance the greater pull of gravity. Forces, therefore, may be measured in terms of the attraction of the earth for a given body. Thus, the English unit of weight, the *pound*, and the Metric unit, the *gram*, represent the pulls of gravity on certain definite quantities of matter. A body weighing 2 pounds will be attracted by the earth with twice as much force as will the body weighing 1 pound, and a body weighing 10 grams with 10 times the force of 1 gram. These bodies are, therefore, said to be capable of exerting *1 pound, 2 pounds, 1 gram, or 10 grams of force,* and by comparing unknown forces with these whose values are known, the unknown values may be determined.

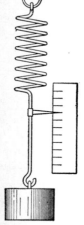

Fig. 2. Elongated Spring

Fig. 3. Spring Balance

Fig. 4. Butchers' Scales

The expression "a force of 2 tons" means that the measure of the attractive force of the earth for the given mass is 2 tons or 4,000 pounds. A very simple method of comparing the pulls of various bodies is by means of a coiled spring, Fig. 2. If a 1-gram weight stretches the spring a certain amount, say 2 divisions of the scale, a 2-gram weight will stretch it twice the distance, or 4 divisions; 10 grams will stretch it 20 divisions, etc. It is, therefore, only necessary properly to incase the spring and to provide a suitable scale in order to have means of determining the value of any unknown force. Such an instrument is called a *spring balance*, Fig. 3, and, in one form or another, is extensively used for butchers' scales, Fig. 4, letter scales, etc.

COMPOSITION AND RESOLUTION OF FORCES

§3. Graphical Representation of Forces. A force is completely defined when its *magnitude, its direction,* and its *point of application* are given. The graphical methods already studied in Practical Mathematics, Part III, have shown that a line may properly represent a force because it has length, corresponding to the magnitude of the force; direction, corresponding to the direction of the force; and a point from which it starts, corresponding to the point of application of the force.

For example, if the lengths of the two lines AB and AC, Fig. 5, are made proportional to the forces which they represent, *i.e.*, in the ratio of 2:3, they may represent two forces of 2 and 3 pounds, respectively, acting at the point A in the direction indicated by the arrows.

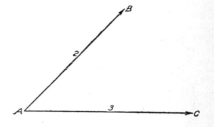

Fig. 5. Graphical Representation of Forces

Again, if a boat is rowed directly across a stream at the rate of 5 miles an hour, while the current flowing 3 miles an hour carries the boat down stream, these forces may be represented by a horizontal line 5 inches long and by a vertical line 3 inches long acting downward.

§4. Resultant of Two Forces Acting in the Same Line. The resultant of two forces is defined as *that single force which will produce the same effect upon a body as is produced by the joint action of the two forces.*

Opposed Forces. In case two forces are acting in opposite directions, it is evident that the effect of one will tend to neutralize the effect of the other and the *resultant will be the difference between the two forces.*

For example, if one tug-of-war team pulls east with a force of 1,000 pounds and another team pulls west with a force of 1,100 pounds, the resultant is a single force of 100 pounds acting in the direction of the stronger team.

Combined Forces. When the forces are acting in the same direction, one force evidently assists the other and the *resultant is equal to the sum of the two forces.*

§5. Resultant of Two Forces Acting at an Angle. When two forces simultaneously act at a point but not in the same direction, the final effect obtained is as though each force had acted independently of the other.

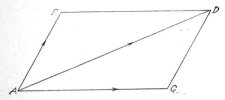

Fig. 6. Parallelogram of Forces

For example, suppose a body at *A*, Fig. 6, is acted upon by forces which are represented by the lines *AB* and *AC*. If at first only *AB* is allowed to act, the body will be carried, say to *B*; then the force *AC*, acting parallel to its original direction, will carry the body to D. Evidently if the order is reversed and *AC* is allowed to act first, the path traveled by the body will be *ACD*. When, however, these two forces are allowed to act at the same instant, the body follows a path along the line *AD*, *i.e.*, along the *diagonal of the parallelogram* formed on the two given forces as sides. When the lines *AB* and *AC* are drawn to represent the forces according to a certain scale, then the diagonal represents in length and direction the combined effect or *resultant* of the two forces.

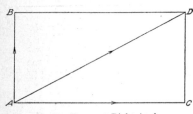

Fig. 7. Forces at Right Angles

If the forces *AB* and *AC* are at right angles to each other, the parallelogram becomes a rectangle, Fig. 7, and the value of the resultant *AD* may be obtained either by plotting the forces and measuring the length of the diagonal *AD*, or by solving for the value of the hypotenuse *AD* by the law of the right triangle (Practical Mathematics, Part III). This result, which is known as the *Law of the Parallelogram*, may now be stated as follows:

If two given forces are represented in direction and in magnitude by two lines, then their resultant will be exactly represented both in direction and in magnitude by the diagonal of the parallelogram of which the lines representing the two given forces are the sides.

When there are more than two forces, *any two* may be selected, as *OA* and *OB*, Fig. 8, and their resultant *OR₁* found. This resultant *OR₁*, considered as one force, and the next force *O C* may be treated in the same manner, and so on until all the forces have been included. The line *OR₃* represents the resultant action upon the body *O* of the

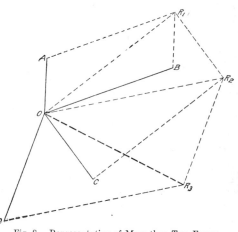

Fig. 8.   Representation of More than Two Forces

four forces shown in the figure. An example of three forces is shown in the traveling crane, Fig. 9, in which the hook can be moved up or down, across the room, and down the room.

Fig. 9.   Electrically Operated Traveling Cranes

Equilibrant. If a body is already being acted upon by one or more forces, then it should be possible to bring into play another *single* force having such a value and direction that no motion shall result; this single force is called the *equilibrant.* In the cases shown in Fig. 6 and Fig. 7, the body at *A*, by virtue of the action of the forces *AB* and *AC*, would tend to move along *AD*. If, now, a force exactly equal but opposite to the resultant *AD*, were to act upon the body, it should neutralize completely the motion due to the forces, *if the resultant AD is really the equivalent of the two original forces.* By setting up practical conditions this fact may be proved experimentally.

Let the two spring balances F_1 and F_2, Fig. 10, be suspended from a beam and let their lower hooks be connected by a string. If, now, a weight *W* is fastened to the string at the point *A*, the two spring balances

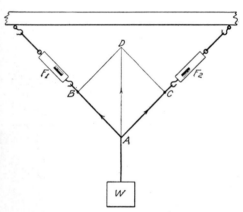

will be stretched until the whole system comes to rest. (Of course, *W* must not be so heavy as to extend F_1 and F_2 beyond the limits of their scales.) This *equilibrivm* will result when the two spring balances are pulling hard enough to develop two forces *AB* and *AC*, whose resultant, the diagonal *AD*, is exactly equal and opposite to the force *W*. If *W* is 12 pounds and the readings of F_1 and F_2 are each 8.5 pounds, it only remains to plot the parallelogram *ABDC* and to determine the value of *AD* in order to prove whether it is equal and opposite to *W*. To accomplish this, support a drawing board vertically back of the strings and, after locating carefully the point *A* on the paper, draw lines in the directions of *AB* and *AC*. Now, if distances be laid off on the lines *AB* and *AC*, equal to 8.5 inches—1 inch to represent 1 pound—and the parallelogram carefully completed, the diagonal *AD* will be found to measure very nearly 12 inches *i.e.*, it is equivalent to a force of about 12 pounds.

Fig. 10.   Experimental Proof of Balanced Forces

This experiment shows that at the moment when the movement produced by attaching the weight *W* stops, the system is in equilibrium and *W* is the equilibrant of the forces F_1 and F_2. To bring

Fig. 11. The First Span of the Quebec Bridge in Process of Erection

Fig. 12. The Ruins of the Bridge Showing the Tangled Mass of Steel after the Collapse

about *balanced conditions* is the problem of the architect and the engineer in every piece of work which they do, whether it be in a structure of steel and cement, a trussed roof, a bridge, or what not.   Unbalanced forces cause destruction, and if a building collapses during the process of construction, the engineer knows that somewhere the size of an I-beam was miscalculated, or a riveted connection was weak, or a foundation was faulty.   The giant cantilever bridge which was being placed across the St. Lawrence River at Quebec in 1906 and 1907 had been the marvel not only of the observing laymen but of engineers as well.   Some idea of the immense size of the structure may be obtained from Fig. 11, the vertical distance from the water to the bridge at the extreme left being 150 feet, and the span 1,800 feet.   This illustration shows how the sections were being built on, the size of each steel rod being supposedly calculated so as to bear the strain which ultimately would be put upon it—a perfect system of balanced forces.   Something was wrong in the calculation of the sizes of the members for, in August, 1907, this mammoth structure collapsed, Fig. 12, without warning, hurling tons upon tons of steel into the waters of the St. Lawrence and carrying nearly 100 workmen to their death.

§6.   **Component of a Force.**   It seems reasonable to suppose that, if two forces may be combined into a single force—the resultant—which completely replaces them, then any force may be split up into two parts or *components*, acting at right angles to each other, and completely representing the original force.

Fig. 13.   Pulling a Freight Car by a Force Acting at an Angle with the Track

For example, if a horse is pulling a car along a track, the wise old fellow has learned from experience to appreciate the fact that he is making a part of his force ineffective unless he pulls in the exact direction in which the car must go.   If he pulls at an angle with the track, Fig. 13, his force F is split up into two parts, one part C_1 acting in the direction the car must go and obviously less than the original; and another part C_2 at right angles to the first, tending to pull the flanges of the wheels against the rails and having no effect on the forward motion of the car.

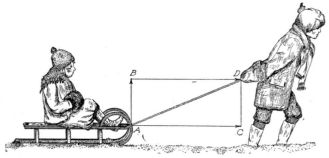

Fig. 14.   Only the Horizontal Component Useful

Again, the small boy who draws sister on his sled is really pulling along AD, Fig. 14, which makes the effective component equal to AC and the useless one equal to AB, the latter force tending to lift the sled at each pull.

Therefore, *the component of a force in a given direction is the effective value of that force in that direction.*

Value of the Component of a Force in Any Direction. Since by definition the two components AB and AC at right angles to each other, Fig. 14, completely represent the pull along AD, it follows that the values or magnitudes of these components must be represented by the sides of a rectangle of which AD is the diagonal. Therefore, *to find the effective component of a force in a given direction, draw a line to represent the force AB, Fig. 15, and from its extremity drop a perpendicular to meet the line representing the given direction AE. The distance cut off on this line represents the value of the effective component AC.* In other words, if the

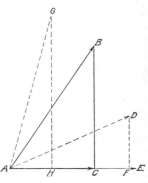

Fig. 15.   Effective Component of a Force

force represented by AB were pulling a body along AE while it, itself, had to act in the direction AB, this force would have a value equal only to AC. If its angle is less, as DAE, its component AF is greater; if its angle is greater, as GAE, its component AH is less. When the angle is 90 degrees, the component is evidently zero and when the angle is zero then the force and its component become one and the same. This agrees with the common observation that the effort necessary to move a body in a fixed direction is greater, the greater the angle which the force makes with that direction.

Suppose it is desired to find the force necessary to hold on the incline a barrel weighing 100 kilos, Fig. 16. The length of the incline AB is 6 meters and the height BC is 2.4 meters. Now let xz represent the force of gravity acting upon the barrel; as gravity must always act vertically downward, only a component of this force will be effective in carrying the barrel down this plane. This component must be found by completing the rectangle on xz as a diagonal, giving yz the component acting down the plane, and xy the component producing a pressure on the plane. Evidently the force which will be necessary to hold the barrel

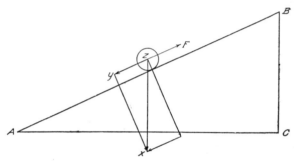

Fig. 16.   Analysis of an Inclined Plane

on the incline will be a force F equal and opposite to yz. By geometry the triangles xyz and ABC can be proved similar and, therefore, their sides are proportional. This gives

$$AB : BC :: xz : yz$$
$$6 : 2.4 :: 100 : x$$
$$6x = 240$$
$$x = 40 \text{ kilos}$$

It will require 40 kilos to keep the barrel from rolling down the incline.

PROBLEMS FOR PRACTICE

1. As a preliminary, solve the following examples in the Metric system, using the approximate reduction units given in Practical Mathematics.

(a) Change 2,000 millimeters to meters; to kilometers.

(b) Change 63 kilos to pounds.

(c) Find the approximate number of centimeters in 12 feet.

(*d*)   How many centimeters in 2.8 kilometers?   In 42 meters?

(*e*)   Change 420 feet to centimeters.   To meters.

(*f*)   How many grams in 7.5 kilos?

(*g*)   Find the value of 4,400 pounds expressed in kilos.

2.   Forces of 6 and 8 pounds act upon a point.   Find their resultant (*a*) if they act in the same direction; (*b*) if they act in opposite directions; (*c*) if they act at right angles.

3.   A steamboat can go down stream at the rate of 15 miles per hour and up stream at the rate of 9 miles per hour.   What is the speed of the current?   Ans. 3 miles.

4.   Find the value of the equilibrant of two forces at right angles to each other, one of 900 grams and the other of 1,600 grams.   Ans. 1836−grams.

5.   A weight of 400 kilos is supported by an iron brace *ABC*, fastened to a wall, Fig. 17.   The brace *BC* makes an angle of 45° with the wall.   Find the pull along *AB;* the thrust of the rod *BC*.

6.   A horse pulls a car with a force of 1,200 lb. but at such an angle that the component at right angles to the track is 400 lb. Find the effective component of the force, *i. e.*, along the track.

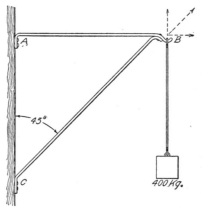

Fig. 17.   Iron Brace Supporting a Weight

7. What force is needed to support 2 tons on a smooth incline, if the grade is 10 per cent?   Ans. 400 lb.

Note: Engineers designate by the term *grade* the rise of an incline per 100 feet of *horizontal distance*, expressed as a per cent.   Where the grade per cent is small, the slope distance is used instead of the horizontal distance.   Thus a "6 per cent grade" means that for a length of slope of 100 feet the rise is 6 feet.

8.   A track is to be laid along rising ground so that (neglecting friction) a force of 100 pounds will just pull a weight of 1 ton up the incline.   What must be the grade?

9.   A boy is pulling a sled in such a way that his effective horizontal pull is 75 lb. and his vertical pull is 25 lb.   Find the actual pull along the rope.   Ans. 79+ lb.

GRAVITATION

§7. Newton's Law of Universal Gravitation. The fact that all bodies when unsupported fall toward the earth has been known since the creation of man, but it remained for Sir Isaac Newton, the great physicist, astronomer, and mathematician, to study successfully this mysterious attraction and to discover its law of action. The law as stated by him is as follows:

Every body in the universe attracts every other body with a force which varies directly as the product of the masses and inversely as the square of the distance between the two bodies.

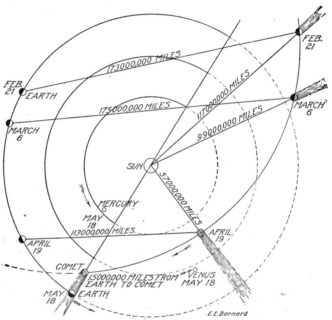

Fig. 18.　Diagram of a Portion of Solar System Including Halley's Comet

It is by the operation of this law that the sun holds planets and comets in their orbits, Fig. 18; that the earth holds the moon in its position, retains the moving things upon its surface, and even prevents the atmosphere, which is so necessary to life, from wandering off into space. The measure of the pull of gravity upon a body is called its *weight* and is found to depend upon the amount of matter in the body and upon its distance from the center of the earth where the attraction of gravity is considered concentrated.

At the poles, for instance, where the surface of the earth is nearest the center, a body weighs slightly more than it does at the equator, while the balloonist who reaches a height of 4 miles above the earth weighs about $\frac{1}{3}$ of a pound less than at the surface of the earth.

§8. Center of Gravity. A body of spherical shape like the earth attracts bodies as if all of its mass were concentrated at its center, and hence the plumb-bob, which the carpenter or brick-layer holds up as a guide in setting his timbers or brick courses, is pulled directly toward the center of the earth. In the same man-

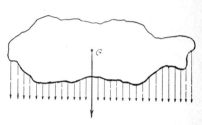

Fig. 19. Graphical Conception of Center of Gravity

ner the attractive force of the earth for a body may be considered, not as a lot of little forces acting on every particle of the body, Fig. 19, as is actually the case, but as a single force acting on a certain point G. This point, called the *center of gravity*, is the point where all of the weight of the body may be considered concentrated. For any regular body like a sphere or a cube, the center of gravity is at the geometrical center; but for irregular bodies like a log or a chair, the center of gravity must be found by experiment, *i.e.*, by suspending the body and a plumb-line successively from points a, b, and c, Fig. 20, marking on the body the paths followed by the plumbline and finding where they intersect.

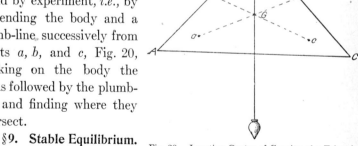

Fig. 20. Locating Center of Gravity of a Triangle

§9. Stable Equilibrium. A body is in stable equilibrium when it is not easily tipped from its position, as, for example, a table, a trunk, or a flat stone resting on its side. If the body, Fig. 21, is tipped up, it revolves about a center O and the center of gravity of the body is raised. The body falls back to its original position on being released, unless the center of gravity G has reached a point G' directly above the center of revolution O, at which point a very

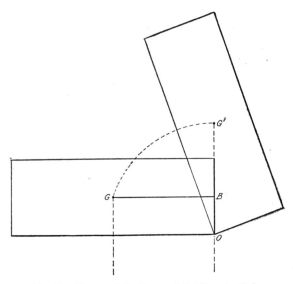

Fig. 21. Measure of the Degree of Stability of a Body

slight additional displacement will send the body over onto its end. Evidently the distance BG' indicates the degree of stability of a body, for it shows to what height the center of gravity must be raised in order to overbalance the body. A ten-pin needs only a touch to topple it over, while a loaded trunk requires considerable force; in the one case the raising of the center of gravity only a fraction of an inch will carry it outside the base, while in the other, the greater weight is combined with a much lower center of gravity. Bodies ordinarily un-

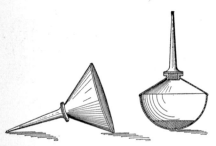

Fig. 22. Loaded Oil Can with Hemispherical Body

stable may easily be made stable by loading the bottom. A clever application of this idea is shown in the loaded oil can, Fig. 22, which always remains upright. In general, a body is stable if a slight displacement tends to raise the center of gravity.

§10. Unstable Equilibrium. When a body has a small base like an inverted cone or an egg on end, Fig. 23, it will either fall over of its own accord, or the slightest touch will throw the center of gravity *outside the base*, thereby causing the body to tip over. Therefore, when a slight movement tends to *lower the center* of gravity, the body is in unstable equilibrium.

Fig. 23.   Examples of Unstable Equilibrium

§11. Neutral Equilibrium. A body which will remain in any position in which it is placed is in neutral equilibrium, as, for example, a sphere, or a cone lying on its side. In general, a body is in neutral equilibrium when a slight displacement neither raises nor lowers its center of gravity.

PROBLEMS FOR PRACTICE

1. What is the object of ballast in a ship?

2. What is the measure of stability of a body?

3. Show how the stability of a body may be determined graphically.

4. Stick a knife blade into a pencil and it may be balanced easily upon the end of the finger, Fig. 24. Locate center of gravity of system; explain stability.

5. Why can an automobile safely round a corner at high speed, while a buggy might easily overturn?

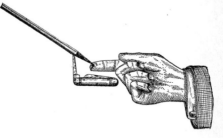

Fig. 24.   Peculiar Example of Equilibrium

6. What is the object of the long stick carried by the tight-rope walker?

7. Why does a person lean forward in climbing a hill?

8. What is the location of the center of gravity of a circular hoop; of a straight iron bar; of the loaded oil can of Fig. 22?

MOTION

§12. Definition. A body is said to be in motion when it is changing its position with reference to a certain point which is considered at rest. All motion is, therefore, relative in that the point of reference, although at rest with respect to the earth, will be moving with respect to the moon or the sun.

Suppose that two men sit at opposite ends of an electric car which is leaving the town at a rate of 10 miles per hour. The men, with reference to the car, or the people in it, are at rest, but with reference to the town, they are in motion at the rate of 10 miles an hour. Now if the man at the rear of the car moves forward, his motion relative to the town is the car rate plus his own walking rate on the car, while with reference to the other man it is merely his walking rate.

Again, if a ship were making 20 miles per hour at sea, a man running on deck from stern to bow, also at a rate of 20 miles per hour, would be making 40 miles per hour relative to the water, while if he ran at the same speed from bow to stern his motion would neutralize the forward motion of the ship, and make him virtually at rest relative to the water.

§13. Velocity. Velocity is the rate of motion of a body and is measured by the number of units of space passed over in a unit of time. If the motion is steady, *i.e.*, if the number of units of space passed over in each succeeding unit of time is the same, the motion is called *uniform*. An example of such motion is found in the movements of the earth and other planets, each of which accomplishes its revolution about the sun in a certain set time. When the motion is not uniform, an average velocity may be calculated by dividing the total distance covered in a given time by the number of units of time. During this interval the body may have changed velocity many times, but for purposes of calculation the effect is as if a uniform rate of motion had been kept up during the entire period. The 20th Century Limited may stop, slow-up for crossings, grades, and curves, and speed up on the straight stretches, but its uniform velocity in miles per hour is obtained by dividing 1,000 miles—the approximate distance from New York to Chicago—by 18 hours. Hence

$$V = \frac{S}{T}$$

where V is the velocity, S is the distance passed over, and T is the time. By means of this expression, any one factor may be obtained if the other two are known.

NEWTON'S LAWS OF MOTION

§14. **First Law—Inertia.** Among the many things which Sir Isaac Newton did for science are included the formulation of three statements on the relation between force and motion. The first law is stated as follows:

Every body continues in its state of rest or of uniform motion in a straight line unless compelled by an external force to change that state.

There are many illustrations of the actions of bodies which are approximately in accord with this law, but the absolute proof is not an easy matter. The fact that a body "at rest remains at rest" is supported by common observation, but when it is in motion, that ever-present *external force* always tends to make the illustration break down. For example, it is easy to start a ball through the air, but it is known from experience that this ball will not continue forever in the same direction, for the resistance of the air and the pull of gravity will soon bring it to earth again. However, if a block is slid successively along a rough board, a highly polished board, a piece of glass, and a sheet of smooth ice, the increasing motion in each successive case as the result of the same force illustrates the effect of cutting down that important external force called *friction*. The wheels of a child's wagon may be made to revolve twice before they stop; a bicycle wheel will run for 30 seconds or more by virtue of its ball-bearings, but the rotor of a steam turbine which is nicely mounted on oil-cushioned bearings will rotate for many hours after the steam is turned off, merely because friction has been reduced to an almost negligible quantity. Finally the fact that the earth and other planets have for ages made their revolutions around the sun without any force to keep them going, and will continue these revolutions for ages to come because there are no external forces to destroy the motion, gives the most convincing proof of the correctness of the law.

This property which every body possesses of resisting a change, whether of rest or motion, is called *inertia*, a polite name for *laziness*. Everyone when riding on a car has felt the backward pull as the car started and the forward push as it stopped—a proof that the body has persisted in its state of rest in the one case and of motion in the other. Water, although very yielding under ordinary circumstances, becomes almost rigid when struck sharply with the open hand or with a broad paddle, simply because of the inertia of the water. The aëroplane successfully "rides the billows of the air" because, by virtue of the propelling force of the motor, the

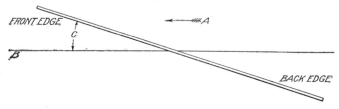

Fig. 25. Principle of the Aëroplane

planes are pushed so rapidly through the air that *the inertia of even as thin a medium as the atmosphere gives the required support to the machine;* without this forward motion, the support is removed and the aëroplane sinks at once to the earth. This effect may be illustrated by pushing against a slight breeze a thin board, Fig. 25, which is held almost horizontal. The tendency to rise on the part of the board and the resistance of the air as it is pushed aside by the moving board will be very marked.

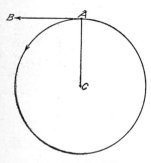

Fig. 26. Centrifugal Force

NOTE: In this connection it has been found that when an aëroplane rises to high altitudes, the motor must be maintained at a much higher velocity in order to provide the requisite support, because the greater the rarity of the air, the less its weight and, therefore, its inertia. Again if a sufficiently high motor velocity can be maintained so that the proper support is obtained with small planes, the actual velocity of the aëroplane is greater because of the reduced friction of these smaller planes against the layers of air.

Centrifugal Force. The average boy knows that if a limber stick is sharpened at one end and a small apple stuck upon it, a vigorous sweep through the air will loosen the apple and send it an amazing distance. What happens is this: The stick in its passage through the air makes the apple, very much against its will, describe an arc of a circle. This resistance of the apple to the change in direction develops along the stick CA, Fig. 26, an outward pull called *centrifugal force*, which increases as the velocity of the sweep increases. It is, therefore, only necessary to make the sweep so vigorous that the centrifugal force becomes greater than the friction between the apple and the stick when the apple shoots off along the tangent AB.

The boy would easily notice three things which influenced the apple to leave the stick, viz, the size of the apple, the length of the stick, and the speed of the sweep. The larger apples always shoot

Fig. 27.   Loop-the-Loop

off with greater ease, which means that the greater the mass the more centrifugal force developed; this fact is made use of in constructing engine fly wheels* with heavy rims so as to give them a

---

*The inertia of a body is proportional only to its mass, but when that same mass is made to rotate in a circle, the effect of the inertia increases with the increase in the distance of the mass from the center of rotation; *i.e.*, the greater the radius, the greater the effect. A flywheel, therefore, with a heavy rim and a large radius will have greater steadying ability than a wheel of the same weight with smaller radius. This factor of a body which determines its resistance to changes in rotational velocity is called its *moment of inertia* and is measured by the expression Mk^2, where M is the mass of the rotating part and k is the *radius of gyration*. Further discussion of moment of inertia would be out of place in this text, and may be found in any encyclopedia or advanced text in Physics.

high inertia and thus steady the moving system.   The same effect is had by increasing the radius of the wheel or the speed of rotation; a too great increase in the latter sometimes causes such a rotating mass as a grindstone to fly apart because of the excessive centrifugal force.   The summer amusement device known as the "loop-the-loop" utilizes the action of centrifugal force in keeping the car on the track throughout the upper half of the loop, Fig. 27, when gravity would otherwise cause a fall of the car.   A railroad track is always inclined inward at every curve and the sharper the curve the greater the inclination.   Evidently if the rails were laid on the horizontal, the centrifugal force developed as the cars passed around the curve might easily tip them over, but the outer rail being raised a certain amount,

Fig. 28.   Car Rounding Curve

Fig. 29.   Motordrome Race Track, Los Angeles, California

there is developed a small component of gravity, Fig. 28, which opposes this tendency to fly outward and brings about equilibrium.

There are many other illustrations of the effect of centrifugal force. The fisherman swings his loaded line about his head and then, letting go at a proper time, allows the sinker to shoot off on a tangent, carrying the line far out into the water. Mud and water fly off of a rapidly revolving carriage or automobile wheel. An oval automobile racing track, Fig. 29, is built like a saucer, so that the slope of the track will allow the force of gravity to neutralize the centrifugal force caused by such a tremendous speed in a circle. This same principle is used in

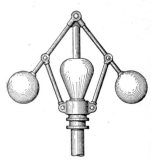

Fig. 30.   Watt's Ball Governor

centrifugal laundry driers, cream separators, honey extractors, and the ball governor for regulating the speed of an engine, Fig. 30.

Fig. 31.   Gyroscope

Gyroscope. A rotating body, because of its inertia, has very great stability of position, *i.e.*, it shows strong resistance to any force tending to change its plane of rotation—to twist it about. This is shown best by the action of the gyroscope, Fig. 31—a wheel with a heavy rim rotating on an axle, the ends of which are pivoted in a ring. When the wheel is rotated rapidly, its inertia will prevent it from tipping and, therefore, will serve to steady anything to which it is attached. Advantage has been taken of this by mounting gyroscopes in ships to do away with the rolling motion, and more recently by Brennan in constructing a one-rail

Fig. 32. Brennan's Monorail Car

car, which is kept upright by rotating two gyroscopes in opposite directions, Fig. 32.

§15. **Second Law.** Newton's second law is stated thus:

Rate of change of momentum is proportional to the force acting and takes place in the direction in which the force acts.

Momentum—quantity of motion in a body—may be defined as *the product of the mass and the velocity.* A steam roller with a weight of 8000 pounds and a velocity of 2 feet per second has the same momentum (8000×2 ft. lb. per sec.) as a 4-pound projectile fired with a muzzle velocity of 4000 feet per second (4×4000 ft. lb. per sec.). But by the law only *variations* in momentum require the expenditure of force; a change of mass in a body cannot occur without the loss of a portion of the body itself, hence, changes in momentum mean *changes in speed.* Everyone who has ridden a bicycle knows that it takes more force to *gain* speed on a smooth level road than it does to keep up this speed when once acquired; and also that the quicker this speed is to be gained, the greater the

necessary force. In like manner, speed once acquired is not destroyed without applying a force equal to that which was necessary to gain the speed in the first place. The earth, having in some way attained its present velocity, and being held in its orbit by the attraction of the sun, is making its yearly revolutions in space without consuming any energy so far as we know. But if any body should

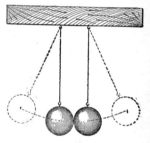

Fig. 33. Elastic Impact

happen to oppose that motion, the disturbing force would need to reckon with the enormous momentum of the earth.

§16. Third Law. Newton's third law is stated thus:

To every action there is an equal and opposite reaction.

The illustrations of this law are many and of common experience. The recoil or "kick" of a gun, the reaction of a boat as a person jumps from it to the bank, the rebounding of two elastic balls after impact, Fig. 33, all go to prove that a force cannot be exerted against a zero resistance but that an equal and opposite force is created in every case.

It is impossible to exert much force upon a light object, because it offers such a slight opposition; this is illustrated by the fact that a person who is pushing against some obstacle which suddenly gives way, is precipitated forward by the sudden lack of resistance. On the other hand, one can push against a wall with all his might and make no impression whatever because the resistance of the wall will meet his greatest effort. Forces, therefore, exist in pairs. To break a string, stretch a rubber band, bite an apple, two equal and opposite forces must be exerted. Such a thing as a single force acting alone is unknown.

PROBLEMS FOR PRACTICE

1. The running time of an overland train from Chicago to San Francisco is 66 hours and the distance is 2,500 miles. Find the average velocity of the train in miles per hour.

2. If an automobile covers 1,260 feet in 10 seconds, find the velocity in feet per second and in miles per hour.

3. What is the effect of a flywheel on an engine? Why?

4. Cream is lighter than milk. How can centrifugal force be used to separate them in the cream separator?

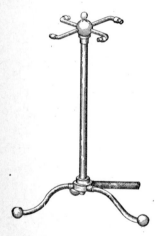

Fig. 34.   Rotary Lawn Sprinkler

5. Why does beating a carpet get the dust out?

6. Why may a string be broken easily by a quick jerk when a steady pull may make it cut the finger?

7. Why does a person who jumps from a moving train have to incline the body away from the direction of the motion in order to alight safely?

8. A grindstone might burst under excessive rotation. Why?

9. Compare the momentum of a 100-pound body moving with a velocity of 40 feet per second, with that of a 20-pound body moving with a velocity of 150 feet per second. Ans. 2nd is $\frac{3}{4}$ of 1st.

10. Explain the rotation of the rotary sprinkler of the type shown in Fig. 34.

11. What speed must a 200-pound motorcycle have to neutralize in collision the momentum of a 1500-pound automobile moving at 8 miles per hour? Ans. 60 miles per hour.

12. How much momentum per second is developed by a 10-inch stream of water, delivering 3,600 cubic feet per minute at a speed of 100 feet per second? (1 cubic foot of water weighs 62.5 pounds.)

PRESSURE IN LIQUIDS AND GASES

LIQUIDS

§17. **Pressure Below a Liquid Surface.** If an empty pail is forced, bottom down, under the surface of a pool of water, Fig. 35, an increasing downward pressure is required until the pail is sufficiently depressed to allow the water to run over the edge. By the time the pail is full all resistance has disappeared and a small upward force is necessary to keep the pail from sinking. It is evident that the pushing aside of the water must develop an upward force on the bottom of the pail, for if the pail is inclined so as to allow it to fill as it is pushed down, the necessary effort becomes very small.

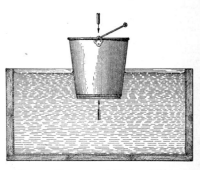

Fig. 35.   Buoyancy of Displaced Water

To show that this force is due to the water, take a wide-mouthed bottle filled with air which is provided with a sheet of rubber bound tightly over its mouth, and force the bottle below the surface of the water. As the depth increases, the rubber diaphragm is pressed further into the bottle by virtue of the increased pressure; careful measurements would show that the *pressure increases in proportion to the depth*, that is, at a depth of 2 feet the pressure is twice as great as at 1 foot.

Pressure Same in All Directions at Equal Depths. If the bottle referred to in §17 is turned successively in an upright, inverted, and horizontal position, while the center of the diaphragm is kept at exactly the same level, no change in the stretch of the diaphragm will be noticed. The same point may be illustrated by filling three tubes of the form shown in Fig. 36, with mercury and immersing them to the same depth in water;

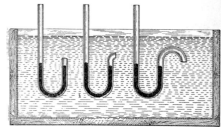

Fig. 36.   Pressure Independent of Direction

the mercury will stand at exactly the same height in all three. Therefore, *at any given depth, a liquid exerts a pressure which is the same up, down, or sidewise, and is measured by the weight of a column of liquid having the given depth and unit area.*

NOTE: The term *pressure*, as applied to fluids, although often used rather freely, always means the amount of force on each unit area. Thus, a pressure of 20 pounds means a force of 20 pounds per square inch; and a pressure of 4 kilograms means 4 kilos per square centimeter.

Total Force on a Given Area. The total force on a given area at any depth is found by multiplying the pressure at that depth by the area. If depth and area are given in the Metric system, the problem is easy, for 1 cubic centimeter of fresh water weighs 1 gram; hence, at a depth of 100 meters, the pressure is $100 \times 100 \times 1 = 10,000$ grams; and if the exposed area is 20 square centimeters, the total force of water is $10,000 \times 20 = 200,000$ grams or 200 kilograms. If depth and area are given in English measure, the problem is the same, but involves more calculation. For example, at a depth of 100 feet, the total force on an area of 34 square inches will be found as follows: 1 cubic foot of water weighs about 62.5 pounds and hence, at a depth of 100 feet, the total weight of water on 1 square foot of area is $62.5 \times 100 = 6250$ pounds. As 1 square foot contains

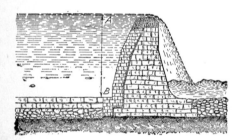

Fig. 37.   Section of Dam

144 square inches, the weight per square inch is $\dfrac{6250}{144} = 43.4$ pounds. But the given area is 34 square inches; therefore, the total force of water on the given surface is $43.4 \times 34 = 1475.6$ pounds.

When different portions of the given surface are under different pressures, as, for example, the side of a tank containing water, an allowance must be made for this inequality by taking the *pressure at an average depth* and applying it over the whole area. At the surface the pressure is evidently zero, but at the bottom it is equal to the weight of a column of water whose height is equal to the extreme depth of the tank; an average of these two pressures, or one-half of the bottom pressure, is used to represent the pressure existing over the whole area. For example, a dam whose height AB, Fig. 37, is 16 feet, and whose length is 50 feet, has a pressure area of 50×16 sq. ft. and an average pressure of $\frac{16}{2} \times 62.5$ lb. per sq. ft. It must, therefore, be able to withstand a total force of water equal to $50 \times 16 \times \frac{16}{2} \times 62.5$ pounds $= 400,000$ lb., or 200 tons.

§18. **Liquids in Connecting Vessels.**   It is a familiar fact that when a liquid is poured into a vessel having connecting tubes, Fig. 38, the liquid will rise to the same level in the vessel and in the tubes. The saying is "Water always seeks its level." This follows from the fact that pressure is proportional to depth only, and hence equilibrium in each tube will only be established when the height of the water is the same as that in the main

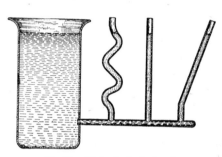

Fig. 38.   Water Seeks its Level

vessel. This principle is made use of in supplying cities with water. A lake or other reservoir is found, which is situated at a sufficient elevation so that when the water is piped to all parts of the city, it will tend to rise at every orifice to a height nearly equal to that of the reservoir. This furnishes sufficient pressure in the system to carry the water to the tops of buildings and throw streams in cases of fire.

Fig. 39.   Earth Section Showing Formation of Artesian Well

When a well is bored, from which water flows without the aid of a pump, it is called an *artesian well*, Fig. 39, and the flow of the water indicates that its source is higher than the orifice of the well.

PROBLEMS FOR PRACTICE

1. A diver goes down in 120 feet of water. What is the pressure on each square foot of his body due to the water?

2. Why does water enter with considerable force through a hole in the bottom of a boat? Upon what does the force depend?

3. A hole 20 square centimeters in area was made in the hold of a vessel 10 meters below the surface of the water. Find the force in kilograms necessary to hold a block against the inrushing water.

4. Find the force acting on the bottom of a box 2 meters long, 3 meters wide, and 4 meters deep, filled with water. Ans. 24,000 kg.

5. Find the total force acting against each of the sides and ends of the box mentioned in Problem 4.

6. A house is supplied with water from a reservoir 400 feet above the first floor level. What will be the pressure in pounds per square inch at this level?

7. A dam is 40 feet high and 200 feet long. Find the total force of the water in tons acting on the dam. Ans. 5000 tons.

8. When the gas in the city mains will support a column of water 5 centimeters high, what is the pressure per square centimeter in the mains? Ans. 5 grams.

PASCAL'S LAW

§19. Transmission of Pressure by Liquids. The fact that in liquids pressure is due to the weight of the liquid and acts in all directions, was found by Pascal to result in a very astonishing principle, viz, *pressure exerted upon any part of an inclosed liquid is transmitted with undiminished force upon all equal areas and at right angles to them.*

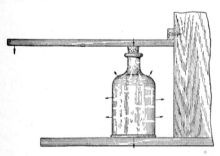

Fig. 40.   Transmission of Pressure by Liquids

For example, take a thin bottle, Fig. 40, completely fill it with water, and, by means of a lever, exert a considerable pressure on the cork. The bottle will probably be shattered owing to the fact that the pressure applied to the cork is instantly transmitted in all directions through the water. Assuming the cork to have $\frac{3}{4}$ square inch of area and to have 100 pounds of force exerted upon it, then every square inch of surface on the inside of the bottle will instantly receive a pressure of $\frac{4}{3} \times 100$, or 133.3 pounds.

§20.   Multiplication of Force. It was soon suggested by Pascal himself that the principle just stated would enable one to multiply an applied force almost without limit. For instance, if the area of the small cylinder *A*, Fig. 41, is 1 square inch, and of the large cylinder *B*, 1,000 square inches, then 1 pound applied on *A* will support a weight of 1,000 pounds on *B;* that is, the force of 1 pound on *A* will

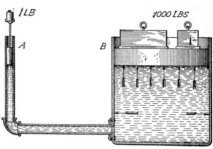

Fig. 41.   Pascal's Principle

be transmitted without loss to every square inch of the piston *B*.

Hydraulic Press. This process of multiplication of a force has been successfully applied in the hydraulic press, an instrument in

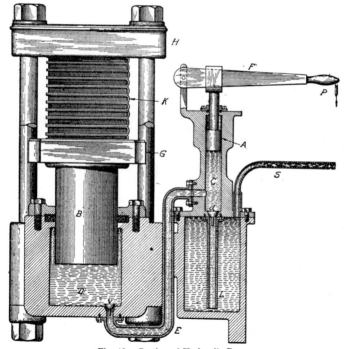

Fig. 42.   Section of Hydraulic Press

common use for producing enormous pressures, such as are necessary to press paper and cotton; to punch holes in iron plates; to cut off steel billets; to extract oil from seeds, etc. The machine consists of two water-tight cylinders C and D, Fig. 42, connected by a pipe E. Pistons A and B are free to move in their respective cylinders and are accurately fitted where they enter the cylinders, so that very little water leaks out. The valve v allows a flow of water into the larger cylinder, but not in the opposite direction, while the valve d prevents water from the supply tank L from flowing back when the piston A is depressed. The piston A is operated by a lever or by steam and when forced down, valve d closes, thus sending the water

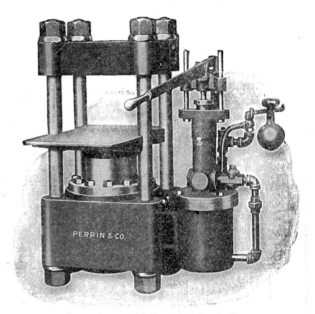

Fig. 43.   Commercial Type of Hydraulic Press
Wm. R. Perrin & Company

through pipe E into the cylinder D. The strokes of A are continued until the desired compression between the plates G and H is obtained. The force on piston A will be multiplied at B *in the ratio of the squares of the diameters of the cylinders*, that is, in the ratio of their areas. Cylinder C may be dispensed with by making a direct connection with E from the city water system or from a private high-pressure system. This method has the advantage that the water continues to flow into the large cylinder until the piston has been moved the required amount.

The modern hydraulic press, shown in Fig. 43, has a cylinder diameter of 14 inches and a vertical movement of the piston of 36 inches; it is capable of exerting a total force of 185 tons.

Gain in Force Lost in Distance. Although the force of 1 pound, Fig. 41, is multiplied 1,000 times in the larger cylinder, it should be noticed that the distance through which the larger piston is moved

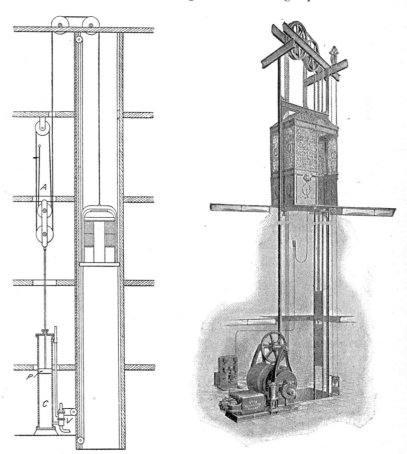

Fig. 44.   Diagram of Hydraulic   Fig. 45.   Diagram of Electrical Elevator
           Elevator

depends absolutely upon how much water is forced over from the cylinder *A*, and *will be* $\frac{1}{1000}$ *of the distance the small piston is de-pressed.* In other words, it will be necessary to depress piston *A* 1,000 inches—say, 100 strokes if the length of stroke is 10 inches—in order to cause a rise of 1 inch in piston *B*. If, therefore, the force on each piston be multiplied by the distance through which it moves, the two products will be found identical, that is, *what is gained by a multiplication of the force is lost in distance*. This important conclusion will be found later to control the action of all machines.

Hydraulic Elevators. Another important illustration of the multiplication of a force is found in the hydraulic elevator, a diagrammatic study of which is shown in Fig 44. Water is admitted into the cylinder *C* above the piston, forcing the latter down and thereby raising the car. The motion of the car is always under the control of the elevator-man by means of the valve *v* which is operated from

Fig. 46. Hydraulic Lift Lock at Peterborough, Canada

the car. When the car should move downward the valve is set so as to allow the water in the cylinder above the piston to flow into the waste pipe and the car settles by its own weight. The pulley block *A* magnifies the motion four times, consequently the piston moves over one-quarter of the space covered by the car. The large amount of space taken up by pumps and other hydraulic machinery necessary for large elevator plants in high buildings, has led to the replacement of many elevators of this type by those controlled by electric motors, Fig. 45; the latter type seems destined to be the prevailing one.

An interesting and unusual application of hydraulic power is illustrated in the hydraulic lift locks at Peterborough, Canada, Fig. 46. The diameter of the cylinders is 8 feet 3 inches, the vertical lift is 65 feet, and the pressure in the presses during operation is 600 pounds per square inch.

PROBLEMS FOR PRACTICE

1. In Fig. 42, what would be the upward force on B if the downward force on A is 80 pounds; the area of piston A is 2 square inches and of B 128 square inches?   Ans. 5120 lb.

2. If the length of the stroke of piston A, Problem 1, is 5 inches, how many strokes will be necessary to compress the books 1 inch?

3. The large cylinder of a hydraulic press, which is 10 inches in diameter, is directly connected to a water system furnishing a pressure of 80 pounds per square inch. Find the force exerted by the large piston.

4. If the piston in Fig. 44 is 8 inches in diameter, the water pressure 120 pounds per square inch, and the gain in distance of the piston due to the pulleys is 4, what total weight of cage and passengers can be lifted?   Ans. 1507 + lb.

5. Referring to the data on the Peterborough lift locks, Fig. 46, given just above these problems, find the total lifting power in each cylinder with a pressure of 600 pounds per square inch acting in each.

6. The cylinders of the press, Fig. 43, are respectively 14 inches and 2 inches in diameter. How many pounds pressure on the small cylinder will develop a force of 185 tons in the big cylinder? How many 36-inch strokes of the small piston will raise the large piston 3 inches?   Answers: 7551 + lb.; $4\frac{1}{12}$ strokes.

SPECIFIC GRAVITY

§21. Loss of Weight of a Body in a Liquid. Nearly everyone has lifted a stone under water and has been surprised at its lightness as compared with its weight when lifted entirely out of the water. A person when entirely immersed in a bathtub full of water can support his entire weight by placing one finger on the bottom. It was this observation that led Archimedes, the Greek philosopher, to the discovery of the principle which bears his name, viz, *that any body immersed in a liquid will lose a weight equal to the weight of the displaced liquid.*

§22. Archimedes Principle. The amount of buoyancy, *i.e.*, the tendency on the part of the liquid to lift an immersed body, may easily be found by the following analysis:

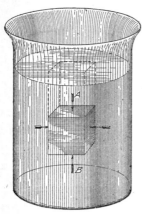

Suspend a cube in a liquid, as shown in Fig. 47, and consider the forces due to the water, which are acting on the various faces. The horizontal forces on the four sides of the cube will vary with the depth but as they will exist as two pairs of equal and opposite forces, they will neutralize each other. The forces on the top and the bottom, however, are not equal, for the bottom face is at a lower level, and the pressure on any exposed surface has already been found to be proportional to the depth. The difference between the forces on *A* and *B* is evidently the weight of a quantity of water having the same volume as that of the cube itself, *i.e.*, the weight of the water displaced. This excess of the upward over the downward force is the *buoyancy*, due to immersion.

Fig. 47.   Proof of Archimedes Principle

Floating Body. Evidently the buoyant force is independent of the weight of the body and also of its depth in the liquid. If the body weighs more than the liquid which it displaces, it must sink, for the force of gravity will be greater than the buoyancy. If, on the other hand, it weighs less than the displaced liquid, the buoyant force exceeds the weight of the body and it must rise to the surface, continuing to rise out of the liquid until the weight of the displaced water is equal to the weight of the body. Hence, *a floating body displaces its own weight of the liquid in which it floats.* A block of wood two-thirds as heavy as water will float a third out of water, because only two-thirds of the block's volume of water is needed to give the necessary upward force. A piece of iron will float on the surface of mercury because it is lighter than mercury. A vessel, Fig. 48, which is being unloaded, rises higher and higher out of the water, and, on being reloaded, sinks so as to displace an additional ton of water for every added ton of freight.

A boat has a length of 200 feet and an average width of 50 feet at the water line. How much cargo will be necessary to depress the boat 1 foot? The area at the water line is $200 \times 50 = 10,000$ square feet. For a depression of 1 foot the volume displaced $= 10,000$ cubic feet. The weight of the displaced water $= 10,000 \times 62.5$ pounds $= 625,000$ pounds. The required weight of cargo is 625,000 pounds.

§23. Density and Specific Gravity. The density of a body is defined as *its weight divided by its volume*, that is, *the quantity of matter in unit volume.* In the Metric system, 1 gram of water occupies 1 cubic centimeter, and therefore the density of water is 1. Archimedes principle furnishes a convenient method of finding the volume of irregular bodies, for the loss of weight of a body when immersed has already been found to be numerically equal to its volume, *when expressed in the Metric system;* that is, a body having a volume of 90 cubic centimeters will lose just 90 grams on being immersed in water. The relation may, therefore, be expressed

$$\text{Density} = \frac{\text{weight in air}}{\text{loss in water}}$$

This loss of weight of a body in water is also found to represent the weight of the displaced water and consequently gives the *exact weight of an equal volume of water.* The ratio of the weight of the body to that of an equal volume of water is called *specific gravity.* The expression becomes in this case

Fig. 48. Ship Displaces Volume of Water Depending on Weight of Cargo

$$\text{Specific gravity} = \frac{\text{weight of body in air}}{\text{weight of equal volume of water}}$$

Evidently the specific gravity of a substance is independent of the system used, and has the same value as the density in the Metric system. Density in the English system, however, has a wholly different value, the unit of weight being the pound and the unit of volume the cubic foot, Table 1.

*TABLE I

Densities in Metric and English Systems

SUBSTANCE	Density in Grams per c. c. = sp. gr.	Density in Pounds per cu. ft.	SUBSTANCE	Density in Grams per c.c. = sp gr.	Density in Pounds per cu. ft.
Charcoal (oak)	0.57	35.	Iron (gray cast)	7.08	442.
Paraffin	0.89	55.5	Zinc (cast)	7.10	443.
Ice	0.92	57.3	Tin (cast)	7.29	455.
Beeswax	0.96	60.	Iron (wrought)	7.85	489.
Sandstone	2.35	146.5	Brass	8.44	527.
Feldspar	2.55	160.	Nickel	8.60	536.
Aluminum (cast)	2.57	160.5	Copper (cast)	8.88	553.
Glass (common)	2.60	162.5	Silver (cast)	10.45	652.
Quartz	2.65	165.	Lead (cast)	11.34	708.
Marble	2.65	165.	Mercury	13.6	848.
Granite	2.75	171.	Gold (cast)	19.30	1205.
Garnet	3.70	232.	Platinum	21.45	1338.

*From Smithsonian Institute Report.

§24. **Methods.** *Solids Heavier than Water.* The specific gravity of a body heavier than water may be found by first finding

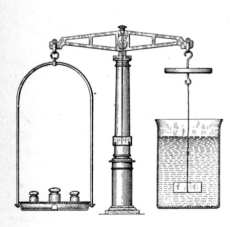

the weight W of the solid in air by means of balances similar to those shown in Fig. 49. A vessel of water is placed underneath the solid so as to completely immerse it. The body will then be found to have lost weight—call this new weight W'. The loss of weight, which is the same as the weight of an equal volume of water, is evidently $W - W'$. Therefore

Fig. 49. Specific Gravity Balance

$$\text{Specific gravity} = \frac{W}{W - W'}.$$

If the solid whose specific gravity is desired is lighter than water, a sinker must be provided, and the method carried through in much the same manner as for a heavy solid.

Liquids. Several methods have been devised for finding the specific gravity of liquids, but the simplest and most common is by means of the *hydrometer*, Fig. 50.   This instrument consists of a glass bulb with a hollow narrow neck in which is fastened a paper scale from which the specific gravity may be read off direct by noting the reading of the scale corresponding to the level of the liquid. The instrument floats in the liquid at such a point that its own weight exactly equals the weight of the displaced liquid. Such instruments are commonly used for testing milk, alcohol, acids, etc.

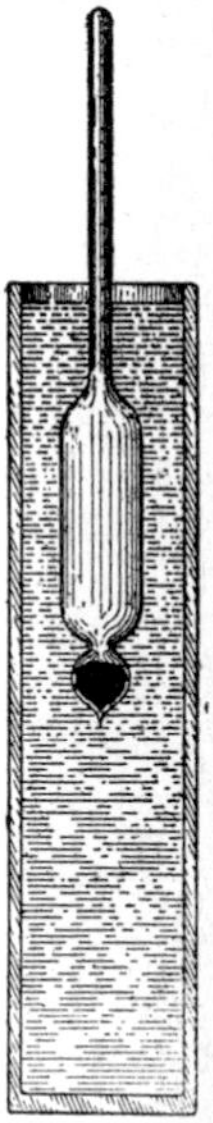

PROBLEMS FOR PRACTICE

1.   A boy's maximum lift is 120 pounds.   The specific gravity of stone is 2.5.   What would be the weight in air of the heaviest stone the boy could lift under water? Suggestion: Weight of stone in water must equal 120 pounds.   Ans. 200 lb.

2.   A boat having a length of 500 feet and an average width of 75 feet sinks 25 feet on being loaded.   How much cargo is put on board?   (1 cu. ft. of water weighs 62.5 lbs.)   Ans. 29,296⅞ tons.

Fig. 50.   Hydrometer

3.   A body weighs 64 grams in air and 40.3 grams in water.   Find the density of the body.   Ans. 2.7.

4.   Will the water line of a boat rise or fall in passing from salt into fresh water?

5.   A pontoon bridge consists of boats 100 feet long and 60 feet wide.   How much will each boat sink when a locomotive weighing 125 tons passes over the bridge?   (Consider each boat separate.)

6.   The specific gravity of a substance is 8.4.   Find the weight n water of 22 pounds of the material.

7.   A hydrometer displaced 28 cubic centimeters of water and 36 cubic centimeters of another liquid.   Find the specific gravity of the unknown liquid.

8.   A 20,000 ton battle-ship displaces how many cubic feet of water?   1 cubic foot of salt water weighs 64.1 pounds.

9.   Commercial hydrometers such as shown in Fig. 50, may be bought for use in liquids of less or greater density than water Which kind will be the heavier ?   Why ?

GASES

§25.   Weight of the Atmosphere.   The fact that the atmosphere has weight is never made noticeable except as the equilibrium between the forces on the inside and outside of the body is disturbed. As a person breathes fresh air into his lungs, the air is simultaneously pressing on the inside and outside of the lungs with the same force, thereby producing a neutral effect.   But let this balance be destroyed by putting one's mouth to an exhaust pump and removing some of the air from the lungs; immediately a pressure is felt from the outside which, if enough air were pumped out of the lungs, might be sufficient to crush in the chest.

Fig. 52.   Can Collapses under Pressure

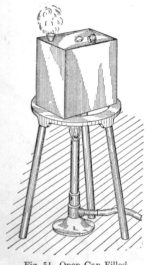

Fig. 51. Open Can Filled with Steam

The effect of the weight of the atmosphere may be shown by the following simple experiment:

Take a thin-walled tin can, Fig. 51, and put into it about 1 inch of water. Heat the water to boiling and after the steam has been coming out for some time, and with the heat still under the boiler, quickly insert the stopper in the can. At the moment the cork is put in, the pressure inside and outside are the same. When the heat is removed the steam will begin to condense and thereby to reduce the internal pressure. This allows the pressure of the air on the outside to make the can collapse. The *weight of the atmosphere* will crush in the sides of the can until it has become a mass of twisted metal, Fig. 52.

Deep-sea fishes, when caught and pulled rapidly to the surface, have been blown up or had their eyes forced from their sockets by the sudden diminution of outside pressure and the consequent expansion of the air within the fish's body. The queer feeling in the ears when a person goes down rapidly into a mine or climbs a high mountain bears testimony to the actual *weight* of the air.

§26. Torricelli's Experiment. If a tube fitted with an air-tight piston, Fig. 53, be placed in a vessel of water and the piston drawn

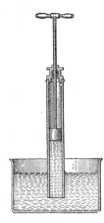

up, the water in the tube will follow the motion of the piston and be drawn above the level of the water outside. It is a common saying that the "water has been drawn up by the *suction*," but in reality it has been forced up by the *outside pressure* of the atmosphere to a height where equilibrium is established between the inside and the outside. In the early days of science the existence of the atmospheric pressure had not been proved and it puzzled the experimenters not a little when it was noticed that a piston like the one shown in Fig. 53 could not possibly draw the water higher than 34 feet. It remained for Galileo to hint at the true explanation, and for Torricelli, his pupil, to discover a method of proof.

Fig. 53. Water Drawn up by "Suction"

He argued that if water would rise 34 feet by virtue of the pressure of the atmosphere, mercury, which is about 13 times heavier than water, would rise, by virtue of the same force, only $\frac{1}{13}$ as high, or about 30 inches. He accordingly provided a glass tube closed at one end and somewhat longer than 30 inches, and filled it with mercury. Placing his finger over the end so as to retain the liquid in the tube and to keep out all air, he quickly inverted the tube and set it in a cistern of mercury in the position shown in Fig. 54. The column immediately fell to a height of about 30 inches and stood still. As the space in the top of the tube was a vacuum, and was, therefore, incapable of exerting any pressure on the mercury in the tube, the column represented the equivalent weight of the atmosphere; *i.e.*, the column of mercury 30 inches high weighed exactly the same as a column of air of the same cross-section and 50 to 100 miles high.

Pascal repeated the experiment and varied it by carrying the tube up on a high mountain. The column fell with increasing altitude, thus proving that the mercury column did really represent the weight of the atmosphere. Evidently this weight per square inch or square centimeter of area may be found by calcula-

Fig. 54. Torricelli's Barometer

ting the actual weight of a column of mercury 30 inches high and 1 square inch cross-section, or 76 centimeters high and 1 square centimeter cross-section. These weights are roughly 15 pounds and 1 kilogram, respectively, and it is, therefore, customary to speak of the *atmospheric pressure as 15 pounds per square inch, or 1 kilogram per square centimeter.* It should now be perfectly clear why the early scientists could not draw the water higher than 34 feet. The strokes of the piston, Fig. 53, produced a partial vacuum in the tube with the result that the outside pressure forced the water higher

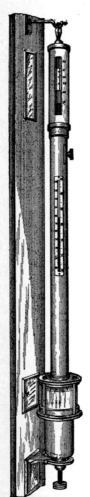

and higher in the tube as the vacuum was increased. But as it has just been shown that the atmosphere can support only 30 inches of mercury or 34 feet of water *with a perfect vacuum above the column*, it is evident that if the well were more than 34 feet deep, the pump could not draw the water up to the spout. Therefore, the length of the tube necessary to repeat Torricelli's experiment with water is something more than 34 feet; for sulphuric acid (density 1.8) the length of the column is $\frac{1.0}{1.8} \times 34 = 18.8 +$ feet; for alcohol (density 0.8) its length is $\frac{1.0}{0.8} \times 34 = 42.5$ feet.

§27. **Barometer.** *Fortin.* If Torricelli's apparatus were placed in a frame, Fig. 55, and the vessel containing the mercury were

Fig. 55. Fortin Barometer

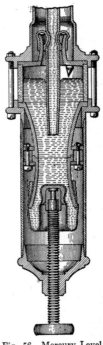

Fig. 56. Mercury Level Regulator

properly supported and inclosed, Fig. 56, the result would be a *barometer*. The scale on the frame enables the observer to determine the height of the column at any time. This style of barometer is called the Fortin, and is the form adopted by the United States weather bureau. The rise and fall of the column of mercury shows the changes in atmospheric pressure and these changes, when properly interpreted by the weather bureau operators, are used as the basis for the weather maps which report to the people of the country the coming of rain storms, frosts, etc.

Aneroid. A barometer of the portable type is called an *aneroid*, Fig. 57, and is used principally in taking elevations. It consists of a metal box, Fig. 58, with corrugated sides in which there is a partial vacuum. The center of the box is in communication with a lever system which records the movements of the box cover corresponding to changes in pressure. A scale outside of the barometer scale enables the observer to determine the elevation by direct readings. These instruments are now made so delicate as to be able to record the difference in level between the table top and the floor.

Fig. 57. Aneroid Barometer

§28. **Height of Atmosphere.** It is a well-known fact that air is elastic and easily compressed. As a result of this elasticity the layers of air near the earth's surface are greatly compressed by the weight of the air above them, *i. e.*, the density of this lower air is increased. As the higher altitudes are reached, however, the density rapidly decreases so that at a height of 3 miles —equal to the height of Mt. Blanc—one-half of the atmosphere has been left below, *i. e.*, the barometer reads approximately 15

Fig. 58. Metal Box in Aneroid Barometer

inches. No one has ever ascended to a greater height than 7 miles, a height attained by a couple of English aëronauts, Glazier and Coxwell, in 1862, who, on account of the cold and rareness of the air, almost lost consciousness before they could open the valve of their balloon. The barometer registered only 7 inches and the temperature was −60° F. As late as 1908 a "sounding balloon" carrying no passengers but provided with automatic recording thermometers and barometers was sent up in Northern Africa to a height of 12 miles. The thermometer recorded a temperature of $-119.7°$ F., which shows why observers cannot go to such heights even if they provide themselves with artificial atmosphere in high-pressure cylinders. From these and other experiments it is estimated that the atmosphere extends to a height of 100 miles or more.

§29. Boyle's Law. The relation of the volume of a gas to the pressure which it sustains was first investigated by Boyle, and was formulated by him into the following law:

The temperature remaining the same, the volume of a given mass of gas varies inversely as the pressure acting upon it.

If the volumes are V and V' and the pressures P and P', this proportion may be expressed in the more usual form thus

$$P V = P' V'$$

or

$$P V = \text{constant}$$

This means that if the pressure exerted upon a body of air is doubled, its volume is halved; if the pressure is tripled, the volume is one-third its initial value, etc.

For example, the volume of a certain amount of air at the ordinary atmospheric pressure—76 centimeters of mercury—is 420 cubic centimeters. What will be the volume of this air when the pressure has been increased to 540 centimeters of mercury? V is evidently equal to 420 cubic centimeters, V' is the unknown, P is 76 centimeters, and P' is 540 centimeters.

$$\therefore \quad PV = P'V'$$
$$76 \times 420 = 540V'$$
$$V' = 59.1 \text{ cubic centimeters}$$

PROBLEMS FOR PRACTICE

1. It takes roughly 12 cubic feet of air to weigh 1 pound. Find the weight of the air in a room $50 \times 100 \times 15$ feet.

2. The can shown in Fig. 51 is 8 inches high, 6 inches wide, and 4 inches thick. Find the total force of the air on the outside, counting 15 pounds per square inch and no pressure on the inside.

3. Why will a bottle in which "suction" has been produced by the mouth, adhere to the tongue?

4.   A circular disk of leather, Fig. 59, having a string fastened to the center may be pressed down on a smooth stone and the latter raised by lifting on the string. Why? If the disk is 3 inches in diameter, how heavy a stone will it lift?

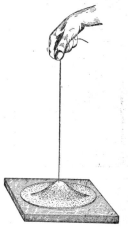

5.   If a tumbler is filled level full with water and a sheet of smooth paper placed over the top, it may be inverted as in Fig. 60, without spilling the water. Explain. Why is the paper necessary?

6.   What is the volume of a mass of air under a pressure of 32 pounds per square inch if it has a volume of 64 cubic feet under a pressure of 40 pounds per square inch?

7.   If the capacity of an inflated automobile tire is 500 cubic inches, and the air inside is under a pressure of 90 pounds per

Fig. 59.   Suction Disk

square inch, how many cubic inches of air at ordinary pressure does it contain? Ans. 3000 cu. in.

8.   How far under water must a diver go to be subjected to a total pressure of 30 pounds per square inch? Ans. 34+ ft.

9.   Why will very little liquid flow from the faucet in a barrel until a hole is made at the highest point?

10.   A vessel connected to an air pump has an opening 3 inches in diameter. If the palm of one's hand were placed over this opening and a perfect vacuum maintained in the vessel, find the pounds of force needed to pull the hand away. Ans. 106+ lb.

Fig. 60.   Illustrating Pressure of Atmosphere

11.   Why do we not feel the enormous pressure of the atmosphere on our bodies?

12.   A pressure tank has a capacity of 5 cubic feet. What will be the pressure on the inside walls if 80 cubic feet of gas are pumped into the tank? Ans. 240 lb.

13.   With an aneroid barometer and authority to travel over all railroads of Illinois, how could one make a relief map of the state ?

PNEUMATIC APPLIANCES

§30. Siphon. The siphon, Fig. 61, is a bent tube used to convey a liquid up over an elevation and down again to a lower level than that from which it started. To

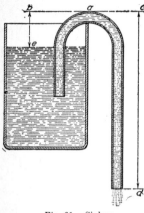

start the flow the tube must first be filled with liquid—either before being put in position or else by suction at the lower end after being placed as in the figure. The water will now run until the supply is exhausted or until the tube is withdrawn. As the air pressures at e and d, Fig. 61, are the same, the force tending to draw the water out of the vessel must be due to the greater length of the column of water, cd, over that of eb, causing an unbalanced condition, which the movement of the water is endeavoring

Fig. 61. Siphon

to restore. Evidently for water the column eb could never equal 34 feet, as, otherwise, a perfect vacuum in the siphon would not succeed in raising the water over the bend a. It is also clear that if

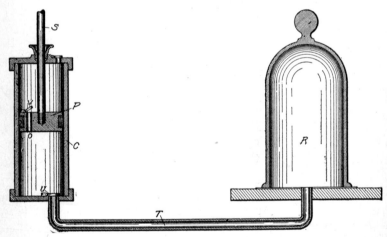

Fig. 62. Diagram of Air Pump

the siphon is to produce any flow, the level e must always be higher than the point d or higher than the surface of the reservoir into which the water is running.

§31. Air Pump. The air pump is an instrument for removing air from a closed vessel, and, in its most common form, works by means of a close-fitting piston P, Fig. 62, which moves up and down in a cylinder C. Connected to the bottom of the cylinder by a tube T is the receiver or vessel R which is to be exhausted of air. A valve u controls the passage of air from the receiver to the cylinder and another valve v performs a like function for the hole c, in the piston. A down stroke of the piston opens valve v and closes valve u. On the up stroke, however, the reverse occurs, and thus the air from the receiver is allowed to flow over to C and equalize the pressure. At each up stroke a portion of the air is removed, and the operation may be continued until the required exhaustion is reached.

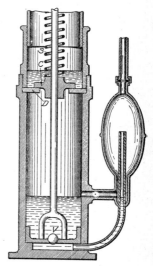

Fig. 63.   Fleuss Pump in Section

Fleuss Pump. One of the most satisfactory of the modern air pumps is the *Fleuss or Geryk* pump, a section of the cylinder of which is shown in Fig. 63. The cylinder is divided into two compartments by a diaphragm D, the opening in which is closed by a collar C held in place by a spring S. Above this collar as well as in the bottom of the cylinder, a heavy oil is used to keep the valves tight. When the piston is raised the valve V closes, the oil above it is raised and the air compressed until the collar on the piston strikes C and raises it; the air and a part of the oil now pass through into the upper chamber. The action is otherwise very much like that of the standard air pump. A very high degree of exhaustion is possible with this pump.

Fig. 64.   Bicycle Pump

§32. Compression Pump. If the valves of an air pump all opened in the opposite direction, air would be forced into the receiver

Fig. 65. Three-Stage Air Compressor. *Ingersoll-Rand Co., New York*

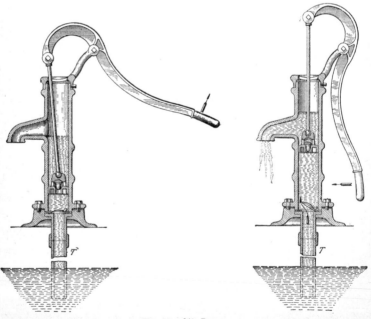

Fig. 66. Lift Pump

instead of being taken from it. Such a pump is the *compression pump*. In the bicycle pump, Fig. 64, the piston itself acts as a valve. It is packed with a cup-shaped disk of leather, which allows the air to pass into the cylinder on the up stroke, but on the down stroke is pressed against the sides of the cylinder and prevents the air from escaping. Compressed air finds many applications in air-drills, air-brakes, pneumatic hammers, etc. A standard three-stage compressor is shown in Fig. 65.

§33. Lift Pump. The common water pump, Fig. 66, has been in use at least since the time of Aristotle—4th century, B. C. It will be seen to have two valves like the air pump, and, in fact, when first started, it is simply exhausting the air below the lower valve so that the water will rise in the tube T. For this reason the well must be something less than 34 feet deep in order to draw water, as otherwise even a perfect vacuum would not bring the water up to a level of the lower valve.

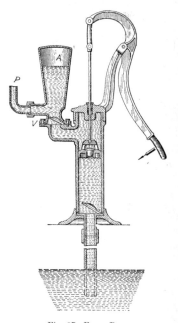

§34. Force Pump. When it is desired to raise the water higher than the pump itself, a *force pump*, Fig. 67, is used. This is similar to the lift pump except for the addition of a third valve and an air chamber A, which serves as a cushion for the water as it is forced above the valve V. The air in this chamber being compressed, keeps up the pressure on

Fig. 67 Force Pump

the stream of water issuing from P, when the piston is on the down stroke, and thus makes the stream a perfectly steady one rather than a series of impulses as in the lift pump. A more complicated and powerful force pump such as is used for fire engines is shown in Fig. 68.

§35. Balloon. Archimedes' principle, which has already been stated for water, must apply equally well for air. Hence, *any body immersed in air is buoyed up by force equal to the weight of the displaced* *air.* A body will, therefore, rise if its own weight is less than that of the air which it displaces. A balloon, Fig. 69, is a large silk bag, varnished so as to be gas-tight and filled either with hydrogen or common illuminating gas. Hydrogen is so much lighter than any other gas, that its lifting power is very great; it weighs approximately .006 pounds per cubic foot, while illuminating gas weighs .05 pounds per cubic foot. As ordinary air weighs .08 pounds per cubic foot,

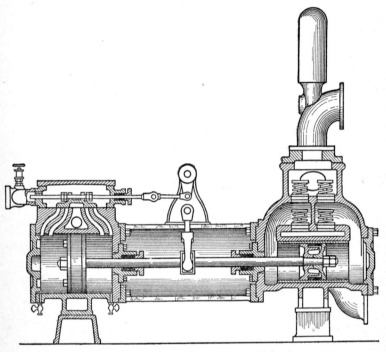

Fig. 68.   Fire Engine with Duplex Pump

it will be seen that the lifting power of hydrogen, viz, .08 − .006 = .074 pounds, is more than twice the lifting power of illuminating gas, .08 − .05 = .03 pounds. However, owing to its cheapness, the latter gas is more often used. Glazier and Coxwell's balloon had a capacity of 90,000 cubic feet and could therefore support 2,700 pounds including bag, basket, passengers, and their baggage. All of the developments in balloons, however, in the last few years have been to produce a *dirigible balloon, i. e.,* one which could be propelled and steered. Fig. 70 shows the U. S. Army Dirigible,

No. 1—designed by Capt. Thomas Baldwin—which has a length of 96
feet, a capacity of 20,000 cubic feet, and is capable of a speed of 20

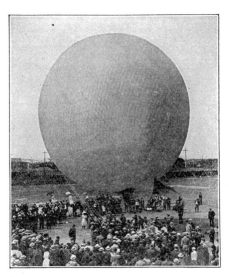

Fig. 69.   Balloon Ready for Flight

miles per hour.   Count Zeppelin, a German nobleman, has produced
the most successful dirigible balloon, Fig. 71, provided with a gas

Fig. 70.   Baldwin's U. S. Army Dirigible Balloon No. 1

bag 446 feet long, with a capacity of 460,000 cubic feet, and a lifting power of 16 tons. This noble air-ship can carry many persons and maintain a speed of over 40 miles per hour.

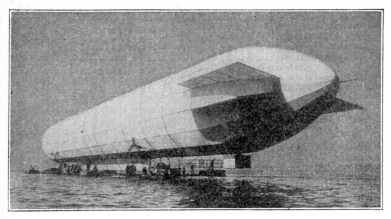

Fig. 71. Count Zeppelin's Dirigible Balloon Rising from Lake Constance

§36. Diving Bell.

Whenever foundations must be laid too far under water to allow a cofferdam to be built, a diving bell is

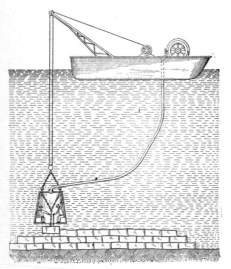

Fig. 72. Diving Bell

most frequently used. This is a heavy bell-shaped affair, Fig. 72, large enough to hold two or more men in its interior, and having an air-supply pipe connected to a pump at its surface. Evidently as the bell is lowered further and further under water, the water pressure will compress the air inside of the bell just as it does the air imprisoned in a glass which is pushed mouth downward under water. The pump must, therefore, supply fresh air and maintain a pressure within the bell exactly equal to or in excess of the water pressure outside. At 34 feet under water, this pressure would be 2 atmospheres, or 30 pounds, 15 pounds of atmosphere and 15 pounds of water; at 68 feet the pressure is 3 atmospheres, etc. The diving bell enables the workmen to carry stones and mortar under the water, to set the stone, and then to return for more. Caissons, which are much used in large under-water excavations are really stationary diving bells which accommodate many workmen; air is supplied in the same manner as in Fig. 72.

§37. **Diving Suit.** A diving suit, Fig. 73, consists of a continuous sheath of rubber from the feet to the shoulders, terminating

Fig. 73. Diver About to Descend

in a metal collar to which is fastened a metal helmet with heavy glass windows. The sleeves are fastened tightly at the wrists so that a pressure may be maintained inside the suit without any leak except through an air valve which is under the control of the diver himself. An air-compression pump, shown at the further end of the boat, supplies fresh air to the diver through a tube, and the pressure is varied inside of the suit to correspond with the depth to which the diver has gone. Only by keeping the pressure inside exactly equal to the pressure outside can the diver carry on his work safely and without hindrance. In the most modern outfits the diver dispenses with the pump and tubing, having mounted on his back a small cylinder filled with compressed air. A valve under the control of the diver will admit air inside the suit at the required pressure and when he wishes to rise he needs only to increase the pressure sufficiently to make him float.

§38. Pneumatic Hammer. The pneumatic hammer, Fig. 74, has been applied with complete success to many mechanical opera-

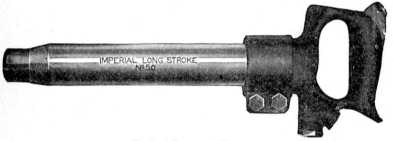

Fig. 74.   Pneumatic Hammer

tions such as driving rivets in bridge and structural steel work, chipping or trimming metal, and dressing or carving stone. The sectional view of a pneumatic hammer, Fig. 75, shows clearly its simplicity of construction and operation. Compressed air is supplied at H and when valve E is opened by pressing the thumb on the trigger T, the air enters the air chamber A. The pressure forces the piston forward to make a stroke upon the head of the tool or rivet placed at F. But just at this instant the piston ports bb are brought in connection with the exhaust port c and the air in

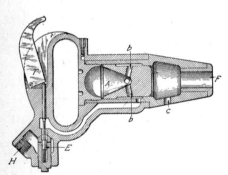

Fig. 75.   Sectional View of Pneumatic Hammer

chamber A escapes into the atmosphere. The pressure being relieved, the piston returns to its former position by virtue of the air pressure in the narrow annular space between the piston and cylinder walls, only to be driven forward again by the filling of chamber A.

§39. Pneumatic Drill. The pneumatic hammer drill, Fig. 76, is much used in mining operations in connection with an air compressor of the type shown in Fig. 65. The steel drill, which is automatically rotated but otherwise remains stationary, is struck many times a minute by the rapidly moving piston or hammer.

Fig. 76.   Pneumatic Drill in Operation

PROBLEMS FOR PRACTICE

1.   Explain why a siphon can not deliver water if the short arm has a height of 34 feet or more.

2.   A pneumatic cash system maintains a pressure of $1\frac{1}{2}$ atmospheres at the compression end and a pressure of 7 pounds at the suction end.   What is the total force driving one of the carriers if its cross section is 7 square inches?   Ans. 108.5 lb.

3. Why does it require more and more force to work the handle of a lift pump during the process of priming?

4. What is the function of the air dome of a fire engine?

5. A diving bell was sunk to a depth of 56 feet. What pressure was maintained inside the bell? (Do not forget the atmospheric pressure.) Ans. 39.+ lb.

6. Find the lifting power of a balloon of 110,000 cubic feet capacity, filled with illuminating gas; filled with hydrogen.

7. The cylinder on the back of a diver has a capacity of 1 cubic foot and the air within is compressed to 40 atmospheres. If he remains at a depth of 34 feet, how many cubic feet can he breathe before the air in the cylinder reaches the existing pressure?

MOLECULAR PHYSICS

MOTION OF MOLECULES

GASES

§40. **Constitution of Matter.** A bit of highly polished wood, which to the naked eye appears perfectly smooth, when examined

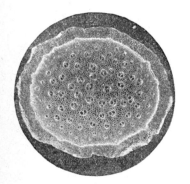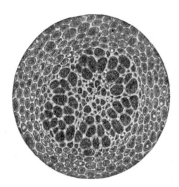

Fig. 77. Magnified Plant Section Showing Cellular Structure

with a small hand magnifier, shows a rough and slightly granular surface; if the piece is placed under a powerful microscope, minute cells of the wood are clearly shown. Fig. 77 shows two sections of a fibrous stem magnified respectively 30 and 250 times. And yet a long series of careful experiments of scientific men tell us that it would take a microscope a thousand times more powerful than now exists to make visible the ultimate particles, called *molecules,* of which the wood cells are composed. A better idea of the extreme smallness of these particles may be gained from an illustration due to Lord Kelvin: "If a drop of water were magnified to the size of the earth, the molecules composing the drop would be of a size between a baseball and fine shot."

However, the scientist goes further and says that in solids and liquids the molecules are very close together but not touching, Fig. 78; while in gases

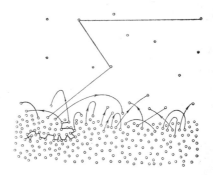

Fig. 78. Supposed Relative Positions of Molecules of a Liquid
Millikan's "Mechanics, Molecular Physics and Heat"

they are, comparatively speaking, very far apart, Fig. 79. This latter statement is easily proved from the fact that when air is liquefied its volume must be contracted 800 times before the molecules are brought close enough together to make the air liquid.

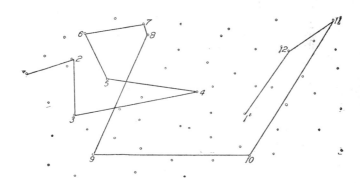

Fig. 79. Supposed Relative Positions of Molecules of a Gas
Millikan's "Mechanics, Molecular Physics and Heat"

§41. **Molecular Motions in Gases.** It must not be supposed that molecules of a gas are hung in space at fixed points like so many captive balloons; many experiments can be performed to prove that, on the contrary, they are continually darting about at a very rapid pace, colliding with other molecules, Fig. 79, or occasionally shooting forward at a higher velocity, like a football player who luckily or skilfully dodges the entire opposing team and carries the ball across the goal line. It seems impossible to give a reason for the fact that the odor of gas or of a strong perfume is carried quickly from one end to the other of a still room except on the supposition that the molecules of the substance are moving rapidly here and there, darting between the molecules of the air, in fact moving more than half as fast as a cannon projectile. Further proof of these movements may be had if a chemist will place a heavy and a light gas—carbon dioxide and hydrogen—in connecting vessels with the heavy one below; in a short time he can find by analysis that the molecules of the two gases have moved from one flask to the other *against the force of gravity.*

According to modern ideas, therefore, *the molecules of all substances are in continual motion and in the case of gases are darting about at a high speed in all directions.* It is interesting, with this property of our atmosphere in mind, to note that the gravitation of the earth is sufficient to hold about its surface enough atmosphere to support 30 inches of mercury while the gravitation of Mars has been able to hold only 7 to 9 inches. The smaller planets and satellites have lost practically all of their atmosphere because their gravitational forces could not prevent the molecules of the air from wandering off into space.

§42. **Gas Pressures.** On the supposition that these molecular motions exist, another peculiar fact may be easily explained: It has already been proved by Torricelli's experiment, page 41, that the atmosphere presses down on the earth's surface with a weight of 15 pounds per square inch. Now if a barometer tube, such as shown in Fig. 54, were enclosed in a glass receiver, Fig. 80, so as to shut out the atmosphere, the sides of the receiver would bear all of this pressure and the column of mercury should immediately drop. As a matter of fact, the mercury column does not change one particle, indicating that there is still some source of pressure on the inside of the receiver. Evidently the *molecules themselves are creating this pressure* in a manner which is made clear by a single illustration. Everyone is familiar with the kick or recoil of a gun when it is fired; if a rapid-fire gun which discharges many bullets per second is substituted, the impulse or kick from each bullet disappears and in its place there is a continuous pressure as long as the stream of bullets continues. It is in this manner that the molecules in the receiver, Fig. 80, bombard the sides of the vessel and the surface of the mercury, the blows occurring so many times per second that there is set up a steady pressure exactly equal to the atmospheric pressure which existed before the receiver was set down over the tube. In other words, the sum of the forces of the millions upon millions of molecules which are beating down upon the mercury surface is equal to 15 pounds per square inch. When a man goes down into a caisson, he feels the change in the air pressure because inside the caisson there are more molecules to beat his ear drum and to enter his lungs, and it takes several moments to accommodate himself to the new pressure. On coming out the reverse is true and the air inside will force itself out in an effort to restore equilibrium. If air is forced into an automobile tire so as to exert 100 pounds pressure, this means that $\dfrac{100}{15}$ or $6\frac{2}{3}$ times more molecules

Fig. 80. Mercury Column Supported by Molecular Vibrations

have been forced in than were present before the tire was inflated and for this reason there are $6\frac{2}{3}$ times as many blows per second. The mercury column in Fig. 80 will fall the moment the number of blows is decreased by the removal of the air inside the receiver and this fall will be in direct proportion to the quantity of air removed.

§43. **Temperature.** If a gas flame were carefully passed a few times over the surface of the receiver, Fig. 80, a rise in the quantity of mercury would be noticed immediately. The number of molecules present must have remained the same, for the receiver was not disturbed, consequently *the heating of the air must have resulted in an increase in the velocity of the molecules.* To say that a body has a certain temperature is, therefore, merely a way of saying that the molecules are moving at some definite rate; this rate is increased when the temperature rises and is diminished when the temperature falls.

LIQUIDS AND VAPORS

§44. **Molecular Motions in Liquids.** The amount of motion in liquids is supposed to be very much smaller than in gases, but the proofs of the existence of this motion are quite as convincing.

Evaporation. It is a well-known fact that if a vessel of water is exposed to the air the water will gradually disappear, supposedly passing into the air. This process, which is called *evaporation,* is easily explained on the assumptions that the molecules of the water are in motion, and that some of the molecules having fewer collisions than others will, therefore, acquire a higher velocity. If these particularly favored ones are moving toward the surface of the water, as shown in Fig. 78, they may shoot out of the liquid, thus getting away from the attraction of their fellows and passing into the air. It is on this principle that moisture is supposed to rise from all exposed water surfaces into the atmosphere, to be deposited later in the form of rain. Evidently when the water is hot, *i. e.,* when the molecules are moving faster, more of them will have acquired the velocity necessary for them to break away from the body of the liquid, thus causing evaporation to occur more rapidly. Consequently, *heat hastens evaporation,* an observation which is confirmed by the fact that evaporation occurs more rapidly on a dry, hot day than on a cold one, and that clothes dry more quickly in the sun or under a hot flat-iron.

If only the fast moving molecules evaporate, those remaining are slower than the average, which leads to the conclusion that *evaporation tends to cool the evaporating liquid.* This is known to be true from the fact that such liquids as ether and alcohol have a marked cooling effect on the hand or body. In fact, it is not at all difficult by passing air rapidly through a vessel containing ether to evaporate it so rapidly that it will freeze water.

Expansion. Fill a flask, Fig. 81, with water and then heat it: the level of the liquid in the tube immediately rises, illustrating the property, common to all liquids, of expansion with heat. The application of heat stimulates the velocity of the molecules and gives them the power to beat their fellows farther apart and thus cause the liquid to assume a greater volume.

§45. Properties of Vapors. A sponge, when dipped into water and then hung in the air, will drip for some time. After the dripping has ceased, a slight squeeze will start it again, showing that before being compressed the sponge contained all of the water it could possibly hold—a condition which is called *saturation*. Air, like the sponge, can hold between its molecules at any given temperature a certain maximum number of water molecules in the form of *vapor* and if this critical number be present, the air is *saturated;* if only one-half the maximum number be present, the air is 50 per cent saturated, etc. When the daily weather report states that *the humidity is 85 per cent*, the quantity of moisture in the atmosphere on that day is 85 per cent of the maximum quantity.

Dew-point. It is clear, therefore, that if air which is near the saturation point is cooled, its molecules come close together—a process corresponding to the squeeze of the sponge. If the cooling is sufficient to make the air pass the saturation point, some water vapor is deposited as moisture, usually upon the body which has done the cooling, a fact which is well illustrated by the gathering of moisture on the outside of a pitcher of ice water in the summer time. *The temperature at which moisture is deposited is called the dew-point.* Using this as a basis, a simple explanation of some of the weather phenomena may now be given.

Fig. 81. Expansion of a Liquid with Heat

Dew and Frost. The vast amount of evaporation going on all the time from exposed water surfaces continually renews the supply of water vapor in the atmosphere but very seldom brings it near the saturation point. After a warm day, however, the earth's surface, especially the blades of grass and the leaves of trees, cool much more quickly than the air, and finally reach a temperature low enough to cool the air near them to the dew-point, which results in the formation of *dew.* If there is not enough moisture in the atmosphere to cause dew to form at a temperature above freezing, the cooling may continue below the freezing point and in such a case the moisture is deposited as *frost*.   Therefore, *whether dew-point is above or below freezing determines whether dew or frost will form*.   If the dew-point is above freezing, then the farmer with perishable crops may rest easy, but if it is below freezing he will know that if the temperature falls below freezing the protecting layer of dew will not form before the tender shoots and the ripened fruit have been frost-bitten.   A

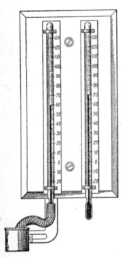

Fig. 82.   Wet- and Dry-Bulb Hygrometer

thermometer in a glass of ice water—with possibly some salt added, if the temperature needs to be below freezing—will show the temperature at which the moisture is deposited on the outside of the glass.   Such observations are usually taken, however, by means of an instrument called a *hygrometer*, Fig. 82, which consists of two thermometers, one being provided with a wet covering over the bulb.   By noting the difference between the readings of the *wet* and *dry* thermometers and consulting a table of values, the humidity and dew-point may be determined.   Acting upon this advance information, the Colorado apple orchardist or the California orange ranchman has kept the temperature of his orchard above freezing by lighting smudges between the trees.

Clouds, Rain, Hail, and Snow.   When a sufficient cooling of the air above the earth's surface brings the temperature down to the dew-point, the condensation of moisture occurs around the dust particles in the air and forms a *cloud*.   If the cooling continues, the mist collects in drops forming *rain*.   If, while falling, the rain passes through a cold air layer, the drops freeze and form *hail*. If the dew-point is below freezing and the air is sufficiently cooled, the moisture will crystallize out in the form of *snow-flakes*

SOLIDS

The facts that liquids expand with heat and that they also give off some of their molecules in the form of vapor, are used as proofs that liquid molecules are in motion.   The same arguments apply equally well in the case of solids.

§46. Expansion. Most solids are so hard and of such close-grained structure that it requires quite a stretch of the imagination to think of them as composed of a vibrating mass of molecules. Evidently, if their temperature governs the rate of their vibrations, an increase in temperature will enable the molecules to spread farther apart and a decrease in temperature will bring them closer together. This property of expansion is used in setting wagon tires and locomotive wheel rims, and must be allowed for in the case of bridge trusses and railroad rails.

§47. Evaporation. On account of the greater attractive force between the molecules of a solid, not many of them at ordinary temperatures allow any of their molecules to escape into the air; nevertheless, there are some which do this. It has been noticed often that snow, during a prolonged spell of cold weather, will disappear without once reaching the melting point, a fact which can only be accounted for on the supposition that the snow has evaporated. Likewise, the lump of camphor which is packed away with one's heavy overcoat during the summer is found in the fall much diminished in size or perhaps gone completely, leaving a strong odor of camphor vapor.

These and other instances of evaporation in solids lead to the conclusion that even in these rigid substances, from which molecular movement would seem as far removed as light from darkness, the molecules are in constant motion, but vibrating between very narrow limits, because of the restraining influence of that prodigious attractive force between the molecules known as *cohesion*.

PROBLEMS FOR PRACTICE

1. The same conditions of air pressure exist within a glass whether it is left open to the atmosphere or whether a glass plate is placed over the top to cut off the pressure of the atmosphere. Explain.

2. If an air-pump receiver has some of the air pumped out, that which remains immediately expands uniformly to fill the space. Why?

3. The molecules of hydrogen gas, of which ether is quite largely composed, move about four times as fast as air molecules. Will this account for its rapid evaporation?

4. Why do clothes dry more quickly on a windy than on a quiet day?

5. Why will a cool wind often bring up a fog? Why are morning fogs cleared up by the sun?

6. A fruit grower in late spring makes a test with his hygrometer and finds the dew-point below freezing. The night is reported cool. In what danger are his buds? What effect will fires between the trees have on the threatened conditions?

7. Why does sprinkling the street on a hot day make the air cooler?

8. The human body throws off large quantities of moisture through the pores of the skin. Why then is the heat so oppressive on a very *damp* summer day?

9. In winter time a pitcher of ice water will show no moisture on the outside. Why?

10. On a cool night, the windows of a room containing many people often show a deposit of moisture. Is this moisture on the inside or outside of the glass; why does it form and what does it indicate?

MOLECULAR FORCES

SOLIDS

§48. Tensile Strength of Materials. Abundant proof has already been given that the molecules of a substance, whether solid, liquid, or gas, are in constant motion. Something must also be done to account for the fact that in a gas the molecules are free to roam about at will; that in a liquid, they slide over each other and yet cling to each other to a certain extent; and that in a solid, the molecules are held together in a very definite shape, in many substances resisting with prodigious force any attempt to pull them apart. It will evidently be necessary to assume a force existing between the molecules which is effective when they are comparatively close together but which loses all its strength—as in the case of a gas—when the molecules are very far apart. This force between molecules of the same kind is called *cohesion*, and between molecules of different kinds *adhesion*. The cohesive force in such metals as steel is enormous, a wire .36 inches in diameter being able to

support a weight of nearly 6 tons. By hanging weights on the end
of wires of the same diameters, but of different material, the relative
breaking strengths—known as *tenacities* or *tensile strengths*—may be
determined. Fig. 83 shows a U. S. standard screw-power machine
used in testing the tensile strengths of metals. It is capable of ex-

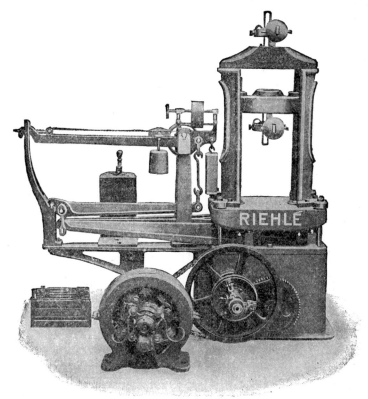

Fig. 83. Standard Screw-Power Testing Machine
Riehle Bros. Testing Machine Co., Philadelphia

erting a maximum pull of 30,000 pounds. Fig. 84 shows the effect of
such a test upon a piece of steel. Note that the sides of the test piece,
instead of being parallel as they were before fracture, taper toward
the broken edge, showing that the molecules were literally *pulled out
of their normal position* before the force of cohesion was overcome.

§49. **Elasticity.** When a solid is bent, twisted, or changed
in shape or size, a *strain* is said to be produced in the body. As
soon as the outside force produces the strain the distortion is re-

sisted by an internal elastic force which tends to restore the body to its original size or shape. That body is *most* elastic, therefore, which will recover from the distorting effects of the greatest force or, what amounts to the same thing, will require the largest force to produce a given distortion. The comparative values of this constant for different materials is obtained by observing the force necessary to produce the same elongation or change in length in wires of the same length and diameter.

Elastic Limit. It is evident that when the force acting on the wire becomes great enough to actually pull the molecules out of

Fig. 84. Piece of Steel Broken Under Tension

position, the elastic force will not be able to restore the wire to its former state, *i. e.*, the wire will have a permanent *set* at the point where the partial rupture occurred. The greatest force the wire can stand without permanent set is called the *elastic limit*.

Hooke's Law. If a wire is so mounted that careful measurements may be made of the change in length when a series of equal weights are added to the wire, the observations will show that *the successive application of equal forces produces a succession of equal stretches, so long as the elastic limit is not reached.* This is Hooke's Law and may be expressed by the equation

$$\frac{F}{F'} = \frac{e}{e'}$$

in which F and F' are any two forces or weights, while e and e' are the corresponding elongations. It has already been shown, Practical Mathematics Part III, that the graph of this relation, *i.e.*, of a direct proportion is a *straight line*.

§ 50. **Equilibrium Between Molecular Forces and Motions.** The facts that the result of the action of a stretching force on a solid is to draw the molecules farther apart; that a compression brings the molecules closer together; and that a rise in temperature of a solid produces expansion; all of these things seem to indicate that a perfect *balance* or *equilibrium* exists at all times between the

Fig. 85. Welding Steel

molecular forces and molecular vibrations of the body. At ordinary temperature the agitated molecules of a solid are able by these vibrations to keep themselves at a definite distance apart; when a pulling force acts upon the solid, it assists the molecular vibrations and stretches the body, but when the force is removed the old condition is resumed.

When the temperature of a solid is raised, the increased rapidity of vibration of the molecules enables them to overcome the cohesive force and thus the molecules move farther apart in order to preserve the balance, *i. e.*, the solid expands. If the temperature is decreased the cohesive force can bring the molecules closer together. In other words, the changes in a solid, under different conditions of stress or temperature, are merely those which will restore the equilibrium existing between the forces acting outward due to molecular motions and those acting inward due to cohesion. Evidently the difference in this equilibrium in different substances is responsible for the creation of such properties as *hardness, brittleness, ductility,* and *malleability.*

Welding. From what has been stated in § 48, it is quite evident that at ordinary temperatures the force of cohesion becomes effective only at extremely minute distances. To lay two pieces of steel together or even to press them together when cold, produces no effect. However, if the temperature of the two pieces of steel be raised to white heat, Fig. 85, the molecular motions have been so stimulated and the molecules have spread so far apart compared to their former condition that when the pieces are again placed in contact, accompanied by a certain amount of pressure, the molecules of each become enmeshed in those of the other so that in cooling the pieces are found to be *welded* together. Throughout the process, a perfect equilibrium has been maintained and the cooling of the welded parts finds the molecules at the joint acting as parts of a single piece of steel.

LIQUIDS

§51. Adhesion Between Liquids and Solids. Almost any solid when dipped into water and withdrawn will bring some water with it. This force of adhesion may be illustrated by suddenly pulling up on a flat board which is lying on the surface of the water. If the board is kept horizontal the pull necessary to separate it from the water will be found considerable. Even when an iron plate is separated from the surface of mercury—which does not "wet" the iron—a large force must be exerted to bring about the separation. The fact that the mercury does not wet the iron merely means that the cohesion between the molecules of mercury is greater than the adhesion between the mercury and the iron.

Behavior of Liquids in Small Tubes. Another example of the adhesion between solid and liquid is given in the behavior of liquids in tubes of small diameter. If a small clean glass tube, Fig. 86,

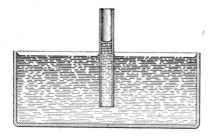

Fig. 86. Ascension of Water in
Capillary Tube

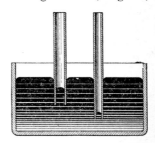

Fig. 87. Depression of Mercury
in Capillary Tube

is immersed in water, the level of the water in the tube will immediately rise above the level of the water outside. If another tube of one-half the diameter is used, the column of water will be twice as high. On the other hand if the same tubes are dried and immersed in mercury, Fig. 87, the column will be depressed *below* the outside level, the greater depression being shown in the smaller tube. The explanation is as follows: It is often noticed that the surface of a liquid is somewhat different from the interior, partaking more of the nature of a film or *skin* on the surface. This is supposed to be due to the fact that a molecule in the interior, Fig. 88, is surrounded by other molecules, all attracting and being attracted by this molecule. The molecules at the surface, however, have none of their fellows above them to balance the downward pull and, as a result, the surface layer of molecules acts like a stretched membrane, causing what is called *surface tension.* Consequently when, as in the case of the capillary tube, Fig. 86, the surface film in the tube

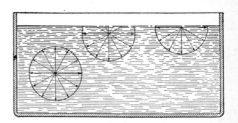

Fig. 88. Diagram Explaining "Skin" Effect
on a Water Surface

catches hold of the sides of the tube by virtue of the adhesion, the film tends to contract and in doing so pulls up water with it until the weight of the water drawn up equals the force of the pull. When the liquid does not wet the tube, as in the case of mercury and glass illustrated in Fig. 87, the surface tension produces a depression because there is only a little adhesive force to work against the strong cohesion between the mercury molecules.

Other Capillary Phenomena. Nature furnishes many examples of capillary action and surface tension. Of the former the most common are the rise of oil in wicks, the wetting of a towel which has only one end in water, the quick spreading of a liquid throughout a lump of sugar when one end is immersed, and the action of blotting paper in absorbing ink. These examples also illustrate surface tension but the membrane (skin) effect on the surface of a liquid is perhaps better shown by such examples as the floating of water bugs on the surface of a pool and the globular form of soap bubbles, rain drops, and molten lead in forming shot.

§52. Solution. A lump of sugar when placed in clear water will be seen to disappear rapidly; the sugar is said to be *dissolved* by the water. Evidently the molecules of the sugar have taken their places between the molecules of water just as the molecules of water vapor passed into the air. It will also be found that some substances will not dissolve in water but will dissolve in, say, alcohol, and *vice versâ*. Water dissolves sugar and salt better than alcohol does, while grease and shellac, although not touched by water, will dissolve readily in alcohol. In order to bring about a solution, the force of adhesion between the molecules of the solvent and those of the dissolved substance must be strong enough to overcome the cohesion of the particles of the substance. To find a *solvent* for a given substance is, therefore, merely to find a liquid whose molecules have a sufficiently strong affinity for the molecules of the substance to break down its cohesion.

Saturated Solution. If sugar is added to water in small quantities, it will soon be noticed that no more sugar is dissolving in the water. The water molecules have admitted as many sugar molecules as possible and the solution is said to be *saturated*. If the solution is heated, more sugar can be taken up but this will promptly crystallize out when the solution resumes its former temperature. The amount of a given substance which, at a given temperature, will produce saturation is always the same for the same solvent.

PROBLEMS FOR PRACTICE

1. If a given wire is stretched .07 inches by a force of 1 pound how far will it be stretched by 14 pounds?

2. The leads for pencils are made by subjecting powdered graphite to enormous hydraulic pressure. Why does this process change the powder to a solid mass?

3. Why must blotting paper rather than a glazed paper be used to take up ink?

4. Why must a blacksmith exert pressure, accompanied by heating, in order to weld two pieces of metal? Why should the surfaces be clean?

5. Candle grease may be removed from clothing by covering the spot with a blotter and passing a hot iron over it. Explain.

EXPANSION BY HEAT

THERMOMETRY

§53. Temperature. The terms *hot* and *cold* as they are generally applied are purely relative, and depend upon the feelings of the person who passes judgment. A room may seem hot to one who has been exercising but will feel cool to one who has been sitting still. A rug may feel warm to the bare feet while a tile floor which is probably at the same temperature may feel cold. Lukewarm water will feel hot or cool to the hand depending upon whether the hand has previously been in cold or hot water, respectively.

The *temperature* of a body, however, has already, page 59, been attributed to the motion of the molecules and surely is a more definite thing than would be indicated by the above examples. This unreliability of body sensations has led to the introduction of mechanical devices for measuring temperature called *thermometers*, which depend for their action on the fact that practically all bodies *expand* with heat.

Methods of Measurement. The first thermometer, made by Galileo, utilized the expansion of air to indicate the temperature, the changes being shown by the rise or fall of a column of colored liquid. About the year 1700 the *mercury* thermometer was invented and proved so reliable and convenient that it has remained the standard form for practical use. *Gas* thermometers are used exclusively in scientific work, particularly for standardizing the mercury thermometers used by thermometer manufacturers and by colleges and universities. *Platinum* thermometers and pyrometers are used for high and low temperatures, and *metallic* thermometers as general weather thermometers and thermostats.

§54. Mercury Thermometers. The mercury thermometer consists of a thick-walled glass tube with a bulb blown on one end into which perfectly clean, pure mercury is introduced. When the mercury has been heated slightly above the highest temperature which the thermometer is expected to register, the open end of the tube is sealed by means of a hot flame; when the mercury cools, it contracts and leaves a perfect vacuum above the mercury column in the tube. The thermometer is now placed successively in a vessel of melting ice, Fig. 89, and in the steam rising from boiling water, Fig. 90, and the position which the top of the mercury column assumes in each case

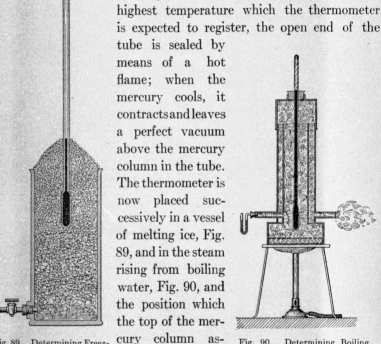

Fig. 89. Determining Freezing Point on a Thermometer

Fig. 90. Determining Boiling Point on a Thermometer

is marked on the tube to indicate the *freezing point* and the *boiling point* of water, respectively.

Centigrade Scale. If the centigrade scale is used the temperature of the melting ice is taken as 0°, while the boiling point is marked 100° and the space between these marks is divided into 100 equal parts. According to this thermometer, one degree of change in temperature means such a change as will cause the mercury column to move over one of these divisions, called a *centigrade degree.*

Jn Important

by the way Johnny!
(wake up)

7. Jackwire

$$F_{2\pi b} = R_8 \sqrt{\frac{2\pi b}{S}} \sqrt{\frac{N_0}{F 2\pi b}}$$

$W = Fs$

Laws of Machines $F_s = R_s$

Laws of Simple Machines

1. Lever

(Scheme) $Fd = Rd'$ $\dfrac{d}{d'}$ $\dfrac{R}{Fd'}$

2. Wheel & Axle $Fr = Rr'$ $\dfrac{r}{r'}$ $\dfrac{Rr}{Rs'}$

3. Pulley $Fs = Rs'$ $\dfrac{s}{s'}$ $\dfrac{Fr}{Rs}$

4. Inclined Plane $FL = Rh$ $\dfrac{L}{h}$ $\dfrac{Rh}{FL}$

$= \dfrac{h}{L}$ $F = Rs'$ $\dfrac{FL}{Rs'}$

Important

Johnny

This scale is used in scientific work the world over and for ordinary purposes in all countries but England and the United States.

Fahrenheit Scale. The Fahrenheit thermometer, which is the common thermometer in England and the United States, differs from the centigrade only in its manner of graduation. The temperature of melting ice is taken at 32° instead of 0° and the boiling point of water is 212° instead of 100°. The space on the stem between these marks is then divided into 180 parts. To compare the readings of the centigrade and Fahrenheit thermometers, it is only necessary to consider that 100 centigrade degrees denote the same difference in temperature as 180 Fahrenheit degrees, Fig. 91.

Therefore, one Fahrenheit degree equals $\dfrac{100}{180}$ or $\dfrac{5}{9}$ of a centigrade degree, and one centigrade degree equals $\dfrac{9}{5}$ of a Fahrenheit degree.

Hence, *to reduce from Fahrenheit to centigrade, subtract 32° and take $\dfrac{5}{9}$ of the remainder.*

To reduce from centigrade to Fahrenheit, take $\dfrac{9}{5}$ of the given temperature and add 32°.

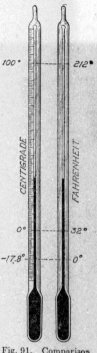

Fig. 91. Comparison of Centigrade and Fahrenheit Scales

EXAMPLES.　1.　Change 72° F. to centigrade.

$$72 - 32 = 40$$

$$\frac{5}{9} \text{ of } 40 = 22.2 + \text{ Ans.}$$

2.　Change −22° C. to Fahrenheit.

$$\frac{9}{5} \text{ of } -22° = -39.6°$$

$$-39.6 + 32 = -7.6° \quad \text{Ans.}$$

The mercury thermometer is usable between the temperatures of −40° C. and 360° C., or between −40° F. and 680° F.

Clinical Thermometer. For taking temperatures of the human body, a form of mercury thermometer called the clinical thermometer is used, Fig. 92. This form has the bore pinched nearly together at one point so that when the mercury cools the column breaks at this constricted part leaving the column above to indicate the highest temperature reached—a permanent record of the temperature until the mercury is shaken down into the bulb.

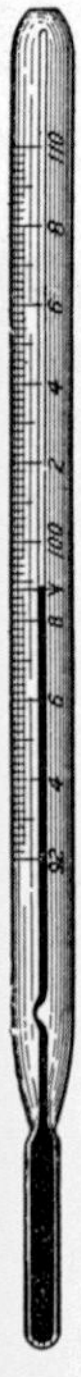

§55. Gas Thermometer. The gas thermometer in the form shown in Fig. 93 is used as the standard with which all mercury thermometers are directly or indirectly compared. It consists essentially of a bulb *B* of glass or platinum (the latter for high temperatures) to the stem of which is attached a flexible tube with a glass tube attached to its other end. The tubes are filled with mercury and the upper end of tube *a* is sealed without leaving any air above the mercury. Now by placing the bulb in melting ice and adjusting the height of tube *a* until the mercury in tube *b* is exactly at the point *c*, the position of the mercury level in tube *a* may be marked on a convenient scale. When the bulb is placed in steam, the heated air within the bulb will expand and then tube *a* must be raised to a considerable height, viz, until the level of the mercury in tube *b* has been brought back to *c*. When this has been done the difference in height of the mercury levels in *a* represents the change from freezing to boiling and may be divided into 100° centigrade or 180° Fahrenheit. After the scale has been thus established the graduations may be extended below the 0° point and above the 100° point and a wide range of temperatures observed.

Fig. 92.
Clinical
Thermometer

§56. Coefficient of Expansion of a Gas. The coefficient of expansion of a gas may be defined as *that fraction of its volume at 0° C. which a certain body of gas will expand or contract for a change of temperature of one degree centigrade.* The value of this fraction is $\frac{1}{273}$. This means that a body of gas in passing from 10° to 11° will expand $\frac{1}{273}$ of its volume at 0°, or in passing from 0° to 100° will expand $\frac{100}{273}$ of the same volume.

Law of Charles. A Frenchman, Charles, discovered that *the expansion coefficients for all gases are the same*, viz, $\frac{1}{273}$. Hence, the bulb *B* of Fig. 93 may be filled with air, hydrogen, nitrogen, or in fact any gas without lessening the reliability of the recorded temperatures. Hydrogen is generally used in the most refined work.

Absolute Temperature. It was shown that, on being heated from 0° to 100° C., a body of gas expands $\frac{100}{273}$ of its volume at 0° C. Evidently, if the gas is *cooled* 100 degrees, *i. e.*, 0° to −100° C., it contracts $\frac{100}{273}$ of its 0° volume. At −200° C., its volume will have been reduced $\frac{200}{273}$, and if this cooling were continued still lower a point would be reached at −273° C., where the volume of the gas would theoretically disappear. This point where the molecules of a gas evidently cease to move is called *absolute zero*, and is made the basis of a new temperature scale, called the *absolute scale*, A. −273° C. is 0° A, 0° C. is 273° A, and 100° C. is 373° A. The main use for this scale is in handling the gas laws in theoretical work, *i. e.*, in determining the volume or the pressure of a gas under changes in temperature.

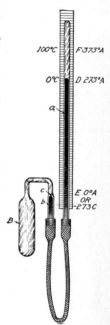

Fig. 93. Standard Gas Thermometer

§57. Low Temperatures. Although the absolute zero of temperature will never be reached, yet it has been approached by the aid of liquid air and liquid hydrogen. Up to thirty years ago the lowest temperature −110° C. had been attained by Faraday. Liquid air, in 1880, lowered this limit to −180° C.; in 1900, Dewar attained a temperature of −260° C. by evaporating liquid hydrogen into a space kept exhausted by an air pump; and in 1911 Kammerlich Ohnes, by evaporating liquid helium reached a temperature *only about 4°* *above absolute zero*. These results in low temperature work form a very convincing experimental proof of the accuracy of the gas laws and of the kinetic theory of gases.

§58. High Temperatures. Both low and high temperatures may be measured by means of the gas thermometer, but in practical work with high temperatures, the common practice is to use either a platinum thermometer or a pyrometer, Fig. 94. The former instrument utilizes the change in electrical resistance of a coil of platinum wire with changes in temperature. The pyrometer con-

Fig. 94. Pyrometer for Determining High Temperatures

sists of two different metals, called a thermo-couple, joined together and placed in a protecting box with one juncture of the thermo-couple at the focus of a concave mirror. When the box is pointed at a furnace door as in the figure or at an observation hole, the radiation from the mirror raises the temperature of one juncture, thus causing a weak electric current to flow through an electrical measuring instrument, the dial of which is so graduated as to give a direct reading of the temperatures. The pyrometer is much used in the pottery and steel industries to enable operators to regulate the temperature of furnaces

PROBLEMS FOR PRACTICE

1. Change 275° F. to centigrade; 110° C. to Fahrenheit; −65° C. to Fahrenheit.

2. What is 85° C. when expressed in the absolute scale? −180° C.?−243° C.? Answers: 358° A; 93° A; 30°A.

3. The bore of a sensitive thermometer is elliptical in shape, Fig. 95, and the graduations are always placed upon the long side of bore. Compare this with a circular bore of the same area.

Fig. 95. Elliptical Shape of Thermometer Tubing

4. Construct a temperature scale with the freezing and boiling points at 0° and 150° respectively, and express the temperatures 20°C., −10°C., and 285°C. in terms of the new scale. Answers: 30° new scale; −15°; 427.5°.

EXPANSION COEFFICIENTS OF LIQUIDS AND SOLIDS

§59. **Liquids.** The expansion of liquids by heat shows itself in a change in volume, *i. e.*, a *cubical* expansion as illustrated by the mercury thermometer. Liquids differ decidedly from gases in that they do not expand uniformly as the temperature rises nor are their coefficients at all alike, as are those for gases. Mercury, however, is better than most liquids in the uniformity of its expansion and for this reason has been selected for use in thermometers.

Maximum Density of Water. The failure of water to contract uniformly with a lowering of its temperature is responsible for what might be considered a *narrow escape of nature.* When water reaches a temperature of 4° C., or about 39° F., it has its smallest volume, *i. e.*, its greatest density. As the temperature is lowered from this point to 0° C. or 32° F. the water *expands*. This means that in winter, the surface water is cooled, sinks, and is replaced by warmer water from below; this sinking of the cold and rising of the warm water goes on until the entire pond reaches a temperature of 39° F. or 4° C. As the cooling continues from this point, the water below 4° C. no longer sinks but floats like oil on the surface until it reaches 0° C. or 32° F. and freezes. As water expands still more on freezing, the ice thus formed floats on the surface getting slowly thicker as the heat is abstracted from the water through the ice, the water, except that immediately below the ice, never getting colder than 4° C. If

TABLE II

Linear Coefficients of Expansion

Aluminum	.000023	Glass	.000009	Silver	.000019
Brass	.000018	Iron	.000012	Steel	.000011
Copper	.000017	Lead	.000029	Tin	.000022
Gold	.000014	Platinum	.000009	Zinc	.000029

it were not for the fortunate expansion of water and ice, the water would cool uniformly to 0° C. and the ice which was formed would sink at once to the bottom; by this process the lakes and ponds would soon be frozen solid, killing all of the fish and producing so much ice that the summer sun might not be able to thaw it out of the lake bottoms. This would produce a permanent glacial condition in all regions except the torrid zone and completely change the character of the earth as a habitation for vegetable and animal life.

§60. **Solids.** *Linear Coefficient.* In the discussion of expansion coefficients of gases and liquids, only the cubical or volume

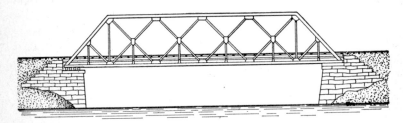

Fig. 96. Arrangement on Bridge to Allow for Expansion

coefficients were mentioned, but with solids much more importance is attached to the *linear coefficient.* This is defined as *the ratio of the increase in length per degree rise in temperature to the total length;* or, in other words, it is *the fraction of an inch which one inch of the substance will expand for 1 degree rise in temperature.* If l_1 and l_2 are the lengths at the temperatures t_1 and t_2, respectively, and c is the coefficient of expansion, then

$$c = \frac{l_2 - l_1}{l_1 (t_2 - t_1)}$$

Some of the most common linear expansion coefficients are given in Table II.

Applications of Expansion. There are many illustrations of the expansibility of solids, most of which are of common observation. *Railroad rails* must be laid, if in winter time, with a space between the rails to allow for the expansion in summer, or if laid absolutely in contact in summer, there will be a comparatively large space between them in cold weather. There is a rather surprising

Fig. 97. Effect of Unequal Expansion of Metals

exception to this behavior in the case of "flush" rails used in street railways, for these rails are welded into one continuous system and yet the fact that only the upper surface of the rail is exposed to the sun while the balance of the rail instead of being surrounded by non-conducting air is buried in much better conductors such as earth and cement, makes the difference between the actual expansion of the rail and the expansion of the surrounding surface material negligible. Again, the *rivets* used in boiler making, bridge work, and steel construction are used *hot* so that, in cooling, the contraction will bring the plates together with prodigious force. *Bridges* need some provision at the terminals for the expansion or contraction caused by changes in temperature, Fig. 96; long lines of *steam pipes* must have *expansion joints*, particularly near corners so that the retaining walls, supports, etc., will not be pulled or pushed out of place by the expanding or contracting pipes.

The unequal expansibility of metals is made use of by riveting or soldering two metals together, Fig. 97. If the temperature is decreased below a normal, the strip will bend one way, and if it is increased above the normal, it will bend the other way. A very familiar illustration of this is the *compensated balance wheel* of a watch, Fig. 98; the metal rim is composed of brass on the outside and steel on the inside, the brass having the greater expansion

Fig. 98. Balance Wheel of Watch Compensated for Temperature

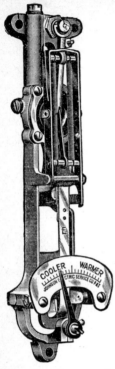

Fig. 99.   Thermostat for Heating System

Fig. 100.   Metal Thermometer Coil

coefficient.   An increase in temperature will increase the radius of the wheel and weaken the elasticity of the hair spring, both of which effects will tend to make the watch lose time; however, the same increase in temperature will make the brass strip in the rim expand more than the steel, thus curling each section *toward the center* and tending to make the wheel vibrate faster. By having large-headed screws in the rim which may be screwed in or out or removed altogether, the adjustment for temperature may be made very accurate. Another important application of unequal expansion is in the *thermostat* or heat regulator, Fig. 99.   A strip E composed of two metals rests between two electrical contact points.   If the room becomes too warm, the strip bends upward and touches a contact point, completing the circuit to a motor which starts, thus closing the drafts in the furnace.   When the temperature becomes too cool the strip bends downward and the motor now opens the drafts.

A *dial thermometer* is made with a coiled spring, Fig. 100, which winds up or unwinds with changes in temperature, up or down, respectively.   This spring motion is communicated to the hand of the dial, Fig. 101, by a system of levers and string connections so that the proper temperature is recorded.   A self-recording type of thermometer, Fig. 102, is made to provide a complete 24-hour record by having the cylinder driven by clock work and the pointer provided

Fig. 101.   Metal Thermometer Complete

with a pen which traces the fluctuations of temperature on a pre-pared record sheet.

The fact that *platinum* and *glass* have practically the same coefficient of expansion makes platinum a very necessary metal in sealing into incandescent lamp bulbs the terminals to which

Fig. 102. Recording Thermometer

the filament is attached. Any other metal would crack the glass on being heated and thus destroy the vacuum in the bulb.

PROBLEMS FOR PRACTICE

1. A brass rod 80 cm. long at 9.7° C. expanded .136 cm. on being heated to 99.2° C. What is the linear coefficient of expansion of brass? Ans. .000018+

2. A glass stopper tightly inserted in a bottle may often be loosened by pouring hot water quickly on the neck. Why?

3. The steel cable from which the Brooklyn bridge hangs is more than a mile long. By how many feet does a mile of its length vary between −20°C. and 30° C.? Ans. 2.9+ feet.

4. Why does the water at the bottom of a pond whose surface is frozen over remain at 4°C.?

ONE CELL OF A HODGES HIGH-DUTY MULTI-STILL

Courtesy of Pure Water Apparatus Company, New York City

PRACTICAL PHYSICS

PART II

WORK AND MECHANICAL ENERGY

§61. Measurement of Work. The term *work* as used in every-day life refers to any form of muscular exertion or the performance of any task whatsoever, *but in Physics work is done only when a force acts so as to move a body over a certain space.* If a laborer, by means of a rope and pulley, raised a barrel of salt to the second floor of a warehouse and held it suspended for a time, he would consider that he was working whether the barrel was moving or not, but according to the true definition, the work stopped when the barrel reached its highest point. Therefore, the amount of work accomplished is measured by the product of the force acting and the distance through which it moves the body. If the barrel of salt just referred to weighed 300 pounds and it were raised 20 feet, the amount of work performed would be 300×20, or 6,000 *foot pounds.* In general, therefore,

$$W = F \times s$$

where W represents the work accomplished, F the force acting, and s the distance passed over by the body.

Units of Work. Evidently the above definition of work makes it possible to have any unit of work desired by coupling any unit of force used with any unit of distance. A *foot pound* means 1 pound of weight acting over 1 foot of space; a *gram-centimeter* means 1 gram acting over 1 centimeter; a *kilogram-meter* means 1 kilogram acting over 1 meter. The units of work most commonly used are the foot pound and the kilogram-meter. If a man raises a 100-pound sack of flour from the floor to his shoulder, a distance of approximately 5 feet, he has done 500 foot pounds of work. In the same manner, if a man weighing 80 kilograms is lifted a distance of 20 meters, 1,600 kilogram-meters of work have been done.

SIMPLE MACHINES

LEVERS

§62. **Law of the Lever.** A lever is a rod free to turn about a fixed axis called the *fulcrum*. Its action may be illustrated by means of a meter stick, Fig. 103, which is supported at a point F, and from which are hung two known weights.

The stick is first adjusted without the addition of the weights, so that it rests in a horizontal position; then a weight of 100 grams placed, say, 40

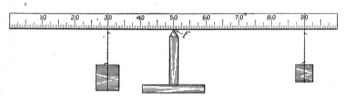

Fig. 103. Example of a Balanced System

centimeters from the fulcrum will destroy this balance, which may be restored by the addition to the other side of 200 grams at 20 centimeters from the fulcrum, or 400 grams at 10 centimeters. In other words, if the product of the weight by the distance from the fulcrum on one side equals the product of the weight by the distance from the fulcrum on the other side, equilibrium is obtained.

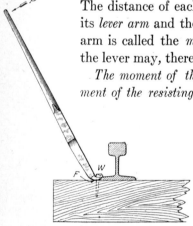

Fig. 104. Crowbar a Powerful Lever

The distance of each weight from the fulcrum is called its *lever arm* and the product of a force by its lever arm is called the *moment* of that force. The law of the lever may, therefore, be stated as follows:

The moment of the acting force is equal to the moment of the resisting force, i. e.,

$$F \, l = F' \, l'$$

where F and F' are the forces, or weights, while l and l' are their respective lever arms.

The examples of the use of the lever principle are many and varied. The laborer on the railroad draws the spikes with a crowbar, Fig. 104, and it is well known that the longer the bar, *i. e.*, the longer the lever arm of P, the more easily the spikes are withdrawn. This is evident from the fact that the distance from W to F is fixed and, therefore, the moment of W is fixed. As this

moment must equal the moment of P, the longer the lever of P, the less force may be exerted to accomplish the work. A chemical balance, Fig. 105, is provided with *equal arms* so that the weights placed in one pan will exactly equal the weight of the body in the other pan. On the other hand, the old-fashioned steelyards or the modern weighing scales are so arranged that a comparatively small counterweight will balance a large mass. In other words, by applying a small force, it is possible to overcome a large resistance.

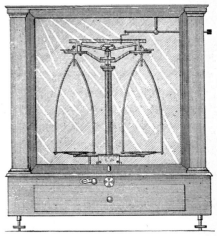

Fig. 105.   Chemical Balance

Addition of Moments. Although the discussion of the forces acting on a lever has been confined to one on each side of the fulcrum, the law holds for any number of forces, and equilibrium will be maintained *as long as the equation of moments is satisfied.*

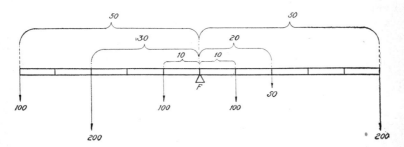

Fig. 106.   Addition of Moments

In Fig. 106, let weights of 100, 200, and 100 grams be placed, respectively, 10, 30, and 50 centimeters from the fulcrum on the left side, and let weights of 50 and 200 grams be placed, respectively, 20 and 50 centimeters from the fulcrum on the right side; it will be found that 100-gram weight will produce equilibrium if placed 10 centimeters from F on the right side. The equation of moments thus becomes

$$(100 \times 50) + (200 \times 30) + (100 \times 10) = (100 \times 10) + (50 \times 20) + (200 \times 50)$$

The law of the lever may be stated in general as follows:

If a system is in equilibrium, the sum of all the moments which tend to rotate the beam in one direction is equal to the sum of all the moments which tend to rotate the beam in the opposite direction.

§63. **Mechanical Advantage.** *The number of times the resisting force is greater than the acting force in any machine is called the mechanical advantage of the machine.* The algebraic statement of the

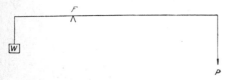

Fig. 107.   Illustrating a Lever of the First Class

law of the lever, $F\,l = F'\,l'$ shows, when placed in the form $\dfrac{F}{F'} = \dfrac{l'}{l}$, that the ratio of the acting and resisting forces is in inverse proportion to the ratio of their respective lever arms.   That is, if the acting force F is to be made very small, the value of l must be large and l' small.   The crowbar shown in Fig. 104 has an l' equal possibly to 1 inch and an l, say, of 72 inches.   The mechanical advantage of the crowbar is, therefore, 72, because the ratio of the force F' applied at the spike head to the force F applied at the end of the bar must be, by the equation just stated, the same as $\dfrac{l}{l'}$.   The balance, Fig. 105, which has its fulcrum set in the middle of the beam, has a

Fig. 108.   Steelyards a Lever of the First Class

mechanical advantage of 1, but as a rule a machine is so designed as to give a distinct advantage either of power or of speed.   What is gained in one direction is lost in the other; a sacrifice of speed is a gain in power. The hydraulic press, Fig. 42, for one stroke of the small piston will raise the large piston only a small fraction of an inch, but the resistance developed is very great. On the other hand, in the sewing machine the power F applied by the feet is many times greater than the resistance F' overcome by the needle, which means that the mechanical advantage is much less than 1 and that l' is many times greater than l. In this case power has been sacrificed for speed, the number of strokes of the needle for one stroke of the pedal showing the enormous gain.

§64. Classes of Lev=ers. Levers are divided into three classes according to the relative position of the acting force, the resisting force, and the fulcrum.

(1) *In levers of the first class*, the fulcrum is between the power (or acting force) and the weight (or resisting force), Fig. 107, giving a mechanical advantage greater, or less, or equal to 1. Examples of this class of lever are to be found in a pair of scissors,

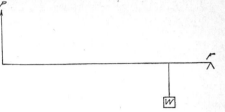

Fig. 109. Illustrating a Lever of the Second Class

Fig. 110. Crowbar May Also be a Lever of the Second Class

Fig. 111. Illustrating a Lever of the Third Class

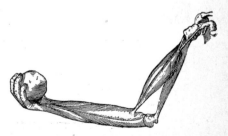

Fig. 112. Forearm a Good Example of a Third-Class Lever

pedal of a piano, pump handle, and the old-fashioned steelyards, Fig. 108.

(2) *In levers of the second class,* the resisting force (or weight *W*) is situated between the power and the fulcrum, Fig. 109. It must be noticed that the *power arm* and the *weight arm* are the distances of the power and the weight, respectively, from the fulcrum. The mechanical advantage is necessarily greater than 1, for the weight arm must be smaller than the power arm, Excellent illustrations of this class of lever are a wheelbarrow and a crowbar thrust under a body and pushed forward, as shown in Fig. 110.

(3) *In the levers of the third class,* the power is between the fulcrum and the weight, Fig. 111. The mechanical advantage, therefore, must always be less than 1, power being sacrificed for speed or motion. The forearm is a good example of this class of lever, Fig. 112.

PROBLEMS FOR PRACTICE

1.   A man weighing 150 pounds carries a hod of brick weighing 75 pounds to a height of 45 feet. How many foot pounds of work are done on the brick? Is this the total work done?

2.   A lever is 4 feet long. Where must the fulcrum be placed in order that 50 pounds at one end of the lever may balance 350 pounds at the other? What is the mechanical advantage of such a lever? Answers: $\frac{1}{2}$ ft. from end; mech. advantage = 7.

3.   Classify the following levers: Oar in rowing a boat, nut crackers, cutting pliers, sugar tongs, claw hammer.

4.   Weights of 100 kilos and 75 kilos are hung from a weightless bar 6 meters long, Fig. 113. The 100-kilo weight is 1.5 meters from *A*, and the 75-kilo weight is 2 meters from *B*. The bar is supported by two men, one at *A* and one at *B*. Find what load each man is carrying. (SUGGES-tion: For load at *B* use

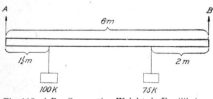

A
B
6m
1½m
2m
100K
75K

Fig. 113. A Bar Supporting Weights in Equilibrium

A as fulcrum, and put upward moment at *B* equal to sum of downward moments of two weights. For load at *A*, reverse process.) Ans. Load at *A* = 100 kg.; at *B* = 75 kg.

5. A man starts a freight car by using a bar as shown in Fig. 114. If the distance from the bend which touches the rail to the end of the bar is 5 feet and from the bend to the point is 2 inches, what force is exerted on the wheel if the man pushes down with a force of 125 pounds? What is the mechanical advantage of the bar?

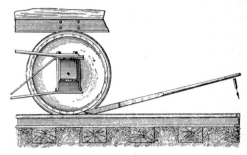

Fig. 114. Starting a Freight Car with a Crowbar

6. With which of the first two classes of levers will a force of 50 pounds raise the greater weight, the lever being 10 feet long and the weight arm 2 feet long? Sketch proof.

7. How much must a boy rolling a wheelbarrow lift in order to raise 200 pounds of material whose center of gravity is 12 inches from the wheel, if the boy's hands are 24 inches farther away?

8. In the steelyards shown in Fig. 108, the distance from the fulcrum to the parcel hook is 1.5 inches. In order to obtain equilibrium how far from the fulcrum must the weight be placed if it weighs 8 ounces and the package weighs 4 pounds? Ans. 12 inches.

9. A ladder rests upon the ground with its foot against a house. Show by figures how the class of lever changes as a man raises it to a vertical position by lifting on successive rungs nearer and nearer the foot. (Take center of gravity of ladder at center rung.)

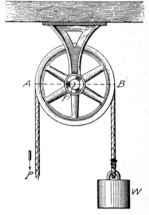

Fig. 115. Fixed Pulley

PULLEYS

§65. **Single Fixed Pulley.** A pulley is really a form of lever, as may be seen from Fig. 115, the center F of the pulley corresponding to the fulcrum, and the two points A and B corresponding to the points of application of the power and the weight. In the case of the single fixed pulley, it is seen that the power and the weight arms are equal to each other, *i. e.*, equal to the radius of the pulley; hence, the mechanical advantage of such a pulley is 1, the acting force passing over the same distance as the resisting load. Such a pulley is often used where a gain in power is not necessary, as in raising brick, gravel, etc., from the ground to the top of a building by hand or by horse. In the latter case a second fixed pulley near the ground is necessary, but this only changes the direction without changing the mechanical advantage of the system.

§66. Single Movable Pulley. In the case of the movable pulley, Fig. 116, the fulcrum is at the point B, which changes its position up and down as the pulley

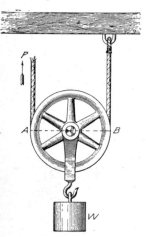

Fig. 116.   Movable Pulley   Fig. 117.   Block and Tackle

is raised or lowered but which is always in a vertical line with the hook to which the rope is attached. The lever arm of the acting force P is, therefore, the diameter D of the wheel, and its moment is PD; the lever arm of the resisting force is the radius of the wheel, and its moment is WR. As D is twice R, the mechanical advantage of the single movable pulley is 2, and P may be one-half of W. It should also be clear that *the force P must pass over twice the distance passed over by W,* thus showing that if friction is neglected, the work put into the machine Pd must equal the work done by the machine Wd', where d and d' are, respectively, the distances moved over by the power and the weight.

§67. **Combination of Pulleys.** When fixed and movable pulleys are combined as in Fig. 117, the machine is called a *block and tackle*. A continuous rope runs from one pulley in the upper block to one in the lower; the power is applied at the loose end of the rope while the weight is hung from the movable block. Since the rope is continuous there must be the same pull on each of the n portions of the rope between the blocks (in Fig. 117, $n = 6$), and therefore, each must support $\dfrac{1}{n}$ of the load. Hence

$$P = \frac{W}{n}$$

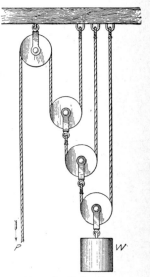

Fig. 118. Pulley System

that is, if n *represents the number of strands between which the weight is divided, the mechanical advantage of the pulley system is equal to* n. As in the case of the single movable pulley the fore end of the rope must be drawn n inches in order to raise W one inch, and the work put into the pulley block is equal, barring friction, to the work got out of it, that is

$$Pd = Wd'$$

PROBLEMS FOR PRACTICE

1. If the mechanical advantage of a fixed pulley is 1, is there any actual advantage in its use for raising materials to the top of a building other than convenience, over the method of carrying the material up ladders by man-power? Analyze.

2. If W, Fig. 118, is 200 pounds, what acting force P is necessary to support the load? (SUGGESTION: Half the weight W is held by second pulley, and so on; top pulley is fixed.) Ans. 25 lb.

3. In a block and tackle with four pulleys in each block, how much weight can be lifted by 50 pounds of acting force?

4. Using a horse, the pulley system, Fig. 117, and a fixed pulley at the ground level, find how far the horse must travel in order to raise a piece of machinery weighing 2 tons a height of 30 feet. How much force must he exert?   Answers: 180 ft.; $666\frac{2}{3}$ lb.

INCLINED PLANE

§68. Mechanical Advantage. The work done in lifting a body against gravity to a certain height as already stated is equal to the product of the weight W by the vertical distance h passed over. Hence, when the barrel, Fig. 119, is rolled up the incline into the wagon, the work done is Wh. But in being rolled up the plane, the barrel passes over the distance l, the length of the plank, and, as already found, page 10, only a component w of the weight is effective down the plane and must be balanced by an equal and opposite force P sufficient to hold the barrel upon the plane. Hence, by similar triangles, the weight W of the barrel will bear the same ratio to this force P that the length l of the inclined plane bears to its height h. That is

$$\frac{W}{P} = \frac{l}{h}$$

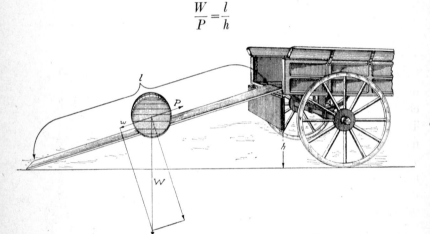

Fig. 119. Illustration of the Use of an Inclined Plane as a Machine

This means that the mechanical advantage of an inclined plane is equal to the ratio of the length to the height. Hence, the mechanical advantage of a 5 per cent grade on a railroad is 20, for the rise is 5 feet in every 100 feet of track. Evidently, then, if the height of the wagon, Fig. 119, is 3 feet and the length of the plank is 15 feet, the inclined plane will develop a mechanical advantage of 5, and a person can, therefore, hold a 300-pound barrel on the plank or, when it is once started, can keep it in motion, with the expenditure of 60 pounds of force.

PROBLEMS FOR PRACTICE

1. A boy who can exert a maximum force of only 80 pounds is called upon to roll a barrel weighing 400 pounds through a doorway 5 feet above the ground. How long a plank will he need? How much work will be done? Answers: 25-foot plank; 2000 ft. lb.

2. The work done in pulling a train of cars for a mile on an 8 per cent grade is the same, barring friction losses, as that done in pulling the same train over 4 miles on a 2 per cent grade. Why then are civil engineers always trying to cut down the grades on railroads?

COMPOUND MACHINES

§69. Law of Machines. The study of the lever and the pulley as types of simple machines shows that, when friction is neglected, *the work put into a machine is equal to the work accomplished by it,* a statement which was first made by Newton and called the *Principle of Work.* This statement is, of course, contrary to a popular idea that machines are devices for doing away with work. There is a compensation always demanded by nature's laws in that *whenever the acting force is a certain number of times smaller than the resisting force, the space over which the smaller force acts must be a corresponding number of times greater than the resisting force.* In other words, whatever is gained in force is lost in distance. The horse which pulls a heavy safe to a third story window with a block and tackle which has a

Fig. 120. Wheel and Axle

mechanical advantage of 8, must walk eight times as far as the safe moves. In the same manner the hydraulic press, Fig. 42, which shows a tremendous mechanical advantage, makes it necessary by this very fact for the small piston to make stroke after stroke in order to carry the large piston through a comparatively short distance.

Compound machines are either variations or combinations of the simpler machines already discussed, and their mechanical advantage may often be most easily found by noting the relative distance over which the resisting and the acting forces move.

§70. Wheel and Axle. The wheel and axle, although a variation of the lever in which the radii of the wheel and of the axle are the arms, can be more easily understood by considering that when the force P, Fig. 120, has unrolled one turn of rope from the wheel, *i. e.*, has acted through a distance equal to the circumference of the wheel, the weight W has been raised a distance equal to one turn of the axle. Therefore

$$P \times 2\pi R = W \times 2\pi r$$
$$PR = Wr$$

in which P and W are the acting and the resisting forces, R and r are the radii of the wheel and axle, respectively, and π is $\dfrac{22}{7}$ as usual. This result shows that the mechanical advantage of the wheel and axle is $\dfrac{R}{r}$ or, in case the diameters are given, $\dfrac{D}{d}$. A spe-

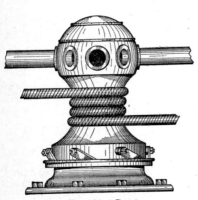

Fig. 121. Capstan

cial case of the wheel and axle is the capstan, Fig. 121, in which the wheel is replaced by handspikes. The mechanical advantage of this machine is the ratio of the length of the handspike to the radius of the barrel around which the rope is wound.

For example, the handspikes of a capstan are 6 feet long, the diameter of the barrel is 10 inches. Find how many men, each pushing with a force of 75 pounds, will be necessary to raise a 1-ton anchor, neglecting friction. The mechanical advantage of the capstan is $\dfrac{6 \times 12}{5}$, or 14.4. Therefore, the force necessary to lift the anchor is $2000 \div 14.4 = 139$ pounds. As each man pushes with a maximum force of 75 pounds, two men can easily do the work.

§71. Gears. *Spur.* Wheels having teeth cut in their periphery are called gears, and two such gears having the same sized teeth and of any diameter may form a part of a simple machine. Gears of the spur type are shown in Fig. 122. Their teeth are very accurately cut so as to mesh perfectly and turn upon each other with as little friction as possible. The mechanical advantage of the transmission will depend upon the relative number of teeth. The small gear goes around as many times to one revolution of the large gear as the number of teeth of the small is contained in the number of teeth of the large. A pair of gears having, respectively, 96 and 12 teeth will have, in any machine combination, a mechanical advantage of 8 or $\frac{1}{8}$ according to which gear receives the acting force.

Fig. 122. Spur Gears

Bevel Gears. When it is desired to transmit motion at an angle with a driving shaft, bevel gears are used. As a rule the motions are at right angles to each other as in Fig. 123. The mechanical advantage of the system is, as stated for spur gears, the ratio of the number of teeth of the driven gear to that of the driving gear. The two bevel gears are called *miter gears* if they are of the same size.

Worm Gears. Another method of transmitting power at right angles is by means of worm gears, Fig. 124, a method which is used

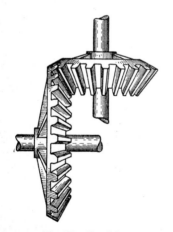

Fig. 123. Bevel Gears

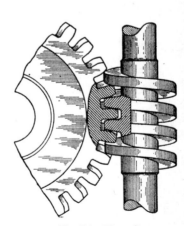

Fig. 124. Worm Gear

when an extremely slow motion is desired. One revolution of the worm advances the gear wheel one tooth and, therefore, it will take as many turns of the worm to produce one turn of the gear shaft as there are teeth in the gear.

Helical Gears. Helical gears are a modification of the ordinary gearing in which the pitch surfaces may be cones or cylinders, Fig. 125. These gears work very smoothly and quietly as the teeth have always two points touching in the plane of the axes, besides being stronger than those of ordinary wheels.

Fig. 125. Helical Gears

Train of Gear Wheels. Gear wheels are often used in a train, Fig. 126, so as to increase the mechanical advantage. In the case illustrated, there are two pairs of gears, each pair having 24 and 11 teeth, respectively. Either pair has, therefore, a mechanical advantage of $\frac{24}{11} = 2\frac{2}{11}$; and the two pairs taken in series have a mechanical advantage of $2\frac{2}{11} \times 2\frac{2}{11} = 4.76$. Hence, *in any compound*

Fig. 126. Train of Gear Wheels

machine the final mechanical advantage is equal to the product of the mechanical advantages of the separate machines.

In the case of a *derrick gear train*, Fig. 127, a combination is made of the crank and axle with two pairs of gears between. Suppose the crank to have a length of 16 inches, the axle a diameter of 4 inches, and the two pairs of gears to have, respectively, 100-10 and 48-8 teeth. The final mechanical advantage is

$$\frac{16}{2} \times \frac{100}{10} \times \frac{48}{8} = 480.$$

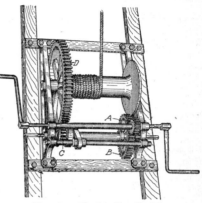

Fig. 127. Derrick Gear Train

§72. Sprocket and Chain. The sprocket and link chain is a form of transmission used extensively in the bicycle, Fig. 128, in the automobile, or wherever the driving and driven shafts are necessarily separated and a belt drive is not suitable. The mechanical advantage is the same as if the two sprockets meshed directly with each other.

Fig. 128. Sprocket and Chain

§73. Screw. A screw consists of a cylinder about which is wound a spiral thread of some form. A thread of square cross-

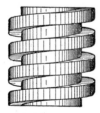

Fig. 129. Square Screw Thread

Fig. 130. V Screw Thread

section is called a *square thread*, Fig. 129, and a thread of triangular cross-section is called a **V** *thread*, Fig. 130. In any case the thread is virtually an inclined plane, as may be shown by wrapping a right-triangular-shaped piece of paper around a pencil, Fig. 131. The hypotenuse of the triangle, representing the length of the inclined

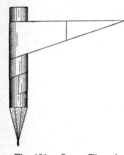

plane, forms the spiral thread of the screw. Now if the nut $M N$, Fig. 132, which has a hole with a continuous groove cut in its side so as to exactly match the thread in the screw, is held while the screw is turned, the screw threads will virtually slide up the inclined plane. If the screw makes exactly one revolution, it will be elevated or depressed just the vertical distance between two consecutive turns of the thread, *i. e.*, a distance $B D$. This distance is called the *pitch* of the screw.

Fig. 131. Screw Thread Really an Inclined Plane

The screw is usually operated by some form of lever like a wrench which is attached to the head of the screw, or like a bar as in the *jackscrew*, Fig. 133. The acting force, in order to raise the resisting body through a distance equal to the pitch d of the screw must make one

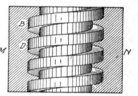

Fig. 132. Screw and Nut

revolution, *i. e.*, must pass over a distance $2\pi l$, where l is the length of the bar. Therefore, *the mechanical advantage of the screw is the ratio of the circumference of the circle moved over by the end of the lever, to the distance between the threads*. That is,

$$P \times 2\pi l = Wd$$

In practice the element of friction is so great that the mechanical advantage is considerably reduced; but if friction is neglected, a jackscrew having 4 threads to the inch and operated by a lever 24 inches long will have a mechanical advantage of

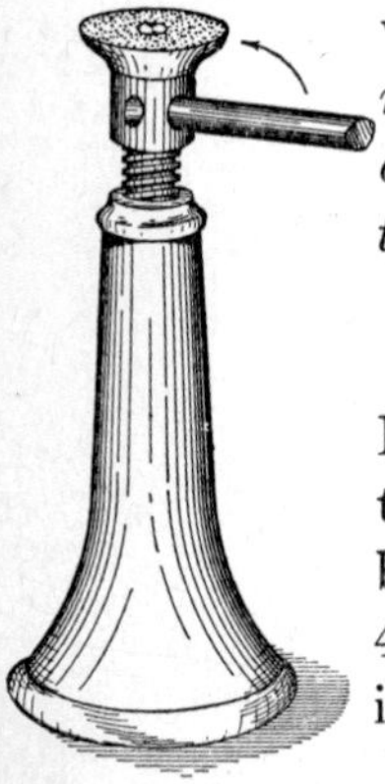

Fig. 133. Jack-screw

$$2\pi \times 24 \div \frac{1}{4} = 2 \times \frac{22}{7} \times 24 \times \frac{4}{1} = 603 +$$

There are many other useful applications of the screw principle, including letter presses, Fig. 134, micrometer calipers, vises,

Fig. 135, lead screws in lathes, clamps, etc., as well as the more simple applications by means of wood and machine screws.

§74. Differential Pulley. In the differential pulley, Fig. 136, an endless chain passes over a fixed pulley A, then down under the movable pulley C, and back over a second fixed pulley B rigidly fastened to pulley A but having a slightly less diameter. The circumferences of A and B have spurs fitting the links of the chain to prevent slipping. If the loose chain is pulled at P so as to turn the fixed block, say, one revolution, this shortens chain e by an amount equal to the circumference of A, $i.\,e.$, $2\pi R$,

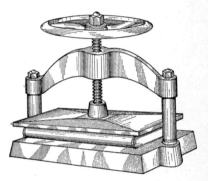

Fig. 134. Letter Press

but lengthens chain d by an amount equal to the circumference of B, $i.\,e.$, $2\pi r$. The actual shortening is, therefore, $(2\pi R - 2\pi r)$ and W, which is attached to a movable pulley, is raised one-half that amount.

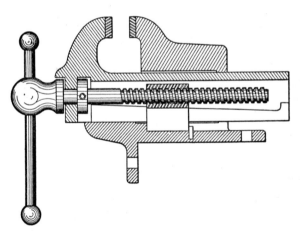

Fig. 135. Mechanics' Vise

Hence, when P moves through the distance $2\pi R$, the weight W moves through the distance $\dfrac{(2\pi R - 2\pi r)}{2}$ and the mechanical advantage of the pulley is the ratio $\dfrac{2\pi R}{\dfrac{2\pi (R-r)}{2}} = \dfrac{2R}{R-r}$. The mechanical

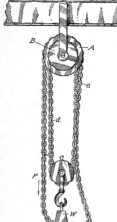

Fig. 136.   Differential Pulley

advantage of such a pulley block is high, but the friction loss is very great.

§75. Water Wheels. A very old and familiar method of utilizing the power of streams is by the use of water wheels of various types. The *overshot wheel*, Fig. 137, depends for its energy upon the amount of vertical fall of the stream. On the circumference of the wheel are buckets into which water flows at the top; the weight of the water together with the force of the current turns the wheel around and thus furnishes the power. The work done per second on the wheel is evidently the weight of water per second multiplied by the height of fall which is practically the diameter of the wheel. This type of water wheel is much used where the fall is considerable and the amount of water small.

Fig. 137.   Overshot Water Wheel

The *breast wheel*, Fig. 138, as its name implies, receives the water about on a level with its axis. Float boards are fixed perpendicular to the circumference and both the weight of the water and the force of the current are utilized. It is not as efficient as the overshot type.

The *undershot wheel*, Fig. 139, is most common in flat countries where the water is abundant and the current rather rapid. It is the least efficient of any of the forms of water wheels in its original form, but a type called the *Pelton wheel*, utilizing this principle, is very efficient, transforming fully 85 per cent of the power into useful work. Fig. 140 shows the manner in which the stream is directed upon the buckets, which are completely enclosed by an iron

casing for the purpose of collecting the waste water and conducting
it away.   This type is manufactured in any size from a small motor

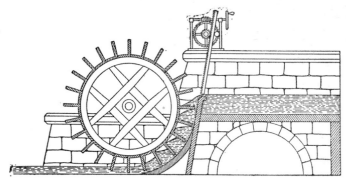

Fig. 138.   Breast Water Wheel

of a fraction of a horse-power for use in city water systems to those
of high power adapted to the extremely high pressures found in the
average western hydro-electric power plant.

The *turbine* is the most modern and efficient form of water wheel,
and is being used exclusively in the many water-power plants which
are being installed throughout the country.   The turbine itself is
completely under water, being mounted inside of a heavy casing,
Fig. 141, into which the water is led from its source through a large
pipe called the *turbine pit*, or *penstock*, shown in Fig. 142, which
represents a section of a Niagara
Falls power plant; the head of
the water is 130 feet.   Entering
the casing the water is forced
by the pressure through fixed
guide vanes *G*, Fig. 143, and
does its work upon the blades
of the turbine wheel, passing into
the tail race at the bottom of
the turbine.   Fig. 144 is a section through the turbine, showing guide vanes *G* and turbine

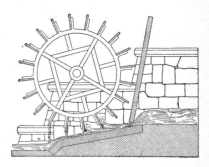

Fig. 139.   Undershot Water Wheel

blades *T*.   The theoretical power of the turbine is evidently the
product of the amount of water passing through per second by
the height of the turbine pit.

Fig. 140.　Pelton Water Motor System

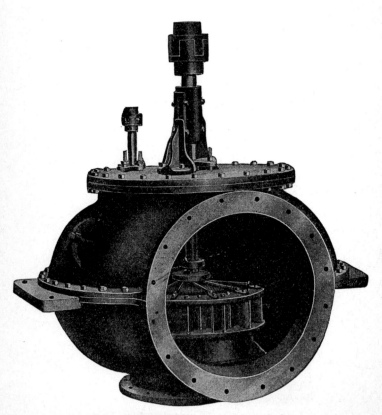

Fig. 141.　Water Turbine Showing Outer Casing

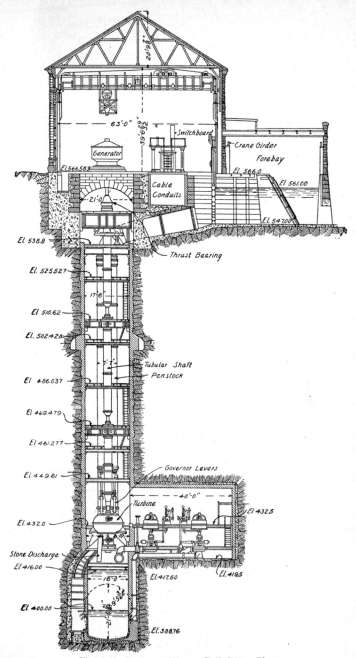

Fig. 142. Section of Niagara Falls Water Plant

PROBLEMS FOR PRACTICE

1. The hay scales shown in Fig 145, consists of a compound lever with fulcrums at F_1, F_2, F_3, and F_4. If F_1o_1 and F_2o_2 are lengths of 6 inches; F_1E and F_2E, 5 feet; F_3n, 1 foot; F_3m, 6 feet; rF_4, 2 inches, and F_4S, 20 inches, how many pounds at P will be required to balance a weight of 1 ton on the platform? (Suggestion: In the calculation, consider entire load as supported at point o_1.) Ans. $3\frac{1}{3}$ lb.

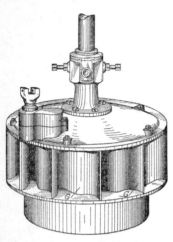

Fig. 143. Water Turbine Outer Casing Removed

2. In the case of a wheel and axle, what must be the diameter of the axle if a pull of 40 pounds on the circumference of the wheel, having a radius of 48 inches, will balance a load weighing 320 pounds suspended from the axle?

3. The sprocket wheel attached to the crank of a bicycle has 18 teeth, while the rear sprocket has 7. How many times does the rear wheel turn for one turn of the pedals? How far does the bicycle go in one revolution of the pedals, the wheels having a diameter of 28 inches?

Fig. 144. Section of Water Turbine Wheel

4. If the capstan of a ship is 12 inches in diameter and the levers are 6 feet long, what force must be exerted by each of 4 men in order to raise an anchor weighing 3,000 pounds?

5. The pitch of a jackscrew is $\frac{1}{2}$ inch, the power of 10 pounds acts through a circumference of 20 feet per revolution. Neglecting friction, how much weight can be lifted?

6. The diameter of the large wheel of a differential pulley is 12 inches and that of the small one is $11\frac{3}{4}$ inches. How much force must be applied to the chain to lift 9,600 pounds? Ans. 100 lb.

7. **The** screw of the letter press, Fig. 134, has 6 threads to the inch and the diameter of the wheel is 12 inches. If a force of 40 pounds is applied to the wheel, what pressure is exerted by the plate? Ans. 9051.+ lb.

8. In the derrick of Fig. 127, the crank arm has a length of 18 inches and the gear wheels A, B, C, and D have 10, 50, 15, and 90 cogs, respectively, while the axle over which the rope runs is 6 inches in diameter. If the rope runs around a movable pulley to which the load is attached, find the mechanical advantage of the derrick. (Suggestion: Use crank and axle as if they were together.) Ans. 360.

Fig. 145. Diagram of Hay Scales

9. A Pelton motor is run from a source 125 feet above the motor and the pipe delivers 5 cubic feet per second. Neglecting friction, how many foot pounds of work are done by the motor?

POWER OF MACHINES

§76. Definition of Power. In the discussion in the preceding sections of the work done by machines, no mention has been made of the *time* occupied by the agent in carrying out the work because the time element does not enter into the problem. The work of raising 10,000 bricks to the third story of a building may be done by man-power in a day while an elevator may be able to do it in 20 minutes, and yet in either case 10,000 bricks have been raised a certain number of feet.

However, in order to determine the ability of an agent to do work, it is necessary to estimate the *rate* at which the work is done. *The rate of doing work is the power or activity of a machine.* The elevator does in 20 minutes what the man does in a day of 8 hours; it is, therefore, capable of delivering 24 times more work per second than the man and is to be rated as a 24 man-power machine.

§77. Horse=Power. The unit of power most commonly used is the *horse-power* and is equal to 33,000 foot pounds of work per minute or 550 foot pounds per second. This unit, which was proposed by James Watt, is probably about a third too high but it has been in use so long that it seems unwise to change it. The power of a man is about $\frac{1}{7}$ h. p., of an ordinary locomotive 600 to 1,000 h. p., and of stationary and marine engines as high as 20,000 h. p.

ENERGY

The energy of a body is its capacity for doing work. A body which has no source of power in itself has energy only by virtue of the work which has been done upon it. A brick may drop from the top of a building only because at some time work was done upon it to place it there. A bullet which is fired from a gun speeds on its way not because of any source of power in the bullet itself, but by virtue of the energy given it by the expanding gases in the gun barrel.

Energy may be displayed in two ways. The brick on top of the building exhibits no evidences of energy until it is pushed over the edge of the wall; its energy is, therefore, that of *position* and is called *potential energy.* On the other hand the bullet, on leaving the muzzle of the gun, has a high velocity and its energy is due entirely to this motion. Such energy is called *kinetic energy.*

§78. Potential and Kinetic Energy. An analysis of the various mechanical sources of energy will show that they fall naturally into one of these two classes and that the action of mechanical devices involve merely the changing of the energy of one class into that of the other. A pile driver, Fig. 146, is equipped with an engine which, by virtue of the kinetic energy of the steam, draws a heavy weight to a certain height, giving it potential energy; this weight, being released, falls, and its potential energy is transformed into kinetic energy, which in turn is expended in a heavy blow on the head of the pile. An archer, by an expenditure of muscular energy, bends his bow, thus giving it a certain amount of potential energy. When the bow is released this energy appears as kinetic energy in the moving arrow which darts away toward the target. The waters of Niagara have at the top of the falls a potential energy which, when expended under control, drives the great turbines at the base

Fig. 146. Pile Driver

of the falls, Fig. 142. A stick of dynamite is an inert mass when lying in the magazine, and yet the chemicals composing it have stored in them a tremendous potential energy which needs only a blow to transform it into kinetic energy of rapidly moving gases.

As energy is the capacity for doing work, its measurement must be in work units. In the case of potential energy, the work done upon the body to give it the potential energy it possesses is the measure of its energy. The pile-driver weight which is raised 30 feet and weighs 1,000 pounds, has a potential energy of 30,000 foot pounds by virtue of the work done upon it against the force of gravity. Therefore, if p. e. denote the potential energy, M the mass in pounds, and h the height in feet, then

$$\text{p. e.} = Mh \text{ foot pounds}$$

The kinetic energy of a body depends upon its velocity and it may be shown that this is measured by the formula

$$\text{k. e.} = \frac{1}{2} Mv^2$$

where k. e. denotes the kinetic energy, M the mass of the body, and v its velocity. As the energy of a body may usually be measured by the work done upon it, the formula for kinetic energy may be neglected in this work.

PROBLEMS FOR PRACTICE

1. An elevator weighing 2,200 pounds and containing 16 people averaging 150 pounds in weight is carried 20 stories of 15 feet each in 50 seconds. Neglecting friction, find the horse-power of the engine which will do this work.

2. A cubic foot of water weighs 62.5 pounds. Find the power of an engine which can pump 500 cubic feet of water per minute from a mine 200 feet deep.

3. The falls of Niagara are about 160 feet high. It is estimated that 700,000 tons of water pass over them per minute. If this energy could all be utilized, what horse-power could be obtained from the falls?

4. A water motor was run from a reservoir 200 feet above the motor. If 25 cubic feet of water passed through the pipes per second and if all of the potential energy of the water were utilized, what would be the horsepower of the motor? Ans. 568.+ h. p.

5. How much work is done in moving a box weighing 700 pounds up a plank 20 feet long and 4 feet high? Ans. 2800 ft. lb.

WORK AND HEAT ENERGY

§79. Nature of Heat. Until the time of Count Rumford and Sir Humphry Davy, the most widely accepted notion of the nature of heat was that it was an elastic fluid, called *caloric*, penetrating the pores of all matter and filling the spaces between the molecules. In order to explain the various manifestations of heat, caloric was endowed with various properties such as indestructibility, absence of weight, difference in the intensity of its affinity for different kinds of matter, etc. However, these explanations were not borne out by experiment; and, in 1798, Count Rumford showed, by a series of experiments with a blunt boring bar and a brass cannon, that the heat developed in boring the cannon had no relation to anything but the friction of the apparatus. He thus proved that heat could not be a material substance, for as long as the motion was maintained *heat could be produced without limit from a limited quantity of matter;* he, therefore, announced his conviction that *heat was in reality a form of motion.* Sir Humphry Davy confirmed Rumford's experiments by showing that two pieces of ice might be melted by rubbing them together, thus proving that heat may be produced by the expenditure of work only.

These experiments lead to the important conclusion that heat must be a form of energy, since it can be produced by an expenditure of energy, and—as is known in the case of the steam engine—can itself be converted into well-recognized forms of energy. This view, which is known as the *kinetic theory of heat*, although only a theory, is today universally accepted as the true idea of the nature of heat; its application to the study of temperature, expansion, etc., has already been given, pages 58 to 63.

HEAT MEASUREMENT

§80. Units of Heat. There are two units of measurement used in determining quantities of heat. The French unit, the *calorie*, is the amount of heat necessary to raise the temperature of 1 gram of water through 1° C. The *British Thermal Unit* (B.T.U.) is the amount of heat necessary to raise 1 lb. of water through 1° F. The former unit is always used in purely scientific work and the latter in engineering tests involving steam and fuels. Thus, for example, when 500 grams of water has its temperature raised 20° C., the water has acquired 500 × 20, or 10,000 calories of heat. In the same manner, if 150 pounds of water is raised from 60° F. to the boiling point 212° F., 150 × 152, or 22,800 B.T.U. have gone into the water.

§81. **Sources of Heat.** The principal sources of heat are the *sun;* the *interior of the earth; mechanical sources,* such as *friction, impact,* and *compression* in which work is transformed into heat; *chemical action,* which includes all chemical combinations accompanied by heat, slow oxidation, etc. Our body sensations tell us of the sun's heat, as well as the heat from the interior of the earth if we go down in a deep mine, the rise of temperature in the latter case being proportional to the depth. Of the effect of friction there are many illustrations, such as the rubbing together of the hands; the sparks thrown from the wheels of a rapidly moving train when the brakes are set; the historic Indian method of kindling a fire by rubbing two sticks together, etc. In the case of impact, the blow itself increases the motion of the molecules and, therefore, increases the temperature, as proved by the fact that a piece of iron may easily be heated too hot to hold by beating it on an anvil with a hammer. The sudden compression of a gas is always accompanied by heat; the cylinder of an automobile tire pump will get hot with use, not from the friction of the piston so much as from the heat of the compressed air which is being forced into the tire. Finally, such chemical action as the combustion of gas or wood is merely the chemical union of the carbon in the burning substance with the oxygen of the air which results in the formation of a new chemical substance and in the production of heat and light.

§82. **Specific Heat.** When the same number of calories of heat is transferred to equal quantities of different substances, *totally different temperatures result.* For example, if 100 grams of water at 80° C. is mixed with 100 grams of water at 0° C., the 200 grams of water will have a temperature of 40° C. Now let 100 grams of lead at 80° C. be mixed with 100 grams of water at 0° C.; the thermometer will not show a temperature of 40° but only about 2.5° C. That is, 100 grams of water and lead were at the same temperature before mixing with equal weights of water at 0° C., yet the hot water, by dropping in temperature a little more than half as far as the hot lead,

TABLE III
Specific Heats*

Hydrogen	3.409	Steel	0.1181
Alcohol	0.602	Iron	0.113
Ammonia (gas)	0.508	Copper	0.095
Ice	0.504	Zinc	0.0935
Air	0.2375	Tin	0.0562
Aluminum	0.218	Mercury	0.0333
Glass	0.2	Lead	0.0315

raised the temperature of its mixture seventeen times higher than the other. Evidently the heat capacity of 1 gram of lead is much less than that of 1 gram of water. (Specific heat of water equals 1.)

The number of heat units taken up by 1 unit of quantity of a substance when its temperature rises through 1 degree is called the specific heat of that substance.

Determination of Specific Heat. One of the simplest methods of determining the specific heat of a substance is by the *method of mixtures.* Suppose that 6 pounds of mercury at 100° C. are poured into 2 pounds of water at 0° C. and that the resulting temperature of the mixture is 9° C. The specific heat S of mercury may be found as follows: 1 pound of mercury will give up S heat units on cooling 1 degree, therefore, 6 pounds, on cooling $(100-9)$ or 91 degrees, will give up 6×91 S, or 546 S units. On the other hand the 2 pounds of water into which the mercury was poured was heated 9 degrees, thus making 18 units of heat gained by the water. These two quantities of heat are equal and hence

$$6 \ (100 - 9) \ S = 2 \ (9 - 0)$$
$$546 \ S = 18$$
$$S = .033$$

This method of determining the specific heat is based upon the assumption that if heat disappears from one substance it reappears in another, *i. e.,* the heat lost in the operation must equal the heat gained, an assumption which follows naturally from the discussion of the Law of the Conservation of Energy given later in Sections 88 and 89. By experiments of this sort, the specific heats of different substances have been very accurately determined, Table III.

*As *specific heat* is a ratio, these values are the same for Fahrenheit and centigrade degrees.

Examples* 1.   80 grams of iron nails at 100° C. are poured into 200 grams of water at 20°.   If the specific heat of iron be taken as 0.113, find the temperature of the mixture.

Let the resulting temperature be x.   The iron, as its temperature drops from 100° to x gives up 80 $(100-x)$ 0.113 calories.   The water in rising $(x-20)$ degrees must have received 200 $(x-20)$ calories.   Equating these two quantities we have

$$80\,(100-x)\,0.113 = 200\,(x-20)$$
$$209.04x = 4904$$
$$x = 23.4+$$

2.   25 pounds of water at 180° F. are mixed with 10 pounds of water at 50°, and 40 pounds at 80°.   Find the resulting temperature.

25 lb. at 180° F. contain, above 0°, $25 \times 180 = 4500$ B.T.U.
10 lb. at 50° F. contain, above 0°, $10 \times 50 = 500$ B.T.U.
40 lb. at 80° F. contain, above 0°, $40 \times 80 = 3200$ B.T.U.

75 lb. at x° F. contain, above 0°, $75x$ $= 8200$ B.T.U.
∴ $x = 109.3°$ F.

PROBLEMS FOR PRACTICE

1.   One kilogram of water at 40°C., 2 kilograms at 30°C., 3 kilograms at 20°C., and 4 kilograms at 10°C., are mixed.   Find the temperature of the mixture.

2.   What temperature will result if 300 grams of copper at 100° C., are placed in 200 grams of water at 10° C.?   Ans. 21.2° C.

3.   It requires 10.9 B.T.U's of heat to warm 25 pounds of aluminum 2° F.   What is the specific heat of aluminum?   Ans. .218.

FRICTION

§83.   Friction Results in Wasted Work.   When a machine is operated it is found that the amount of work obtained from the machine is always less than the amount put into it.   This loss is due to friction produced by the rubbing of the moving parts and by the resistance of the air, which consume a certain amount of energy and bring into the operation of any machine the factor of *wasted work*.   If it were possible to do away with all of the friction in a machine, the work put in would always equal the work gotten out; but there will always exist some inequalities in the rubbing surfaces and the lubricant which is applied to reduce the friction will never entirely eliminate it, resulting in a loss of mechanical advantage— a certain amount of work which can never be regained.

*In these and subsequent problems no account is taken of the heat used up by the vessel which contains the mixture.   In actual experiments this small amount of heat would need to be considered.

On the other hand, friction is sometimes of great service. The brakes on electric cars and railroad trains, the belts over pulleys, and the driving wheels of locomotives are instances of the utilization of frictional resistance. Before considering what becomes of this wasted work, a few of the most general laws of friction will be discussed.

§84. Sliding Friction. *Laws.* The laws of sliding friction here given must be considered as only rough approximations on account of the impossibility of obtaining accurate results. Fair observations may be obtained, however, by the use of the device shown in Fig. 147.

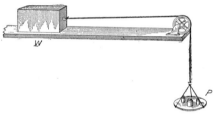

Fig. 147. Determination of Coefficient of **Friction**

(1) *The friction between two solid surfaces is greater at the start than after motion has begun.* This is easily seen if it is considered that each surface is a series of waves and that the crests of one surface sink into the hollows of the other.

(2) *After the motion has started, the friction between solid surfaces is practically independent of the speed of the motion.*

(3) *Friction between two surfaces is proportional to pressure;* that is, doubling the total weight of block W and load makes it necessary to double the force P required to maintain a steady motion.

(4) *Friction is independent of the extent of surface if the total force pressing the two surfaces together is constant;* that is, it requires the same force to draw a brick on its side as on its end. For this reason the guides for engine crossheads, the bearings of cranks, etc., are made large, so that the pressure will be less per unit of area. The friction will be the same, but as it is distributed over a considerable area, there will be less wear and less heating.

(5) *Friction is greater between surfaces of the same material than between those of different materials,* because the bodies have the same molecular structure. For this reason the axles of railway cars are made of steel, while the boxes on which they revolve are made of brass, or some other metal, ordinarily an anti-friction one.

(6) *Friction is diminished by polishing or lubricating the adjoining surfaces.* The joints of men and animals are lubricated by a

liquid called the synovial fluid, and the friction thus reduced to a minimum. When oil, grease, or graphite is placed on a surface, the hollows are filled with a substance whose particles move on each other with less friction than do the metals and, therefore, such friction is a friction of the lubricant rather than of the surfaces themselves.

Coefficient. The coefficient, or measure, of sliding friction is expressed by the equation

$$f = \frac{P}{W}$$

in which f is the coefficient, P is the force necessary to overcome friction, and W is the pressure perpendicular to the surfaces in contact. For example, if W, Fig. 147, weighed including the load, 2,000 grams and it required a force P of 800 grams to draw W along the plank, the coefficient

$$f = \frac{P}{W} = \frac{800}{2000} = 0.4$$

Fig. 148.   Modern Roller Bearing

§85.   Rolling Friction. If two masses of iron, one in the form of a rectangular block and the other in the form of a cylinder, are moved separately along a surface, it will be found that the rolling cylinder offers much less resistance to the motion than does the block; in fact the coefficient of rolling friction may be only $\frac{1}{100}$ of the sliding friction coefficient for the same metals. A heavy freight car can be pushed along the track by a couple of men, whereas the same car, deprived of its wheels, would require many men to slide it along the track. On the other hand, rolling friction requires a smooth surface and if the road is rough and yielding, as when a carriage wheel rolls over a sandy road, the rolling friction may become greater than the sliding friction under the same conditions. Ball and roller bearings, Fig. 148, represent the highest type of bearing where friction is reduced to a minimum.

EFFICIENCY

Friction has been found an ever-present factor in the operation of any machine and the extent to which it has been eliminated determines in most machines the amount of useful work to be obtained from it and, hence, determines the *efficiency*. *Efficiency is, therefore, the ratio of the useful work to the total work put into the machine.* Thus

$$\text{efficiency} = \frac{\text{useful work}}{\text{total work}}$$

For example, a wheel and axle whose diameters are, respectively, 20 inches and 4 inches, will, in raising a weight of 400 pounds a distance equal to one revolution of the axle, perform $400 \times 4\pi$, or 1600π inch-pounds of work. But it is found that 133.3 pounds of force are necessary to do this work and as the distance through which the force acts is 20π inches, the work put into the machine is $133.3 \times 20\pi$, or 2666π inch-pounds. The ratio $\dfrac{1600\pi}{2666\pi} = 60$ per cent, the efficiency of the wheel and axle.

§86. Efficiency of Machines. Simple machines like the lever often have such a small friction factor that their efficiency is practically 100 per cent. The same is true of the inclined plane, the efficiency here running from 90 per cent to 100 per cent. It is practically assured, however, that if a machine has a high mechanical advantage it will have a correspondingly low efficiency. The jackscrew, although having an enormous mechanical advantage, often gives only 25 per cent of the work put into it, and the same is true of the differential pulley, another machine of high mechanical advantage. The various forms of gears and chain drives, as developed in the automobile, are of high efficiency—probably between 90 per cent and 100 per cent—and the ordinary pulley block has an efficiency of 40 to 60 per cent. Water wheels of the overshot and undershot variety return, respectively, about 85 per cent and 30 per cent of the work put into them, while the water turbines, such as shown in Fig. 144, will give back 80 per cent to 90 per cent of the work done by gravity.

PROBLEMS FOR PRACTICE

1. A block and tackle with a theoretical mechanical advantage of 8 was found to require a force of 300 pounds to raise a weight of 1,000 pounds. Find efficiency of block and tackle. Ans. $41\frac{2}{3}\%$.

2. A jackscrew has 4 threads to the inch and the lever used to operate it is 3 feet long. If the efficiency of the jackscrew is 32 per cent, how much force must be exerted on the lever to raise a weight of 2 tons?

3. The Niagara turbine pits are 136 feet deep and their average horsepower is 5,000. Their efficiency is 85 per cent. Find pounds of water discharged per minute by each turbine. Ans. 1,427,000 lb.

MECHANICAL EQUIVALENT OF HEAT

§87. Wasted Work Appears as Heat. It has already been learned that the friction between the moving parts of a machine always results in the disappearance of a certain amount of work, a sort of *mechanical interest* demanded by nature for the use of the machine. There are abundant evidences about us that this wasted work is transformed into heat. The friction between our hands and the rope as we slide rapidly down to the ground may develop enough heat to burn our hands; the heating of drills by rubbing, of pieces of iron by pounding, of car axles by rubbing when the bearings become dry, all show that heat appears wherever there is friction. Count Rumford was the first to show that a continuous supply of heat could be produced by turning a dull drill in the bore of a cannon, a heat which was intense enough to boil water and which continued as long as the drill turned. Other experiments of a similar nature were devised by an English physicist, Joule, who proved in many ways that not only is heat produced by friction, but that *the amount of heat is proportional to the work done*, that is, there is a definite *mechanical equivalent of heat*.

§88. Joule's Experiments. Joule's first test of his conclusions regarding the mechanical equivalent of heat was by heating a certain quantity of water by means of a set of paddles, Fig. 149, which were rotated in the water by a system of dropping weights. Evidently the work done by the weights in falling a certain distance may be calculated, and by knowing the exact amount of water, and its temperature before and after the work is done, the number of calories of heat may be obtained. The amount of work necessary to produce one calorie of heat is the mechanical equivalent sought. The most accurate determination of this important constant was made by Rowland, in 1880, at Johns' Hopkins University. He found that it required 427 gram meters of work to raise one gram of water 1° C. Expressed in English units, 778.8 foot pounds of work are necessary to raise the temperature of one pound of water 1° Fahrenheit; i. e., 1 B. T. U. = 778.8 foot pounds.

Joule also proved the equivalence of heat and work by free expansion of air, by compression of air, and by the electric current. In all of the experiments he found approximately the same value, proving without question that no work is really wasted but that its disappearance means the appearance somewhere else of the equivalent amount of heat.

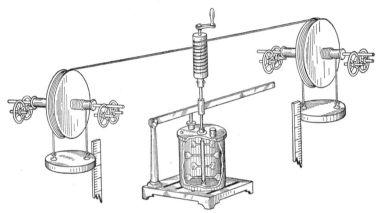

Fig. 149.   Joule's Apparatus for Determining Mechanical Equivalent of Heat

§89.   Conservation of Energy.   Growing out of these experiments is the following important principle:

Whenever energy is expended on a machine or device of any kind, an exactly equal amount of energy always appears either as useful work or as heat.

It is, therefore, possible to follow a certain amount of energy through a series of transformations, from potential energy to kinetic and back again to potential with the perfect assurance that if heat losses are given their proper values, the sum total of the separate energies will be equal to the original amount. This great principle of conservation of energy may be more briefly stated thus:

Energy may be transformed but it can never be created or destroyed.

§90. **Perpetual Motion.** From the statement just given of the principle of conservation of energy, it is evident that to build a machine which would in any way return *more* energy than was used by the machine in producing it is an impossibility. In fact, as friction is always present to some degree in a machine, the amount of energy obtained *must be less* than the amount put in. Probably no one law of nature has been more vigorously attacked in an effort to prove its fallacy than that of conservation of energy. Men seem possessed with the idea that it is possible in some way to defeat the law of nature and get something for nothing; and so from the earliest times, attempts have been made to "discover" perpetual motion. Many men have wrecked their lives mentally and financially on this rock and the patent office is filled with the derelicts. Sometimes it is a Keeley who skillfully transmits additional power by underground methods and produces a motor with apparently extraordinary efficiency—higher than 100 per cent—and traps the unwary investor who allows his desire for fabulous returns to warp his judgment. But Keeley's fraud is discovered and the law still stands. Several years ago an enthusiastic but badly trained inventor made extravagant claims for a liquid-air apparatus by which 2 gallons of liquid air could be used to manufacture 6 or 8 gallons more, and so on—a proposition which, as it contemplated *creating energy*, at a rapid rate, contrary to the law of nature, was soon proved fallacious. The principle of conservation of energy stands today as perhaps the most important law of nature, a sort of bed rock upon which the whole structure of science rests.

HEAT ENGINES

The discussion of the relation of heat and work has, up to this point, been confined to the transformation in one direction only, viz, from work into heat. The reverse process is, however, in many ways more important and its application is of frequent occurrence. Any device for transforming heat into work is called a *heat engine* and examples of such machines fall naturally into three distinct classes, *steam engines*, *steam turbines*, and *gas engines*. Of these the steam engine was developed first and from some standpoints may be considered the most important, although the applications of the two other types, have increased enormously within the last decade.

§91. Steam Engine. The steam engine of today is surprisingly similar to the first commercial engine designed by James Watt, in 1768, the only great improvement since that time being the *compound expansion of the steam*. The method of operation is as follows: Steam generated in a boiler passes through a pipe into the steam chest M, Fig. 150, and thence through the passage O to the cylinder A where its pressure forces the piston U toward the left. This motion pushes rod E back and thus rotates the shaft H of the engine, which in turn moves the eccentric I so as to give the slide valve X a motion contrary to that of the piston. At the proper moment in the stroke, the slide valve cuts off the steam from the passage O and when the piston has reached the end of the stroke, the valve is in position to admit steam at the left end of the cylinder and at the same time to allow the steam already in the right end of the cylinder to pass out through the exhaust port. The motion of the piston towards the right in response to the force of the steam causes the same shift of the slide valve to the left and the process is repeated automatically. Fastened to the shaft are two large fly wheels P whose immense inertia makes the motion steady under a load and carries the crank G past the *dead points*.

Condensing and Non-Condensing. It is usual in stationary engines to lead the exhaust steam to a chamber in which a spray of cold water is introduced to condense the steam. This chamber is kept at a low pressure—about 1 pound—by means of an air pump so as to reduce the back pressure of the exhaust steam on the face of the piston and thus increase the effective pressure of the steam on the other side of the piston plate. The requirement of the condenser and pump increases the weight and cost of the engine and hence the smaller types of stationary and locomotive engines are operated as non-condensing, *i. e.*, the steam is used at a higher pressure and the exhaust is forced directly into the air, giving at each stroke the sharp *puffs* which are so characteristic of a locomotive.

Compound Expansion. The sharp puff of a non-condensing engine shows that the full force of the steam has not been spent when the cylinder is opened to the exhaust. To obviate this waste of energy, engines are provided with more than one cylinder so that steam which has been used in one cylinder can be admitted into another of larger capacity before being allowed to pass into the

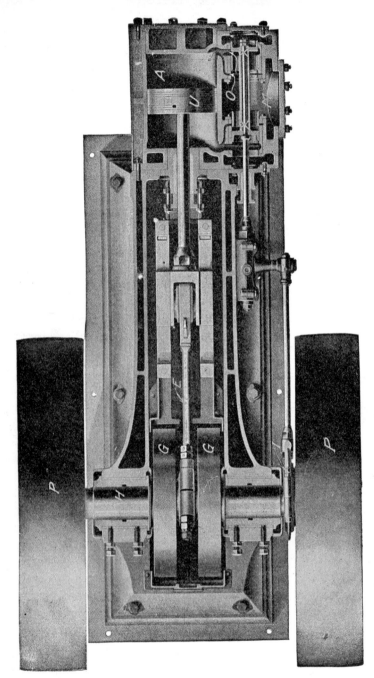

Fig. 150. Part Section of a Modern Steam Engine

exhaust. By automatic devices, valves C_1, D_2, and E_2, Fig. 151, are opened simultaneously and thus permit steam from the boiler to enter the small cylinder A, while the partially spent steam in the other end of the same cylinder passes through D_2 into B, and the more fully exhausted steam in the upper end of B passes out through E_2. At the upper end of the stroke of the piston P and P_1, C_1, D_2, and E_2 automatically close, while C_2, D_1, and E_1 simultaneously open and thus reverse the direction of motion of both pistons. These pistons are attached to the same shaft. Fig. 152 shows a compound expansion engine of the type known as *tandem-compound*. It has been found possible to increase the efficiency still more by having a series of three or four such cylinders cross-compounded, and engines thus equipped are called *triple* or *quadruple expansion engines*.

Locomotive Engine. The fact that the locomotive must carry its boiler plant with it, *i. e.*, that it shall be a unit in itself, has re-sulted in the development of many special features. The *tubular* boiler was the result of the demand for a large quantity of steam in a short space of time. The water in the boiler, Fig. 153, surrounds a large number of iron tubes through which the fire and hot gases are drawn, thus bringing the water into more direct con-

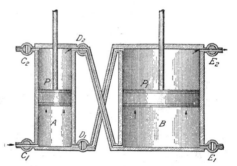

Fig. 151. Diagram of Compound Expansion Device

tact with the flames than would be possible in a boiler of the ordi-nary type. Another device which came early in the development of the locomotive and was due to Stevenson is the principle of *forced draft* by the use of the exhaust steam. By placing the end of the exhaust pipe, Fig. 153, partly up the smokestack, the discharge of the steam draws the smoke and flames through the pipes of the boiler, thus increasing the draft and the intensity of the fire.

The steam pressure developed in locomotives may be as high as 200 pounds per square inch, although the average demand is con-siderably less; the horse-power developed varies from 500 to 1,000. In some of the larger and more modern types, the principle of compound expansion has been utilized with a resulting saving in steam consumption of about 20 per cent.

Fig. 152.   Tandem-Compound Expansion Engine

Efficiency. It is evident from the principle of conservation of energy that every pound of steam which does work upon the piston head of an engine must as a result of that effort be cooler than before. It must also be clear that any heat units lost in the process or not abstracted from the steam will represent a loss of energy which must count against the efficiency of the engine. Any one who has stood near a locomotive and felt the heat radiated from its surface and has seen the hot exhaust steam pass out through the smokestack realizes that the losses of transformed heat are enormous. As a matter of fact these losses are so great that even an ideal engine cannot transform more than 25 per cent of the energy of the fuel used and most engines fall far short of that. The best quadruple expansion stationary engines will show an efficiency of about 17 per cent while locomotives and the like do not show more than 5 to 8 per cent. And yet it must not be imagined because of this low

Fig. 153. Section of Locomotive

efficiency that the steam engine in its various forms is an inferior machine from a mechanical point of view. No device in the whole field of engineering has been the subject of more thought and effort on the part of the best brains of the scientific world than the steam engine and these enormous losses must be recognized as inherent. A comparison of the efficiencies given above with that of 85 to 90 per cent for water turbines indicates in a measure the reason for the desire of power companies to utilize water instead of steam power to run their generating plants.

§92. **Steam Turbine.** The first heat engine of which there is record was a steam turbine, designed by Hero of Alexandria about 200 B. C., so that this type of engine, although only recently developed to any extent, is older than the reciprocating engine. The fact that James Watt took out a patent in 1784 for a turbine shows that some of the advantages of this type were appreciated even then

Fig. 154.   De Laval Steam Turbine

and it is probable that if Watt had put his marvelous inventive mind to the turbine problem as he did to that of the reciprocating

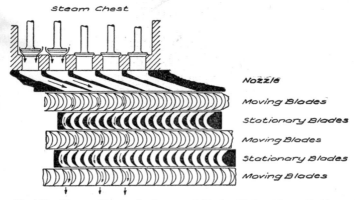

Fig. 155.   Diagram Showing Stationary and Moving Blades of Steam Turbine

pumping engine, the former might have been developed one hundred years before it really came into prominence.

The steam turbine, although using steam under pressure as the source of power, makes use of the *velocity* of the steam as it issues from an orifice, while the reciprocating engine uses the *static pressure* on the piston. Fig. 154, which is an element of the De Laval turbine, shows clearly how the steam impinges upon a series of

Fig. 156.   110-H. P. Terry Steam Turbine

curved vanes, thereby turning the wheel or *rotor* to which the vanes are attached. But the entire energy of the steam is not exhausted by one impingement, so a series of elements are mounted on the same shaft with stationary blades in between, as shown in Fig. 155, by which the steam can be made to do the work as long as there is enough energy left to make its use economical. A commercial form of small power turbine is shown in Fig. 156.

The applications of steam turbines have been tremendously increased during the last few years, not only in ocean travel, on such ships as the Lusitania and Mauretania, but in commercial power plants like the Commonwealth Edison Company at Chicago. The ordinary steam turbine uses steam at about 150 pounds pressure,

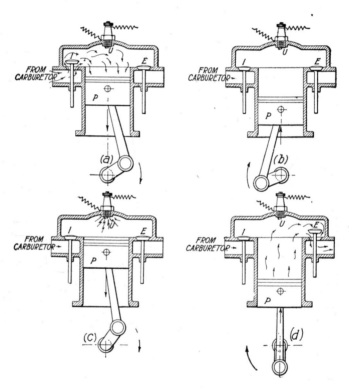

Fig. 157. Diagram Showing Cycle of Operations in Gasoline Motors

but it has lately been found possible to design *low-pressure turbines* which operate on steam from about one-pound pressure down to a very high vacuum. These turbines are able to take the exhaust steam from the high-pressure reciprocating engines and reclaim most of the waste energy. An astonishing example of this has lately been shown in the New York Subway power plant where the exhaust from two reciprocating engines supplying about 12,000 h.p. was turned into a low-pressure turbine, practically doubling the available energy. Of course this gain is not attained without some compensating losses, such as extra cost of condenser, cost of maintenance, etc., but when these losses are all counted in, there is still a decided gain in the use of the turbine.

§93. **Gas Engine.** Within the last fifteen years the internal combustion engine has assumed an important place in the mechanical

Fig. 158.   Franklin Air-Cooled Gasoline Motor

world, replacing the steam engine in many medium-sized power plants and controlling practically without challenge the new fields of automobile, motor-boat, and aëroplane. A gas, or gasoline, engine operates by properly timed explosions of a mixture of gas and air in one or more cylinders; the cycle of operations is divided into four stages: *admission of the mixture, compression, explosion,* and *exhaust,* Fig. 157, the cycle being accomplished in two complete strokes of the piston. The first stage (a) assumes the piston P moving out and the valve I to the gas supply opening to admit the mixture. As the piston starts back (b) valve I closes and the mixture is compressed ready for the explosion which now occurs (c) through the aid of a spark at U from a magneto or spark coil. The force of the explosion drives the piston sharply back and gives the flywheel the only impulse of the cycle. On the return of the piston (d), the exhaust valve E opens and allows the burned gases to be

Fig. 159. Westinghouse Gas Engine

expelled, thus completing the cycle. Owing to the fact that it is only during the third stroke that the engine is receiving energy from the exploding gas the flywheel of a gas engine is made very heavy so as to store up enough energy to last through the three other parts of the cycle. Gas engines may be divided broadly into three general classes: high-speed; moderate-power stationary; and large gas engines.

High-Speed Engines. The high-speed gas engines, which are used principally in automobiles and motor-boats, and which develop generally not more than 15 horse-power in a single cylinder, are commonly vertical and multi-cylinder, use gasoline as fuel, and have jump-spark ignition. This highly specialized type has had enormous development in the past few years and has practically reached standard forms and proportions. It is of extreme lightness and compactness, runs at high speed, and has no governor. An excellent example of an air-cooled type is shown in Fig. 158.

Moderate-Power Stationary Engines. Gas engines for stationary purposes are of all powers up to about 200 horse-power in a single cylinder, Fig. 159. These engines are characterized by longer strokes, more moderate speeds, greater weight, and the use of a governor. They show an extraordinary variety in form and arrangement, although, like the high-speed engines, they are practically always single-acting. They are also made to use any of the liquid or gaseous fuels. The ignition is usually hot tube or electric spark.

Large Gas Engines. Large gas engines, developing 250 horse-power and over in a single cylinder, are the latest development in gas-engine practice. They are horizontal, double-acting, with water-cooled pistons and rods. They use low-tension electric ignition. The fuel most commonly used in them is blast-furnace gas, though producer gas, coke-oven gas, and natural gas are sometimes used.

EXAMPLE. The total pressure on a piston of a steam engine is 9,000 pounds. How much work is done in one stroke of length 18 inches? How many B. T. U. of heat did the steam lose in this operation?

The work in one stroke is $9,000 \times 1.5 = 13,500$ foot pounds. Now, 779 foot pounds of work are required to produce 1 B. T. U. of heat, hence $\frac{13500}{779}$ or 17.3 B. T. U. were lost by the steam.

PROBLEMS FOR PRACTICE

1. In what way does the action of steam in the turbine engine differ from the action of steam in the ordinary reciprocating engine?

2. What is the function of the flywheel on an engine and what property makes it so useful?

3. If the average pressure of the steam in a steam-engine cylinder is 100 pounds per square inch and the diameter of the piston is 10 inches, how much work is done in 100 strokes of 30 inches.*

---

* A cylinder with a diameter of 10″ and a piston stroke of 30″ is called a 10×30 cylinder.

CHANGE OF STATE

FUSION

§94. Heat of Fusion. The fact is well known that water may become ice or steam by simply taking from or adding to the water a certain amount of heat. Any one of the three conditions mentioned is called a *state* of matter and all of the known substances can be made to *change their state* by changing their condition of temperature and pressure. Now, if a thermometer be placed in a glass with some finely chopped ice, it will register 0° C. and will continue to register the same temperature until all of the ice is melted, notwithstanding the fact that the ice has been taking heat from the surrounding air for a considerable time. Evidently this heat does not show itself by the thermometer but is used in melting the ice—in tearing apart the molecules of the ice so as to make them assume the character of water without increasing their total kinetic energy. *The number of heat units necessary to melt one weight unit of any substance without producing any change in its temperature is called the heat of fusion.* This phenomenon is only another evidence of the possibilities of transformation of heat into a different form of energy, viz, into potential energy of partially separated molecules. It represents the work done in bringing about the change of state. The fact that this heat disappeared as far as the thermometer was concerned was the reason for the early scientists calling it *latent* or *hidden* heat, and this name is still in use to a large extent.

Measurement. A fairly exact determination of the heat of fusion for ice is a simple matter.

Weigh into a metal vessel—a baking powder can for example—a known quantity of water, say, 200 grams. Heat this water in the vessel to a lukewarm temperature, say 50° C., and then, taking the temperature carefully, say 48.7°, drop in a piece of ice about the size of a goose egg. Stir the water continually until the ice is all melted and then read the temperature again, 18.4°. Weigh the calorimeter and water again and the difference between this weight and the previous one will be the weight of the ice, 62 grams. Following the plan used on page 111, an equation may be written expressing the exchange of heat in the process. The ice has evidently been the gainer and the water the loser; 200 grams of water have been cooled from 48.7° to 18.4°, giving up during this cooling process 200(48.7 − 18.4), or 6,060 calories. On the other hand 62 grams of ice were melted and the water thus formed was raised to 18.4°. Let L represent the number of calories of heat necessary to melt one gram of ice. Then the heat gained by the ice is $62L + (62 \times 18.4)$. The equation then reads

$$200(48.7 - 18.4) = 62L + (62 \times 18.4)$$

$$62L = 4919.2$$

$$L = 79.3$$

Careful determinations of this constant give the value 80 calories for the heat of fusion of ice; expressed in terms of the Fahrenheit degree and pounds of water, it is 144 B. T. U.

§95. Melting Points of Crystalline Substances. When any crystalline substance, like ice, zinc, or cast iron, changes from a solid to a liquid state, the change always takes place at a definite temperature for each substance. Melting points are determined with far less accuracy than most heat constants; a list of melting points for some of the common substances is given in Table IV.

TABLE IV
Melting Points

Substance	Temperature Degrees C.	Substance	Temperature Degrees C.
Ether	−117	Zinc	418
Mercury	−39.4	Silver	908
Ice	0	Gold	1072
Paraffin	46	Copper	1082
Wood's metal	65 to 70	Cast iron	1100 to 1200
Sulphur	114	Wrought iron	1600
Tin	232	Platinum	1775
Lead	327	Iridium	1950

The laws governing the fusion of crystalline substances may be stated as follows:

(1) *The temperature of solidification and of fusion are the same.*

(2) *After fusion begins, the temperature of the mass remains at the melting point until the process is completed.*

Substances like glass, wax, etc., which are called *amorphous*, have no definite melting point, but soften gradually until they become liquid. For this reason, such substances can be heated until they become plastic and can then be moulded or rolled into any desired shapes.

§96. Change of Volume on Solidifying. Almost every one has had some experience with the expansion which takes place when water freezes, as, for example, the breaking of bottles and crocks when filled with water and left out in the cold. Water is almost unique in this respect, and the fact that the ice by virtue of this expansion becomes of less density than the water and floats upon the surface avoids the disastrous effects of a "heavier than water" ice which would sink as soon as it is formed, thus clogging the lakes and rivers of the earth.

Cast iron and type-metal (an alloy of lead, antimony, and copper) are among the few metals which, like water, expand on solidifying and these metals make sharp castings. Such metals as gold, silver, and lead must be stamped in order to obtain sharp impressions upon their surface.

§97. Factors Influencing the Melting Point of Substances.

Pressure. If a body of water were just about to freeze, it would of course tend to expand in doing so; and the application of a pressure on the surface would retard the freezing until a slightly lower temperature had been reached, *i. e.,* its freezing point would be depressed. In like manner a substance which contracts on solidifying should have its solidifying point raised by pressure as, in this case, the pressure would assist the molecules in their attempt to come closer together. Hence *pressure lowers the melting point of substances which expand on solidifying and raises the melting point of substances which contract on solidifying.* This may be strikingly illustrated by a simple experiment.

Fig. 160.　Illustration of Effect of Pressure on Melting Point of Ice

Mount a block of ice, Fig. 160, between two tables, loop a small wire around the ice, and hang about 20 pounds of weight on the wire. In a half-hour or so the wire will have cut its way through the ice, showing a filmy trace of its path and leaving the block as solid as before. The pressure of the wire melts the ice and lowers its temperature slightly, but as the wire settles down and relieves the water formed of this pressure, it immediately freezes again above the wire.

Substances in Solution. A pure substance has been found to have, under standard conditions, a definite melting or freezing point, but when another substance is dissolved in the given liquid the passing of the given liquid into the solid state is delayed until the temperature is lowered several degrees below the standard freezing point of the pure liquid. This may be illustrated by the following simple experiment:

Make a mixture of 3 parts of pulverized ammonium nitrate and 1 part of ammonium chloride and place about half a glass full of this mixture in two-thirds of a glass of water. Stir the solution and note the effect upon a thermometer placed in the glass; a temperature of about $-10°$ C. will be recorded. The presence of the salt in the water has depressed the freezing point 10 degrees. A mixture of 35 parts of common salt and 100 parts of water will produce a temperature of about $-21°$ C.

The presence of the salt molecules between those of the water evidently has made it more difficult for the freezing of the water to take place, for the cohesive force of the water must now overcome not only the vibratory motions of the water molecules but those of the salt molecules as well. As a result the temperature at which these forces can be overcome is lower than in the case of a pure liquid and, as might be expected, the lowering is proportional to the amount of salt added. When the crystals finally form in the presence of the salt molecules, the latter are pushed aside and do not partake in this formation; in other words, the water freezes out of the solution as pure water. *The lowest temperature obtainable with any solution is the temperature at which the solution becomes saturated.*

Evidently, then, a *freezing mixture*, of which ordinary salt and ice is the most common example, is merely a combination of two substances which form a solution whose freezing temperature is below $0°$ C. When ice and salt are put together, they go into solution and in doing so both are melted; this process, in the case of the water, as has already been found, requires 80 calories of heat per gram, and consequently the demand for heat as the ice is melted must be satisfied by taking it from the mixture itself, a process which reduces its temperature far below the freezing point. The best proportions for this freezing mixture are three parts of snow or finely shaved ice to one part of common salt; three parts of calcium chloride and two parts of snow will produce a temperature of $-55°$ C. Freezing mixtures are mainly used as mild refrigerants where carbon dioxide or liquid ammonia would cause too low a temperature.

VAPORIZATION

§98. Heat of Vaporization. Evaporation, as already explained, represents the passage into the air in the form of water vapor of the rapidly moving liquid molecules. If the liquid is heated, it is reasonable to suppose that more and more molecules will escape as the temperature rises, until finally at a certain given temperature, molecules in the body of the liquid as well as at the surface will rise in the form of vapor. The liquid is now said to be *boiling*. Just as it was found, when one gram of ice was melted, that 80 calories of heat were consumed in pulling apart the molecules of the ice, so it is found that *a definite amount of heat, called the heat of vaporization, is required to change one gram of liquid into vapor*. When the nature of vapor, with its high molecular velocities, is considered, it might be supposed that the heat of vaporization would be larger than the heat of fusion. This is quite true, for accurate measurements of this constant give as its value *536 calories per gram*. When the vapor thus formed returns to a liquid form, *i. e.*, when it *condenses*, the amount of heat liberated is exactly equal to the amount which was originally required to produce the vapor.

Measurement. The quantitative determination of the **heat of vaporization** may be made as follows:

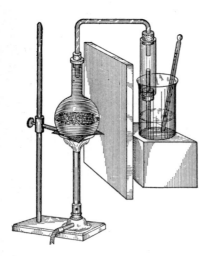

Fig. 161.   Apparatus for Determining Heat of Vaporization

Set up a flask of water with a Bunsen burner underneath, Fig. 161, and a cork in the top through which runs a glass tube. This tube leads over to a device called a *steam trap* which is provided to catch the steam which condenses as it passes through the tube. Boil the water in the flask and, when the steam is flowing freely through the trap, insert the end of the trap in a known quantity of water, say 300 grams, whose temperature has been brought about 10° below room temperature, *i. e.*, to 10° C. Let the steam flow into the water until the temperature reaches about 30°, then withdraw the tube and take the highest temperature of the water accurately. Let this be 32.4°. A second weighing of the water shows that it has increased in weight 11.2 grams, which evidently represents the amount of steam which was condensed in the water. The water in being heated from 10° to 32.4° has absorbed 300 (32.4 −10) calories. If x represents the number of calories of heat given up by 1 gram of steam in condensing at 100°, then 11.2 grams of steam in condensing gave up 11.2x calories. But the condensed steam cooled from 100° to 32.4° and in doing so gave up 11.2 (100 −32.4) calories. Putting these operations in the usual equation form, it reads thus:

$$11.2x + 11.2\ (100-32.4) = 300\ (32.4-10)$$
$$11.2x = 6720 - 757.1$$
$$x = 532.4 \text{ calories}$$

The heat of vaporization when expressed in terms of the Fahrenheit degree and the British thermal unit is *966 B. T. U.*

§99. Boiling. When water is first heated over a flame, the air which is present is driven off in tiny bubbles which rise to the surface and escape without noise. When the water nearest the flame is raised to the boiling point, bubbles of vapor are formed, which also rise through the water, but are condensed by the cooler layers before getting to the surface. This formation and condensation of steam bubbles produces the sound known as singing or simmering. The "water-hammer" in steam pipes is of a somewhat similar nature but on a larger scale. When the entire mass is heated practically to the boiling point, the steam bubbles rise to the surface and break with the characteristic noise. This is called *ebullition*, or *boiling*. Just as in the case of melting, the temperature of the liquid during the boiling process remains absolutely stationary. The fact that the bubbles which formed at the bottom of the vessel were condensed as they passed through the cooler layers of water near the top, shows that the cooling lessens their resistance to collapse, *i. e.*, in order to exist as steam the vapor molecules must have sufficient internal pressure to resist the atmospheric pressure. In other words, *the boiling point of a liquid is the temperature at which the pressure of the saturated vapor is equal to the pressure acting upon the surface of the liquid.*

Laws of Ebullition. (1) *Every liquid has its own boiling point which is always the same for that liquid under the same conditions.*

(2) *The presence of salts in solution raises the boiling point of a liquid.*

(3) *An increase of pressure on the surface of a liquid raises the boiling point and a decrease lowers it.*

§100. Pressure and the Boiling Point.

Under a standard atmospheric pressure of 76 centimeters of mercury, water boils at 100° C., but by varying the pressure upon it with the aid of an enclosed vessel or by a change in its altitude, it may be made to boil at any temperature. A striking experiment which illustrates this point may be performed as follows:

Fill a round-bottomed flask half full of water and boil it vigorously. While the water is still boiling quickly insert a rubber stopper in the mouth of the flask and, reversing the flask, place it upon the triangle support in 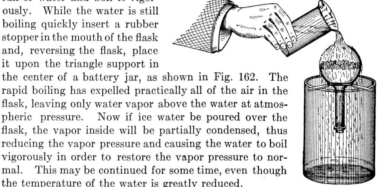 the center of a battery jar, as shown in Fig. 162. The rapid boiling has expelled practically all of the air in the flask, leaving only water vapor above the water at atmospheric pressure. Now if ice water be poured over the flask, the vapor inside will be partially condensed, thus reducing the vapor pressure and causing the water to boil vigorously in order to restore the vapor pressure to normal. This may be continued for some time, even though the temperature of the water is greatly reduced.

Fig. 162. Water Boiling under Reduced Pressure

At the top of high mountains the boiling temperature is considerably lowered. For examples, at the summit of Mt. Blanc (15,780 ft.) the temperature of boiling water is 182.7° F., or 83.7° C., and on top of Pike's Peak (14,147 ft.) 185.7° F., or 85.4° C. On the other hand, in a boiler of a steam engine in which the pressure is 100 pounds per square inch, the boiling point of water is 311° F. or 155° C.

The boiling points of a few substances at atmospheric pressure are given in Table V.

§101. Distillation.

The differences in the boiling points of substances have an important practical application in the separation of liquids from solids or of liquids from each other. In the case of solids in solution, the vapor which rises from the liquid is practically pure, thus giving a simple method of bringing about the separation. In order to capture the vapor which is formed, however, it must be condensed by a suitable apparatus called a *still*, Fig. 163. The still consists essentially of two parts, a *retort* in which the liquid is vaporized, and a *condenser* in which the vapor is reduced to liquid form again. Suppose it is desired to distill some pure alcohol from

TABLE V
Boiling Points

Substance	Temperature Degrees C.	Substance	Temperature Degrees C.
Liquid air	−188	Chloroform	61.2
Ammonia	− 38.5	Alcohol	78.4
Sulphurous anhydride	− 10.1	Mercury	357.
Ether	34.9	Sulphur	444.5

a mixture of alcohol and water. The mixture is poured into the retort B and then heated to about 90° C., which is above the boiling point of alcohol but below that of water. As a consequence, a vapor which is very rich in alcohol and which contains a comparatively small amount of water vapor passes through the pipe A into a helical coil, or *worm D*, which is surrounded by cold water. The

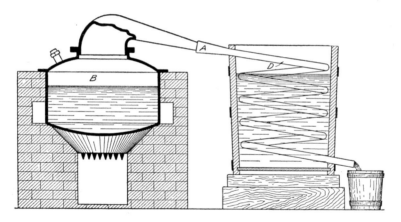

Fig. 163. Commercial Still

vapors condense in passing through the worm and drip into a suitable vessel. If the distillate must be more free from water vapor, it is put through the still a second time and possibly several times, until the required concentration is reached. This process is called *fractional distillation* and is used in the manufacture of liquids such as alcohol and the various products of petroleum. In the latter case its process is particularly valuable because of the many distillates like gasoline, benzine, naphtha, and kerosene which come off from petroleum at different temperatures.

LIQUEFACTION OF GASES

§102. Critical Temperature and Pressure. When water is boiled in a closed vessel, the space above the water first becomes filled with water vapor (steam) whose density increases up to the saturation point, after which just as much vapor condenses as is formed. Now if this water vapor without any liquid present were placed in a closed vessel and its temperature raised above 100° C., the vapor would require a greater and greater pressure applied to the interior of the vessel in order to condense it, until the temperature passed 365° C., when it would be found that no pressure however great could bring the steam back to water. In other words, there is for every substance a temperature, called the *critical temperature*, above which it cannot be liquefied. The pressure which will produce liquefaction when the gas is at the critical temperature is called the *critical pressure*. The critical temperatures and pressures of some substances are given in Table VI.

The critical temperatures of the so-called *permanent* gases like hydrogen and air are seen to be extremely low and some special means must be employed to liquefy them. Carbon dioxide (CO_2) and ammonia, however, have moderately high critical temperatures, and liquefaction can be produced by pressure alone.

§103. Liquid and Solid Carbon Dioxide. A study of Table VI shows that carbon dioxide may be liquefied at ordinary tem-

Fig. 164. Carbon Dioxide Cylinder

peratures by applying a pressure of 73 atmospheres, or about 1,100 pounds. This gas is extensively used for soda fountains and for purposes of refrigeration, the "liquid carbonic acid," as it is more often called commercially, being kept in heavy steel tanks, Fig. 164, sufficiently strong to stand a pressure approximately equal to that which was necessary to liquefy the gas. When the tank is tipped with the valve end down and the valve is opened, the liquid escapes and of course instantly expands into a gas at atmospheric pressure. This sudden change from liquid to gas, as has been learned, demands a great amount of heat which must come from the immediate neighborhood. In consequence the surrounding air, the

TABLE VI

Critical Values for Gases

SUBSTANCE	CRITICAL TEMPERATURE DEGREES C.	CRITICAL PRESSURE IN ATMOSPHERES	BOILING POINT AT ATMOSPHERIC PRESSURE DEGREES C.
Hydrogen	−240	14	−252
Air	−140	39	−182
Carbon dioxide	31	73	− 80
Ammonia	130	115	− 33
Ether	190	37	38.5
Alcohol	243	63	78
Water	365	200	100

gas, and the liquid carbon dioxide are tremendously reduced in temperature, so much so that the liquid, as it issues from the valve, solidifies into a snowy powder of solid CO_2 which may be collected in a bag, Fig. 164. Solid CO_2 has a temperature of $-80°$ C.

§104. **Liquid Air.** The fact that the critical temperature of carbon dioxide is $31°$ C. makes it possible to liquefy this gas by pressure alone. But not so with air, whose critical temperature is so low ($-140°$ C.) that some radically different method must be used to bring about the desired change of state. Linde devised a method and an apparatus, Fig. 165, which illustrate the essential principles of all the methods now in use. Air is admitted into a two-cylinder air compressor, the larger cylinder e giving a pressure of 16 atmospheres and the smaller cylinder d giving 200 atmospheres. The air enters the low-pressure cylinder, is cooled by passing through a coil in the jacket of the cylinder about which water is circulating, and then goes into the high-pressure cylinder. From here it passes through a device f for removing the moisture in the air, thence through a brine tank g which reduces its temperature to perhaps $-10°$ C., and from there it passes through pipe p_2 into the inner tube of a triple-walled copper worm w, shown in section. The inner tube is, therefore, in contact with the high-pressure cylinder of the compressor; the middle tube is in communication by means of pipe p_1 with the low-pressure cylinder; and the outer tube leads to the atmosphere. The air pressures in the three tubes are, respectively, 200, 16, and 1 atmospheres. At the lower end of the two inner tubes are hand valves a and b by which the air in the tube of higher pressure may be admitted to that of lower pressure. To return to the air which had begun to flow through the inner tube, it passes down to the valve a and when this is opened the air expands to 16 atmospheres, cooling itself in the process and flowing back through the middle tube. In flowing back, this cooler air cools the on-coming air in the inner tube and then passes through pipe p_1 to the high-pressure cylinder, to be compressed again and

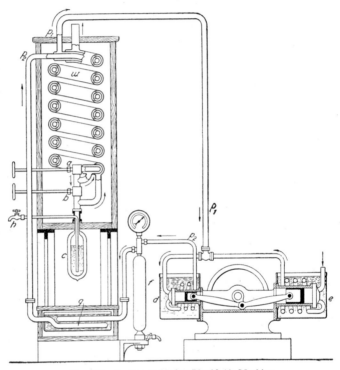

Fig. 165.   Section of Linde's Liquid Air Machine

continue its second journey. The second time this air expands from the high- to the low-pressure pipe it is colder than before and it is readily seen that this cycle can be kept up until a sufficiently low temperature is reached to allow the expansion from the low-pressure pipe through valve b to the atmosphere to accomplish the final drop in temperature. When this temperature is reached the liquid air will drip from the open valve b into the "Dewar flask" c, which is a special double-walled flask, Fig. 166, with all the air removed from between the walls. That part of the air coming from valve b

which is not liquefied escapes into the open air through the outer tube.

The liquid air proves to be a light-blue liquid considerably lighter than water, which boils at −182° C., and maintains this temperature until it all evaporates. It is impossible to confine it in any way, as there is no container sufficiently strong to withstand the pressure if the temperature of the liquid air approaches ordinary atmospheric temperature; it must, therefore, be made as needed; a requirement which can easily be met in case it is being used for refrigeration purposes.

By suitable variations of the method just given for air, all the other known "permanent" gases such as oxygen and hydrogen, may be liquefied. When liquid hydrogen was allowed by Dewar to expand into a vacuum, its temperature was reduced to −260° C., within 13° C. of the supposed absolute zero. By this study it is seen that all substances under the proper conditions of temperature may be made to assume successively the three states of matter. The state in which they exist at ordinary temperature is what might be called their normal state; some substances like platinum must have their temperature raised to an extremely high point be-

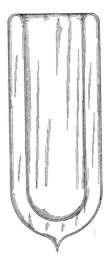

Fig. 166. Section of Dewar Flask

fore they will fuse and finally vaporize; while others like air must be carried to the other extreme of temperature in order to attain the solid state.

§105. **Ice Manufacture.** In a large majority of modern ice plants, the low temperature used in making the ice is produced by the expansion of liquid ammonia. Ammonia will be found from Table VI to have a critical temperature of 130° and can, therefore, be liquefied by pressure alone. At ordinary temperatures, 21° to 23° C. or 70° to 75° F., the pressure necessary to produce liquefaction is about 10 atmospheres, or 155 pounds. The method is as follows: The compressor, Fig. 167, forces gaseous ammonia at 155 pounds pressure into a condenser consisting of a long coil of pipes over which cool water is running, where the temperature of

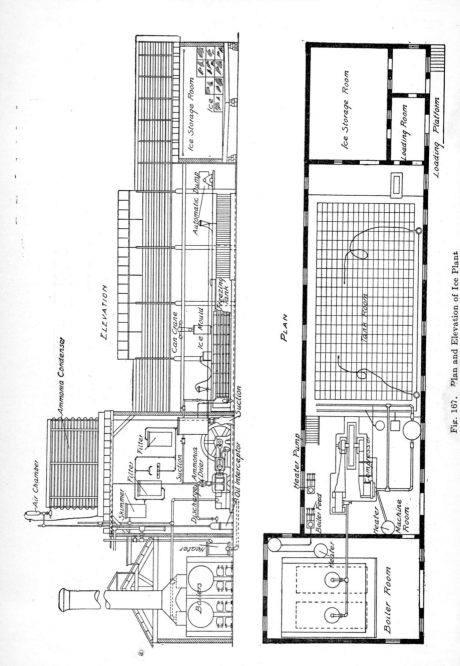

Fig. 167. Plan and Elevation of Ice Plant

the ammonia gas is sufficiently lowered to liquefy it.   It now flows from the condenser down to the freezing tank which, as its name indicates, is where the ice is made.   This tank, which covers an area depending upon the capacity of the plant, is a shallow wood affair, filled with brine in which are immersed the ice cans in rows, as shown in the plan of Fig. 167.   Between every second row of cans is placed a coil of pipe through which the liquid ammonia circulates, usually entering at the bottom.   When the cans are filled with distilled water, a valve connecting these coils with the suction of the compressor is opened and, the pressure being relieved, the liquid ammonia immediately vaporizes, taking the heat necessary for this process from the surrounding brine which in turn takes the

Fig. 168.   Cold Storage Room for Fish and Poultry

heat from the water in the cans and freezes it.   This process is kept up continually, the cakes of ice as soon as they are ready being lifted by a crane and sent off to the storage house, and the can filled again.

In *cold storage warehouses* the expansion coils are themselves arranged along the sides of the rooms, Fig. 168, and by virtue of their low temperature, keep the room at a low temperature; or else brine, which has been cooled by having the expansion coils immersed in them, is circulated through the pipe coils in the room. The former method is generally used for low temperature rooms such as are needed for fish, poultry, etc.

PROBLEMS FOR PRACTICE

1. How many pounds of ice at 32° F. put into 12.5 pounds of water at 120° F. will cool the mixture to 48° F.? Ans. 5.625 lb.

2. What would a person need in order to obtain palatable drinking water from sea water? Give the process.

3. Why is salt thrown on an icy sidewalk? Explain.

4. How could liquid air be made to assume a temperature higher than − 182° C.? How lower than − 182° C.?

5. Two small cakes of ice may be pressed together hard enough to make them stick. Explain.

6. What temperature will result from mixing 400 grams of ice at 0° C. with 400 grams of water at 80° C.?

7. Why does snow on some days pack easily and on others fail to hold together?

8. Why is a "steam burn" so much worse than one resulting from boiling water, although the temperature is the same?

9. Does water boil at 212° F. in a steam boiler? If not, what has changed the boiling point and to what extent?

10. Ten grams of steam were condensed in 160 grams of water at 5° C. What was the resulting temperature? Ans. 42.11°+C.

11. In the case of fractional distillation, why is there always some water distilled over with the alcohol although the boiling point of water is never reached?

12. Find the number of calories necessary to change 500 grams of ice at 0° C. into steam at 100°. Ans. 358,000 calories.

13. Why is type metal used for the casting of type?

14. On a summer day hard ice cream when placed even in contact with the ice in a refrigerator will melt. Explain.

15. A "carbonic acid gas" cylinder contains liquid carbon dioxide. If the tank is set upright in a soda fountain, CO_2 gas may be drawn off at will. What is the condition inside the cylinder when the gas ceases to flow? Where is the liquid?

16. If 2 pounds of steam condenses in a radiator and imparts its heat to the air of a room 15×12×7 feet, how many degrees centigrade will the air be warmed? (1 cubic foot of air weighs .08 pounds. Specific heat of air is .24.) Ans. 44.36° + C.

17. Why is the steam issuing from a kettle invisible just in front of the spout, while showing as a white cloud farther away?

HEAT TRANSMISSION

CONDUCTION

§106. Solids. When a metal rod is held in a flame the rod soon becomes too hot to hold in the hand. The molecules of the flame are moving very rapidly and communicate their motion to the molecules of the metal which, in turn, stimulate the molecules next to them. This process of inter-molecular transfer of heat is called *conduction*. Solids differ in their ability to conduct heat, a fact which may be illustrated by the following experiment:

Take a piece of brass tubing and insert in one end a plug of wood which shall have the same diameter as the outside dimension of the tubing, Fig. 169. Wrap a piece of paper around the juncture of the two solids and hold the paper in a Bunsen burner. The paper in contact with the brass will be untouched while that in contact with the wood will be badly charred. The brass conducts away the heat, while the wood, because of its low conductivity, cannot remove the heat before it has burned the paper.

Fig. 169. Illustration of Conduction of Solids

The conductivities of a number of substances are given in Table VII.

§107. Liquids and Gases. All *liquids* except mercury and molten metals are poor conductors, water, as will be seen from Table VII, being 500 times poorer than silver as a conductor of heat. A test tube full of water may contain ice in the lower end and be heated to boiling at the upper end at the same time, showing that it takes

TABLE VII
Heat Conductivity
Silver as the standard

SUBSTANCE	RELATIVE CONDUCTIVITY	SUBSTANCE	RELATIVE CONDUCTIVITY
Silver	100.	Marble	.5
Copper	86.	Water	.2
Brass	24.	Glass	.05
Iron	20.	Wood	.03
Lead	8.	Sawdust	.012
Mercury	2.	Flannel	.004

some time for the heated water molecules to communicate their motion to their fellow molecules. A very striking illustration of the poor conductivity of water is shown in Fig. 170. The glass bulb is immersed in water and its stem dips down into water, by which the expansion of the air in the bulb may be indicated. Some ether poured on the surface of the water and ignited will burn merrily while the air thermometer shows hardly any change in the level of the indicator column.

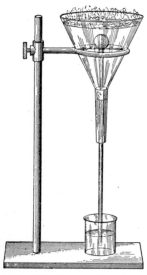

Fig. 170. Water a Poor Conductor of Heat

Gases are such poor conductors that it has been questioned whether they conduct at all. They certainly do conduct heat to a certain extent but can be classed as non-conductors for all practical purposes. A hot flatiron may be touched without a burn if the finger is moistened, as the layer of vapor which is instantly formed acts as a non-conductor, and protects the finger. Feathers, furs, felt, sawdust, all owe their low conductivity to the presence of air in the spaces between the particles. Snow is a poor conductor for the same reason and acts as a blanket over the earth to prevent the vegetation from being killed by the cold of the winter, as evidenced by the greater luxuriance of the ground vegetation in years when snow covers the ground throughout the winter.

§ 108. **Relation of Conductivity to Sensation.** The difference in the conductivity of bodies leads a person sadly astray in his estimate of the temperature of bodies. If, on a winter day, one picks up a piece of wood, a stone, and a piece of iron from the ground with the bare hand, he will estimate that the iron is the coldest, the stone next, and the wood the least cold. On the other hand, the same objects picked up from the ground under the summer sun will feel *hot* in the same order that in the winter they felt cold. This merely means that the iron, being the best conductor, seems to show the most extreme cold or heat. As a matter of fact the thermometer would show no difference in the temperature of the three substances.

§109. Davy Safety Lamp. An important application of the high conductivity of a metal was made by Sir Humphry Davy in his safety miners' lamp, in which the flame was completely incased in wire gauze, thus preventing the flame from igniting the inflammable gases which might exist in the mines. The principle may be illustrated by holding a piece of wire gauze, Fig. 171, over a Bunsen burner and touching a lighted match to the gas *above* the gauze. The gas will not ignite below the gauze. On the other hand, if

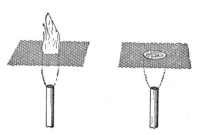

Fig. 171. Principle of Davy Safety Lamp

the gas is lighted *below* the gauze it will not burn above it. The metal wires are such good conductors that they conduct the heat away and prevent the gas from reaching the kindling temperature.

PROBLEMS FOR PRACTICE

1. In cold weather a person keeps warm by means of a woolen blanket, and in summer may keep a piece of ice from melting by means of the same blanket. Explain.

2. Why do steel workers who must be near hot furnaces always wear heavy flannel shirts the year round?

3. A steel bit should in winter be heated before putting it in a horse's mouth. Would this be necessary with a raw-hide bit? Explain.

4. Why will hoods made of newspaper and placed over plants protect them from frost?

CONVECTION

§110. Convection Currents. It was shown in Fig. 170 that water was a very poor conductor of heat. There is a way, however, that it may transfer heat much more efficiently, viz, by *convection currents*. If a vessel of water is heated at the bottom, Fig. 172, the change in density of the bottom layers makes this heated water rise and the colder water at the side, moving in to take its place, sets up a current as shown by the arrows. These currents soon distribute the heat throughout the vessel. In the same way the heated air which rises from a stove or radiator, Fig. 173, tends to bring cold air from another part of the room to take its place and thus makes the influence of the radiator felt throughout the entire room.

Winds and Ocean Currents. If any one will consult a government weather map, Fig. 174, he will find marked upon it certain places of *low* and *high* pressure which have been created by unequal heating of the earth's surfaces or by other agencies. This lack of equilibrium will bring about a movement of the air from the high to the low areas in order to restore the balance, which movement is responsible for the winds which prevail at any time. If the difference of pressure is considerable, the wind will be high; if the differ-

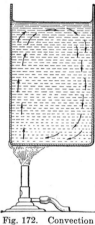

Fig. 172. Convection Currents in Water

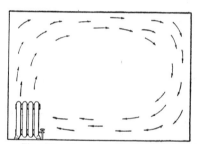

Fig. 173. Convection Currents in Air

ence is only slight, the movement is gentle. The winds are, therefore, nothing more than convection currents. The principle is strikingly illustrated on the seashore by the sea and land breezes so characteristic of such a locality. During the day time the land is heated more rapidly than the sea, for the sea has much the greater heat capacity. Hence, the air over the land being hotter rises and the cooler sea air blows in towards land to restore the equilibrium. This constitutes the day sea breeze. At night, the earth cools off more quickly than the sea and the direction of motion of the air is reversed, giving a land breeze which blows all night.

Ocean currents are the result of the heating of the sea water in the tropics and the blowing of the heated surface water along certain lines followed by the prevailing winds. These currents are subject to certain variations but in general follow a rather definite track.

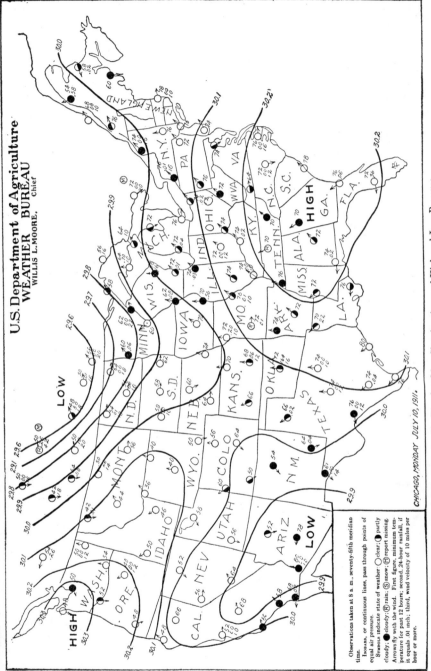

Fig. 174. Daily Weather Map Showing Areas of High and Low Pressure

U.S. Department of Agriculture
WEATHER BUREAU
WILLIS L. MOORE, Chief

CHICAGO, MONDAY JULY 10, 1911.

Observations taken at 8 a. m., seventy-fifth meridian time.

Isobars, or continuous lines, pass through points of equal air pressure. Shadows indicate state of weather: ○ clear; ◑ partly cloudy; ● cloudy; ⊙ rain; Ⓢ snow; Ⓡ report missing. Arrows fly with the wind. First figure, minimum temperature for past 12 hours; second, 24-hour rainfall, if it equals .01 inch; third, wind velocity of 10 miles per hour or more.

RADIATION

§111. Nature of Radiation. When a person stands near a grate fire or a radiator, he is conscious of receiving quite a large amount of heat; if he stopped to think how he receives this heat he would be puzzled, for neither of the methods already discussed, by which heat is transferred, seems to apply here. The air is such a very poor conductor of heat that no help can come from that source, and the convection currents caused by the radiator are all *towards* the source of heat, except those from above the radiator, which certainly cannot aid one standing at the side. There must, therefore, be a third method of transfer of heat, by which heat may be carried

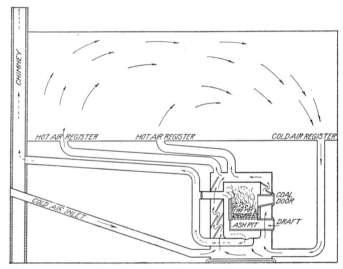

Fig. 175. Hot-Air System of Heating

over intervening space without the help of any known medium; such heat is called *radiant heat* and the method of transfer is called *radiation*. In order to account for the transmission of this heat scientists have created a medium called the *ether,* a medium no one has ever seen or can see but which is supposed to exist everywhere and which is capable of transmitting by a wave motion the heat and light energy with the enormous velocity of 186,000 miles per second. The sun's heat and light are transmitted by the ether and as this source is really responsib 'e for life on the earth, it is seen that radiation is by far the most important mode of transfer of heat.

HEATING AND ·VENTILATION

§112. Heating of Buildings. There are three methods in common use for supplying heat to a building, viz, hot air, hot water, and steam. In *hot-air heating*, the air which is to be supplied to the rooms of the house is drawn from the fresh-air duct, warmed by passing it over the outer jacket of the furnace, Fig. 175, and

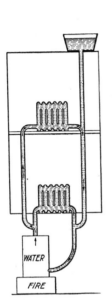

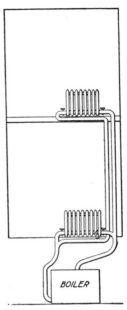

Fig. 176.   Hot-Water
Heating System

Fig. 177.   ˈSteam Heating
System

then delivered to the rooms. After giving up its heat it is returned through the cold-air register, mixed with more fresh air, and reheated. The amount of heat is, of course, regulated by having the registers on and off as well as by increasing or decreasing the draft.

In *hot-water heating*, the system is represented, Fig. 176, by a closed circuit of pipes and radiators with a furnace to heat the water at the lowest point in the circuit. A large pipe leads directly from the heater to the highest room to be heated, above which there is a small reservoir to keep the pipes full of water and allow for the expansion of the water when heated. This method relies entirely on convection currents to transfer the heat, but this very fact makes the system a very adaptable one to the entire range of temperatures, for a slow fire will produce gentle currents while a hot fire will make

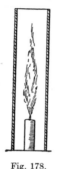      

Fig. 178.   Fig. 179.   Fig. 180.

Illustrations of Good and Bad Flame Ventilation

the circulation more rapid. In this system of heating, the radiators and pipes must be comparatively large.

In *steam heating*, the system is more simple than in that for hot water, as no reservoir is necessary, Fig. 177. Steam flows from the boiler to the radiators where it is condensed, giving up its heat of vaporization and flowing back to the boiler again. Steam heating is a very useful method for large buildings, but is not so suitable for dwellings because of the impossibility of regulating the temperature to the demands.

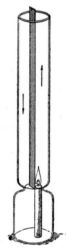

Fig. 181. Chimney with Partition

§113. **Ventilation.** In hot-water and steam heating no provision is made for ventilation. Sometimes, however, by indirect radiation through heating coils, fresh air from the outside is warmed and admitted to the rooms by methods similar to a regular hot-air system. In respect to ventilation, no heating system has been devised which is quite the equal of the open grate fire, for ventilation must be accomplished by having a *complete convection circuit*. A lighted candle, when placed under a chimney of either form shown in Fig. 178 and Fig. 179, will flicker and smoke or go out because the openings are not so placed as to allow circulation about the flame. On the other hand, if the chimney is kept open at both top and bottom, Fig. 180, the candle will burn brightly and steadily, the cold air entering below and driving out the warm air at the top. If a partition is placed in the chimney, Fig. 181, the candle will burn brightly even though there is no inlet at the bottom, for the partition allows a current of cold air to flow down on one side while the hot air is passing up on the other side.

PROBLEMS FOR PRACTICE

1. Why do large power plants require a high chimney?

2. A thick glass tumbler will break while a thin one will not, if suddenly filled with hot water. Explain. Liquid air poured into the heavy glass will also crack it. Is this due to the same cause?

3. If a door is opened between a warm and a cold room and a lighted candle is placed at the top of the door, in what direction will the flame be blown? Explain.

INDEX

INDEX

*The page numbers of this volume will be found at the bottom of the pages;
the numbers at the top refer only to the section.*

Note.—For page numbers see foot of pages.

Note.—For page numbers see foot of pages.

Note.—For page numbers see foot of pages.

Note.—For page numbers see foot of pages.

Note.—For page numbers see foot of pages.